AN INTRODUCTION TO THE LAW ON FINANCIAL INVESTMENT

This book provides a wide-ranging overview of the law and regulatory rules applicable to investment in financial instruments.

Part 1 introduces the reader to the basic principles and structure of the law relating to financial investment. It explains the legal nature of financial instruments, the rationale for regulation and the history and development of the system of regulation in the United Kingdom. It includes an analysis of the main principles and regulatory techniques introduced by the Financial Services and Markets Act 2000. Part 2 examines investments and investors. It explains the legal nature and structure of the main forms of financial investment and examines the legal principles and regulatory rules that are relevant to institutional investment and private investors. Part 3 deals with finance and governance. In essence this part aims to explain the legal mechanisms through which investors supply money to companies seeking investment and the governance techniques that have been developed to allow investors to monitor investments and hold company directors accountable for their actions. Part 4 discusses how markets and market participants operate and are regulated. It examines the nature of financial markets, their regulation and the legal rules that promote 'clean' markets. There is also discussion of the role and regulation of the different types of participants who deal in the markets.

An Introduction to the Law on Financial Investment

Iain MacNeil

School of Law
University of Glasgow

·H A R T·
PUBLISHING

OXFORD AND PORTLAND, OREGON
2005

Hart Publishing
Oxford and Portland, Oregon

Published in North America (US and Canada) by
Hart Publishing c/o
International Specialized Book Services
5804 NE Hassalo Street
Portland, Oregon
97213-3644
USA

Hart Publishing is a specialist legal publisher based in Oxford, England.
To order further copies of this book or to request a list of other
publications please write to:

Hart Publishing, Salter's Boatyard, Folly Bridge,
Abingdon Road, Oxford OX1 4LB
Telephone: +44 (0)1865 245533 or Fax: +44 (0)1865 794882
e-mail: mail@hartpub.co.uk
WEBSITE: http//www.hartpub.co.uk

British Library Cataloguing in Publication Data
Data Available
ISBN 1–84113–478–3 (paperback)

eset by Hope Services (Abingdon) Ltd.
Printed and bound in Great Britain on acid-free paper by
Page Bros Ltd, Norfolk

CONTENTS

PREFACE

The law relating to financial investment comprises many strands drawn from different branches of the law. Some parts are drawn from basic common law principles that would be recognisable to a medieval merchant if he were to experience transmutation into the modern world. Other parts are linked with features of modern markets that would be barely recognisable to a market practitioner from one generation past. Taken together, the different strands present a complex picture of the nature of investment and the process of investing. Definition of the nature of investment is complicated by the presence of a diverse range of investments with fundamental differences in the legal obligations of issuer and investor; and a clear view of the principles of the law relating to the process of investment is obscured by the presence of different markets with their own history and mode of operation and the differing emphasis placed on investor protection and freedom of contract in different circumstances and transactions.

In the past, the law relating to financial investment could have been regarded as comprising mainly private law as contract and trust were the two main pillars of the legal framework that enabled the creation of 'investments'. Both contract and trust remain central to the creation of 'investments' and the process of investing in the modern world, but the growth of regulation during the twentieth century has led it to become the third pillar of the legal framework of investment. Regulation has become an important influence not just for the process of investing, with which it is most commonly associated, but also for the nature of investments and the rights of investors. Underlying the structure and approach of this book is a belief that a rounded view of the law relating to financial investment requires an understanding of the role, function and interplay of each of these three pillars.

As the title of the book suggests, its purpose is to provide an introduction to the legal principles and regulatory rules that are relevant to financial investment. The structure and approach are intended to define and provide an analytical framework for the core legal issues that arise in relation to financial investment. The book is intended to provide a general overview of the law in this field rather than a detailed treatment of all the issues. The reader who requires more will hopefully find that further detail is readily available from the many valuable research sources on which I relied in writing the book. It follows, of course, that the book is not intended to provide legal or investment advice in respect of particular transactions or circumstances, in respect of which specific advice should always be sought.

Iain MacNeil
Glasgow
2 November 2004

ACKNOWLEDGEMENTS

This book is the result of many years of observation and analysis of the law relating to financial markets, from both an academic and practical perspective. I am grateful to the many people who have assisted, perhaps unwittingly, the development of my understanding and ideas over the years. In particular I should thank Michael Hesketh, my mentor during my early career in the financial markets of the City of London; Angelo Forte and Roderick Paisley at Aberdeen University, who encouraged my endeavours in this field; my colleagues in Glasgow, Fraser Davidson, Jenny Hamilton and Gillian Black, who read and commented on drafts; Richard Hart, for his enthusiastic uptake of my proposal; and last, but not least, my wife Alison and children Roddy and Pippa for their enduring support.

TABLE OF CASES

UNITED STATES OF AMERICA

TABLE OF LEGISLATION

EUROPEAN UNION

Directives

INTERNATIONAL

United Kingdom

Statutory Instruments, Rules etc

United States of America

Financial Services Act 1999, *see* Gramm-Leach-Bliley Act 1999

Statutory Instruments, Rules etc

Part 1

Investment, Law and Regulation

1

The Nature of Investment

What is investment? The answer to that question depends on the context in which the term is being used. It is possible to identify three distinct meanings that are commonly given to the term. The first is what can be termed an economic definition of investment.

According to this view investment means that individually, as a company or as a country, we forgo the consumption of goods today in order to achieve greater consumption in the future. On this view, investment can take any form and has no particular association with the manner in which an economy is organised or the mechanisms through which investment occurs. Buying a spade with which to plant potatoes in one's garden is, from this perspective, as much 'investment' as buying a potato future in the commodities market or a share in a company that operates as a potato merchant. This approach also distinguishes investment from saving, which simply transfers consumption from one period to the next.

The economic approach to investment also distinguishes investment in real assets (such as land or machinery) from investment in financial instruments such as shares and bonds. Investment decisions relating to real assets (sometimes termed 'direct investment') are most often made within an enterprise and focus on the extent to which wealth can be created by using existing and future resources to produce goods and services now and in the future with greater value than the resources consumed. Investment decisions relating to financial instruments are generally made by investors outside these enterprises and are primarily concerned with providing finance to fund the direct investment projects of enterprises.[1] Investment in financial instruments is termed 'portfolio investment' because investors generally aim to diversify their holdings of financial instruments across a portfolio. This book is primarily concerned with portfolio investment.[2]

---

[1] From the perspective of the enterprise requiring finance such decisions are referred to as financing decisions because they concern the manner in which (direct) investment decisions are financed.

[2] There is, however, some discussion of direct investment as portfolio investors do make some direct investments (eg in land).

A second meaning of investment is what can be termed the legal definition of investment. This focuses on investment as property and the legal rules associated with ownership of that property. The legal view of investment is intrinsically liked with the economic view because the objective of the legal rules is to create a link between the forgoing of consumption today and the delivery of greater consumption in the future. If legal rules do not provide a sufficiently strong link between the two, it is unlikely that investment (in the economic sense) will occur. In other words, legal rules must be devised so that investors have confidence in their ability to enforce their claims at some point in the future. This means that the law must make clear the nature of the claim held by the investor and make available enforcement procedures that will provide consistent enforcement of those claims over the long term.[3]

A third meaning of investment is what can be termed the process of investing. This focuses on the procedures, institutions and legal rules that are associated with investment (in the economic sense). This view encompasses matters such as the role of markets and financial institutions in channelling surplus funds (such as savings) into investment as well as the regulation of markets and their participants. Investment is more likely to occur when investors believe that they are treated fairly during the process of investment. This can be understood in different ways in different contexts. For example, it can refer to the information provided by a company when it invites the public to buy its shares. Equally, it can be taken to refer to the extent to which financial markets are 'clean', meaning that they are free from manipulation and insider dealing. For private investors, it will often relate to the quality of information and advice provided at the time of making an investment decision as well as the suitability of investments that are sold to them.

Each of these three aspects of investment is central to what follows in the book. The discussion below provides a brief overview of some of the main issues, while much of the detail is dealt with in later chapters.

1.1 The economic nature of investment

The central feature of the economic nature of investment is the forgoing of current consumption in the expectation of achieving greater consumption in the future.[4] A willingness to forgo current consumption in favour of investment is

---

[3] The significance of consistent enforcement over the long term becomes particularly clear in the context of equity investment, which by its nature is of an indefinite duration.

[4] See R Pike and R Dobbins, *Investment Decisions and Financial Strategy* (Oxford, Philip Allan, 1986) ch 3.

normally only possible when resources are not required for current consumption. In such circumstances, surplus resources or savings will be present in the financial system and will in principle be available for investment. That is not to say that they will be automatically invested. Whether they are invested or not will depend on many different factors, two of which are particularly important.

The first is the risk associated with investments and the risk preferences of the potential investors who have savings to invest. The second is the extent to which financial institutions perform the function of financial intermediation.

1.1.1 Risk

The risks associated with a particular investment can be classified as:[5]

- *Uncertainty of income* (sometimes referred to as project or business risk). This risk arises when an investment, such as a company share, does not have a fixed income.
- *Default risk.* This risk arises in respect of debt securities (which are essentially loans raised by enterprises) and is the risk that a loan will not be repaid at the due date.
- *Interest rate risk.* The valuation of investments is sensitive to the prevailing level of interest rates and therefore changes in interest rates cause changes in market values.[6]
- *Inflation risk.* This is the risk that the return on an investment that carries a fixed income (eg government securities) will be less in real terms than expected at the time of purchase as a result of higher than expected inflation.

The extent to which investors are willing to assume these risks depends on their risk preferences. Risk preferences are measured by reference to the utility (subjective satisfaction) that an investor derives from an increase in wealth at any given level of wealth. It is generally assumed that investors are risk averse, meaning that as wealth increases they derive less utility from further increases in wealth.[7] This means that investors generally require additional expected

---

[5] See J Rutterford, *Introduction to Stock Exchange Investment* 2nd edn (Basingstoke, Macmillan, 1993).

[6] Modern portfolio theory uses a 'risk-free' rate of return to measure risk and expected return from securities. The 'risk-free' rate of return is based on the yield available from government securities, which are regarded as a proxy for a 'risk-free' investment. Expected returns from other securities can be compared with this risk-free rate. Changes in interest rates cause changes in the yield on government bonds and hence changes in the expected return of a particular security (eg a company share) by comparison with the 'risk-free' rate of return.

[7] A risk-averse investor will always refuse a fair gamble. Assume for example that Brown is offered a 50% chance of winning £500 and a 50% chance of losing £500. If, at a given level of wealth, Brown declines the offer, she is risk-averse. If she accepts she is a risk preferrer. See Rutterford (above n 5) p 54 for more detail.

return for taking on additional risk.[8] The specific additional return required by a particular investor in respect of a particular investment will depend on the particular utility of wealth characteristics of that investor. While that is not capable of precise expression, it underlies investment decision-making by risk-averse investors, who attempt to achieve either the highest return for a given level of risk or the lowest risk for a particular desired return.[9]

Modern portfolio theory distinguishes between those risks that can be avoided and those that cannot.[10] Specific risk relates to particular events relevant to particular investments, such as a company losing its main customer. These events are specific to individual companies and are not dictated by general movements in the economy as a whole. Specific risk can be reduced through diversification, which has the effect of balancing out across many investments the specific risk attached to each. In this sense, diversification reduces the overall risk of a portfolio. Market risk refers to the risks arising from general movements in the economy, for example a recession. Within a single-country portfolio this risk cannot be avoided, but for an international portfolio, diversification can reduce the risk. The availability of data on historic price movements of specific investments by comparison with the market as a whole (the beta coefficient) now enables investors to measure the relative degree of risk in their portfolios by comparison with the market as a whole.[11]

Different investments involve different levels or risk and offer different types of return.[12] The most basic distinction is between equity-based investments and fixed interest investments. The main feature of equity-based investments is that they offer no guarantee in respect of either return of capital or income. In that sense they are risk capital. Fixed interest investments (such as bank deposits, gilts and corporate bonds) on the other hand offer a guarantee in respect of both return of capital and income. In that respect they are safer investments than equity-based investments, but holders do nevertheless face the risk of default (eg if the borrower becomes insolvent).

---

[8] In principle, the nature of the additional risk does not matter. Inflation and interest rate risk arising from poor macro-economic management could have a similar effect to the risk of uncertain income arising from generally poor standards of management in the corporate sector.

[9] The former would be appropriate in circumstances where the level of risk is constrained (eg trustees with limited powers of investment) and the latter to circumstances where the investments are designed to fund specified liabilities (eg in the case of a pension fund investing to meet the cost of pension payments).

[10] See generally Pike and Dobbins (above n 4) ch 8.

[11] See *ibid* pp 142–44 for an explanation of beta.

[12] The nature of particular forms of investment is discussed in more detail in Ch 4. See also Ch 7.2 for a discussion of equity and fixed interest investments.

1.1.2 Financial intermediation

The second factor that determines whether funds available for investment are invested is the role played by financial intermediaries. Included in this category are banks, investment management firms, insurers, unit trusts and investment trusts.[13] They act as intermediaries in the sense that they take money from their customers and in turn provide their customers with a financial instrument (such as a deposit, unit trust, life policy or share). That process has a fundamental effect on investment because it allows the intermediary to create investments with characteristics that could not be created by an investor acting alone.[14]

This transformation occurs in relation to maturity and risk. The first refers to the ability of intermediaries (such as banks) to borrow short and lend long. For example, a bank that takes a large number of short-term deposits (eg repayable on demand) is able to lend that money on a long-term basis (eg in the form of a mortgage) because not all the depositors will want to be repaid at the same time. The second refers to the role of an intermediary in changing the risk faced by an investor. A unit trust, for example, is able to transform risk because a single unit in the fund offers diversification across the entire portfolio held by the trust, whereas a single share in a company leaves the investor with a high degree of specific risk. In both instances a financial intermediary is able to offer a product to the investor that would not be available if the investor were to deal directly (on an individual basis) with a long-term borrower or a company.[15]

An additional feature of intermediation is that it offers a solution to the problem of asymmetric information in financial markets. This refers to circumstances in which there is an imbalance in the information available to parties who may potentially enter into a contract. Investors (particularly private investors) often face this problem as they may lack either relevant information or the ability to interpret that information. If this problem is left unresolved it has the potential to hold back the growth of financial markets as, if investors lack the information needed to distinguish good investments from

---

[13] It is also possible for intermediation to occur between these financial intermediaries and investors—this occurs, for example, when a financial adviser recommends a financial product to a potential investor. See Ch 6 for further details.

[14] The important role of intermediation in investment is evidenced by the substantial proportion of investments held through investment funds (such as unit and investment trusts and life policies). See the Myners Report (*Institutional Investment in the United Kingdom: A Review* (2001), available at www.hm-treasury.gov.uk (8 Nov 2004)) for statistics.

[15] This is not to say that intermediation is always necessary. There are many instances in which companies are able to raise finance directly from investors (typically through financial markets).

bad, they are likely to pay only average prices for all securities, with the result that high-quality issuers are likely to be deterred from raising capital.[16] Intermediaries can resolve this problem at relatively low cost by selecting and monitoring investments on behalf of a group of investors.

1.2 The legal nature of investment as contract and property

The fundamental challenge for the law is to devise rules that will allow investment to occur. In essence this means devising rules that will provide legal rights to potential investors (surplus economic units) that will encourage them to become investors. The purpose of such rules is to determine the rights and obligations of an investor in relation to the entity in which the investment is made, other investors and the outside world. Without such legal rights, surplus resources or savings are unlikely to be channelled into investment because investors will be faced with legal risk as well as business risk.

Contract is the primary mechanism through which rights and obligations associated with investing are created. The essence of contract is that it creates rights and obligations only for the parties to the contract. An important example in the investment context is the 'statutory contract' which links a shareholder with a company and the other shareholders.[17] The contract comprises the memorandum and articles of association of the company and defines, inter alia, voting rights, the right to dividends and the distribution of power between the shareholders and the board of directors. While there is a core of mandatory rules that cannot be altered by this 'statutory contract' it is, in the United Kingdom at least, a relatively small part of company law.[18]

---

[16] This is known as the problem of adverse selection. It is discussed in more detail in Ch 2 at 2.1. See also P Spencer, *The Structure and Regulation of Financial Markets* (Oxford, OUP, 2000) ch 2.

[17] The statutory contract is created by s 14 of the Companies Act 1985 and is central to the operation of companies and to the definition of the rights of shareholders. The contract comprises the memorandum and articles of association. The articles control the internal organisation of a company. They define the rights attached to securities issued by the company, how resolutions are to be adopted in general meeting etc. While company law provides standard forms of articles that can be used by companies, they are free to alter the standard articles as they wish. The result is that, subject to compliance with the mandatory rules of company law, there is considerable freedom as to how a company is organised. This means that there is no standard model of shareholders' rights that is applicable to all circumstances. While particular types of investment (such as ordinary shares) are generally associated with similar rights in all companies, and some of these rights are guaranteed by mandatory rules in company law or listing rules, it is important to bear in mind the significance of the articles in determining the rights of shareholders.

[18] See generally I MacNeil, 'Company Law Rules: An Assessment from the Perspective of Incomplete Contract Theory' (2001) *Journal of Corporate Law Studies* 107.

It is nevertheless common for investors to be described as 'owners' of investments. From this perspective, investments are not just contracts but are also a form of property and investors are not just party to a contract but also own a 'thing'. The implication is that investors have 'ownership' rather than just contractual rights. But how is it possible for contractual rights to become property? The following sections attempt to explain this transformation, which is central to the legal meaning of investment.

1.2.1 Property—ownership of things

The two key concepts in property law are ownership and things. Ownership is the bundle of legal rights held by an owner in respect of a thing. Not all things, however, are capable of being owned.[19] Those things that are capable of being owned fall into two categories. A distinction is first made between tangible (corporeal) and intangible (incorporeal) things. A painting or a plot of land, for example, is tangible, but copyright in the painting or a right to rent from land is intangible. Tangible property is divided into real (or immoveable) property and personal (moveable) property. Real property is land and buildings while personal property is all other types of property. In English law, tangible personal assets are referred to as 'choses in possession' or chattels and intangible personal assets are 'choses in action' or claims. In Scotland, the respective terms are 'corporeal moveables' and 'incorporeal moveables'. Investments are generally regarded by the law as falling into the category 'choses in action' ('incorporeal moveables' in Scotland).[20]

Ownership of a thing can take different forms. Divided ownership occurs when each person owns a thing that is legally distinct from other similar things. An example is a bearer security that promises to pay the bearer on demand. Each security is a thing in its own right, with rights and obligations that can be determined without reference to any other similar security. Undivided (or *pro indiviso*) ownership occurs when two or more people hold

---

[19] The meaning of a 'thing' in this context is defined by DN MacCormick at para 1097 of the entry 'General Legal Concepts' in T Smith and R Black (eds) *The Laws of Scotland, Stair Memorial Encyclopedia* (Edinburgh, Butterworths, 1990) vol 11:

Things are conceived as durable objects existing separately from and independently of persons, subject to being used, possessed, and enjoyed by persons, and thus capable of being transferred from one person to another without loss of identity.

The reference to 'durable' does not rule out a temporary existence—eg a right exercisable within a certain period of time.

[20] This categorisation is not inevitable. It is based on a distinction between a financial instrument (eg a share certificate) and the rights represented by that instrument. In the United States, for example, registered securities (such as company shares) are considered to be tangible property.

a thing as an undivided whole, without separate parts being attributed to each co-owner. A further distinction can be made, in the case of undivided owner-ship, between common property and joint property. In the case of common property (in England, tenants in common) each co-owner has a share in the *pro indiviso* whole that is separate in a legal, though not a physical, sense from shares held by other co-owners. An example is a share in a company, which is an undivided fractional part of the issuing company.[21] There are no particular parts of the share capital or assets of the company associated with a share and the issuer owes only one set of obligations to each class of shareholder. Other examples are registered debt and units in unit trusts.[22] A co-owner of any form of common property is entitled to transfer her share to another person.

Joint property (in England joint tenants) arises when there is no distinct legal title held by each of the co-owners in the *pro indiviso* whole. An example is the joint ownership of trust property by trustees (eg pension fund trustees or unit trust trustees). This type of ownership has been decribed as 'elastic'[23] as it vests in the persons who are for the time being trustees. A joint owner does not have a legally distinct share of joint property that can be transferred to another person. For example, a purported transfer by an individual trustee without the agreement of the others is of no effect.

As far as the nature of ownership rights are concerned, a basic distinction can be drawn between real and personal rights. Real rights can be exercised against the whole world, whereas personal rights can be exercised only against specific persons. The classic example of a real right is that of an owner of prop-erty against a thief. The true owner is able to vindicate his right by reclaiming stolen property because he has a real right in the property that can be exercised against everybody. The classic example of a personal right is a contractual obligation owed by a debtor to a creditor. The right is personal because it can only be exercised against the debtor. Rights in investments (or in other words the legal rights that comprise the investment itself) can only ever be personal rights because they are in essence contractual rights.[24]

1.2.2 Contractual rights as a form of property

The rights of an investor are determined principally by contract. In the case of a company, for example, the rights of an ordinary shareholder are contained in the 'statutory contract' represented by the memorandum and articles of association.[25] In the case of a lender to a company (such as a debenture holder)

---

[21] See J Benjamin, *Interests in Securities* (Oxford, OUP, 2000) para 2.14.
[22] See Ch 4 for the meaning of those terms and also Benjamin (above n 21) para 11.62.
[23] K Reid 'Co-ownership' in Smith and Black (eds) (above n 19) vol 18 (*Property*) para 35.
[24] The detail of these contractual rights is discussed in Ch 4.
[25] See above n 17.

the rights of the holder are determined by a loan agreement (often supplemented by the taking of a security interest to guard against the possibility of default by the borrower). In both instances, the financial and control rights (in the form of voting) associated with the investment are determined contractually. There are, however, some aspects of rights in investments that are determined not by a contract between an issuer and investor but by the law relating to the type of entity in which the investment is made. An important example is the right of a shareholder in a limited company to limited liability. Although this forms part of the 'statutory contract', that contract does not bind outsiders (eg the company's creditors) who are not party to the contract. Limited liability is a statutory rule relating to the nature of the investment entity that binds outsiders (eg creditors) as well as insiders (shareholders). [26]

Historically, the characterisation of contractual rights as property in the legal sense was based on a distinction between those contractual rights that were closely associated with an individual and those that were not. In the latter case the contractual rights were considered a thing (property) that was capable of being transferred to any other person whereas in the former they were not. A debt, for example, was considered property because it represented an obligation to pay money and the payment of money by A to B is, from A's perspective, the same as payment of money from A to C. B was therefore permitted to assign the debt owed to her by A to C. However, an obligation to paint a portrait or to take up employment could not be considered property because the obligation was intrinsically linked with a particular individual and could not be considered a thing capable of transfer to another person. Underlying this distinction was the general legal view of property as something that is capable, in principle, of being owned by anyone.[27]

---

[26] Limited liability was made available by the Limited Liability Act 1855. The general availability of limited liability was an important development for investment. It reduced the risks attached to investment by limiting the liability of shareholders to the extent of the company's issued capital. In partnerships, it was not possible to limit the liability of the partners in this way. Early forms of company that preceded registered companies had used various devices to limit liability but the general availability of such limitation for registered companies provided a standard form of organisation that would become the model into which most investment would be channelled. It also made possible the diversification of investment portfolios, although it was some time later before the benefits of diversification were fully appreciated. Associated with the (statutory) recognition of limited liability was the recognition of the company as a legal person distinct from its members (shareholders). See generally P Davies, *Introduction to Company Law* (Oxford, OUP, 2002) chs 2 and 3.

[27] See JA Penner, *The Idea of Property in Law* (Oxford, OUP, 1997) who explains this approach by reference to the concept of the separability of a thing from a particular person. He says (p 113):

> Separability is a conceptual criterion of property which defines the objects of property and gives rise to transferability. To be conceived as an object of property a thing must first be considered as separable and distinct from any person who might hold it, and is for that reason rightly regarded as alienable.

The significance of recognising contractual rights as property was that it made those rights transferable,[28] and this was crucial for the early development of commerce and financial markets during the medieval and early modern period. English law had previously restricted the transfer of contractual obligations.[29] Subsequent developments in the law liberalised the rules relating to the transfer of obligations and thereby laid the foundations for the creation of markets in transferable financial instruments.[30] In essence, therefore, it was the recognition that the contractual rights of an investor were an item of (transferable) property that was the crucial legal foundation for the development of modern financial markets. Without it, investors would be faced with the prospect of being 'locked in' to particular investments because there would be no market in which to sell and an investor could only be released from his obligations with the consent of the remaining investors.

1.2.3 Rights associated with the holding of investments

It is common nowadays for investors to hold investments through intermediaries rather than directly.[31] Two explanations can be given for this trend. First, there are some investors (both professional and private) who may find it convenient to have a professional custodian hold investments on their behalf. Fund managers, for example, generally prefer to focus on portfolio management rather than be involved in the administrative arrangements associated with ownership and transfers of ownership of investments. Second, the introduction of dematerialised title to securities has encouraged indirect ownership because transfers of title through the system are possible only through a member.[32] If a member holds securities as custodian on behalf of investors, transfers are generally simpler and less costly.

It is in respect of third parties (such as custodians) who hold investments on behalf of investors that the real property rights of an investor become

---

[28] Transferability is the logical consequence of categorising a thing as property (in the legal sense) rather than a criterion by which a thing is or is not considered to be property. See Penner (above n 27) pp 113–114.

[29] On the rationale for the restriction in English law on the transfer of contractual obligations see GH Treitel, *The Law of Contract*, 11th edn (London, Sweet & Maxwell, 2003) p 672. Scots law on the transfer of contractual rights was less restrictive than the law in England: K Reid, 'Transfer of Ownership' in Smith and Black (eds) (above n 19) vol 18 (*Property*) para 652.

[30] On the historical evolution of the law relating to the transfer of obligations see R Zimmerman, *The Law of Obligations* (Oxford, OUP, 1996) pp 66 and 67. He notes that transferability (through assignment) was first recognised in England by the practice of financiers operating under Jewish law.

[31] The legal mechanism through which this occurs is normally trust. See 1.3.4 below for an overview of trust and see Ch 6 for more detail on the operation of trusts.

[32] See Ch 4 for more detail.

apparent. An investment is in essence a bundle of personal rights held by the investor, but when that bundle of rights is 'deposited' with an intermediary such as a custodian, the investor has real rights against the custodian. The legal nature of the investment (as a bundle of personal rights) is unchanged but there is a new legal relationship between the investor and the intermediary under which the property of the investor is deposited with the intermediary and in respect of which the investor has real rights.[33] Another way of expressing this is to say that an investor's ownership of an investment is a right that is good against the rest of the world (a real right) even though the rights represented by the investment can only be enforced against particular persons (personal rights). The position can be illustrated by reference to a simple example. A share issued by company X to Y is, as between X and Y, essentially a contractual arrangement. However, when this share is held on Y's behalf by custodian C, the law views Y as having a real right in respect of the share. The implication of this is that the share is not available to C's creditors should C become insolvent because the share is the property of Y and not C.[34]

This is not to say that there are not important issues that fall to be agreed by contract between an investor and an intermediary who holds securities on his behalf. Such issues include the manner in which control (voting) rights associated with an investment are to be exercised, the purposes for which the intermediary is entitled to use the investments (eg to lend to others) and the persons to whom they may be entrusted for safekeeping. These (personal) rights are, however, distinct from the real rights relating to the investment in that they are enforceable only against the custodian, whereas the real right is a right to enjoy the benefits of ownership that is good against the whole world.

Another important consideration in respect of the holding of investments is the distinction between fungible and non-fungible property. The distinction is relevant to any situation in which there is an obligation to re-deliver property, such as when a custodian re-delivers securities held on behalf of a client. Property is fungible if it is a commodity that has no definitive characteristics and can therefore be replaced by a similar weight, number or measure of the same commodity. Examples are money, and commodities such as grain and oil. Property is not fungible if it has definitive characteristics (eg a painting, a

---

[33] Benjamin (above n 21 at para 13.10) sums up the position as follows: 'intermediation is not only compatible with property rights in relation to intangibles: it is their precondition'.

[34] The position would differ if the law recognised Y as having only a contractual (personal) right against C. This would be the case if Y deposited money with a bank. A deposit becomes the property of the bank and a depositor has only a contractual (personal) right to the return of the money. In principle, therefore, there is no 'property' which can be identified by Y as belonging to him in the event of the bank's insolvency and therefore Y will have to claim as a creditor in any insolvency procedure rather than being able to require the return of his 'property'. See generally J Wadsley and GA Penn, *The Law Relating to Domestic Banking*, 2nd edn (London, Sweet & Maxwell, 2000) ch 3.

house or a dog). Undivided securities (such as company shares of the same class) are always fungible because they are identical parts of a single unit (such as the capital of a company).[35] It follows that a re-delivery obligation in respect of such securities can be satisfied by delivery of any of the relevant class of security. In principle, this makes possible the pooling of securities of the same type held for different clients by custodians, as they are able to satisfy re-delivery obligations by using any of the securities in the pool. Without that capability, custody of investments would become more complex and costly.

1.2.4 Legal title to investments

As noted earlier, property in the legal sense is a thing that has the potential to be owned by anyone. For a particular person to own a thing requires that a legal title to it becomes vested in that particular person. The process by which legal title become vested in a particular person varies as between different categories of property. In the case of registered securities (the principal example being company shares) legal title is constituted by entry of the owner's name in the relevant register. The registered owner is the legal owner and in the case of company shares, no other interest can be recorded in the shareholders' register.[36] A distinction can be drawn between an investment and a document, certificate or other token that represents the investment. A share certificate, for example, is not itself an investment but simply evidence that the holder is a shareholder.[37] The investment is the bundle of rights held by the shareholder. The distinction between the certificate and the investment is illustrated by the approach to forged transfers. Suppose that A steals B's share certificate, forges B's signature on a transfer form, submits it to the issuer and has his name inserted on the shareholders' register. Assuming that B is able to show that A's ownership claim is false, he is entitled to have his name reinstated on the register. This remains true even if C has taken the certificate from B in good faith and for value as the certificate does not have the character of a negotiable instrument.[38]

---

[35] Not all securities are fungible. Some money-market instruments, for example, have distinctive serial numbers and are regarded as non-fungible.

[36] Section 360 of the Companies Act 1985 prohibits the recording of notice of a trust on the shareholders' register of companies incorporated in England and Wales. The prohibition does not apply to companies incorporated in Scotland. The legal owner will often not be the 'ultimate' investor (the person whose money has bought the investment) as legal title to securities is nowadays often held in trust (by a trustee or custodian) for the ultimate investor. Indeed, scrutiny of the shareholders' register of many companies will in itself often reveal very little in terms of the true ownership of the company.

[37] Companies Act 1985 s 186.

[38] See Ch 4 for more detail on transfers of financial instruments.

In the case of bearer securities, a distinction between a certificate and the underlying investment cannot be drawn in the same manner. Bearer securities are regarded as tangible moveable property and can be transferred simply by delivery.[39] There is, in principle, no need for a record of ownership and any (unidentified) holder is the legal owner.[40] This gives effect to the principle that a bearer security should have a negotiable character, meaning that it is possible for a transferee to take a better title than that held by the transferor. Suppose that the same circumstances mentioned in the paragraph above occur in relation to a bearer security. While B can recover the stolen certificate while it remains in the possession of A, he cannot recover it from C, if C is a bona fide purchaser for value (a 'holder in due course').

These examples illustrate the different interests that the law relating to transfer of registered and bearer securities have recognised. In the case of registered securities, priority has been given to security of title and there has been a strict application of the principle *nemo dat quod non habet* ('no one can give what he does not have'). In the case of bearer securities, priority has been given to security of transfer (to a holder in due course), reflecting the historic concern of the law merchant to facilitate the transfer of rights in the market through negotiability.[41]

Paper certificates have been replaced in many instances by an electronic record of ownership, both for registered and bearer securities. This process is referred to as dematerialisation. Its main attraction is that it eliminates the need for transfer of paper certificates, thereby making the trading of securities less cumbersome and securities markets more efficient. Dematerialisation has been adopted in many countries including the United Kingdom. It results in an issue of securities to investors being recorded electronically by the issuer or its agent, with the investor receiving confirmation that this has occurred. Confirmation does not have the status of a document of title as it merely intimates that title is recorded in the electronic register.

Legal title to securities can be immobilised, meaning that arrangements are made for securities to be issued on the basis that there will be, in perpetuity, only one legal owner. This is a separate process from dematerialisation in that its main effect is on the ownership link between an issuer and investor. It involves legal title to an entire issue of securities being taken by a central

---

[39] Historically, this treatment evolved through a legal fiction under which the debt itself became merged with the negotiable instrument issued in respect of it, with the debt being considered to be 'locked-up' inside the investment (see Benjamin, above n 21 ch 3). In the US, but not the UK, this approach was applied to registered securities.

[40] In practice many bearer securities are held (on behalf of the ultimate owners) by central securities depositaries (mainly for security reasons) but this does not limit their 'bearer' status.

[41] See Benjamin (above n 21, paras 3.21–3.26) on the historical significance of negotiability before assignment became available as a means to transfer choses in action (incorporeal moveable property in Scotland).

securities depositary (CSD). Investors to whom the securities are issued are recorded in the books of the CSD as holding the appropriate number of securities. However, these book entries do not give legal title to the investor as that remains with the CSD. The investor in this situation has no direct link with the issuer and his rights are derived from those held by the CSD.[42]

1.2.5 Transferring legal title to investments

As noted earlier, the categorisation of investments as property means that they are, in principle, transferable. Put another way, the bundle of rights representing an investment issued to A can be transferred to B. However, a potential impediment to transfer arises from the fact that the rights being transferred are essentially contractual (personal) rights. As a general rule,[43] contractual rights are transferred by assignment and that process reflects the fact that such rights are limited by comparison with real rights.[44] Assignment operates on the basis that a transferee takes the rights held by the original holder.[45] Suppose, for example, that A assigns his life assurance policy to B, who in turn assigns it to C. Assume also that the insurer is entitled to set aside (avoid) the policy on the basis of misrepresentation (eg because A lied about his health when taking out the policy). In these circumstances, the insurer has the same remedy against a subsequent holder (assignee) of the policy (B and C).

Assignment remains the method by which most investments other than registered securities (primarily shares) are transferred. However, the potential risks to a transferee (buyer) arising from the rule discussed above is often removed by the issuer of the relevant instrument accepting disapplication of the rule, so that a transferee takes free from any defects in the title of the original or subsequent holders.

Shares are transferred by a different legal process, which is referred to as novation. This is a general principle of contract law that allows a new creditor to be substituted for an existing creditor. The agreement of the debtor (company), existing creditor (seller) and new creditor (buyer) is necessary. The

---

[42] Issues arising where (as is common) there is a chain of custodians linking the CSD with the ultimate investor are discussed in Ch 10.

[43] Negotiable instruments are an exception as the process of negotiation can result in a transferee having superior rights to the original creditor or a prior holder. Such instruments (and their legal infrastructure) were developed to overcome the limitations imposed on the transfer of contractual obligations by the process of assignment. In the United States, registered securities are considered to be tangible property and can be transferred by indorsement and delivery of the relevant certificate.

[44] Personal rights are those that can only be exercised against a limited group (eg between parties to a contract) whereas real rights are good against the whole world (eg ownership).

[45] The principle is encapsulated by the Latin maxim *assignatus utitur jure auctoris* (the assignee takes the rights of the assignor).

process differs from assignment in that the new creditor does not succeed to the rights of the old creditor but enters a new contractual relationship with the debtor.[46] It is possible for novation to occur in respect of company shares because of the existence of the 'statutory contract' between shareholders and the company and the shareholders *inter se*. The terms of the (new) contract (with the new member) are contained in the memorandum and articles of the company, which together form the 'statutory contract'. The agreement of the debtor (issuing company) to the process of novation is shown by it entering the name of the new shareholder (buyer) on the register and removing the name of the previous shareholder (seller).[47] Novation differs from assignment in that a transferee (buyer) is not exposed to the risk (albeit relatively minor in the context of modern financial markets) of her title being affected by defences available to the issuer against the original holder.

1.3 The process of investment

As the focus of this book is on portfolio rather than direct investment, it is assumed that all investments are made through the financial markets. In other words, the process of investment is viewed as comprising the institutions, legal rules and procedures that together form the framework within which investments are issued, bought and sold in financial markets. An overview of that framework follows below and is developed in more detail in subsequent chapters.

1.3.1 Law and markets

Markets (whether organised or not) provide a forum in which investments can be traded.[48] From the legal perspective, contract law provides the basic framework within which markets operate. The role of contract law in markets of any kind is primarily to facilitate transactions or, put another way, to make it possible for private bargaining to occur. This can be understood in two ways. The first is that contract law must provide certainty that bargains will be enforced. Uncertainty surrounding the enforcement of bargains is likely to discourage investment because, even if the legal rights represented by the investment (as a form or property) are quite clear, there will be confusion over whether and on

---

[46] Strictly speaking, therefore, novation is not transfer but its economic effect is the same.

[47] There may be circumstances in which the issuer can, according to its articles, refuse to register a transfer but these will be comparatively rare. See Ch 4 for more detail.

[48] See Ch 9 for a more detailed discussion.

what terms any transfer is to take place. Put another way, there would be little point in the law recognising the transferability of investments if it were not able to provide certainty in respect of the enforcement of bargains under which such transfers are to take place.

Second, facilitation can be understood as meaning that contract law is structured so as to minimise transaction costs for the parties.[49] The most important way in which contract law pursues this objective is through the provision of standard contract terms. These mainly take the form of default rules, which are rules that apply unless disapplied or altered by the parties. Default rules are relevant both to the making of contracts that define investors' rights (such as the 'statutory contract', comprising the memorandum and articles of association in the case of companies[50]) and to contracts under which investments are transferred.[51] The benefit of default rules is that they limit transaction costs by allowing parties to avoid drafting a new agreement every time they contract. They also provide flexibility by allowing the parties to adapt the standard terms to a form that is best suited to their own circumstances.

There are three techniques employed by the law to give effect to standard contract terms.[52] The first, and most straightforward, is that it is possible for a contract to refer to a set of standard conditions that govern the contract. This technique (incorporation by reference) enables several hundred pages of the rules of the London Stock Exchange to be incorporated into the one-page contract note that is the contract for the sale or purchase of securities on that exchange. The second technique is that terms can be implied into contracts even when they have not been expressly agreed between the parties. The rationale for this is that a reasonable person in the position of the contracting parties would have agreed to the inclusion of the term. A third technique (of less relevance in modern financial markets) is that the parties will be bound by a well-established trade custom.

Underlying the concern with providing a legal framework for markets that combines certainty with low transaction costs is the perception that allocative efficiency will be maximised under these conditions. Allocative efficiency refers to the extent to which (scarce) resources are allocated through financial markets to those enterprises that are likely to put them to the best use.

---

[49] As to the economic significance of transaction costs in determining whether and to what extent trading in legal rights (such as investments) is likely to occur see RH Coase, 'The Problem of Social Cost' (1960) 3 *Journal of Law and Economics* 1 and O Williamson, *The Economic Institutions of Capitalism* (New York, Macmillan, 1985).

[50] The standard articles reduce transaction costs in setting up a company and determining shareholders' rights.

[51] Standard contracts for the transfer of investments (eg as regards time of payment and delivery of legal title) reduce transaction costs in the process of managing investments.

[52] See generally Treitel (above n 29) chs 6 and 7, and in respect of Scotland, W McBryde, *Contract*, 2nd edn (Edinburgh, W Green, 2001) chs 7 and 9.

Financial markets play a role in allocating resources (in the form of finance) to enterprises in two ways. First they act as a conduit through which enterprises can raise money directly from investors. Secondly, they provide a mechanism through which securities can be traded to those who value them most highly.[53] Both of these functions contribute most effectively to allocative efficiency when transactions costs are low because it is in these circumstances that market participants are likely to engage in transactions. As transaction costs progressively increase, it is likely that financial markets will perform their functions less effectively and allocative efficiency is likely, in aggregate, to decline.

1.3.2 Regulation

Markets in which contract law pursues only the objective of facilitation of private bargaining may encounter problems. If, for example, there are no controls over the terms that may be agreed between parties, those with a weak bargaining position may have little choice but to accept bad bargains. This has long been regarded as unfair (as well as inefficient in that it is likely to discourage contracting and therefore also the process of investment) and contract law has therefore adopted a regulatory as well as a facilitative objective. That regulatory role involves the making of mandatory rules which must be observed and which cannot be excluded by agreement between the parties.[54] Such rules differ fundamentally from the main body of rules in contract law, which are default rules in the sense that they can be changed by express agreement between the parties. The most obvious examples of the regulatory role played by contract law are the relatively recent statutory controls over contract terms,[55] although there are also much older examples of common law controls over freedom of contract.[56] These regulatory rules are mandatory in the sense that they cannot be avoided by contracting round them.

---

[53] According to the 'Coase Theorem' (above n 50) all legal rights (including financial instruments) will, at least in a world with no transaction costs, be traded to those who value them most highly. The presence of transaction costs will progressively limit the extent to which this process occurs.

[54] In this sense, the term 'regulation' can be applied to any circumstances in which mandatory rules limit the operation of private ordering through contract.

[55] The Unfair Contract Terms Act 1977 and the Unfair Terms in Consumer Contracts Regulations 1999. Both aim to protect consumers (broadly speaking, persons acting in a private rather than a business capacity) by prohibiting or limiting the use of contract terms that are patently unfair (eg terms that exclude liability for breach of contract).

[56] eg the law relating to restraint of trade. See also s 310 of the Companies Act 1985 which renders void any contract that attempts to exempt or restrict the liability of a director (to a company) for breach of duty.

While these aspects of the law's regulatory approach to the process of investment are important, the term 'regulation' is nowadays understood more specifically to refer to rules and procedures created by statute and administered by dedicated agencies. Some elements of regulation, in this more limited sense, have a relatively long history, but the modern form of regulation started in the United States in the early 1930s, largely as a response to the events that culminated in the Wall Street Crash of 1929.[57] In the United Kingdom, there was less inclination to introduce statutory regulation as there was a strong tradition of self-regulation in financial markets. That tradition survived, in varying forms, until the introduction of the Financial Services and Markets Act 2000, which created a system of statutory regulation with a single regulator responsible for investment business in the UK.

The rationale for statutory regulation is that the general commercial law (primarily contract law) does not provide an adequate basis for the operation of investment markets. Investment has two characteristics that differentiate it from other commercial activities, where general commercial law may be adequate.[58] The first is the presence of information asymmetry. In the absence of regulation, investors may lack the information required to make informed investment decisions. There is therefore information asymmetry between the investor and the entrepreneur who wants to attract investment. Such asymmetry is likely to deter investment and, if sufficiently serious, may prevent the emergence of markets for investments. Second, investment often exposes investors to systemic risk. That is the risk that, even if the entity in which they invest or the entity holding their investment is sound, its solvency may be threatened by the collapse of another entity to which it is linked through the financial system. This risk arises most obviously in banking, but is also present in investment. Statutory regulation, such as the system established by the Financial Services and Markets Act 2000 in the United Kingdom, aims to improve the operation of financial markets by creating rules and procedures that limit the risks posed to investors by systemic risk and information asymmetry.

1.3.3 The common law

Despite the expansion in statutory regulation of investment in recent years, the common law remains a significant influence for the process of investment. This results mainly from the central role of trust and fiduciary duty in the organisation of investment entities and in the process of intermediation.

---

[57] See JA Grudfest, 'Securities Regulation' in P Newman (ed) *The New Palgrave Dictionary of Economics and the Law* (Basingstoke, Palgrave Macmillan, 2002) pp 410–19.
[58] These issues are examined in more detail in Ch 2.

Trusts are a legal device that enables the legal ownership of property to be separated from the enjoyment of the benefits that flow from that property.[59] They are commonly used as the legal structure under which investments are held and managed in the United Kingdom.[60] Occupational pension funds and unit trusts are structured as trusts, thereby enabling large numbers of small investors to have an interest in a fund that is legally owned by the trustees.[61] Custodians (sometimes referred to as nominees) hold investments on trust for their customers, thereby simplifying and centralising the administrative aspects of the ownership of investments.

Fiduciary duty arises in circumstances in which the law recognises a relationship of trust between two parties. In the investment context, important instances of fiduciary duty are the duty owed by a trustee to a beneficiary of a trust, a director to a company and an agent to a principal. Underlying the law in each instance is the objective that a fiduciary should not allow her own interest to conflict with that of the person to whom the duty is owed and should act at all times in the best interests of that person.[62]

Fiduciary duty is central to the process of investment. In the case of investment advice, for example, an independent adviser is considered the agent of the client and therefore owes a fiduciary duty to the client. Trustees of a unit trust or an occupational pension scheme owe a fiduciary duty to trust beneficiaries (unit-holders or relevant employees respectively) and therefore investment (and other) decisions must be made according to the high standards the law demands from a fiduciary. In some respects, statutory regulation has replicated much of the content of fiduciary duty in regulatory rules. This is evident in rules such as suitability, which governs the standard of advice required from a financial adviser. However, as the courts have made clear, regulation has not superseded the common law and, in many respects, the wide-ranging and flexible nature of fiduciary duty represents a more appropriate legal basis for governing the process of investment than regulatory rules that are often (at least for private investors) complex, counter-intuitive and inaccessible.[63]

Fiduciary duty also arises when an agent acts on behalf of a principal. This occurs in many instances during the process of investment, common examples

[59] This brief introduction ignores the different doctrinal bases of trust law in Scotland and England. The English law of trusts recognises that ownership rights can be split between a legal owner (the trustee) and a beneficial owner (the beneficiary of the trust). Scots law does not recognise the possibility of ownership rights being divided in this way. In Scots law one is either a legal owner (including a common or joint owner) or not an owner. See Ch 5 for discussion of the nature of the rights of a beneficiary of a trust in Scotland.

[60] The role of trusts is discussed in more detail in Ch 5.

[61] See Ch 5 for more detail on the nature of the ownership interest.

[62] For a classic statement of the content of fiduciary duty see *Aberdeen Railway Company v Blaikie Bros* (1854) 1 MacQueen 461 (HL).

[63] See Ch 6 for more discussion of the relative roles of the common law and regulatory rules.

being a broker buying shares for a client or an independent financial adviser providing advice to a client. The agent is taken to be in a position of trust as regards the carrying out of the mandate of the principal and is therefore subject to the full rigour of fiduciary duty.[64]

The common law of tort (delict in Scotland) is also important in the context of investment. Liability can arise in tort in circumstances in which the common law holds that one person owes a duty of care to another. For example, in the case of *Hedley Byrne v Heller*[65] it was held that a bank owed a duty of care to a third party who relied in the course of business on a reference given by the bank in respect of a customer. In the investment context, the law of tort is relevant when financial advice is given to a potential or actual customer or when information or an opinion is provided on which others rely in making investment decisions. Liability in tort is particularly important as a means of redress when there is no contractual relationship between the parties, such as when a sales representative 'advises' a potential customer regarding the sale of a financial product.[66]

Common law criminal offences have now become of relatively minor significance as far as the process of investment is concerned. Two related reasons can be given for this. One is that they have not proven to be an effective mechanism for punishing what may be termed 'wrongdoing' in financial transactions. Fraud is the most obvious example: it is difficult to collect adequate evidence to show intent to commit fraud and there is the added complication of ensuring that a jury is able to understand the often complicated factual circumstances associated with fraud in financial transactions. Another reason is that there has been a substantial expansion in the range of 'regulatory' criminal offences, which have been created as part of the system of financial regulation and company law. They include insider dealing, market manipulation, misleading investors and a whole array of more minor and technical offences. Moreover, there is an increasing tendency, as evidenced by the new market abuse regime,[67] for the regulatory system to ignore the criminal law altogether and to resort to sanctions imposed by the financial regulator rather than by courts.

---

[64] See generally G Fridman, *Fridman's Law of Agency*, 7th edn (London, Butterworths, 1996) ch 8.

[65] [1964] AC 465. It was held in this particular case that the bank had not actually breached its duty of care (because its reference included a disclaimer of liability) but the principle has nevertheless had a far-reaching impact in respect of potential liability for negligent financial advice.

[66] See the cases discussed in Ch 6.3.

[67] See Ch 9 for more detail.

1.3.4 Investment entities

Earlier in this chapter, reference was made to the role of financial institutions in the process of financial intermediation. Nowadays, much of that process (at least as far as financial investment is concerned) takes place through specialised investment entities and legal structures. A distinction can be drawn between two types of entity or legal structure through which the process of financial intermediation takes place. The first are what may be termed fiduciary entities, which hold investments on trust for their clients.[68] As they act in a fiduciary capacity, they are subject to the rigorous standards required by the law from fiduciaries.[69] In this category are unit trusts, pension funds and custodians. The second category can be termed non-fiduciary entities. In the latter category are insurers and deposit-taking institutions. They have a contractual rather than a fiduciary relationship with their customer and this has important implications for the nature of the relationship between the parties and the rights of the 'investor'. In the case of both insurance and deposits, the institution becomes the owner of the money it receives from the 'investor', who has only a contractual claim against the institution to perform the obligations contained in the relevant contract. Moreover, such an institution does not normally[70] have a fiduciary duty to the customer, with the result that the normal principles of contract law (including *caveat emptor*[71]) apply.[72]

As well as undertaking the function of financial intermediation (in the economic sense discussed in section 1.1 of this chapter), investment entities also undertake the function of re-packaging investments in a form suitable for investors. For example, unit trusts, in addition to providing risk diversification, also transform the legal mechanism under which an investor owns a company share. If an investor were to own the share directly, her rights would be determined primarily by the 'statutory contract' under section 14 of the Companies Act 1985. If she owns the share indirectly through a unit trust, it is the trustees who are the legal owner (and therefore party to the

---

[68] In English law, the client of such an entity can be described as the beneficial owner of the investment. In Scotland the client will either be the beneficiary of a trust or the principal in respect of an agency agreement.

[69] See Ch 6 for more detail.

[70] It may be assumed in special circumstances. See Wadsley and Penn (above n 34) paras 3-009–3.013.

[71] Meaning 'buyer beware'. The expression emphasises that contracts are generally made 'at arm's length' with the result that each party must look after their own interests.

[72] It is of course true that the principle of *caveat emptor* has been modified considerably by the regulatory obligations imposed on financial institutions (see eg the relevance for life insurers of the regulatory obligation to treat with-profits policyholders fairly, discussed in Ch 4.10).

'statutory contract') and she is a beneficiary of the trust. A similar process occurs in occupational pension schemes, which operate under the legal structure of trust. In both instances, the transformation of the legal nature of the rights of the 'ultimate investor' makes possible the achievement of the economic objectives inherent in pooled investment funds (primarily risk diversification and economies of scale).

2

Regulation of Investment— Rationale and Development

Chapter 1 drew a distinction between 'regulation' and the broader set of legal principles and rules applicable to financial investment. This chapter examines the rationale for regulation in the sphere of financial investment and its historical development. The scale and complexity of the system of regulation in the modern world is such that its existence is often taken for granted. It is true that the case for regulation is now broadly accepted, but there are at least two good reasons for exploring the rationale for regulation. The first is that such an examination is likely to provide guidance as to the objectives of a regulatory system in the sense that any system of regulation must reflect the rationale for its creation.[1] It does not, however, provide direct guidance as to the techniques by which those objectives are given effect and it is for this reason that regulatory systems around the world differ despite often sharing common objectives. The second reason for exploring the rationale for regulation is that it provides a clearer picture of the costs and benefits of regulation by focusing attention on the movement from an unregulated to a regulated world. Ultimately, the value of any system of regulation must be judged by a comparison between those benefits and the costs that arise from implementing regulation.[2]

The development of regulation prior to the Financial Services and Markets Act 2000 is also discussed in this chapter. The objective is to put the current system into historical perspective and to provide some indication of how attitudes towards financial regulation and the role of financial markets have

---

[1] See A Ogus, *Regulation: Legal Form and Economic Theory* (Oxford, Clarendon Press, 1994) ch 1.

[2] This is not to say that policy considerations that do not have a well-defined economic value (eg a desire to limit the extent to which individuals might experience hardship through being over-indebted) cannot form part of the assessment of whether regulation is necessary. Indeed, it might well be said that the more fundamental the rationale for a particular form of regulation, the more difficult it is to engage in cost–benefit analysis because it is more difficult to calculate the costs and benefits relevant to broad policies (eg the reduction of financial crime) than it is in the case of regulatory techniques (eg disclosure) that have a narrower field of application.

changed over time. Finally, this chapter also provides an introduction to the emerging regulatory framework for financial investment at the international level.

2.1 The need for regulation

Why do financial markets require regulation? To answer this question we need to consider the legal framework under which markets operate without regulation. There are two aspects to consider. The first is the structure and operation of the market itself as distinct from the transactions taking place in the market. In an unregulated market, there will in principle be unrestricted and free access to the market place for buyers and sellers. In other words there will be no requirement for licensing or authorisation as a condition for engaging in a particular activity. Nor are there likely to be 'market rules' relating to the structure and the operation of the market, such as standard rules determining when payment or delivery is due under contracts or rules governing the conduct of participants in the market.[3]

The second aspect is the legal framework governing transactions in the market. The essential elements of that legal framework are property law and contract law, which together define ownership interests and their mode of transfer. In principle, a market can operate without regulation in circumstances in which the law is sufficiently developed to provide certainty in respect of ownership interests[4] and their transfer and to punish the most obvious forms of fraudulent activity. Indeed, markets in many goods and services operate successfully on this basis without any 'regulatory' intervention.

However, an unregulated market may operate in a manner that ultimately leads to the conclusion that some form of regulation is necessary.[5] First, unrestricted access to the market may have a damaging effect if unscrupulous individuals are permitted to participate. This is a particular problem in financial markets because of the nature of the product being sold and the relationship between the product and the seller. A simple financial product such as a bank deposit account provides an example. It gives the depositor a contractual claim

---

[3] Such 'market rules' can be distinguished from contract law although both govern the conduct of contracting parties. The former are concerned primarily with the structure and operation of the market, the latter with the rights and obligations of the contracting parties. Market rules are associated with organised markets whereas ad hoc contracting can be governed only by contract law.

[4] It was noted in Ch 1.2 that ownership rights in financial investments are essentially contractual rights which are considered to be 'property'.

[5] See generally Ogus (above n 1) chs 3 and 10.

against the bank which can only be satisfied if the bank has sufficient funds to meet the claim. The depositor does not 'own' the deposit in the legal sense as the money deposited in the bank is owned by the bank.[6] Instead, the depositor relies on the on-going ability of the bank to repay deposits when they fall due. The trust placed by the depositor in the financial soundness of the bank is central to the transaction but, in most cases, is something that the depositor cannot independently verify. Without regulation of entry, the market is in principle open to those who would abuse this trust by running a bank in a way that threatens the interests of depositors.

The second problem, which compounds the first, is that the presence of information asymmetry is particularly severe in financial markets.[7] Two examples illustrate the problem. Consider first the position of a small group of shareholders who between them own and manage a company. They want to raise more capital through an offer of shares to the public. Clearly, their knowledge of the company and its prospects are superior to the new investors they hope to attract into the company. Applying the normal principles of contract law to the offer of new shares would result in very limited disclosure of information to the new investors because contract law generally does not require information to be volunteered to the other side. Without regulation, new investors would lack the confidence to buy the new shares. One might argue at this point that the investors could require information as a condition of investing. Well-informed investors might well do so but others might lack the ability to define the necessary information. In any event, the lack of a minimum standard of information disclosure would have the potential to discourage investment and cause confusion among investors.

Another example is that of a private individual buying a pension. The product itself is often complex and so too are the tax rules and the relationship between private and state pensions. In many cases an individual will face making an important decision relating to retirement without a proper understanding of the relevant issues. This can arise simply as a result of inherent complexity in the investment even when there is adequate information available.

Unlimited access and information asymmetry may both threaten the existence or scale of the market. Unlimited access to the market poses a risk in that reputable suppliers of the same service may not be able to differentiate themselves sufficiently from disreputable suppliers and so may be unable to achieve higher prices (reflecting their financial soundness and reliability).

---

[6] *Foley v Hill* (1848) 2 HL Cas 28. See generally J Wadsley and GA Penn, *The Law Relating to Domestic Banking*, 2nd edn (London, Sweet & Maxwell, 2000).

[7] The effect of information asymmetry on the operation of markets was first elaborated by G Akerlof in 'Market for Lemons: Quantitative Uncertainty and the Market Mechanism' (1970) *Quarterly Journal of Economics* 222.

Information asymmetry poses a problem in that those who lack information on which to base decisions (such as the investors in the capital of the company described above) may decide not to invest or to limit their investment to less than it would have been had they had more information. It can be seen, therefore, that both suppliers and buyers of financial products may, in an unregulated market, have incentives either to withdraw from the market or to limit their involvement in it.[8]

There may also be problems in punishing fraudulent activity in an unregulated market. The criminal law of fraud is a relatively blunt instrument, which is capable of dealing with very obvious instances of fraud (eg when an instrument of transfer is forged in an attempt to gain ownership of an investment) but it is less well suited to dealing with conduct which is not expressly 'criminal' but nevertheless is damaging to the operation of financial markets. For example, investors are likely to be discouraged from investing if company profits are routinely overstated in prospectuses offering shares to the public, but it is not always the case that this type of misleading behaviour would be categorised as fraud.[9]

At this point, it can be asked if unregulated markets and their legal infrastructure can evolve in a manner that resolves the problems outlined above. In respect of the first issue, unrestricted access, economists have argued that there are powerful theoretical reasons for believing that self-regulation on the part of market participants will restrict market access in circumstances where the existence or scale of the market is threatened by open access.[10] The history of regulation in the London Stock Exchange (LSE) tends to support such a view. Having initially operated as a forum that was in principle open to all buyers and sellers, the LSE limited access to its members (who were required to satisfy a 'fit and proper' test) in 1801.[11] The effect was to enhance and expand the

---

[8] This process is often referred to by economists as 'adverse selection', a concept first developed in the field of insurance to describe the process by which the presence of information asymmetry in the formation of insurance contracts is likely to lead to insurers providing cover primarily to the riskiest individuals or properties because they lack the information to evaluate risk accurately.

[9] See J Birds (ed) *Boyle & Birds' Company Law*, 5th edn (Bristol, Jordans, 2004) para 19.36 for a discussion of common law fraud in the context of public offers of securities.

[10] See, for theoretical analyis, P Spencer, *The Structure and Regulation of Financial Markets* (Oxford, OUP, 2000) pp 30–33; and for an historical perspective C Day, 'Bits and Pieces and Moral Authority: The Paradox of Success in the Unregulated 19th Century New York Capital Markets', available at http://ssrn.com/abstract=572163 (8 Nov 2004).

[11] R Michie, *The LSE: a History* (Oxford, OUP, 1999) observes (at p 31) that:

> Essentially, what the professionals wanted so as to ensure speed and trust was a market in which all present were active participants, ready to buy or sell when the opportunity arose, and each possessing a reputation for honouring their part of a bargain. In turn, those who did not fit these criteria or meet the standards set would be excluded from the market.

trading capacity of the market because control over entry provided a higher level of confidence among market participants that the chains of credit typically associated with transactions would be honoured. In respect of the second issue, the rules governing transactions in the market, it is more difficult to judge the extent to which evolution and adaptation could provide a solution. It is certainly true that the common law is inherently adaptable[12] but the problem is that it may not be able to evolve quickly enough to meet the needs of rapidly developing markets. Another problem is that the common law is generally based on default rather than mandatory rules,[13] with the result that any 'investor protection' rules that arose from the common law could in principle be avoided by contract.

Financial market regulation can also be justified by reference to systemic risk. This is the risk of failure of an individual institution having a 'domino' effect, leading to the collapse of other institutions and a threat to the entire financial system. This risk is present particularly in chains of transactions that are linked by credit, where the scale of credit is large by comparison with the capital of the participants.[14] Systemic risk is present particularly in the banking sector, where extended chains of credit are common, but it is also present in securities markets, where firms may be linked by credit chains as a result of settlement obligations arising from buying and selling securities. However, systemic risk justifies only a limited form of financial regulation in respect of the financial resources of market participants. This form of regulation is generally referred to as prudential supervision and is mainly implemented through capital adequacy rules that require sufficient regulatory capital to be available to cover the risks arising from banking and trading in financial markets. The objective of prudential supervision is to ensure that shareholders rather than customers bear the risk of loss arising from regulated activity.

Finally, regulation can be justified simply by paternalism. On this view, the state supplies regulation because it knows what is best for its citizens and acts so as to protect them. While in principle it can be used to justify extensive regulation of financial markets, paternalism is most persuasive as a basis for regulation in relation to private investors. Professional and institutional investors are better able to look after their own interests and therefore require less protection from the state.

---

[12] An example is the manner in which the general principles of contract law were adapted to suit the needs of insurance contracts in the eighteenth and nineteenth centuries through the development of the duty of disclosure, which resolved the problem of information asymmetry.

[13] See Ch 1.3.2.

[14] See, for example, the account of the collapse in 1998 of Long Term Capital Management (LTCM) in S Valdez, *An Introduction to Global Financial Markets* (London, Macmillan, 2000) p 343. LTCM had borrowings of 50 times its shareholders' capital.

2.2 Regulatory models and techniques

Once the need for regulation of financial markets has been identified, the question of the form that regulation should take needs to be addressed.[15] The most basic issue to be determined is whether regulation should be supplied by government or by the market itself. The former is typically referred to as statutory regulation and the latter as self-regulation. They are not mutually exclusive. It is possible, as shown by the system of regulation created by the Financial Services Act 1986, for a hybrid to be created combining statutory regulation and self-regulation. The attraction of a statutory system is that it removes regulation from the control of market participants and provides a clear legal framework for the exercise of the regulator's powers. Self-regulation offers the potential for regulation that is more flexible and responsive to market developments but it inevitably suffers from the risk that the system will evolve in a manner which favours the narrow interests of market participants over the broader public interest. In the main, most countries, including the UK, have now concluded that a heavy reliance on self-regulation is no longer appropriate in financial markets, but some have continued to recognise that it can be beneficial to allow for some degree of self-regulation within the system.[16]

A second issue to be considered is the manner in which the scope and operation of the system of regulation is defined. There are two possibilities. Functional regulation defines a particular type of activity (eg 'investment business') and regulates any person engaging in this type of activity. Institutional regulation focuses on particular types of institution (eg banks) and regulates whatever business is conducted by that institution. Both have strengths and weaknesses. Functional regulation takes account of the fact that particular activities are often carried on by different institutions as distinctions between different types of financial institution have become increasingly blurred. It can, however, give to rise to problems of co-ordination when different regulators are responsible for different parts of an institution's business. Institutional regulation allows the entire business of an institution to be controlled by a single regulator, but may lead to variable regulatory treatment of institutions in respect of the same business if different regulators are responsible for different categories of institution.

[15] See generally A Page and R Ferguson, *Investor Protection* (London, Weidenfeld & Nicolson, 1992) ch 6.

[16] Elements of the self-regulatory approach in the UK survive in the fields of corporate governance and takeover regulation (see Ch 8). See E Ferran, 'Corporate Law, Codes and Social Norms—Finding the Right Regulatory Combination and Institutional Structure' (2001) 1 *Journal of Corporate Law Studies* 381.

Two other issues are linked with the choice between the institutional and functional principle of regulation. The first is the choice between a single or multiple regulators for the financial sector and the second is the issue of legal separation of different financial activities. As was historically the case in the UK prior to 1998, some countries adopt a system of multiple financial regulators, with responsibility typically being divided between the banking, insurance and securities sectors. This division of responsibility between regulators can be organised on the functional (as was the case in the UK) or institutional principle. Irrespective of the manner in which it is organised, the presence of multiple regulators is likely to raise problems, particularly in a liberal financial environment in which financial conglomerates can engage in a variety of activities. It was precisely this problem that was one of the main reasons for the UK moving to a single financial regulator in 1998. However, there is an important reason why multiple regulators survive in many other countries. It is that they are linked with legal restrictions on combining different types of financial activity within a single organisation or under common ownership. The purpose of such restrictions is to limit the accumulation of different types of risk within a single organisation. This can serve the interests of shareholders in the relevant institutions as well as the regulators, at least in circumstances in which there are real concerns over the ability to monitor and manage risk. The best known example is probably the now-largely-repealed Glass-Steagall Act in the United States which prohibited commercial banks from engaging in non-banking business and thereby created a 'firewall' between commercial banking on the one hand and securities and investment banking business on the other.[17]

A number of different techniques are available to regulate the financial sector. It will become apparent in later chapters that the system of regulation in the UK represents a combination of all the techniques referred to below.

Disclosure aims to resolve the information asymmetry which forms a substantial part of the rationale for regulation. Its function is to make information available so as to allow investors to make informed choices, with the result that the market operates more efficiently (eg in the investment context by allocating capital more efficiently to competing uses). Recognition of the role of disclosure obligations as a device to resolve information asymmetry has a long history, which pre-dates the modern (post 1930s) phase of financial regulation. Two examples are particularly noteworthy. First, the common law, from the mid-eighteenth century onwards began to develop an obligation of disclosure in insurance contracts as a device to resolve the information disadvantage of an insurer in respect of insured risks. Second, the Companies Acts from 1844 onwards imposed disclosure obligations on the issuer of a prospectus

---

[17] See M Nance and B Singhof, 'Banking's Influence over Non-Bank Companies after Glass-Steagall: A German Universal Comparison' (2000) 14 *Emory International Law Review* 1305.

offering shares to the public. This occurred at a time when the Stock Exchange was a private body and there was no system of financial regulation in the modern sense. More recently, the need for mandatory disclosure has at times been questioned. For example, in the United States, it has been argued that the extensive disclosure obligations mandated by the Securities and Exchange Commission ignore the capacity of markets to require the disclosure of information when it is required for efficient decision-making.[18] However, there now appears to be broad acceptance of the role of disclosure as a regulatory device.[19]

Allied to disclosure are a number of related devices. Registration is a device for making information available to the public at large.[20] The most obvious example is the requirement imposed on companies by the Companies Act 1985 to register information at Companies House. This is in addition to the information that has to be sent directly to shareholders. The purpose of registration is to make the information available to the public at large so that it can be used for any purpose in connection with the relevant company (eg lending, providing trade credit). Audit is intended to provide reassurance to investors that financial statements represent a 'true and fair' view of a company: they provide some reassurance relating to the quality of information. Risk warnings are intended to encourage an evaluation of risk on the part of investors, who might not otherwise attempt to relate the characteristics of a particular investment to their own financial position. Cooling-off periods provide investors with an opportunity to re-consider a transaction and to withdraw from it. They were introduced as a response to high-pressure sales techniques and modify the general rules of contract law by allowing the investor to withdraw from a legally binding transaction.

No modern system of financial regulation relies entirely on disclosure (and its related devices). Nowadays, authorisation (or licensing) has become a standard technique. The objective is to create a perimeter from which unauthorised persons are excluded and within which the regulator can exert control over authorised persons. The authority of the regulator ultimately rests on its ability to punish non-compliance with exclusion from the regulated activity. The regulator is typically given a wide discretion to grant authorisa-

---

[18] See H Jackson and E Pan, 'Regulatory Competition in International Securities Markets: Evidence from Europe in 1999—Part 1' (2001) 56 *Business Law* 653.

[19] This is reflected in the approach taken by the International Organisation of Securities Commissioners (IOSCO)—see 'Objectives and Principles of Securities Regulation' at www.iosco.org (11 Nov 2004). The nature and function of IOSCO is discussed in 2.5 below. See also K Lanoo, 'The Emerging Framework for Disclosure in the EU' (2003) 3 *Journal of Corporate Law Studies* 329.

[20] Page and Ferguson (above n 15 at p 50) distinguish registration in principle from certification and licensing but note that, historically, there has been a tendency to combine registration with licensing.

tion. In the UK, this has taken the form of requiring the applicant to satisfy a 'fit and proper' test as well as other specific requirements.

Another feature of modern systems of financial regulation is prudential supervision. This focuses on controlling the solvency and liquidity of participants in financial markets. The purpose of such controls is to ensure that customers are not threatened by the risks to which financial institutions are exposed in the normal course of their business. In the case of banks, the most obvious risk is credit risk, which is the risk that borrowers will default on loans to such an extent that the solvency of the bank is threatened. In the case of securities firms (or banks involved in securities business) the main risk is market risk, which is the risk that the value of the firm's holdings of securities will fall to such an extent as to threaten its solvency. Regulators attempt to protect customers from these risks by requiring banks and securities firms to have minimum levels of shareholders' capital (sometimes referred to as regulatory capital) and to hold a certain proportion of their assets in a liquid (readily-realisable) form. This has the effect that, if the firm were to face financial difficulties, losses would be borne by shareholders before customers became affected. In this sense, prudential supervision uses regulatory capital to protect customers. Shareholders in financial institutions, on the other hand, receive no special protection from the system of prudential supervision. They are assumed to face the normal risks arising in any business, which includes insolvency.

Conduct of business rules are an important part of the UK system of regulation. They are rules that control the manner in which individual financial transactions are conducted. They impose different types of obligations in different circumstances. Many are in effect disclosure (or related) obligations, such as the rules that require disclosure of information to a customer before a transaction is agreed. Others go beyond disclosure and limit the freedom of action of authorised persons or have important implications for the structure of the market.[21] Central to the operation of conduct of business rules is the system of customer classification used in the Financial Services Authority (FSA) rulebook.[22] The effect of this system is to provide different levels of investor protection in different circumstances. Private investors are given very extensive protection by conduct of business rules but professional investors are subject to much less regulation in their dealings with each other.

Portfolio regulation is a technique that restricts the investments that can be made by a financial institution or a person managing investments. Historically, trustees have been subject to such restrictions under the Trustee Investment

---

[21] The rules on 'suitability' (governing the provision of financial advice to private investors) fall into the former category, whereas the rules relating to 'polarisation' (discussed in Ch 6) fall into the latter.

[22] See Ch 10 for more detail.

Acts and the system of prudential supervision in respect of banks, building societies and insurers has also adopted this technique. It has also been adopted in the system of regulation for collective investment funds. The general objective has been to protect customers by limiting exposure to the riskier classes of investments.

Powers of intervention are another regulatory technique. They were employed by the Insurance Companies Act 1982, the Financial Services Act 1986 (FSA 1986) and the Banking Act 1987 (all now superseded by the Financial Services and Markets Act 2000 (FSMA 2000)). Their purpose, broadly speaking, was to permit the regulator to intervene in the business of a regulated firm when there were grounds for concern. For the purposes of UK authorised persons, the concept of intervention has been superseded by the power of the regulator to impose requirements on permission or vary the permission of an authorised person. This is a narrower power by comparison with the power of intervention previously provided by the FSA 1986 because it rules out direct intervention by the regulator in the running of the business. The powers of intervention contained in FSMA 2000 are now confined to those necessary to give effect to the relevant provisions of the EU single market directives.[23]

Finally, compensation schemes can also be considered to be a regulatory technique. Prudential supervision attempts to protect customers from insolvency but it cannot provide a guarantee that insolvency will not occur. The purpose of compensation schemes is to provide a guarantee to investors that they will be compensated for losses resulting from the insolvency of an authorised person. A requirement that an authorised firm be a member of an approved compensation scheme represents a technique available to a regulator to bolster the confidence of customers in the firms they use to conduct financial transactions. However, it does not remove all risk from customers as compensation schemes generally include a co-insurance provision (requiring the customer to bear a proportion of the loss) and limit the size of any financial award.[24]

2.3 Regulation in the United Kingdom prior to the Financial Services Act 1986

The perception that the pre-FSA 1986 period in the UK was dominated by self-regulation is both right and wrong. It is wrong in the sense that, historically, there were several instances of statutory intervention in the working of the

---

[23] See generally 2.5 below.

[24] Compensation following insolvency of an authorised person is discussed in Ch 6.

financial markets. It is right in the sense that, to a substantial extent, statutory intervention had a less significant influence on the operation of markets than self-regulatory rules.

Trading in financial securities was already well established in London in 1697 when an Act was introduced to regulate trading. At this time, the market was mainly in government securities[25] and there was no distinction between brokers (acting as agents on behalf of their customers) and dealers acting as principals ('jobbers' or, in modern parlance, 'market-makers'). The Act required brokers and dealers to be licensed, limited the number of brokers to 100, fixed maximum commission levels and required transactions to be recorded. It was a temporary measure and lapsed when it was not renewed in 1707.

In 1801, the Stock Exchange in its modern form came into existence. It controlled admission of members and required an annual application for re-admission, thereby opening up the possibility of exclusion if a member's conduct was considered unacceptable. From 1812 onwards all members of the London Stock Exchange had to confine their business to buying and selling securities, the objective being to limit the risk arising from a member's bankruptcy.[26] At this stage the securities market was essentially a market in government securities. However, over the course of the nineteenth century there was a transformation in the nature of the securities traded on the United Kingdom securities markets.[27] By the end of the century corporate securities comprised a substantial part of the market. This was made possible by several key developments in corporate law during that period. One was the possibility to incorporate a company by registration, which was introduced by the Companies Act 1844. Before that time incorporation was not freely available.[28]

[25] See Michie (above n 11 at p 18), who describes the emergence of securities markets in the UK as follows:

> The real foundation of the securities market, that eventually led to the formation of the London Stock Exchange, took place in the year 1693 when the government, for the first time, borrowed by creating a permanent debt that was transferable. Previous to that the government's borrowing had been on a short-term basis, with the debt being either redeemed or refinanced, depending on the state of the national finances, when it became due.

[26] The Stock Exchange was concerned that if members were involved in other forms of trade (as they had been previously) bankruptcy could lead to trade creditors other than Stock Exchange members having claims on a member's assets. Given the extended credit and settlement chains that often existed in Stock Exchange dealings, this posed a risk for the operation of the Stock Exchange.

[27] The sheer scale of company promotions during certain periods in the nineteenth century makes the twentieth century pale by comparison. For example, Michie (above n 11 at p 56) refers to there being 624 joint-stock companies promoted in 1824–25. Of these only 127 survived until the end of 1826. This was before the advent of the disclosure and registration obligations introduced by the Companies Act 1844.

[28] See, regarding the history of incorporation, P Davies, *Gower's Principles of Modern Company Law* 6th edn (London, Sweet & Maxwell, 1997) ch 3.

A second factor was the general availability of limited liability as a result of the Limited Liability Act 1855.[29] A third factor, which was crucial for future developments in investor protection, was the emergence of disclosure obligations in respect of public offers of securities. At this stage, the Stock Exchange regarded itself primarily as a market for secondary trading in securities and therefore it made no attempt to regulate disclosure in relation to offers of shares to the public.[30] That was seen as a matter for the common law, which made available a range of remedies to investors who bought securities on the basis of prospectuses that were misleading or omitted material facts.[30a]

The establishment of provincial stock exchanges during the nineteenth century also had an impact on the development of regulation within the London Stock Exchange (LSE). The provincial exchanges were mainly involved in trading government securities and shares in local companies. Their role in financing and trading in the shares of railway and canal companies was particularly important. They did not, in the main, compete directly with the LSE because they could not offer the liquidity or range of securities available on the LSE. There was therefore a substantial volume of business passed from brokers and jobbers in provincial exchanges to the London market, a process that was eased by the introduction of the telegraph and later telephone links. The manner in which this business was conducted had an important impact on regulation within the Stock Exchange itself. There were two main concerns. Brokers were concerned that outsiders (provincial brokers and and banks) had direct access to LSE jobbers and that commissions were being forced down by competition to attract business from provincial exchanges. Jobbers were concerned that they were being bypassed as brokers made markets in securities and brokers were concerned that jobbers had direct contacts with sources of business outside the Stock Exchange. This threatened the operation of the 'single capacity' market model in which jobbers were limited to acting as principals (making markets) and brokers as agents.[31] The Stock Exchange

---

[29] See H Hansmann and R Kraakman, 'The Essential Role of Organizational Law' (2000) 110 *Yale Law Journal* 387.

[30] This is not to say that the Stock Exchange admitted the securities of any company to listing. The position was described as follows:

> the Stock Exchanges guard the public, in so far as they are able, in declining to admit to quotations the questionable enterprises of 'shady' promoters, but they do not in any manner thereby indicate any opinion, personal or official, as to the value of such issues, or their real genuineness or soundness. That is entirely beyond their province, and the persons buying issues that have been 'listed' should scrutinise the property and investigate the value for themselves.

(GR Gibson, *The Stock Exchanges of London, Paris and New York: A Comparison*, New York, 1889, 37, quoted in Michie, above n 11, ch 3 p 96).

[30a] See Birds (above n 9) pp 618–25.

[31] Michie (above n 11 at p 113) notes that this model ('single capacity') was effectively enshrined in the Stock Exchange Rules from 1847 onwards, but was not enforced.

responded to both concerns by introducing rules which were to remain in place (albeit in modified form) until the 'Big Bang' in 1986.[32] In 1909, dual capacity was prohibited with the result that members could only act as a broker or a jobber. From the legal perspective, the requirement of single capacity introduced a strict division between the activities of agents (brokers acting for clients in accordance with fiduciary duties) and principals (jobbers acting on their own account with no duty owed to other parties). In 1912, minimum commissions were introduced, thereby limiting the possibility of competition between members based on transaction cost.

In the United States, the Wall Street Crash of 1929 was an important influence in the introduction of the new statutory system of regulation established by the Securities Act 1933 and the Securities and Exchange Act 1934. In the United Kingdom, there was a more limited reaction to the crash. Attention was focused not on the activities of the Stock Exchange but on those outside the Exchange who were engaged in promoting securities to the public. One particular concern was the growth in unit trusts. They had existed for at least 50 years, having become popular in the 1870s, but had expanded considerably in the 1930s following the adoption of the more flexible legal structure (imported from the USA) which allowed continuous creation and redemption of units by the manager.

The Prevention of Fraud (Investments) Act 1939 made two significant changes to the existing law.[33] First, it required dealers in securities either to be licensed or be granted exempt status. Members of a recognised stock exchange were automatically granted exempt status and it was open to any dealer to apply for an individual exemption. Many of the banks (commercial and merchant), insurance companies and investment trusts gained exempt status. The result was that 'licensed dealer' status was largely confined to fringe operators who were not members of an exchange or well-established financial institutions. The second change made by the Act was the introduction of Conduct of Business Rules governing the manner in which transactions are conducted. Although, under the 1939 Act, these rules were confined to the relatively small category of 'licensed dealer', they were later to take on a much more extensive role under the Financial Services Act 1986. Following some amendments made to the 1939 Act by later Companies Acts, it was re-enacted in 1958.

Although the Bank of England was nationalised in 1946 and provision was made for it to assume a statutory role in regulating the banking sector, it continued to rely on its traditional informal role in supervising banks.[34] There was no authorisation requirement and no formal rules governing the way a bank

---

[32] See below 2.4.

[33] See generally R Pennington, *The Law of the Investment Markets* (London, BSB Professional, 1990) paras 2.07–2.13.

[34] See generally Wadsley and Penn (above n 6) ch 1.

carried on its business. The Bank was reputed to rely on its power and status as the Central Bank and the disciplining effect of a 'raised eyebrow' in supervising the banking sector. This approach remained in place until 1979 when the first EC[35] Banking Directive required the introduction of a statutory system of banking regulation. The informal system of banking regulation that operated before 1979 facilitated the expansion of merchant banks' involvement in the securities markets. Members of the Issuing Houses Association had a long history of organising company flotations and had also developed fund management business. The post-war period brought a new development in the form of takeovers and mergers. The conduct of takeovers raised important issues for shareholders and the market and a solution was sought through self-regulation rather than statutory control. The Notes on Takeovers and Amalgamations were introduced in 1959 and later became the Takeover Code, administered by the Takeover Panel. The Panel and the Code still survive today, sustained by a reputation for sound rule-making, rapid decision-making and effective enforcement.[36]

2.4 The Financial Services Act 1986

The Financial Services Act 1986 represented the beginning of the modern era of regulation of investment business in the United Kingdom. It was introduced during a time of significant change in the financial sector both within the United Kingdom and elsewhere. A number of changes had occurred before 1986, which had fundamentally altered the structure and operation of financial markets in the UK. Exchange controls were removed in 1979, encouraging the flow of investment into and out of the UK and the internationalisation of the UK financial markets. Significant changes also occurred in the London Stock Exchange. First, restrictions on outside ownership of member firms were removed as a result of a series of changes in the rules of the Exchange, thereby permitting foreign (mainly US) firms to take an ownership interest and start the process of formation of financial conglomerates. Second, in response to the threat of being taken before the restrictive trade practices court, the Stock Exchange abandoned its 'single capacity' rule and allowed members to act in a 'dual capacity'. The effect of this change was that members could now act at the same time as agents for clients and as principals trading in securities on their own account (ie they could become combined broker/dealers rather than having to choose between being one or the other). This change, taken together with the replacement of 'face-to-face' dealing on the floor of the Exchange with a new computerised dealing system (the Stock Exchange Automated

---

[35] For EC see below n 55.
[36] See Ch 8 for more detail on the Takeover Panel and Code.

Quotation System or SEAQ), came to be referred to as the 'Big Bang',[37] reflecting the fundamental transformation in the operation of the Exchange that occurred on the day (27 October 1986) that these two reforms took effect.

Significant change was also evident in the retail financial market. The mortgage market expanded rapidly as the Bank of England liberalised the mortgage-lending regime and this in turn led to a rapid expansion in the market for endowment life assurance as a mechanism to repay mortgages. This reflected the trend established in the 1970s whereby life assurance came to be regarded as much as a form of investment as a form of financial protection against early death.

The Financial Services Act 1986 made two significant changes to the existing regulatory regime. First, it created a single regulatory structure for all 'investment business'. The underlying rationale was that all those involved in this business should operate on a 'level playing field' with consequent benefits for investor protection and the promotion of competition among providers of financial services.[38] Second, it effectively ended the tradition of self-regulation, despite giving the appearance of continuing, in a limited form, that type of regulation. The Act provided for the creation of a regulator responsible for all investment business, the Securities and Investment Board (SIB) as well as self-regulatory organisations (SROs) responsible for the regulation of particular parts of the investment industry.[39] The SROs were ultimately accountable to the SIB in that they had to be 'recognised' by SIB, a process that required them to meet certain standards laid down by the Act. There was, however, some semblance of self-regulation in that the SROs were able to make and enforce their own rulebooks largely without interference from SIB. Under this structure, recognised investment exchanges (such as the London Stock Exchange) were exempt from the Act. However, as was the case with the SROs, this did not result in a system of self-regulation free from outside control as to gain 'exempt' status an exchange was required to satisfy recognition requirements laid down by the Act.

---

[37] See J Littlewood, *The Stockmarket, Fifty Years of Capitalism at Work* (London, Pitman, 1998) ch 27 and L Gower, *'Big Bang' and City Regulation* (1988) 51 *MLR* 1.

[38] See *Review of Investor Protection* (1984 Cmnd 9125) paras 1.11–1.20. The review was carried out for the Department of Trade and Industry by Professor Gower and became known as the 'Gower Report'. Its proposals for a fundamental change in the regulation of investment were given effect by the Financial Services Act 1986.

[39] Five SROs were recognised when the Financial Services Act 1986 took effect: the Financial Intermediaries, Managers and Brokers Regulatory Association (FIMBRA); the Investment Management Regulatory Organisation (IMRO); the Securities Association; the Association of Futures Brokers and Dealers (AFBD); and the Life Assurance and Unit Trust Regulatory Organisation (LAUTRO). The number fell to four in 1991 when the Securities and Futures Authority (SFA) was formed by a merger of the Securities Association and the AFBD and to three in 1994 when the Personal Investment Authority (PIA) was formed by the merger of LAUTRO and FIMBRA.

Within a relatively short period following its introduction, it became clear that the Financial Services Act 1986 system of regulation was not working as well as had been hoped.[40] The first major problem to become apparent was the system of rule-making created by the Act. Each regulator was responsible for making and enforcing rules in respect of persons they had authorised to engage in investment business. However, the rulebook of the SIB (the senior regulator) was given a special status because the rulebook of the other regulators had to provide protection at least equivalent to that afforded by the SIB rulebook.[41] This led to a tendency on the part of the other regulators to take an overly cautious and legalistic approach in writing their rulebooks, which in turn resulted in complex rulebooks which could not be easily compared across the different investment sectors. This problem, as well as some others, was addressed by the 'new settlement', the term given to a package of amendments to the FSA 1986 introduced by the Companies Act 1989. The rule-making system was amended in two ways. First, the 'equivalence' standard for SRO rule-making was changed to a test of whether there was adequate investor protection, with the result that it was no longer necessary to make direct comparisons with the SIB rulebook. Second, an effort was made to improve the consistency and coherence of rules across the system as a whole by introducing a tiered system of rules comprising principles, core rules and third-tier rules. The first two tiers were to be the responsibility of the SIB, with SROs assuming responsibility for the third tier. Principles were intended to articulate the basic values and objectives of the regulatory system and core rules were intended to flesh out the principles in a manner that was relevant to all investment business. It was only the third tier rules that were intended to deal with the detailed aspects of rule-making which were applicable only to individual investment sectors.

A second source of difficulty was in the effective enforcement of rules made by regulators operating under the FSA 1986. This was particularly evident in the Maxwell affair, in which it became clear that IMRO had failed properly to supervise authorised members who were involved in managing pension funds associated with the Maxwell group of companies. The essence of the Maxwell affair was that assets were improperly removed from those funds, with the result that pensioners suffered considerable hardship. The review of the entire system prompted by that failure[42] commented that IMRO's monitoring had been too mechanistic and insufficiently alert, its analysis of information had

---

[40] See generally J Black, *Rules and Regulators* (Oxford, Clarendon Press, 1997) ch 3.

[41] FSA 1986, s 10 and sch 2 para 3.

[42] As well as two other regulatory failures: SIB's supervision of London FOX, a recognised investment exchange that traded futures and options on soft commodities and agricultural products; and home income plans, which raised issues regarding the interface of regulatory responsibility as between SIB, FIMBRA and LAUTRO.

been too uncritical, it had failed to recognise and judge risks and its response to the crisis when it broke was inadequate.[43]

A third problem was the ability of the system to cope with new financial products. This was tested most obviously in relation to personal pensions, a new form of individual pension plan which came into existence at the same time as the FSA 1986 came into effect. While there were general rules (and later core rules) governing such sales in place from the very outset of the operation of the FSA 1986 system of regulation, there were no detailed rules in place until much later. Irrespective of whether responsibility for this episode lies with the companies and advisers selling personal pensions or with the regulators, it is clear that the system failed quite comprehensively to provide adequate protection to investors.[44]

A fourth problem, brought clearly into focus by the collapse of Barings bank,[45] was that the existence of separate regulators compounded the inherent difficulty of regulating 'conglomerates' which were engaged in a number of different types of activity such as merchant banking, commercial banking, stockbroking and investment management. It became clear from the investigation which followed the collapse of Barings that having separate regulators dealing with the banking and securities activities of such an organisation made it much more difficult to monitor the overall exposure of the group to a fall in financial markets. This incident was generally regarded as a significant factor in the decision made by the new Labour government in 1998 to strip the Bank of England of responsibility for banking supervision.[46] In that year, a single financial regulator, the Financial Services Authority, was created, with the intention that it would ultimately assume responsibility for the entire financial sector, including banking and insurance.[47] That policy was later given effect by the Bank of England Act 1998 and the Financial Services and Markets Act 2000.

---

[43] See A Large, 'Financial Services Regulation: Making the Two Tier System Work' (Securities and Investment Board, May 1993).

[44] See for more detail J Black and R Nobles, 'Personal Pensions Misselling: The Causes and Lessons of Regulatory Failure' (1998) 61 *MLR* 789 and G McMeel, 'The Consumer Dimension of Financial Services Law: Lessons from the Pension Mis-Selling Scandal' (1999) 3 *Company Financial and Insolvency Law Review* 29.

[45] See by way of background the report of the Board of Banking Supervision into the collapse of Barings, Session 1994–95 HC 673, discussed in C Brown, 'Report of the Board of Banking Supervision Inquiry into the Circumstances of the Collapse of Barings' (1995) 10 *Journal of International Banking Law* 446–452.

[46] This is made clear by the Treasury and Civil Service Committee, 6th Report 1994–5, 'The Regulation of Financial Services in the UK' vol 1, p V (conclusions and recommendations). Nor had the Bank of England emerged unscathed from the aftermath of the collapse of the Bank of Credit and Commerce International (BCCI) in 1991: see The Treasury and Civil Service Committee report 'Banking Supervision and BCCI—International and National Regulation' HC 177 (1991–92).

[47] The creation of the FSA did not in itself require statutory intervention. It was achieved simply by changing the name of the SIB, which had been created as a company limited by guarantee. The name change in itself transferred no additional regulatory responsibility to the FSA.

2.5 International investment

International portfolio investment has become a significant factor for financial markets.[48] It can take a variety of forms. The following are common examples:

1 Purchase, in the home state of the investor, of a security issued by a company incorporated and listed in another country.
2 Purchase, in the home state of the investor, of a security issued by a company incorporated in another country but with a secondary listing[49] in the investor's home country.
3 Purchase, outside the home state of the investor, of a security issued by a company incorporated and listed outside the home state of the investor.
4 Purchase of an indirect form of overseas investment. This could be purchase of a depositary receipt[50] or of shares in an investment trust or units in a collective investment scheme in the investor's home country, where the underlying investments are securities issued by a company incorporated and listed in another country.

Functionally, these different techniques are equivalent in the sense that they have the capacity to expose the investor to the same investment and currency risks. However, the legal and regulatory treatment of the different techniques is quite different. The main reason is that each instance involves a different interaction between the regulatory system of the home state of the investor and that governing the issuer and the process of investment. In order to understand this interaction, three different aspects are examined in turn: the development of international regulation, the EU regulatory regime and the principles that are relevant for determining which country's regulatory system governs a particular transaction.

---

[48] See, for example, p 27 of the Myners Report (*Institutional Investment in the United Kingdom: A Review*, published by HM Treasury 2001, available at www.hm-treasury.gov.uk (8 Nov 2004)) which shows that overseas investment in United Kingdom equities rose from 7.0% in 1963 to 29.3% in 1999; and paragraph I.2 of the explanatory memorandum to the European Commission's proposal for an amended directive on investment services and regulated markets (2002/0269 COD, later enacted as the MiFID directive referred to below) which notes that over the period 1998–2003 cross-border equity trading in the EU grew at a rate of 20–25% per annum. Factors contributing to its growth were: widespread abandonment of exchange controls (eg in 1979 in the UK); wider appreciation of the diversification effect of international investment; and a desire to tap into faster economic growth in emerging economies.

[49] See Ch 7 for an explanation of the term.

[50] See Ch 4 for an explanation of the term.

2.5.1 International regulation?

There is no international system of regulation for portfolio investment comparable to that which exists in individual countries. The European Union has introduced directives relating to investment (they are considered below) but they leave much of the detail of regulation to be determined by the Member States. At the broader international level, there is no regulatory authority that can make rules binding individual states. Attention has therefore focused on the development of 'soft' law and co-operation between regulators in different countries in the enforcement of domestic laws.

'Soft law' consists of codes and standards that are adopted voluntarily by states, regulators or markets. Once implemented in national or regional legal systems (eg the EU) 'soft law' can acquire binding force. An example is the capital adequacy standards that were originally developed as 'soft law' by the Bank for International Settlements and have subsequently been implemented in many national legal systems. In the investment field, international 'soft law' has been developed mainly through the International Organisation of Securities Commissioners (IOSCO). Formed in 1973 to promote co-operation among US securities regulators, IOSCO now has an international membership that accounts for all the major financial centres.[51] Its work includes the development of standards that can be implemented at national level. Particularly important in this regard are IOSCO's *Objectives and Principles of Securities Regulation* and *International Disclosure Standards for Cross Border Offerings and Initial Listings by Foreign Issuers*. These two documents, taken together, establish the underlying standards for securities regulation and the form and content of an internationally acceptable offering document.[52]

Also of significance in this respect is the work of the Financial Stability Forum (FSF). Formed in 1999 by the G-7 Group it focuses specifically on international aspects of financial market operation and in particular on systemic risk and the relationship between macro-economic regulation of the economy and micro-regulation of financial markets. The FSF has laid particular emphasis on transparency of capital flow between countries and the operation of market forces (as a technique for exerting economic discipline over countries that do not comply with prevailing international standards).

---

[51] See www.iosco.org for general background, documents and standards.

[52] See D Arner, 'Globalisation of Financial Markets—An International Passport for Securities Offerings?' (London Institute of International Banking, Finance and Development Law, 2002). The United Kingdom has implemented IOSCO's *International Disclosure Standards* in its Listing Rules—see Ch 7 for more details on listing and public offers.

Another aspect of the emergence of international 'soft law' has been the movement towards harmonisation of accounting standards. There is no body with authority to set mandatory international accounting standards and therefore international investors are faced with the problem of trying to interpret accounts that have been prepared on different bases. Countries can be split in two distinct groups in terms of their approach to accounting.[53] On the one hand, there are countries where business finance is provided mainly by banks and whose approach to accounting is largely based on taxation considerations: the preparation of accounts is geared towards the calculation of tax liabilities and the company law often contains detailed provisions on how the accounts are to be prepared and presented. On the other hand, there are countries in which business finance is dominated by equity finance and accounting is driven more by the disclosure requirements of financial markets and professional standards than company law and tax considerations. Moreover, even within the second category, there are important distinctions between for example the 'detailed rule' approach of the Generally Accepted Accounting Principles in the US and the 'principles' approach adopted in the International Accounting Standards adopted by the International Accounting Standards Committee.

While some progress is being made, the prospects for harmonisation or convergence in international accounting standards appear more remote than in respect of securities regulation. The main body that is promoting international harmonisation is the International Accounting Standards Committee (IASC). Formed in 1973, the IASC is engaged in an effort to harmonise and improve accounting principles for the benefit of the public. Its standards are essentially recommendations in that, in themselves, they have no binding authority although they can achieve binding authority through adoption (in whole or part) by the relevant national authorities. The EU, for example, requires all listed companies to report according to International Accounting Standards (IAS) by 2005.[54] Moreover, as the IASC's standards are generally broad and allow alternative practices, it is open to question how far they can achieve the harmonisation objective.

[53] See generally D Arner (above n 52).

[54] See Reg 1606/2002 [2002] OJ L243/1. Detailed disclosure standards will be set by the European Securities Committee, whose function is to advise the Commission on the detailed implementation of the securities directives.

2.5.2 The EC regulatory regime

The EC regime for investment business reflects the broad objective of creating a single (or internal) market in services and capital within the EC.[55] The EC Treaty provides:[56]

> The internal market shall comprise an area without internal frontiers in which the free movement of goods, persons, services and capital is ensured in accordance with the provisions of this Treaty.

The main Treaty provisions that give effect to this objective in the field of investment are:

Article 56—Free movement of capital
Article 43—Freedom of establishment
Article 49—Freedom to provide services

The principle of free movement of capital in Article 56 prohibits restrictions on movements of capital between Member States and between Member States and third countries.[57] It is therefore no longer possible for EC Member States to limit direct or portfolio investment through restrictions on capital movements. The Treaty does, however, authorise the EC, by way of exception to the general principle, to adopt restrictive measures relating to capital movements to or from third countries.[58]

Freedom of establishment arises from the prohibition contained in Article 43 against restrictions on nationals of a Member State establishing a business in another Member State. The prohibition applies irrespective of the form of the business as Article 43 refers expressly to the setting up of agencies, branches and subsidiaries. It includes the right to take up and pursue activities as a self-employed person and to set up and manage undertakings. The term 'nationals' includes companies that are formed under the laws of a Member

---

[55] The Treaty on European Union (sometimes referred to as the Maastricht Treaty) entered into force on 1 November 1993. It created the European Union and amended and renamed the European Economic Community (EEC) Treaty (1958), which is now known as the European Community (EC) Treaty. Legislative measures relevant to the single market are adopted under powers contained in the EC Treaty. Hence, they are referred to in this book as EC measures and the single market is referred to as the EC single market. Moreover, the EC single market measures apply (sometimes with qualifications) to the broader area referred to as the European Economic Area (EEA).

[56] Art 14(2).

[57] This Treaty provision was introduced by the Maastricht Treaty on European Union in 1993. The principle of free movement of capital between Member States had already been established by Council Directive 88/361, [1988] OJ L178/5. See generally JA Usher, *The Law of Money and Financial Services in the European Community* (Oxford, OUP, 1994) ch 2.

[58] Art 57(2). Unanimity is required in the EU Council 'for measures under this paragraph which constitute a step back in Community law as regards the liberalisation of the movement of capital to or from a third country'.

State and have their registered office, central administration or principal place of business within the Community. The main impact of this for financial investment is in respect of the right of providers of financial services to establish operations in EC countries other than their home country.

Freedom to provide services is in principle different from freedom of establishment in that it relates to the right to provide services on a temporary basis within another Member State (a 'host' state). This differs from operating a business from a permanent establishment in another Member State. However, freedom of services does not, in principle, allow the service provider to escape the control of the Member State in which the service is provided as Article 50 provides that the activity can be pursued 'under the same conditions as are imposed by that state on its own nationals'. Freedom to provide services is of particular significance for the development of 'remote' services such as those delivered over the Internet.

The Treaty provisions relating to establishment and services are directly effective,[59] meaning that in principle they give rise to rights that can be enforced by individuals in national courts. Why, then, have they given rise to such a complex array of secondary legislation governing EU financial markets? There are two main reasons. First, the early case-law of the European Court of Justice dealing with these rights focused on discrimination with the result that the emphasis was on eliminating discriminatory treatment of foreign nationals. It was only later that the European Court of Justice (ECJ) began to prohibit trade barriers adopted by Member States that were equally applicable to nationals and foreign nationals and even when this occurred there was considerable doubt over the restrictions that could be imposed by Member States on foreign nationals exercising their right of establishment or freedom to provide services.[60] This confusion was apparent in the competing claims made in the case of *Commission v Germany*[61] regarding the extent to which the German Insurance Supervisory Authority could regulate the activities of foreign insurers and brokers operating in its territory. Second, the Treaty rights, although directly effective, are subject to exceptions, some of which are contained in the Treaty and some that have been developed by the ECJ.[62] The result of these exceptions was that it was possible for Member States to limit the operation of the Treaty rights (and in particular freedom to provide services) on the basis that restrictions were imposed for the 'general good' of their citizens. The solution adopted by the EC was to limit the operation of this exception by creating

---

[59] See generally S Weatherill and P Beaumont, *EC Law,* 3rd edn (London, Penguin, 1999) ch 11.

[60] See generally *ibid,* ch 17.

[61] Case 205/84, [1986] ECR 3755.

[62] See further I MacNeil, 'Does the EC Have a Single Market in Insurance?' (1995) 10 *Butterworths Journal of International Banking and Financial Law* 122.

a system of regulation that removed the need for Member States to take action to protect their citizens.

The initial approach of the EC was to focus on harmonisation of the laws of the Member States as a means of pursuing the market integration objective. It soon became clear that this approach would not work as the harmonisation proposals became bogged down by political disagreements. In the mid-1980s, the approach was changed so as to focus on the principle of mutual recognition of laws of different Member States combined with minimum harmonisation. The objective of mutual recognition was to recognise the laws of each Member State as being equivalent to each other, with the result that it would no longer be necessary, in principle, to apply the laws and regulatory rules of state A to the supply of services in that state by a supplier based in state B. For example, mutual recognition would allow a bank based in the UK to engage in banking business in Germany without having to go through an authorisation process in Germany. The objective of minimum harmonisation was to create the conditions under which the assumption of equivalence between the laws of a home and a host state was factually correct. If it were not, it would not be possible for mutual recognition to work because there would remain differences between the laws of Member States that would eventually make the system unworkable.

The principles of minimum harmonisation and mutual recognition led directly to the development of the two key principles adopted in the EC financial market directives, the 'single licence' and 'home country control'. The former provides that an authorisation granted in the home state provides a basis for engaging in relevant business in a host state through a branch or through the provision of services. It does not extend to conducting business through a subsidiary, which is a legal person formed under the laws of the host state and is therefore governed by the laws of the host state. Home country control is a technique for allocating regulatory responsibility between home and host states. As implemented by the EU directives, it results in a home state assuming primary responsibility for all business undertaken under an authorisation that it has granted. The main exception to this principle is that a host state remains able to apply its conduct of business rules to transactions occurring within that state. There also remained in place, however, a residual exception based on the concept of the 'general good', which permitted Member States to limit the operation of the principle of freedom of services (and by implication the 'single licence' and 'home country control') on the basis that such restrictions were necessary for the protection of investors in that country.

The principles of 'single licence' and 'home country control' are given effect in the field of investment by the Markets in Financial Instruments Directive[63]

---

[63] Dir 2004/39/EC [2004] OJ L145/1. This directive became effective on 30 April 2004 and replaces the Investment Services Directive (93/22/EC [1993] L141/27) as from 30 April 2006.

(MiFID) and the Capital Adequacy Directive[64] (CAD). The former is concerned mainly with authorisation and supervision of investment firms and regulated markets, while the latter is concerned with capital adequacy requirements (regulatory capital) for investment firms and banks with a substantial securities trading business.[65] From the perspective of cross-border investment, there are a number of relevant issues that are dealt with by these directives.

It is for individual Member States to designate regulated markets. The consequence of such designation is that they become subject to the rules of the MiFID. In the past, the focus on 'regulated markets' in the Investment Services Directive (ISD), MiFID's predecessor, adopted what has been referred to as the 'public utility' approach to market regulation.[66] This evolved during the era when national stock exchanges often enjoyed a monopoly (legal or de facto) over securities trading and the main regulatory concern was to control the *modus operandi* of the exchange so as to limit anti-competitive behaviour.[67] Associated with this was the desire on the part of some EC states to protect their financial market from competition from more developed markets following liberalisation and also from 'alternative markets'.[68] The 'concentration' provision in the ISD reflected these concerns. It gave Member States the option of requiring that transactions in securities be carried out on a regulated market when certain conditions are met.[69] In effect, the 'concentration' provision gave Member States the option of prohibiting the execution of transactions on 'alternative' markets.[70] The rationale for the provision was that there were benefits for investors in having transactions centralised in a large and liquid market. However, the concentration provision attracted criticism on the basis that it was not compatible with the competition provisions of the EC Treaty[71] and has now been repealed by the MiFID.

---

[64] Dir 93/6/EC [1993] OJ L141/1.

[65] For a general overview see N Moloney, *EC Securities Regulation* (Oxford, OUP, 2002).

[66] See G Ferrarini, 'The European Regulation of Stock Exchanges: New Perspectives' (1999) 36 *CMLRev* 569.

[67] See, for example, J Littlewood (above n 37) pp 317–18 regarding concerns over anti-competitive practices in the London Stock Exchange in the early 1980s.

[68] See Ch 10 for a discussion of alternative markets.

[69] See Art 14(3) of the ISD. Those conditions are that: the transaction must involve an instrument dealt in on a regulated market in that Member State; the investor must be habitually resident or established in that Member State; the investment firm must have the right to carry out the transaction in the relevant Member State. The latter right can arise from the use of 'passport' rights (establishment or services), thereby precluding the use of the concentration provision to protect national markets from foreign competition.

[70] It did not, however, give a Member State the option of prohibiting the execution of the transaction on a regulated market in another Member State.

[71] See M Tison, 'The ISD and its Implementation in the EU Member States' Working Paper 1999-17 University of Ghent Financial Law Institute at www.law.ugent.be/fli/WP (8 Nov 2004).

One of the main achievements of the EC regulatory regime is to facilitate market access. This works in two ways. First, it facilitates access on the part of investment firms in country A to regulated markets in country B. It does this by requiring country B to ensure that investment firms authorised in country A can become members of or have access to the regulated markets in country B.[72] That in itself does not provide a right of remote access to a regulated market in country B for an investment firm in country A. However, where the regulated market in country B operates without a requirement for a physical presence, there is a right to have remote membership or access.[73]

The EC regime also facilitates access by a regulated market in country A to investment firms in country B. In circumstances in which a regulated market in country A has no requirement for a physical presence on the part of investment firms, that regulated market has the right to provide 'appropriate facilities' in country B so as to enable investment firms to exercise their right of remote membership or access.[74] There is no definition of 'appropriate facilities' but it seems clear that if remote access is to operate properly, such facilities must include those required to provide pre- and post-trade transparency to the investment firm in the other country.[75]

By way of derogation from the basic principle of 'home country control', the EC regime provides that a Member State is entitled to apply its Conduct of Business Rules to transactions taking place in its own territory.[76] For example, an investment firm authorised and supervised by country A will be required to comply with the Conduct of Business Rules of country B when it provides services in country B, despite the fact that country B has no role in the authorisation or supervision of the firm. This represents a significant practical limitation on the operation of the single market in financial services within the EU because it requires compliance with the Conduct of Business Rules of each Member State in which investment services are provided.

The MiFID Directive[77] introduces some changes that are designed to promote the objective of capital market integration within the EC. This recognises the increasing role that market based financing (both equity and debt) is playing in the financing of European enterprises, which, outside the United Kingdom, have tended historically to rely more heavily on bank loans. It gives

---

[72] Art 32 of the MiFID.

[73] Art 33 of the MiFID.

[74] Art 42(6) of the MiFID. See also art 46 regarding the provision of clearing and settlement facilities in country B for the settlement of trades conducted in a market in country A.

[75] Market transparency is one of the objectives of the ISD. See Ch 9 for a discussion of the meaning of the term and its implementation.

[76] MiFID art 19. It is envisaged that common conduct of business rules for the EC will eventually be adopted under art 19(10).

[77] See above n 63.

a more prominent role to alternative markets on the basis that they provide valuable competition to recognised exchanges and can contribute to market efficiency provided adequate transparency rules are in place to enable investors to observe activity across the market as a whole.[78] It also includes measures to limit the conflicts of interest that arise when investment firms perform a wide range of services under one roof (eg combining own-account trading with client-oriented services) and measures to ensure that investment firms make use of the wide array of order–execution facilities that have become available as alternative markets have proliferated. Another concern is to overcome the potential for countries to create barriers to the exercise of the Treaty freedoms by investment firms. This potential has arisen as a result of the formulation of the ISD in terms of generic principles (largely unsupported by operational guidance) and the ample scope for restrictions created by the 'general good' principle. Finally the new directive extends the scope of regulation to include investment advice, financial analysis and commodity derivatives, which are currently excluded from the ISD.

2.5.3 Regulation of international portfolio investment transactions

While the EC regime discussed above is relevant to some international investment transactions, there are many to which it is not applicable, such as transactions undertaken outside the EC. In the absence of any developed international system of financial regulation, it then becomes important to determine which country's system of regulation will be applicable to a particular transaction. It is important to resolve this issue because it has the potential to affect the manner in which the transaction is carried out and the obligations owed by parties involved in its execution (including brokers, market-makers and exchanges). In the main, securities law applies to relevant transactions within a country irrespective of the company law that governs the issuer.[79] The result is that the securities law of country A will generally apply to transactions within that country even if the law applicable to the issuer of securities[80] or to

---

[78] See Ch 9 for more details on the structure and regulation of investment markets.

[79] See Ch 3 for details of the jurisdictional scope of FSMA 2000.

[80] There are two approaches to this issue. The first, adopted in the UK, is that a company is governed by the company law of the country in which it is incorporated. The second is that a company is governed by the company law of the country in which its seat (*siège réel* or head office) is located. Irrespective of which approach is applied, the result is that an investor in one country buying a security issued by a company governed by the company law of another country will have his rights as a shareholder defined by the company law of that other country. In this sense, the applicable company law acts as a fixed definition of shareholders' rights irrespective of where shares are traded or held.

the transfer of legal title[81] is that of another country. The corollary is that, in the main,[82] the securities law of country A will not apply to securities transactions in other countries even when entered into by an investor who is a national of country A.

Unlike national systems of financial regulation, the listing rules of stock exchanges do not directly give rise to conflict of law issues.[83] Listing rules require an issuer to observe the listing rules, primarily in the form of disclosure requirements, without reference to national legal systems. In principle, company A, incorporated in the UK, and company B, incorporated in the Cayman Islands, are both bound by the listing rules in the UK in the same way if their securities are listed on the London Stock Exchange.[84] Nor are the sanctions available to the listing authority dependent on national legal systems because the ultimate sanction (removal of listing) does not require enforcement through national courts.[85] For this reason, listing rules can be regarded as the first true form of international securities regulation because they are capable of regulating issuers of securities without reference to the jurisdiction in which the issuer of securities or the investors in those securities are based.

---

[81] The determination of the applicable law in respect of transfers of securities is important because different countries may have different rules regarding what constitutes a valid transfer and the respective rights of transferor and transferee. Under UK company law, the legal owner of a share is the person who is registered in the company's register of shareholders. Where a UK court is faced with a question of which law applies to a transfer it will normally apply the law of the place where the shareholders' register is located, on the basis that this is where the transfer occurs. See G Cheshire, *Cheshire & North's Private International Law*, 13th edn (London, Butterworths, 1999) pp 175–77.

[82] There are some exceptions to this general principle. The most significant are the 'extraterritorial' provisions of the US securities laws. See S Choi and A Guzman, 'The Dangerous Extraterritoriality of American Securities Law' (1996) 17 *Journal of International Business Law* 207.

[83] See Ch 7 for more detail on listing rules.

[84] See Ch 7 for a discussion of the modification of this principle in the case of 'secondary' overseas listing.

[85] In the UK, however, suspension of listing can be challenged before the Financial Services and Markets Tribunal: see FSMA 2000 s 77(5).

3

The Regulatory System in the United Kingdom

This chapter examines the regulatory system currently in place in the United Kingdom. It provides an overview of the structure and objectives of regulation, the role of the regulator and the techniques that are employed in regulating transactions, firms and individuals.

3.1 The Financial Services and Markets Act 2000

The failings associated with the system of regulation created by the Financial Services Act 1986 (FSA 1986) were widely regarded as serious, but it was less obvious that they were indicative of a systemic failure in the system of regulation.[1] Any system of regulation can be expected to experience some problems and it is a matter of judgement as to whether such difficulties can be resolved within the system or whether the system requires replacement. Many of the changes that have been introduced by the Financial Services and Markets Act 2000 (FSMA 2000) could have been introduced under FSA 1986. With the benefit of hindsight, it seems clear that much of the impetus for the introduction of the new Act was a desire to abandon a system that was associated with failure rather than to initiate 'root and branch' reform.

FSMA 2000 cannot be viewed as being a fundamental change in the system of financial regulation in the same way that FSA 1986 was. The move to a single statutory regulator for the entire financial sector, arguably the most significant of the changes made to the regulatory system, took place while the FSA 1986 was still in force. Although much was made of the abandonment of self-regulation as a result of the introduction of FSMA 2000, the reality was that the Securities and Investment Board (the predecessor of the Financial Services Authority (FSA)) had effectively operated in this way for much its

---

[1] See, as regards these failings, Ch 2.

existence. Moreover, at the level of the regulatory rules, much of the detail of the pre-FSMA 2000 regime has simply been carried over into the new FSA Handbook.

As was the case with FSA 1986, the FSMA 2000 is largely a statutory framework. It sets out some basic principles and provides various powers to the regulator. Unlike the FSA 1986, the objectives of FSMA 2000 are explicitly stated by the Act.[2] They are:

Market confidence

The market confidence objective is maintaining confidence in the financial system. The financial system includes financial markets and exchanges, regulated activities and other activities connected with financial markets and exchanges. This objective therefore extends beyond activities which are regulated activities under the Act. Market confidence does not imply a policy of preventing all failures but involves minimising the impact of failures and providing mechanisms to protect consumers.[3]

Public awareness

The public awareness objective is promoting public understanding of the financial system. This includes awareness of the benefits and risks associated with different kinds of investments and the provision of appropriate information and advice. The financial system has the same meaning as in the paragraph on *market confidence* above.

The protection of consumers

The consumer protection objective is securing the appropriate degree of protection for consumers. In considering what is appropriate, the FSA must have regard to risk, expertise, the need for information and advice and the general principle that consumers should take responsibility for their decisions. 'Consumer' is defined broadly and includes (a) past, present and potential customers of authorised persons or appointed representatives[4]; (b) companies and persons entering into transactions in a business capacity; and (c) persons who derive rights from persons who are 'consumers'.[5]

---

[2] FSMA 2000 ss 3–6.

[3] See FSA publication *Reasonable Expectations: Regulation in a Non-Zero Failure World* (Sept 2003).

[4] See Ch 6 for an explanation of this term.

[5] FSMA 2000 s 138(7).

The reduction of financial crime

The reduction of financial crime objective is reducing the extent to which it is possible for a business carried on (a) by a regulated person or (b) in contravention of the general prohibition against carrying on regulated activity without authorisation, to be used for a purpose in connection with financial crime. Financial crime includes any offence involving fraud or dishonesty; misconduct in, or misuse of information relating to, a financial market; or handling the proceeds of crime. The offence includes an act or omission that would be an offence if it took place in the United Kingdom. The Act itself establishes offences falling within the scope of this objective, such as making misleading statements and engaging in market manipulation.[6]

The Act also refers to principles of good regulation to which the FSA must have regard in carrying out its duties.[7] They are:

(a) the need to use its resources in the most efficient and economic way;
(b) the responsibilities of those who manage the affairs of authorised persons;
(c) the principle that a burden or restriction which is imposed on a person, or on the carrying on of an activity, should be proportionate to the benefits, considered in general terms, which are expected to result from the imposition of that burden or restriction;
(d) the desirability of facilitating innovation in connection with regulated activities;
(e) the international character of financial services and markets and the desirability of maintaining the competitive position of the United Kingdom;
(f) the need to minimise the adverse effects on competition that may arise from anything done in the discharge of those functions;
(g) the desirability of facilitating competition between those who are subject to any form of regulation by the Authority.

The manner in which the statutory objectives and the principles of good regulation determine the FSA's approach to regulation is considered below in the context of authorisation, rule-making and risk assessment and supervision.

The Cruickshank Report[8] on competition in UK banking recommended that the FSMA 2000 should be reviewed within two years of its taking effect. HM Treasury accepted that recommendation and began its review in November 2003. The limited nature of the review was made clear by the Treasury statement[9] that marked the opening of the review, which referred to

---

[6] FSMA 2000 s 397.

[7] FSMA 2000 s 2(3).

[8] *Competition in UK Banking: A Report to the Chancellor of the Exchequer* (2000), available at www.hm-treasury.gov.uk (10 Nov 2004).

[9] See the statement by the Financial Secretary to the Treasury Mr Stephen Timms, 'Two-Year Review of the Financial Services and Markets Act 2000 and Financial Services and Markets Act two year review: Changes to secondary legislation' Government response at www.hm-treasury.gov.uk (14 April 2005).

the FSMA 2000 system as a 'resounding success' and 'a framework which works well'. There are three main strands to the review, covering:

(a) The impact of the FSMA 2000 on competition, which is being assessed by the Office of Fair Trading, which has wide-ranging responsibility for competition matters in the UK and has a statutory responsibility under FSMA 2000 to keep the FSA Handbook of Rules and Guidance under review.

(b) The second strand of the review covers aspects of the practices of the FSA and the operation of the Financial Ombudsman Scheme. A number of issues are being examined under the first heading. They include compliance costs arising from the complexity of the FSA Handbook, the volume of consultation papers issued by the FSA and the role of cost–benefit analysis in rule-making. The main issues being reviewed in connection with the operation of the Financial Ombudsman Scheme are the relevance of 'wider implication' cases and the possibility of permitting Ombudsman decisions to be appealed to the courts.[10]

(c) The third strand of the review deals with the boundary of regulation. The two main issues that have been identified here are the impact of the regulatory regime on capital raising for small businesses and on the provision of financial advice (eg by organisations such as Citizens Advice Bureaux).

The review was completed in autumn 2004 and will lead to some amendments to the FSMA regime and FSA practice.

3.2 The Financial Services Authority (FSA)

The FSA is empowered to carry out the regulatory functions conferred on it by FSMA 2000. These functions include those transferred to the FSA from the Chief Registrar of Friendly Societies, the Friendly Societies Commission, the Building Societies Commission and the regulatory functions previously carried out by the Treasury in respect of insurance. The FSA had already taken over responsibility for banking supervision from the Bank of England as a result of the Bank of England Act 1998.

The Treasury and the Bank of England do, however, retain a significant role in the system of financial regulation established by FSMA 2000. A memorandum of understanding agreed between the three organisations in 1998 set out the respective role of each, as follows:

(a) The Bank of England is responsible for the overall stability of the financial system. This remit includes monitoring payment systems and broad overview of the financial system as a whole.

---

[10] See, for more detail, Ch 6.4.

(b) The FSA has statutory responsibility for authorisation and prudential supervision of banks, building societies, insurers and investment firms, supervision of financial markets and associated clearing and settlement systems.

(c) The Treasury is responsible for the overall institutional structure of regulation and the legislation which governs it. It has no operational responsibilities for the activities of the FSA or the Bank of England but does nevertheless have considerable influence on regulatory policy through oversight and order-making powers granted by FSMA 2000.

The FSA existed prior to the Act, having been created in 1997 as result of a change in the name of the Securities and Investments Board (SIB). As was the case with SIB, the FSA is a private company limited by guarantee, subject to the provisions of the Companies Act 1985. Its constitution must comply with the provisions of schedule 1 FSMA 2000 which deals with, inter alia, organisational structure, the maintenance of monitoring and enforcement arrangements in respect of rules imposed by or under the Act, investigation of complaints against the FSA and the Authority's immunity from liability in respect of the exercise of its functions. Schedule 1 provides that the Authority must have a chairman and governing body appointed by the Treasury. The majority of the members of the governing body must be non-executives.

While the FSA was established with the intention of creating an independent regulator, the Act does provide for a degree of accountability to government ministers, Parliament and stakeholders.[11] The most significant form of ministerial control is the power of the Treasury to appoint and remove the chairman and members of the governing body of the FSA. This gives the Treasury a significant role in influencing the manner in which the FSA approaches its regulatory remit. It is possible for the Treasury to require the FSA to alter its rules but only when they have a significantly adverse affect on competition[12] or in order to comply with the UK's EC or international obligations.[13] Probably of greater long-term significance for the structure and operation of financial markets is the Treasury's power to make regulations setting out the requirements to be met by exchanges and clearing houses seeking 'recognised' status. That power has the potential effectively to bring the major exchanges under the regulatory control of the Treasury rather than the FSA. It is also possible for the Treasury to commission value-for-money audits and to arrange independent inquiries into regulatory matters of serious concern.[14]

---

[11] See generally A Page, 'Regulating the Regulator—A Lawyer's Perspective' in E Ferran and C Goodhart (eds) *Regulating Financial Services and Markets in the 21st Century* (Oxford, Hart Publishing, 2001).

[12] FSMA 2000 s 163.

[13] FSMA 2000 s 410.

[14] See ss 12 and 14 FSMA 2000 respectively.

Some measure of Parliamentary scrutiny of the FSA is made possible by the requirement that its annual report be laid before Parliament.[15] The FSA is also in principle subject to Select Committee scrutiny but serious doubts have been expressed over the effectiveness of such oversight.[16]

The main mechanism for securing accountability to stakeholders has been the requirement that the FSA establish Consumer and Practitioner Panels.[17] The FSA must consider representations made by either Panel and if it disagrees with it, must give the Panel a statement in writing of its reasons for disagreeing.

As regards the potential liability of the regulator for losses suffered by investors as a result of regulatory failures, the Act provides that neither the FSA nor any person who is, or is acting as, a member, officer or member of staff of the Authority is to be liable in damages for anything done or omitted in the discharge, or purported discharge, of the Authority's functions.[18] This exemption does not apply to acts or omissions shown to have been in bad faith[19] or acts or omissions which are unlawful as a result of section 6(1) of the Human Rights Act 1998.[20] A similar exemption was provided for the FSA/SIB and self-regulatory organisations (SROs) by section 187 of FSA 1986. Neither the Authority nor its members, officers or staff act on behalf of the Crown.[21] Even without this statutory exclusion of liability, it would be difficult to establish a claim in negligence as the courts have been reluctant to recognise that regulators owe a duty of care to the customers of regulated firms.[22]

---

[15] FSMA 2000 sch 1 para 10(3).

[16] See Page (above n 11) at p 134.

[17] FSMA 2000 s 8.

[18] Pt IV of sch 1.

[19] The meaning of bad faith in the context of financial regulation was considered in *Melton Medes Ltd v SIB* [1995] 3 All ER 880 and *Three Rivers DC v Bank of England (no 3)* [2000] 2 WLR 1220. In *Melton Medes* it was held (Lightman J referring to Wade *Administrative Law,* 6th edn (1988) p 782 citing *Bourgoin SA v Ministry of Agriculture Fisheries and Food* [1985] 3 All ER 585) that bad faith, in the context of the statutory immunity provided to SIB by s187(3) FSA 1986, was to be understood in the context of misfeasance in public office and not the wider meaning given to the term in administrative law. Bad faith, in this sense, connoted either (a) malice in the sense of personal spite or a desire to injure for improper reasons or (b) knowledge of absence of power to make the decisions in question. It was also established in *Melton Medes* that an allegation of bad faith would be struck out as an abuse of process unless there were prima facie evidence to justify the allegation. In *Three Rivers DC* it was established that the tort of misfeasance in public office involves an element of bad faith. It follows that establishing a case based on misfeasance in public office will suffice to show that an act or omission is in bad faith.

[20] This section deals with contravention by a public authority of rights contained in the European Convention on Human Rights, which was implemented in the UK by the Human Rights Act 1998.

[21] Sch 1 FSMA 2000 (para 13).

[22] It was established in *Yuen Kun Yeu v A-G of Hong Kong* [1987] 2 All ER 704 PC and *Davis v Radcliffe* [1990] 2 All ER 536 that a banking regulator does not owe a duty of care to depositors in a licensed bank, with the result that the regulator cannot be liable in negligence for loss suffered by depositors as a result of a bank failure.

A more realistic alternative, and one that might not always fall within the statutory immunity of the Authority, is a claim in respect of the tort of misfeasance in public office.[23] Moreover, the FSA is in principle subject to judicial review.[24] It was established in *R v SIB ex p IFFA*[25] and *R v SIB ex p Sun Life Assurances plc*[26] that in principle SIB (the FSA's predecessor) was amenable to judicial review, although both cases failed on the merits. The same principle would appear to apply to the FSA. However, the relatively narrow grounds on which judicial review can be sought means that in most instances it does not provide a realistic basis for challenging acts or decisions of the FSA.[27]

3.3 Authorisation

The FSMA 2000 adopts the basic rule, on which most systems of financial regulation are based, that authorisation is required to engage in regulated activities.[28] Authorisation is achieved, in most cases, by applying to the FSA for permission to engage in the relevant activity. An applicant must meet the 'threshold conditions' contained in the Act before permission will be granted.[29] These conditions cover a number of issues and in particular leave considerable discretion to the FSA in deciding whether two requirements are met. The first is whether the applicant has adequate financial resources in relation to the regulated activities he seeks to carry on, and the second is whether the applicant is a fit and proper person (natural or legal) having regard to all

[23] It is in principle possible for a regulator to be liable for the tort of misfeasance in public office but that requires (a) intent to injure the plaintiff or (b) knowledge or reckless indifference as to the illegality of the act and (c) the losses caused by the act or omission to be foreseeable (*Three Rivers DC v Bank of England (no 3)* [2000] 2 WLR 1220). It is conceivable that a challenge to the statutory immunity of the FSA for liability in negligence could be mounted on the basis that it is a disproportionate interference with the right of access to a court under article 6(1) of the European Convention on Human Rights (as incorporated into UK law by the Human Rights Act 1998). In *Osman v United Kingdom* (2000) 29 EHRR 245, the European Court of Human Rights reached such a view in respect of the (common law) immunity of the police from liability in respect of negligence. A UK court is, however, not bound by such a decision (s 2 of the Human Rights Act 1998).

[24] Judicial review is a process by which the decisions or acts of public bodies can be challenged before the courts.

[25] [1995] 2 Butterworths Company Law Cases 76.

[26] [1996] 2 Butterworths Company Law Cases 150.

[27] There are three possible grounds for judicial review: illegality; irrationality; or procedural impropriety. See generally ch 11 of D Foulkes, *Administrative Law*, 8th edn (London, Butterworths, 1995).

[28] This is the 'general prohibition' contained in s 19 FSMA 2000.

[29] See generally M Blair (ed) *Butterworths Annotated Guide to FSMA 2000* (London, Butterworths, 2002) pp 59–62.

the circumstances. Both tests formed part of the authorisation procedure under FSA 1986. Special provisions apply to firms from other Member States who wish to become authorised by exercising rights under the EC financial market directives or the EC Treaty. There are also a number of important exemptions from the requirement for authorisation. These issues are discussed below.

3.3.1 Permission

Permission is normally granted only for specified activities.[30] That in itself constitutes authorisation for the purposes of the Act, with the result that any form of permission means that the criminal offence of engaging in unauthorised activity cannot be committed. However, engaging in activity in respect of which a person does not have permission is a regulatory contravention which will result in disciplinary action being taken by the FSA. It is not, however, a criminal offence and the contravention has no effect on the validity of a contract. The scope of permission can be varied at the request of an authorised person subject to meeting the 'threshold conditions' in relation to all permitted activities. The Authority is empowered to vary or revoke permission in three circumstances: first, when an authorised person fails to satisfy the 'threshold conditions'; second, when an authorised person fails, within 12 months, to carry on a regulated activity for which he has permission; and third, when it is in the interests of consumers.

3.3.2 EEA (European Economic Area) and Treaty Firms

It is also possible for authorisation to be achieved by an EEA firm exercising its rights under the various EC Directives which give effect to the EC Treaty principles of freedom of establishment and freedom to provide services.[31] This is referred to in FSMA 2000 as the exercise of 'passport rights' by EEA firms. The EC Directives relating to banking, insurance and investment are based on two principles. The first is a 'single licence' under which a firm authorised in an EEA state is entitled to provide services or establish a branch (but not a subsidiary) in other EEA states. The second is 'home country control' under which a firm is supervised by its home state in respect of all its business conducted under the single licence.

Subject to satisfying certain conditions associated with the exercise of these rights (mainly the giving of notice to its home state regulator), an EEA firm

---

[30] See generally Pt IV of FSMA 2000.
[31] See Ch 2.3.

qualifies for authorisation in the United Kingdom.[32] It is also possible for an EEA firm to gain authorisation for an activity in respect of which there is no EEA right to carry on the activity in the manner proposed by the applicant. For this to occur, the firm must have authorisation in its home state and the laws of the home state must provide equivalent protection or conform with a relevant provision of EC law.[33] This possibility is referred to by FSMA 2000 as the exercise of 'treaty rights' and is designed to ensure that the UK conforms with EC law relating to freedom to provide services.[34]

Implementation in the UK of the EC Directive on Electronic Commerce[35] has given an even more significant role to the principles of the single licence and home country control. The Directive applies to what are termed 'information society services' (ISS), which are in essence any services provided for remuneration at a distance by electronic means at the request of a recipient of services (eg on-line share dealing or banking). It extends the principle of home country control to these services with the result that providers of such services are free to provide them in other Member States. It does not allow such providers to escape the requirement to be authorised in respect of such activities by their home Member State.[36] It does, however, mean that ISS providers can operate in other Member States without having to comply with the conditions that would otherwise apply to the provision of services, such as the giving of notice to its home state regulator.

3.3.3 Exemptions

A number of exemptions from the general prohibition against engaging in regulated activity without an authorisation are provided by FSMA 2000. Section 285 establishes the general framework under which investment exchanges and clearing-houses[37] are regulated. It provides that investment exchanges and clearing-houses which have been 'recognised' by the FSA are

---

[32] FSMA 2000 s 31(1)(b) and sch 3.

[33] FSMA 2000 s 31(1)(c) and sch 4.

[34] The EC Treaty rules relating to freedom of services are broader than the regime established by the financial market directives, hence the need for this rule.

[35] Dir 2000/31, OJ 2000 L178/1, implemented in the UK (in respect of financial services) with effect from 21 August 2002 by the Electronic Commerce Directive (Financial Services and Markets) Regulations 2002 (SI 2002/1775); the FSMA 2000 (Regulated Activities) (Amendment) (No 2) Order 2002 (SI 2002/1776); and the FSMA 2000 (Financial Promotion) (Amendment) (Electronic Commerce Directive) Order 2002 (SI 2002/2157).

[36] See art 3(1) of the Directive, which requires Member States to ensure that ISS services provided by a service provider from its territory comply with the national provisions applicable to taking up the relevant activity.

[37] See Ch 10 for more detail regarding the nature and operation of exchanges and clearing-houses.

exempt from the general prohibition in section 19 of the Act. There are two important aspects of exempt status. First, the exemption is not a true exemption from the regulatory framework of the FSMA 2000 because exchanges and clearing-houses can only become recognised if they meet certain criteria.[38] Moreover, for certain purposes (eg the reduction of financial crime objective in section 6 FSMA 2000) recognised investment exchanges (RIEs) and recognised clearing-houses (RCHs) are treated as regulated persons. Second, the scope of the exemption is limited. For an RIE it relates to activities carried on as part of the business of an exchange or in connection with the provision of clearing services. For a RCH it relates to activities connected with the provision of clearing services by the clearing-house. There is no exempt person status in respect of other activities undertaken by RIEs or RCHs. Any application for permission in respect of such other activities is to be treated as an application relating only to that other activity.

Authorised representatives are also exempt from the requirement for authorisation. They are persons (human or legal) who act on behalf of an authorised person in carrying on a regulated activity. They cannot themselves be authorised persons. Organisations such as banks and building societies which were previously authorised under the Banking Act 1987 or Building Societies Act 1986 and exempt (as authorised representatives) under the FSA 1986 are now required to obtain permission to carry on the activities previously undertaken in their capacity as authorised representatives. The exemption applies only if:[39]

- the appointed representative is a party to a contract with an authorised person, referred to as the principal, which permits the appointed representative to carry on regulated activities; and
- the principal has accepted responsibility in writing for the conduct of those regulated activities.

The consequence of accepting responsibility for the actions of an authorised representative is that the principal bears responsibility for them in any disciplinary action taken by the FSA or civil action taken by a customer. There is, however, a limitation of the principal's liability in respect of criminal offences in that the knowledge and intentions of the appointed representative are not attributed to the principal unless in all the circumstances it is reasonable for them to be attributed to him. The type of activity carried on by appointed representatives and some aspects of the relationship between the principal and appointed representative are controlled by regulations made by the Treasury.[40]

---

[38] See Ch 9 for more detail.

[39] FSMA 2000 s 39.

[40] The Financial Services and Markets Act 2000 (Appointed Representatives) Regulations 2001, SI 2001/1217 as amended by SI 2001/2508. See Ch 6 for more detail.

Although appointed representatives do not require authorisation, they require approval under the 'approved persons' regime if they undertake 'controlled functions' in respect of the principal's business.[41]

Members of designated professions are also exempt from the general prohibition against engaging in regulated activity without authorisation. This is mainly an issue for firms of accountants and solicitors, who in the normal course of their business may find themselves engaging in regulated activities (eg an accountant engaging in tax-planning advice on pensions or a solicitor arranging for the investment of a trust fund). The main problem faced by the regulatory system is differentiating between cases in which such activity can safely be left outside the regulatory perimeter (leaving it to be controlled by the relevant professional body) and cases in which the scale of the regulated activity justifies treating members of professions on an equal footing with other authorised persons.

The central provision of the Act is that a professional firm or person can only be exempt if the carrying on of regulated activity is incidental to the provision of professional services.[42] Whether or not regulated activity is incidental to a profession is determined by the 'Professions Order'[43], which distinguishes between completely non-exempt activities and non-exempt activities that are subject to conditions. If the 'incidental business' requirement is breached there is no exemption available and the firm or person can be considered to be undertaking unauthorised activity. However, the likelihood of that occurring is reduced by the requirement that designated professional bodies should make rules that give effect to the 'incidental business' requirement. Moreover, the firm or person must not receive from any other person any pecuniary reward (such as commission) for which he does not account to his client. This is not a prohibition on charging clients for services comprising regulated activities. The intention is that there should be no payment made to the member of the profession that is hidden from the client.

The Treasury is authorised to designate professional bodies for the purposes of this exemption. To qualify for designation a professional body must show that it has rules which satisfy the conditions mentioned above. It must also demonstrate the legal basis for its regulatory function in respect of the profession. Following designation, responsibility for oversight of professional bodies lies with the FSA. It is required to keep itself informed of the manner in which professional bodies exercise their supervisory function and the way in which members of the profession carry on their activities. The FSA also has residual

---

[41] See below 3.7.
[42] FSMA 2000 s 327(4).
[43] The FSMA 2000 (Professions) (Non-exempt activities) Order 2001, SI 2001/1227.

powers to 'knock out' the exemption for the professional body in whole or in part or to 'knock out' a particular firm.[44]

3.3.4 Jurisdiction

The 'general prohibition' contained in section 19 FSMA 2000 applies to the carrying on of regulated activity in the United Kingdom. Section 418 identifies five cases in which a person carrying on a regulated activity, who would not otherwise be regarded as carrying it on in the UK, will be regarded as carrying it on in the UK. They relate to cases in which persons based in the UK (according to various criteria) carry on regulated activities overseas (whether in the EC under Treaty or Directive rights or elsewhere in the world). The general principle is that such persons are treated as carrying on regulated activity in the UK and therefore subject to the FSMA 2000 system of regulation. This is consistent with the general 'home country control' principle that is now well established in the EC and gaining increasing acceptance across the world.[45]

3.3.5 Unauthorised activity

Engaging in regulated activities without authorisation is a criminal offence.[46] It is not, however, a criminal offence for an authorised person to engage in activities for which no permission has been granted by the FSA, but this may give rise to disciplinary action. An agreement made by a person acting in contravention of the general prohibition (ie an unauthorised person) cannot be enforced against the other party.[47] The latter is entitled to recover any money or property transferred and compensation for any loss sustained as a result of having parted with it.

3.4 Regulated activities

The definition of regulated activities is central to the system of regulation because it defines the sphere of activity in respect of which authorisation is required. Section 22(1) FSMA 2000 provides as follows:

---

[44] See respectively ss 328 and 329 FSMA 2000. For more detail see Ch 22 of *Blackstone's Guide to FSMA 2000* (M Blair ed) (London, Blackstone, 2001).

[45] See E Lomnicka, *The Financial Services and Markets Act: An Annotated Guide* (London, Sweet & Maxwell, 2002) pp 626–27 for more detail.

[46] FSMA 2000 s 19.

[47] FSMA 2000 s 26. In effect, a party entering an agreement with an unauthorised person is given the option of enforcing the agreement. That section does not apply to unauthorised deposit-taking, in respect of which there is a special provision in s 29.

An activity is a regulated activity for the purposes of this Act if it is an activity of a specified kind which is carried on by way of business and—

(a) relates to an investment of a specified kind;

(b) in the case of an activity of a kind which is also specified for the purposes of this paragraph, is carried on in relation to property of any kind.

This rather opaque formulation creates two routes through which activity may be regulated. The first is that it is a specified activity relating to an investment of a specified kind.[48] The second is that it is a specified activity carried on in respect of any property. The purpose of paragraph (b) of section 22(1) is to bring within the scope of regulation activities that would not otherwise be regulated. For example, property (land and buildings) is not a specified investment but paragraph (b) allows direct property investment to be brought within FSMA 2000 in certain circumstances. This has occurred in respect of direct property investment undertaken by collective investment schemes and stakeholder pension schemes.[49]

The Treasury is authorised to make an order defining what is meant by a specified activity or specified investment and has made the Financial Services Services and Markets Act 2000 (Regulated Activities) Order 2001[50] (generally referred to as the 'RAO'). The RAO provides a more detailed definition of specified activities and investments than the Act itself. Before turning to the detail of the RAO, it should be noted that, to fall within the scope of FSMA 2000, the relevant activity must satisfy three requirements. First, the activity must be carried on by way of business. Whether an activity is carried on in this manner is determined by an order (the 'Business Order'[51]) made by the Treasury. Persons (natural or legal) acting solely for their own account do not fall within the scope of the Act. Second, the activity must relate to a specified investment or be carried on in relation to property of any kind. Investments are defined in schedule 2 to the Act and the RAO and are discussed in more detail in Chapter 4. Finally, the activity must be of a kind specified by schedule 2 FSMA or the RAO. The activities specified by the RAO are set out below.[52]

---

[48] Paragraph (a) of s 22(1) (quoted above).

[49] Arts 51 and 52 respectively of the RAO.

[50] SI 2001/544.

[51] See the FSMA 2000 (Carrying on Regulated Activities by Way of Business) Order 2001 (SI 2001/1177) for more detail.

[52] This section is intended to provide an overview of the RAO. As each regulated activity is subject to detailed conditions and exceptions, reference must be made to the RAO to decide whether a particular activity falls within its scope.

Accepting deposits

This activity has been the traditional foundation on which banking regulation has been based in the UK. It reflects the emphasis in banking regulation on the protection of depositors. Certain types of deposit made other than in the context of banking business (eg a deposit that is a pre-payment for goods) are excluded from the RAO.

Insurance

Effecting or carrying out a contract of insurance as a principal is a regulated activity. The RAO excludes from its scope the activities of EEA insurers carried out under freedom of services and in relation to co-insurance, in respect of which there are EC Directives in force. Annuity contracts (such as personal pensions or 'insured' group pensions) are included within the definition of insurance. Breakdown insurance is excluded from the RAO.

Dealing in investments as a principal

This category applies most obviously to market-makers[53], whose business consists principally of buying and selling investments with a view to making a profit. The RAO makes clear that this category of specified activity applies only to persons engaged in dealing as a business and not persons who deal in investments in the course of carrying on a separate business (eg fund management).[54]

Dealing in investments as agent

Buying, selling, subscribing for or underwriting securities or contractually-based investments as an agent is a specified activity. There are exclusions from this type of activity. An important one relates to transactions arranged by an agent who is not an authorised person where the client enters the transaction on advice given by an authorised person. The limitation of this activity to securities or contractually-based investments has the effect of excluding mortgage broking and general insurance broking from this activity although, as discussed below, these two activities will soon be subject to regulation.[55]

---

[53] On the role of market-makers, see Ch 10.
[54] Art 18A of the RAO (inserted by SI 2001/544) makes clear that companies who purchase their own shares to be held in 'treasury' under s 162A of the Companies Act 1985 do not engage in regulated activity.
[55] See the comment below re 'advising' for more detail.

Arranging deals in investments

Making arrangements for another person (whether as principal or agent) to buy, sell, subscribe for or underwrite particular investments[56] is a specified kind of activity. This category is intended to deal with persons involved in making arrangements for other persons in circumstances in which they are not the agent of that person. An example would be a person operating, on an independent basis, a system that enables investors to buy and sell securities from each other.

Managing investments

Managing investments belonging to another person, in circumstances involving the exercise of discretion, is generally a specified kind of activity.

Managing the investments of an occupational pension scheme (defined in the RAO as a scheme limited to providing benefits to a defined category of employees) is, subject to exceptions, a specified activity.[57] The exceptions are wide-ranging. Authorisation is not required if a trustee[58] does not hold himself out as providing an investment management service or if the trustee is not acting in a business capacity. A trustee does not act in a business capacity when:

- routine investment decisions are delegated to an authorised person with relevant permission, an exempt person or an overseas person; or
- the trustee is a beneficiary of the scheme (eg an employee); or
- the trustee has no part in routine investment decisions.[59]

The activity of managing investments is not carried on by a person acting under a power of attorney if all routine investment decisions are taken by an authorised person with permission to carry on this activity.

Safeguarding and administering investments

This is a regulated activity if the assets include any investment which is a security or contractually based investment or may do so. It is immaterial that the title to assets is held in uncertificated form.[60] An authorised person with permission to engage in this activity is a 'qualifying custodian'. Mere introduction of a customer to a qualifying custodian is not a regulated activity.[61]

---

[56] See art 25 of the RAO.

[57] See p 78 of *A Practitioner's Guide to FSA Regulation of Designated Investment Business* (T Cornick ed) (Old Woking, Surrey City & Financial Publishing, 2002) for more detail.

[58] A trustee is responsible for the investment of trust funds and an occupational pension fund is a trust fund.

[59] Art 66(3) of the RAO and art 4 of the Business Order (SI 2001/1177).

[60] See Ch 4 as to the meaning of uncertificated securities.

[61] Art 42 of the RAO.

Sending dematerialised instructions

This category is intended to bring within the scope of FSMA 2000 persons involved in sending instructions relating to the transfer of legal title to securities that are held in dematerialised form (ie ownership is recorded in a computer system rather than on a paper certificate). The activity relates to instructions sent within a relevant system in respect of which an Operator is approved under the Uncertificated Securities Regulations 2001.[62] There are exemptions from the scope of this activity, notably in respect of system participants and takeover offers.

Collective investment schemes[63]

The following are specified activities:

(a) establishing, operating or winding up a collective investment scheme;
(b) acting as trustee of an authorised unit trust scheme;
(c) acting as the depositary or sole director of an open-ended investment company (OEIC).

These activities are also specified for the purposes of section 22(1)(b) FSMA 2000, with the result that they are regulated activities when carried on in respect of property of any kind (eg investing scheme assets in land and buildings, which are not specified investments).

Stakeholder pension schemes[64]

Establishing, operating or winding up a stakeholder pension scheme is a specified kind of activity and is also specified for the purposes of section 22(1)(b) FSMA 2000.[65] Operating an occupational pension scheme is not a specified activity under the RAO, but, as noted above, managing the investments of such a scheme may be a specified activity.

Advising on investments

This is generally a specified activity. Included within the scope of the activity is advice given to a person in his capacity as agent for an investor or potential investor. Generic investment advice in newspapers and other publications is excluded if it does not advise on particular investments or lead or enable persons to deal in securities.

---

[62] See Ch 4.
[63] The structure, operation and regulation of collective investment schemes is discussed in Ch 4.
[64] See Ch 4 for the meaning of this term.
[65] See the comment on collective investment schemes in the text above.

There are two important gaps that will be soon filled. The first is general insurance broking. This is excluded because article 53 of the RAO is limited to advice on securities or contractually based investments. The latter category includes 'qualifying contracts of insurance' (which are particular types of life assurance) but excludes general insurance contracts and 'non-investment' life assurance.[66] A similar position existed under FSA 1986. The Insurance Brokers Registration Act 1977 controlled the use of the term 'insurance broker' but was not a comprehensive system of regulation as it was possible to fall outside the scope of the Act by describing oneself as something other than a broker (eg adviser, consultant or agent). Self-regulation of the sale of general insurance was established in 2000, in the form of codes adopted by the General Insurance Standards Council, but that was to prove no more than a transitional phase as the government announced in late 2001 that general insurance sales and advice would become subject to FSA (ie statutory) regulation. The RAO has now been amended so as to bring general insurance broking within the scope of regulation.[67] This change became effective on 14 January 2005 and a new section of the FSA Handbook entitled Insurance: Conduct of Business Sourcebook (ICOB) was created for this purpose. ICOB will also implement two European Community measures that have significant implications for general insurance broking, the Insurance Mediation Directive[68] and the Distance Marketing Directive.[69]

The second is mortgage broking. Mortgages were excluded from the activity of advising for the same reason as was explained above in relation to general insurance contracts. The extension of regulation to cover mortgages is discussed in more detail below.

Firms that are already authorised (as a result of having permission to engage in other activities) and wish to conduct or to continue to conduct general insurance broking and/or mortgage broking will require a variation in their permission.

---

[66] The main example of 'non-investment' life assurance is term assurance, which (in a variety of forms) provides cover against premature death and provides no payment if the policyholder survives the policy term.

[67] See the FSMA 2000 (Regulated Activities) (Amendment) (No 2) Order 2003, SI 2003/1476 (arts 2 and 9(1), amending art 53 of the RAO).

[68] Dir 2002/92/EC [2003] OJ L9/3. While the Directive in terms does not apply to 'direct sales' (see art 2(3)), it is open to member states to implement more stringent provisions (see para 19 of the preamble to the directive). The UK has chosen to do this by defining insurance mediation to include 'direct sales' so as to avoid consumer confusion and to create a level playing field between 'direct' and 'intermediated' sales. See FSA Consultation Papers 160 *Insurance Selling and Administration—the FSA's High-Level Approach to Regulation* (Dec 2002) and 187 *Insurance Selling and Administration and Other Miscellaneous Amendments* (June 2003) for more detail. See also Ch 6 for an explanation of 'direct' and 'intermediated' sales.

[69] Dir 2002/65/EC [2002] OJ L 271/16.

Lloyd's

Advising a person to become, or continue or cease to be, a member of a particular Lloyd's syndicate is a specified kind of activity. Generic advice on whether to become a member of Lloyd's is not included in this activity. Managing the underwriting capacity of a Lloyd's syndicate as a managing agent at Lloyd's is a specified kind of activity. The arranging of deals in contracts of insurance at Lloyd's by the society of Lloyd's (ie the activity of a Lloyd's broker) is a specified activity.

Funeral plan contracts

Entering as provider into a funeral plan contract is a specified activity, subject to exclusions.[70]

Regulated mortgage contracts

Mortgages often represent a major and often the largest long-term financial committment of households. Despite this, mortgages were not included in the definition of investments under FSA 1986 with the result that neither mortgage lending nor advising on mortgages fell within the scope of regulated activities under that Act. The regulatory gap was eventually filled in 1997 by a self-regulatory 'Mortgage Code', which was overseen by a body called the Mortgage Code Compliance Board.[71] However, it soon became clear that some form of statutory regulation would be introduced. The Treasury's initial proposal was to bring mortgage lending with the scope of regulated activities and appropriate provisions were included in the RAO. They did not, however, come into effect as originally planned in September 2003. Instead, regulation of mortgage lending was introduced at the same time as regulation of mortgage advice on 31 October 2004. From that date, a number of activities that are undertaken in respect of 'regulated mortgage contracts' are specified activities,[72] and a new part of the FSA Handbook, the Mortgage Conduct of Business Rules (MCOB), has taken effect.

To qualify as a 'regulated mortgage contract', the following conditions must be met:[73]

---

[70] See art 60 of the RAO.

[71] See FSA Consultation Paper 70, *Mortgage Regulation: The FSA's High Level Approach* p 8 for more detail.

[72] See the FSMA 2000 (Regulated Activities) (Amendment) (No 1) Order 2003, SI 2003/1475.

[73] See art 61 of the RAO. Loans that do not fall within this definition (eg a mortgage which is a second charge) may be subject to regulation under the Consumer Credit Act 1974. Responsibility for licensing under that Act lies with the Office of Fair Trading (OFT). For more detail on the precise split between the FSA and OFT as regards mortgage regulation, see ch 4 of FSA Consultation Paper 70 (above n 71).

(a) the borrower must be an individual or trustee;
(b) the contract must be entered into after mortgage regulation comes into force (31 October 2004);
(c) the lender must take a first charge over UK property;
(d) the property must be at least 40 per cent occupied by the borrower or his immediate family.

The following are specified activities in respect of such contracts:

• entering into or administering;[74]
• arranging;[75]
• advising.[76]

The introduction of mortgage regulation has consequences for all firms engaging in mortgage business. Unauthorised firms will require authorisation while authorised firms will require a change in their permission. Authorised representatives (aka 'tied agents') do not have the option of becoming authorised for the purposes of mortgage advice, as the FSMA does not permit the same person to be both exempt from authorisation[77] in respect of some activities and authorised for others. Professional firms that carry on regulated activity that is incidental to their profession can engage in a similar fashion in arranging and advising on mortgages. This activity does not include recommending particular products to clients, for which authorisation is necessary. With the introduction of mortgage regulation, the scope of the financial promotion regime[78] has been extended to include promotion relating to arranging and advising in respect of regulated mortgage contracts.

Agreeing to carry on activities

Agreeing to carry on most of the activities referred to above is a specified activity.[79] This brings within the scope of FSMA 2000 persons who have not yet commenced the relevant activity but have agreed to do so. It has implications for persons who plan to provide services in respect of which they do not currently have permission.

---

[74] Art 61 of the RAO.
[75] Art 4 of SI 2003/1475 (creating a new art 25A of the RAO).
[76] Art 13 of SI 2003/1475 (creating a new art 53A of the RAO).
[77] Under s 39 FSMA 2000, appointed representatives are exempt from authorisation.
[78] See 3.5 below.
[79] Exceptions are accepting deposits, effecting and carrying out contracts of insurance or carrying on any of the collective investment scheme activities or activities in relation to stakeholder pension schemes.

Exclusions applying to several specified kinds of activity

This part of the RAO excludes certain types of activity from its scope. They are:

(a) some of the activities of trustees and personal representatives;
(b) activities carried on in the course of a profession or non-investment business which are a necessary part of that business and are not remunerated separately;
(c) activities carried on in connection with the sale of goods or the supply of services;
(d) transactions between members of corporate groups and joint enterprises;
(e) activities carried on in connection with the sale of a body corporate;
(f) activities carried on in connection with employee share schemes;
(g) various activities carried on by an overseas person.

3.5 The financial promotion regime

The financial promotion regime had no direct counterpart under FSA 1986. It has two main purposes. First, it prohibits financial promotion on the part of unauthorised persons. Authorised persons are permitted to engage in financial promotion and when they do so are regulated by FSA rules.[80] Second, it unites in a single regime a variety of regulatory controls relating to financial promotion that had in the past existed under FSA 1986, the Banking Act 1987 and the Insurance Companies Act 1982. These controls related to the advertising, marketing and sales techniques used to promote the financial products falling within each of the three regulatory regimes (above) that pre-dated FSMA 2000. Of particular significance in the context of investment were the controls over advertising (s 57 FSA 1986 and rules made under it), unsolicited calls (s 57 FSA 1986 and relevant rules), promotion of unregulated collective investment schemes (s 76 FSA 1986) and promotion of certain long-term insurance contracts (s 130 FSA 1986). By consolidating these controls, the Financial Promotion Regime provides a single point of reference for determining whether a person can engage in financial promotion.

Financial promotion is not the same as regulated activity. While the distinction introduces considerable complexity into the regulatory system, it has been justified on the basis that the FSA should be able to take action when an unauthorised person attempts to induce a potential customer into a transaction without waiting until regulated activity has commenced. Under FSA

---

[80] These rules form part of the Conduct of Business Rules (COBs) rather than being part of the financial promotion regime itself.

1986, 'investment business' included 'offering' to engage in such business, with the result that promotion fell within that Act's definition of regulated activity.[81] That is no longer the case as under FSMA 2000 an unauthorised person contravenes the general prohibition only at the stage of agreeing to carry on a regulated activity and not before.[82] It has also been justified on the basis that the territorial scope of the financial promotion regime should be broader than that of 'regulated activities' so as to limit promotions aimed at the UK from overseas persons falling outside the scope of the RAO.

Section 21 of the FSMA forms the basis of the financial promotion regime. It provides:

(1) A person ('A') must not, in the course of business, communicate an invitation or inducement to engage in investment activity.
(2) But subsection (1) does not apply if –
  (a) A is an authorised person; or
  (b) the content of the communication is approved for the purposes of this section by an authorised person.

A number of points can be made.[83] First, 'in the course of business' appears to mean in the course of any business and not just regulated activity. 'Communicate' appears to include not just the source of the communication but also persons involved in its delivery (in whatever format) to the potential customer. 'Engaging in investment activity' is defined by section 21(8) as:

(a) entering or offering to enter into an agreement the making or performance of which by either party constitutes a controlled activity; or
(b) exercising any rights conferred by a controlled investment to acquire, dispose of, underwrite or convert a controlled investment.

'Controlled activities' and 'controlled investments' are defined (at some length) in an Order made by the Treasury under section 21 FSMA 2000.[84] These categories do not correspond with 'specified activities' and 'specified investments' under the RAO.

The restriction on financial promotion does not apply to a communication if the content of the communication is approved for the purposes of section 21 by an authorised person. The approval process is controlled by Conduct of Business Rules made by the FSA.[85] As far as territorial application is concerned the prohibition applies to communications originating outside the UK that are capable of having an effect within the UK[86] but does not generally apply to

---

[81] See sch 1 p 2 FSA 1986.
[82] See art 64 of the RAO. The reference to 'agreeing' indicates that there must be a legally binding contract for the carrying on of a regulated activity.
[83] See generally p 57 of *Blackstone's Guide to FSMA 2000* (above n 44).
[84] The FSMA 2000 (Financial Promotion) Order 2001 SI 2001/1335 (as amended).
[85] See FSA Handbook, COB 3.
[86] FSMA 2000 s 21(3).

communications made to persons receiving it outside the UK or which is directed only at persons outside the UK.[87]

3.6 Rule-making

The nature of FSMA 2000 is that it is an enabling statute. It contains only a basic framework for the system of financial regulation, leaving much of the detail to rules made by the regulator. The rule-making powers of the FSA are therefore central to the whole system.

The FSA has both general and specific rule-making powers. The general rule-making power authorises the FSA to make such rules applying to author-ised persons with respect to them carrying on any activities (whether or not regulated activities) as appear necessary or expedient for the purpose of protecting the interests of consumers.[88] Statutory recognition that rules may apply in different ways to different persons or activities allows the Authority to continue the practice of distinguishing between different types of customer and investor in its rulebook.[89] There are also specific rule-making powers.[90] Also relevant here are the FSMA provisions relating to the manner in which the FSA carries out its functions. One of the FSA's general functions under the Act is making rules and the Act requires that in discharging its general functions, the Authority must have regard to, inter alia, the principle that the costs of regulation should be proportionate to the benefits.[91]

The rule-making procedure under FSMA 2000 is more formal and detailed than that under FSA 1986.[92] The FSA must publish a draft of proposed rules for public consultation and must take account of any representations when making the rules. Such representations are likely to be made by the Consumer[93] and

---

[87] Article 12 of the Financial Promotion Order (n 84 above).

[88] FSMA 2000 s 138. Consumers are defined very broadly by sub-s 7 and can range from pri-vate customers to market counterparties (see Ch 10 for categorisation of customers under FSMA 2000).

[89] See s 156(1) FSMA 2000.

[90] See ss 144–47 FSMA 2000 which empower the Authority to make price stabilising rules, financial promotion rules, money laundering rules and control of information rules. The specific powers do not limit the general rule-making power: s 138(3) FSMA 2000.

[91] FSMA 2000 s 2(3)(c). The costs of regulation are borne initially by authorised persons and ultimately by investors (assuming that such costs are passed down the chain of transactions).

[92] See s 255 FSMA 2000.

[93] 'Consumer' includes persons falling within the (broad) definition in FSMA 2000 s 138(7) and also persons who would be consumers within that definition if the relevant activities were carried on by an authorised person. This brings within the definition of 'consumer' persons who deal with an unauthorised person carrying on regulated activities. Authorised persons are not consumers (sub-s 7). The FSA must ensure that the Consumer Panel fairly represents the inter-ests of persons using services in a private (ie non-business) capacity.

Practitioner Panels which the Authority is required to establish and maintain.[94] The consultation draft must be accompanied by an explanation of the purpose of the proposed rules. The FSA must also, in most circumstances, publish a cost–benefit analysis with a draft of the rules. If the rules differ significantly from the consultation draft, the FSA is required to publish details of the difference and another cost–benefit analysis.

The FSA has used these powers to make its rulebook, the Handbook of Rules and Guidance.[95] The Handbook is divided into several blocks, which are in turn divided into topics. There are six blocks as follows:

1 High-level standards. They contains, inter alia, statements of principle applicable to businesses and approved persons.
2 Business standards. This contains the prudential sourcebooks for banks, insurers and investment firms as well as the *Conduct of Business* ('COB') and *Market Conduct* (MAR) sourcebooks.
3 Regulatory processes. Included in this block are the *Authorisation* (AUTH), *Supervision* (SUP) and *Enforcement* (ENF) manuals.
4 Redress. This contains the complaints and compensation sourcebooks.
5 Specialist sourcebooks, including those applicable to collective investment schemes, recognised exchanges, the Lloyd's insurance market and listing rules.
6 Glossary and Index.

The status of each provision in the Handbook is indicated by a letter attached to it as follows:

R indicates rules, which can be general rules made under section 138 FSMA 2000 or rules made under other specific powers provided by the Act.
D indicates directions and requirements given under various powers conferred by the Act.
P indicates Statements of Principle for Approved Persons made under section 64 of the Act.
C indicates 'safe harbours' (conclusive descriptions of compliant behaviour in respect of the market abuse regime) specified under section 119(2) of the Act.
E indicates evidential provisions, which are discussed below.
G indicates guidance given under section 157.

It will be clear from this structure that the FSA Handbook comprises diverse provisions that have different effects. Some have no binding effect (guidance).

---

[94] See ss 8–10 FSMA 2000.
[95] The handbook is available online at www.fsa.gov.uk (10 Nov 2004). See the Reader's Guide to the Handbook for details regarding structure and content.

Others are binding but are expressed with differing levels of detail (principles and rules). Others serve the purpose of more clearly delimiting the scope and application of related rules (safe harbours and evidential provisions).

Evidential provisions are intended to make clear when compliance with or contravention of one rule (A) will result in compliance with or contravention of another rule (B). An evidential provision must either provide that contravention of rule A tends to establish contravention of rule B or that compliance with rule A tends to establish compliance with rule B. Evidential provisions do not create presumptions but they come close to doing so.[96] Their effect is to move the burden of proving compliance with rule B on to a firm when it is in contravention of rule A and of proving contravention of rule B on to the FSA when a firm is in compliance with rule A.

'Safe harbours' differ from evidential provisions in two important ways. First, they relate only to the market abuse regime. Second, behaviour in conformity with a safe harbour is, by virtue of section 122 FSMA 2000, conclusively not market abuse. In this sense, safe harbours provide guarantees in respect of behaviour while evidential provisions do not.

Guidance can consist only of information and advice and therefore cannot impose obligations.[97] It can take the form of general guidance given to the public, regulated persons or a class of regulated persons or, alternatively, specific guidance given to an individual or firm.[98] Compliance with guidance provides no immunity from regulatory action taken by the FSA in respect of a contravention of the Act or rules made under it, but the FSA has made clear that action will not normally be taken against a firm or individual in respect of behaviour in line with general or specific guidance.[99]

Finally, the FSA may also, in some circumstances, give directions. For example, when it decides to modify or waive the application of a particular rule, the FSA gives a direction to that effect. There are normally particular conditions attached to the making of directions.

3.7 Approval of individuals

In the main, the FSA and rules made under it impose obligations on authorised persons, most of whom are companies and partnerships rather

---

[96] See the analogy with the Highway Code in M Threipland, 'Rules and Guidance' ch 12 in *Blackstone's Guide to the FSMA 2000* (above n 44).

[97] See ss 157 and 158 FSMA 2000.

[98] The FSA can make a reasonable charge for guidance given to a person on request.

[99] See FSA Policy Statement, *The FSA's Approach to Giving Guidance and Waivers to Firms* (Sept 1999).

than individuals. However, there are instances in which obligations are imposed also on individuals. The 'approved person regime' established by sections 59–70 FSMA 2000 is an important development in this respect. It had no direct counterpart under FSA 1986, although similar arrangements were introduced by the self-regulatory organisations that preceded the FSA. The purpose of the approved person regime is to ensure that the FSA is able to 'vet' individuals who are to be employed by authorised persons to carry out significant functions. An application for approval in respect of the relevant individual must be made to the FSA by the authorised firm and approval will be granted only if the FSA is satisfied that the individual is a fit and proper person to perform that function.

Section 59 FSMA 2000 limits the performance of controlled functions[100] to approved persons (natural or corporate). An authorised person ('A') must take reasonable care to ensure compliance with this provision, both in respect of persons directly employed by A and also in respect of persons employed by a contractor of A (including an appointed representative). The FSA may designate a function as a controlled function if one of the following conditions is met:

(a) the function is likely to enable the person responsible for its performance to exercise a significant influence on the conduct of the authorised person's affairs, so far as it relates to the regulated activity; or
(b) the function will involve the person performing it in dealing with customers of the authorised person in a manner substantially connected with the carrying on of the regulated activity; or
(c) the function will involve the person performing it in dealing with the property of customers of the authorised person in a manner substantially connected with the carrying on of the regulated activity.

A 'grandfathering' provision applies to persons performing the equivalent of a controlled function before the general prohibition against engaging in regulated activity without authorisation (s 19 FSMA 2000) entered into force (on N2 day, 1 December 2001). Such persons are to be treated as 'approved' by the FSA for the purpose of performing that function after section 59 became effective.[101]

The 'approved person regime'—contained in the APER section of the FSA Handbook—does not apply to firms who carry on business in the UK which falls within the 'EEA' and 'Treaty firm' category of authorisation[102] if the issue of whether a person is fit and proper to perform a specified function is reserved to the 'home' state regulator. This is intended to give effect to the 'single

---

[100] Controlled functions are defined in general terms by s 59 (4)–(9) and more specifically by the FSA Handbook—see AUTH 6.2.1G and SUP 10 (SUP 10.4.5R lists 27 controlled functions).
[101] SI 2001/2636 (Pt VI).
[102] See s 31 and schs 3 and 4 of FSMA 2000. See also Ch 2.5.2.

licence' and 'home country control' provisions of the EU directives covering the financial sector.[103]

3.8 Risk assessment and monitoring

The FSA now operates what it refers to as a 'risk-based' system of regulation. The risks to which this refers are those that pose a risk to the achievement of the statutory objectives set by FSMA 2000.[104] This is a fundamentally different perspective of risk from that of an authorised firm that is managing risk within its business. Essentially the risk with which the FSA is concerned is the risk of regulatory failure in the sense that failure to achieve the statutory objectives can be described as regulatory failure.[105]

In identifying and assessing risks the FSA focuses on their impact (the scale of the effect on the statutory objectives if the issue or event crystallises) and their probability (the likelihood of the particular issue or event crystallising). Firms that are assessed by the FSA as being 'low impact' (in the sense of posing little risk to the achievement of the statutory objectives) do not have an individual risk assessment or mitigation programme. They are monitored through the more traditional approach of scrutinising returns made by firms and conducting sample exercises to monitor compliance standards.

For those firms subject to individual risk assessment, the FSA identifies the following types of risk:

(a) Firm specific risk. This is the risk that arises from the structure and method of operation of a particular business. It can be broken down into two components:
    (i) Business risk. This is the risk that arises from the nature of the business. For example, in banking there is a risk of customers defaulting on loans and in general insurance there is the risk posed by the multiple occurrence of insured risks (eg as a result of an earthquake).
    (ii) Control risk. This risk arises from the way in which a business is organised and operates. It includes issues such as the management structure, internal controls and the way in which the business sells financial products to or advises customers.

---

[103] See FSA Handbook, SUP 10.1.10G for more detail. Note, however, that the 'EEA Investment Business Oversight Function' (defined by SUP 10.7.6R) is a controlled function and will require approval (which may be combined with approval for another controlled function eg a significant management function).

[104] See above 3.1.

[105] See generally FSA publication, *The Firm Risk Assessment Framework* (Feb 2003).

(b) Environmental risk. This category describes risks that are external to the firm but which directly or indirectly affect firm specific risk. It comprises the following types of risk:

(i) Political/legal. This would include threats to a firm's business posed by changes in legislation.

(ii) Socio-demographic. An example would be the long-term effect on an annuity provider of increasing life expectancy.

(iii) Technological. An example is the threat posed to recognised investment exchanges by developments in computerised dealing systems.[106]

(iv) Economic. Changes in interest rates may, for example, increase loan defaults for banks.

(v) Competition. Some firms may face pressure from new competition (domestic or international).

(vi) Market structure. This may be affected by changing customer preferences (eg a preference for home ownership over renting) or regulatory developments.[107]

The next step is to link these risks to the statutory objectives. This is achieved through an assessment of how these risks affect one or more of seven regulatory risks, which are termed 'risk to objectives' (RTO) groups. In essence the RTOs provide a technique for mapping business and control risks on to the statutory objectives. The RTOs are as follows:

Financial failure. This is the risk posed to market confidence and consumer protection from the failure of a firm.

Misconduct and/or mismanagement. An example is the risk to consumer protection and market confidence arising from 'mis-selling'.[108]

Consumer understanding. This is the risk posed to the consumer protection and public awareness objectives by lack of understanding on the part of consumers of products bought from firms.

Incidence of fraud or dishonesty. This poses a threat to the financial crime, consumer protection and market confidence objectives.

Incidence of market abuse. This also poses a threat to the financial crime, consumer protection and market confidence objectives.

Incidence of money laundering. This poses risks for the financial crime objective.

Market quality. This is the risk posed to market confidence and consumer protection arising from possible deterioration in the functioning of a market.

---

[106] See Ch 10 for more discussion.
[107] See the discussion of 'polarisation' in Ch 4.
[108] See Ch 6 for a discussion of 'mis-selling'.

In respect of each firm, the business and control risks are scored against the RTO groups. This process provides an overall probability score in respect of each statutory objective that falls into one of the following catgeories: high, medium high, medium low or low. The next step is for the FSA to develop a risk mitigation programme (RMP) by reference to the score of a particular firm.[109] In doing so the FSA takes account of the principles of good regulation by aiming to ensure that the intensity of the RMP is proportionate to the risk posed by the firm. The RMP is then communicated to the firm together with an indication of the regulatory period, which is the period between formal risk assessments. The period varies between 12 and 36 months according to the risk profile of firms and when longer than 12 months, an interim risk assessment will be undertaken which may result in changes to the RMP.

3.9 Compliance and enforcement

All authorised firms are expected to establish procedures and working practices that will ensure the firm is in compliance with FSMA 2000 and rules made under it.[110] Contravention of the Act or a rule is likely to result in a range of measures being taken against the relevant firm, and in some cases, individuals within the firm. These measures include disciplinary action taken by the FSA, a criminal prosecution or a private action in damages brought by a client for breach of statutory duty.

3.9.1 Disciplinary measures

The FSA has a range of disciplinary measures at its disposal.

Public censure

The most straightforward sanction is public censure,[111] which simply involves publication of the fact of a contravention of the Act or rules made under it by an authorised person. The FSA is not required to establish a contravention of the Act or its rules according to any objective standard before issuing a public censure.[112] This sanction relies on the deterrent effect that adverse publicity can have on reputation in the financial market.

---

[109] See Annex 7 to FSA Publication *The Firm Risk Assessment Framework* for an example of an RMP.

[110] Principle 3 of the FSA's Principles for Business (PRIN) states that 'A firm must take reasonable care to organise and control its affairs responsibly and effectively, with adequate risk management systems'.

[111] See s 205 FSMA 2000.

[112] See FSA Handbook, ENF 12.3 regarding factors relevant to the issue of a public censure.

Financial penalty

Another option is to impose a financial penalty. This was a power that the FSA lacked under the FSA 1986 regulatory system: only the self-regulatory organisations (SROs) were empowered to impose financial penalties and that was a matter of contractual agreement between the SROs and authorised persons rather than a statutory power. There is, in principle, no limit to the amount of the penalty but the FSA is required to publish guidance on its policy regarding penalties and the amount of penalties.[113]

Variation or cancellation of permission

Although not categorised by FSMA 2000 as disciplinary measures, there are several other options that might be considered by the FSA in response to a contravention. One is a variation in the regulated activities included in an authorised person's 'permission'.[114] This might occur if it became clear that a firm was not capable of conducting part of its business to an appropriate standard. A second, and more drastic, response would be complete cancellation of permission to engage in any regulated activity. That, in itself, does not result in withdrawal of authorisation because a separate direction from the FSA is required for that to occur.[115] The purpose of this procedure is to ensure that when an authorised person is no longer able to engage in regulated activity as a result of cancellation of permission, it remains subject to the jurisdiction of the FSA because it is still an authorised person.

Prohibition orders

The FSA may prohibit an individual (ie a human person) from performing any regulated activities carried on by an authorised person if it considers that the individual is not a fit and proper person to carry on that function.[116] The prohibition may apply to any or all regulated activity and may prohibit employment by a particular firm or type of firm. An order may also prohibit an individual from performing functions in relation to the regulated activity of an exempt person (such as an appointed representative or a recognised investment exchange or clearing house) and persons covered by an exemption under Part XX (provision of financial services by members of the professions). In most cases the FSA will consider whether the particular unfitness can be

---

[113] See ss 206 and 210 FSMA 2000. The guidance is published at ENF 13.
[114] This is possible at the FSA's initiative under s 45 FSMA 2000.
[115] FSMA 2000 s 33.
[116] FSMA 2000 s 56.

adequately dealt with by withdrawing approval or other disciplinary sanctions, for example public censure or financial penalties, or by issuing a private warning.[117] The FSA will consider making a prohibition order only in the most serious cases of lack of fitness and propriety.[118] In the case of an individual who is not an approved person, a prohibition order may be the only enforcement option.[119] The FSA will also take into account other enforcement action against the individual by the FSA, other agencies or professional bodies.[120]

It is an offence for an individual to perform or agree to perform a function in breach of a prohibition order. The offence is one of strict liability (not requiring *mens rea*) but it is a defence for the accused to show that he took all reasonable precautions and exercised all due diligence to avoid committing the offence. The FSA may, on the application of the individual named in a prohibition order, vary or revoke it.

An authorised (or exempt) person is required to take reasonable care to ensure that no function of his, in relation to the carrying on of a regulated activity, is performed by a person who is prohibited from performing that function by a prohibition order. Such orders are recorded in the register maintained by the FSA.[121] Reasonable care would appear to require that an authorised person search the register before engaging any employee. Any breach of this duty of care is actionable at the suit of a private person who suffers loss as a result of the contravention.[122]

Approved persons

The FSA is empowered to take disciplinary action against approved persons if two conditions are met.[123] The first is that the person is guilty of misconduct. This will occur if an approved person has failed to comply with the FSA's Principles for Approved Persons or has been knowingly concerned in a contravention on the part of an authorised person. The second is that it is appropriate in all the circumstances to take action against the approved person. In this regard, statements made by the Authority shed some light on what will be considered appropriate circumstances:[124]

---

[117] FSA Handbook ENF 8.4 sets out the FSA's policy on making prohibition orders. The Authority considers that a prohibition order is a more serious penalty than the withdrawal of approval (in relation to an approved person) because a prohibition order will usually be much wider in scope.

[118] FSA Handbook, ENF 8.5.2G sets out the factors to be taken into account in deciding whether to make an order against an approved person.

[119] See FSA Handbook, ENF 8.6.1AG

[120] See FSA Handbook, ENF 8.4.3G

[121] As required by s 347 FSMA 2000.

[122] FSMA 2000 s 71(1).

[123] FSMA 2000 s 66.

[124] FSA Consultation Paper 26, *The Regulation of Approved Persons* (1999) paras 98 and 115 respectively.

For example, action will be unlikely where an individual's behaviour was in compliance with the rules imposed on his firm in respect of his controlled function

and

> The FSA does not consider that it would be appropriate to discipline senior managers, approved for the purpose of [s 59 FSMA 2000], simply because a breach of the regulatory requirements has occurred in an area for which they are responsible. There will only be a breach of a Statement of Principle where there is personal culpability.[125]

The Authority must bring disciplinary proceedings against an approved person within two years of becoming aware of the misconduct. The criteria relevant to the Authority's decision to take disciplinary action under this section are set out in the FSA Handbook.[126] It is also possible that the Authority might simply give a private warning rather than take formal action.[127] The FSA is also empowered to take action against persons registered with SROs under arrangements that pre-dated the 'approved persons regime', in respect of contraventions occurring before the FSMA 2000 took effect.[128] The Authority will generally be able to take action against such persons in respect of contraventions that relate to activities which, if performed after the commencement of FSMA 2000, would be considered 'controlled activities'.

The sanctions available to the FSA if misconduct on the part of an approved person is established are a financial penalty or public censure.

3.9.2 Disciplinary procedure and sanctions

The disciplinary procedure provisions of FSMA 2000 attracted considerable attention during the committee stages in Parliament as debate focused on their compatibility with the Human Rights Act 1998.[129] The main issue was the compatibility of the procedures with article 6 of the European Convention on

---

[125] See FSA Handbook, APER 3.2.1E for factors relevant to determining if approved persons are in compliance with the Principles. See above 3.7 for APER.

[126] See ENF 11.4.1G.

[127] See FSA Handbook, ENF 11.3.1G.

[128] See the FSMA 2000 (Transitional Provisions and Savings) (Civil Remedies, Discipline, Criminal Offences) (No 2) Order 2001, SI 2001/3083, art 9.

[129] The Act gives effect in the United Kingdom to the European Convention on Human Rights. See the First (H of L 50 I–II; H of C HC328 I–II) and Second (H of L 66; H of C HC465) Reports of the Joint Parliamentary Committee on Financial Services and Markets. Para 147 of the First Report notes:

> According to the Progress Report [on the Bill] 'The main focus of comment on the draft Bill has been on the disciplinary process. There has been a perception that the FSA internal procedures may lack fairness and transparency, or be unduly costly and burdensome, and that the FSA will be able to act as prosecutor judge and jury.'

Human Rights (ECHR) which provides for the right to a fair trial. Potential contraventions were identified by reference to the following:[130]

(a) the extent to which the disciplinary procedure and the role of the FSA provided for a fair trial;
(b) the absence of legal assistance to secure representation for persons appearing before the Financial Services Tribunal;
(c) the standard of proof to be required in hearings before the Financial Services Tribunal;
(d) the use of compelled evidence in disciplinary proceedings; and
(e) the absence of legal certainty in the definition of market abuse.

The disciplinary framework ultimately adopted by the Act took account of these concerns. The relevant powers of the FSA are spread across various provisions of the Act and in the relevant part of the FSA Handbook (designated DEC). The key points are as follows:

(a) The first stage in the disciplinary process is the issue of a 'warning notice' to a firm or individual. This gives reasons for the proposed action and allows a period of time during which representations may be made to the FSA.
(b) The Regulatory Decisions Committee (RDC) is responsible for reaching decisions on disciplinary matters raised in a warning notice.[131] The members of this Committee are independent of the FSA.[132] When making decisions the RDC meets in private and is required to adopt procedures that will result in the case before it being dealt with fairly.
(c) Following intimation of the RDC's conclusions to the FSA, either a decision notice or discontinuance notice will be issued to the firm or person concerned. A decision notice must set out the action that the FSA proposes to take and, if relevant, draw attention to any right of appeal to the Financial Services and Markets Tribunal and any right of access to material relevant to the decision. If there is no referral to the Tribunal, a final notice will be issued before the relevant action is taken. If there is a referral to the Tribunal (or a subsequent appeal to the court), the Authority must give the relevant person a final notice before taking action in accordance with the direction of the Tribunal or court.
(d) The Financial Services and Markets Tribunal has a wide-ranging jurisdiction over many of the FSA's decisions, including those of a disciplinary

---

[130] See Annexes C and D to the Joint Committee First Report on the draft Bill (above n 129).
[131] See FSA Handbook DEC 4.1.
[132] This gives effect to the requirement of s 395 FSMA 2000 that such decisions must be made by persons independent of those who investigated the matter.

nature.[133] It is not an 'appeals' tribunal in the strict sense as it determines matters *de novo* and is able to consider fresh evidence that was not available to the RDC. The Tribunal must determine what (if any) is the appropriate action for the FSA to take. Decisions of the Tribunal may with permission be appealed to the courts on a point of law.[134]

(e) The Act makes provision for persons to whom notices are issued to have access to material that the Authority relied on in making the decision regarding issue of the notice.[135] The objective is to give effect to the right to a fair trial (article 6 ECHR), which includes the right to have knowledge of and comment on evidence relied on in the proceedings.

(f) In respect only of market abuse cases that are referred to the Financial Services and Markets Tribunal, there is a legal assistance (or 'legal aid') scheme.[136]

The sanctions available to the Authority are either a financial penalty of such amount as it considers appropriate or publication of a statement of the person's misconduct.

3.9.3 Prosecution of criminal offences

There are a number of criminal offences created by FSMA 2000. They include:

- breach of the general prohibition against carrying on regulated activity without authorisation[137]
- the making of false claims to being an authorised or exempt person[138]
- the use of misleading statements and practices to induce another person to enter into an investment agreement[139]
- engaging in market manipulation[140]
- misleading the Authority.[141]

---

[133] See pp 204–5 of *Butterworths Annotated Guide to FSMA 2000* (above n 29) for details of the Tribunal's jurisdiction. The tribunal is composed of a legally qualified President and a panel of persons comprising (a) a lawyer, (b) other persons qualified by experience or otherwise to deal with matters of the kind that may be referred to the Tribunal (sch 13 to FSMA 2000).

[134] FSMA 2000 s 137. Permission means that of the Tribunal or the relevant court (Court of Appeal in England, Court of Session in Scotland).

[135] FSMA 2000 s 394.

[136] This reflected advice given to the government during the passage of the bill through Parliament that the market abuse regime could be considered 'criminal' rather than 'civil' for the purposes of human rights law. Categorisation as 'criminal' would increase the likelihood of triggering the requirement of article 6(3)(c) ECHR that legal assistance be provided 'when the interests of justice so require'.

[137] FSMA 2000 s 23.

[138] FSMA 2000 s 24.

[139] FSMA 2000 s 397.

[140] FSMA 2000 s 397(3).

[141] FSMA 2000 s 398.

In England and Wales, prosecutions in respect of offences under FSMA 2000 may be instituted by the FSA, the Secretary of State (Department of Trade and Industry) or by or with the consent of the Director of Public Prosecutions. In exercising its powers, the FSA must comply with any conditions or restrictions imposed by the Treasury. In Scotland, prosecutions for offences under FSMA 2000 remain the responsibility of the Crown Office.

A contravention that is a criminal offence may or may not be pursued through the criminal courts. A decision on whether to prosecute or take disciplinary action will depend on a range of factors, including the likelihood of securing a criminal conviction.[142] The FSA has made clear that prosecution will not normally be pursued alongside disciplinary measures.

FSMA 2000 also provides for personal criminal liability on the part of certain individuals in circumstances in which an offence is committed by an organisation with the consent or connivance or as a result of the negligence of that individual. The provision[143] applies to officers of a company[144], partners in a partnership and officers or members of the governing body of an unincorporated association. The Treasury has power to extend this section to bodies established outside the United Kingdom.

3.9.4 Civil action for damages

A contravention of FSMA 2000 or a regulatory rule opens up the possibility of an action in damages at the suit of a private person.[145] A private person includes any individual, unless he suffers the loss in the course of carrying on any regulated activity and any person who is not an individual (eg a company) unless he suffers the loss in question in the course of carrying on a business of any kind.[146] Non-private persons can take action in three circumstances only:

(a) where the rule that has been contravened prohibits an authorised person from seeking to make provision excluding or restricting any duty or liability;

(b) where the rule that has been contravened concerns the misuse of unpublished information (ie market abuse); or

(c) where the action can only be brought in a fiduciary capacity by a non-private person on behalf of the private person.[147]

---

[142] See FSA Handbook, ENF 15.5.1G.

[143] FSMA 2000 s 400.

[144] The term includes controllers (large shareholders) who are individuals, and members of a Limited Liability Partnership (see SI 2001/1090).

[145] FSMA 2000 s 150.

[146] Art 3 of the FSMA 2000 (Rights of Action) Regulations 2001, SI 2001/2256.

[147] Art 6 of SI 2001/2256.

The basis of an action under section 150 is that the contravention represents a breach of statutory duty which has caused loss to the investor. As it is of most direct relevance to private investors, the requirements for a successful action are discussed in Chapter 6.[148] The equivalent provision in FSA 1986 was little used and it is likely that this will remain so under FSMA 2000.

---

[148] See 3.4.4.

Part 2

Investments and Investors

4

Investments

This chapter explains the legal nature and characteristics of different types of investment, focusing in particular on those that fall within the scope of FSMA 2000. It assumes that the reader is familiar with the concepts discussed in Chapters 1 and 3.

In Chapter 1 it was noted that investments are personal rights over incorporeal moveable property (intangibles). The nature of these rights is the subject of this chapter. For some investments, such as company shares, investors' rights are largely determined in the market (through contract) with little regulatory control. In the case of other forms of investment (eg some forms of investment fund) there is much less scope for private bargaining as the investor's rights are largely determined by regulation. As will be seen, regulation can control both the (contractual) relationship between an issuer and investor and the legal structure of an investment entity.

It was also noted in Chapter 1 that legal title to investments can be constituted in different ways. The main distinction is between registered and unregistered securities. The implications of this distinction for the mode of transfer of investments and the rights acquired by a transferee are considered in this chapter.

In Chapter 3, the scope of the regulatory system established by FSMA 2000 was discussed. Central to the scope of that system is the concept of a 'specified investment' because any 'specified activity' carried on by way of business in respect of a 'specified investment' or specified property of any kind is a regulated activity falling within the Act.[1] The Regulated Activities Order (RAO) defines both specified activities and specified investments. The scope of the former was outlined in Chapter 3 while the scope of the latter is explained in this chapter by reference to the main categories of investment.

There is no discussion in this chapter of 'product wrappers' into which investments may be organised. They include Individual Savings Accounts

---

[1] See s 22 FSMA 2000. 'Specified activities' and 'specified investments' are discussed in Ch 3.

(ISAs), Personal Equity Plans and Investment Trust Savings Plans. These 'wrappers' are not in themselves investments or property (in the legal sense).[2] They are essentially contractual arrangements for the administration of investments, designed mainly to take advantage of various tax-incentives. They do not alter the legal nature and structure of the underlying investments that are included in the 'product wrapper'.

4.1 Direct property investment

A distinction can be drawn between direct property investment and investment in financial instruments (portfolio investment). The former is investment in real (tangible) things such as land and buildings. The latter form of investment represents a more complex relationship between persons and property. An investor in a financial instrument cannot identify physical property over which she holds legal rights (eg a company shareholder has no direct ownership in respect of assets owned by the company). Thus, although the holder of a financial instrument is commonly termed its owner, the nature of ownership differs fundamentally from direct investment in property. A direct property investor has real rights that can be exercised against tangible property (eg taking possession), whereas a portfolio investor has personal (contractual) rights that cannot be exercised in that way.[3]

Direct property investment is familiar to most people in the form of home ownership. It is also undertaken by companies who buy premises and by fund managers who buy property as part of their portfolios. While direct investment in property gives an investor a real right in the property, this is not to say that the investor has exclusive rights in the property because more than one real right can exist in respect of the same property.[4] Common examples of the co-existence of real rights are when security interests are granted over property (eg a mortgage) or the grant of the real right of possession through a lease. The co-existence of such real rights can have important implications for the direct

---

[2] They cannot be considered property as they are personal to the account holder. No one person's tax exemption or incentive may be transferred to another. They therefore fail to meet the basic criterion of property that it should be capable of being owned by anyone. For an overview, see J Gray, 'Personal Finance and Corporate Governance: The Missing Link: Product Regulation and Policy Conflicts' (2004) 4 *Journal of Corporate Law Studies* 187 at 208–210.

[3] See Ch 1 for a discussion of real and personal rights. It was noted in Ch 1 that the holder of a financial instrument may have real (proprietary) rights against persons who hold the instrument on his behalf. Such rights do not, however, transform the nature of the financial instrument. They relate to the manner in which rights are held rather than their nature.

[4] See Ch 1 for a discussion of property rights in the context of investment.

investor, such as for example restricting the ability to sell or take possession of the property.

Direct property investment is not a specified investment for the purposes of FSMA 2000. It follows that regulated activities that are defined by reference to specified investments (eg dealing, managing, advising) do not, when carried out in respect of direct property investment, fall within the scope of FSMA 2000. However, a distinction must be drawn between direct property investment and activities relating to the financing of that investment. The most common form of finance is secured lending, commonly referred to as a mortgage.[5] Neither mortgage lending nor advising on mortgages (aka mortgage broking) fell within the scope of regulation under FSA 1986 or FSMA 2000. However, as from 31 October 2004, entering into (ie lending), administering, arranging or advising on mortgages became regulated activities.[6]

4.2 Government and public securities

Government (sometimes referred to as 'Treasury') and public securities are loans raised by the government and public authorities. They are specified investments for the purposes of FSMA 2000.[7] The term 'gilt-edged stock' or 'gilts' is used in respect of government borrowing because of the security attaching to the loan as a result of the government's promise to repay the loan. Loans are raised for different periods at different interest rates, and are categorised as being short (up to 5 years), medium (up to 10 years) or long (over 10 years) dated. The interest rate is fixed. The par value, at which the loan will be redeemed, is normally £1. However, gilts need not be issued at par and the prices at which they trade will reflect movements in interest rates since their issue.[8]

Gilts are registered securities and are therefore transferred by the legal process of novation.[9] Legal title is now generally held in dematerialised form[10] and transfers normally take place through CREST.[11] It does, however, remain

---

[5] Although the term 'mortgage' is now commonly used throughout the United Kingdom, it has no technical meaning in Scotland, where a security interest over land granted by a borrower to a lender is termed a 'standard security'.

[6] See Ch 3.4 for an explanation of regulated activity.

[7] See art 78 of the Regulated Activities Order (SI 2001/544). Instruments issued by the National Savings Bank are excluded from the definition of specified investments.

[8] See, regarding the structure and movements in interest rates, ch 4 of K Pilbeam, *Finance and Financial Markets* (Basingstoke, Palgrave, 1998).

[9] See 4.4.3 below for an explanation of novation.

[10] Legal title is recorded and transferred electronically rather than by the use of paper records.

[11] The operation of CREST is discussed later in this chapter and also in Ch 9.

possible for transfers of certificated securities to be effected outside the CREST system by means of a stock transfer.[12]

4.3 Deposits

A deposit is an arrangement under which the depositor transfers ownership of the deposit to the deposit-taker (normally a bank or building society) who is free to use the deposit in the course of its business, which will normally mean that the deposit becomes part of the institution's funds available for lending to borrowers. The depositor has a contractual claim for the repayment of the deposit on the agreed terms (eg as to interest and time).[13] It is normal for deposit agreements to provide for repayment on demand or subject to a period of notice being given by the depositor.

Deposits are specified investments for the purposes of FSMA 2000 and the business of deposit-taking falls within FSMA 2000 because deposit-taking is a specified activity (under the RAO).[14] While this represents an expansion of the scope of the FSMA 2000 regulatory system by comparison with that created by FSA 1986 (which did not cover the business of deposit-taking), it is in reality just a transfer to the FSMA 2000 of the system of banking regulation previously contained in the Banking Act 1987.

4.4 Company shares

Company shares are specified investments for the purposes of FSMA 2000.[15] This section considers their nature, legal title and transfer. It assumes that the reader is familiar with the more general analysis of these issues presented in Chapter 1.

---

[12] See s 1 of the Stock Transfer Act 1963.

[13] As ownership of the deposit is transferred to the deposit taker, a depositor has no real (proprietary) right in respect of the deposit: *Foley v Hill* (1848) 2 HL Cas 28.

[14] See arts 5 and 74 of the RAO (SI 2001/544). Note that mortgage-lending is not included within the definition of the regulated activity of deposit taking although it is often funded by deposits—see Ch 3.4 regarding the regulation of mortgage lending.

[15] See para 11 of sch 2 to FSMA 2000 and art 21 of the RAO.

4.4.1 Nature of company shares

It was noted in Chapter 1 that a share is a form of intangible personal property (in Scotland, incorporeal moveable property). That observation, however, leaves unresolved the more fundamental issue of what the property actually comprises.[16] So too does the statutory definition of a share as '[a] share in the share capital of a company'.[17] However, related statutory provisions make clear the nature of a share. Membership of a company is dependent on owning a share[18] and members are parties to the statutory contract[19] between each member and the company and between the members *inter se*. The statutory view is therefore essentially of a share as a contractual relationship.

Judicial definitions of a share support that view. In *Borland's Trustee v Steel Bros & Co Ltd* it was said that: [20]

> A share is the interest of a shareholder in the company measured by a sum of money, for the purpose of liability in the first place, and of interest in the second, but also consisting of a series of mutual covenants entered into by all the shareholders inter se in accordance with s16 of the Companies Act 1862 [now s14 of the Companies Act 1985]. The contract contained in the articles of association is one of the original incidents of the share. A share is not a sum of money settled in the way suggested, but is an interest measured by a sum of money and made up of various rights contained in the contract, including the right to a sum of money of more or less amount.

A similar approach was adopted in *Commissioners of Inland Revenue v Crossman*.[21] In this case, the interest of a shareholder was defined as being 'composed of rights and obligations which are defined by the Companies Act and by the memorandum and articles of association of the company'. Even those definitions that focus on the property rather than contractual characteristic of shares recognise that the property is essentially a set of contractual rights.[22] In this respect the position of a shareholder is different from a trust

---

[16] See, for an historical analysis of this issue, R Pennington, 'Can Shares in Companies be Defined?' (1989) 10 *Company Lawer* 140–44.

[17] Companies Act 1985 s 744.

[18] Companies Act 1985 s 22. This is the case for a company with a share capital—see also s 352.

[19] See s 14 Companies Act 1985.

[20] [1901] 1 Ch 279 at 288, per Farwell J.

[21] [1937] AC 26, 66 per Lord Russell of Killowen.

[22] See R Pennington, *Pennington's Company Law*, 8th edn (London, Butterworths, 2001) at p 6 for a definition of a share as

> a species of intangible movable property which comprises a collection of rights and obligations relating to an interest in a company of an economic and proprietary character.

G Morse (ed) *Palmer's Company Law*, 25th edn (London, Sweet & Maxwell, 1992) para 6.001 provides the following definition:

> A share in a company is the expression of a proprietary relationship: the shareholder is the proportionate owner of the company but he does not own the company's assets which belong to the company as a separate and independent legal entity.

beneficiary who (at least in English law) has an equitable interest in the assets comprising the trust fund.

Shareholders' rights are defined by company law and by a company's memorandum and articles of association, which together form a company's constitution. Company law recognises that the memorandum and articles of association form a 'statutory contract' between shareholders and the company and among the shareholders *inter se*.[23] However, a company owes only one set of obligations to shareholders rather than a separate obligation to each, with the result that the nature and enforcement of the statutory contract are problematic.[24]

Companies can have different classes of shares with different rights.[25] Ordinary shares are by far the most common category and if there is only one class of share they are assumed to be ordinary. In respect of ordinary shares, the articles of association of companies normally provide that each share carries one vote.[26] If the articles are silent on the matter the default rule of company law is that each share carries one vote.[27] While this is assumed to be standard practice nowadays, there have been variants, particularly in continental Europe, where in the past voting rules were derived from the principle that each member rather than each share carried a vote.[28] It is possible for the articles to provide that a certain class of share has no voting rights but this is less common nowadays, particularly in the case of public listed companies, in respect of which institutional investors have an established policy opposing the creation of non-voting shares.[29] Enhanced voting rights attaching to particular shares are also possible, for example allowing a particular shareholder to veto certain decisions or actions of the company. Shareholders' agreements, although not part of the articles of association of a company, may attach special conditions to voting rights in certain circumstances.

---

[23] Companies Act 1985 s 14(1).

[24] E Ferran, *Company Law and Corporate Finance* (Oxford, OUP, 1999) observes at p 619 that:

> The nature of the contract formed by a company's memorandum and articles is somewhat obscure and the extent to which the courts will enforce provisions contained in those documents is uncertain.

See J Benjamin, *Interests in Securities* (Oxford, OUP, 2000) p 35 regarding the historical development of the nature of shares and the obligations of companies to shareholders.

[25] See also Ch 7.1.

[26] See art 54 of Table A (Regulations for Management of a Company Limited by Shares) in the Companies (Tables A to F) Regulations 1985, SI 1985/805.

[27] Companies Act 1985 s 370(6).

[28] See CA Dunlavy, 'Corporate Governance in Late 19th Century Europe and the United States, The Case of Shareholder Voting Rights' in KJ Hopt, H Kanda, MJ Roe, E Wymeersch and S Prigge (eds) *Comparative Corporate Governance—The State of the Art and Emerging Research* (Oxford, OUP, 1998).

[29] See E Ferran (above n 24) p 246.

Ordinary shareholders have no legal right to payment of a dividend. Companies are free to retain profits or distribute them to shareholders as they see fit and the balance between retention and distribution will vary over time and across different industry sectors. Ordinary shareholders ultimately control this issue through voting on dividend resolutions at the annual general meeting.

Taken together, the right to dividends (at the company's discretion) and the right to vote are the essence of what is 'owned' by an ordinary shareholder. This becomes clearer if the focus of the enquiry into the nature of ownership moves from the assets of the company to its earnings and dividends. The company itself, as an independent legal person, owns the assets, but shareholders are entitled to dividends which are paid from earnings (profits). That entitlement is realised through the power of shareholders to vote on a resolution for the payment of dividends.[30] When shares are issued or transferred, it is essentially these rights that are allocated to the owner, hence the assumption in finance theory that the value of a share is the present value of the future stream of dividend income.[31] Viewed in this light, shareholders are holders of legal title to a stream of income in the form of dividends. A share price (or in the aggregate, the market capitalisation of a company) is simply an estimate of the present value of that right and has no necessary link with the value of the company's assets or the share capital recorded in the company's accounts.

Preference shares, as the name suggests, provide investors with preferred rights in respect of any or all of voting, dividends and rights on liquidation of the company. Preference shares normally carry a right to dividend expressed as a percentage of their par value. The dividend is often stated to be cumulative and will be assumed to be so unless the articles provide otherwise. This means that if the company fails to pay the dividend in one year, the preference shareholders are entitled to payment in the following year(s) before any distribution of profit can be made to the ordinary shareholders.

If a company becomes insolvent, ordinary shareholders are in a weak position. Preferred creditors, ordinary trade creditors and preference shareholders rank ahead of them in terms of claims on the remaining assets of the company. As liquidation is most often the result of insolvency, ordinary shareholders often face the prospect of being paid little or nothing in a liquidation. This is the price to be paid for their equity interest in the company: they are better rewarded than other stakeholders if the company does well and they suffer more if the company fails. Preference shareholders are in a better position than ordinary shareholders but may also face the prospect of losing much of their investment on insolvency.

---

[30] Company law controls the circumstances in which a dividend can be paid. See Ch 7 for more detail.

[31] See Pilbeam (above n 8) ch 9.

4.4.2 Legal title

A shareholder is the registered owner of shares in a company. Every company is required to keep a register of its members and this register is *prima facie* evidence of the legal title of the shareholder to the relevant shares.[32] The register is not conclusive evidence of membership of the company because (a) section 22 of the Companies Act 1985 also requires agreement for a person to become a member; (b) it may be that the requirements of the company's articles of association have not been met (eg as a result of pre-emption rights in a private company[33]); or (c) in the case of dematerialised shares settled through CREST, there may be a discrepancy between the issuer company's register and the Operator register of members.[34] In the case of listed companies, whose shares must be freely transferable, the register will in practice be conclusive in almost every case.

In the past, a share certificate provided evidence of ownership of shares. While it is still possible for this to occur, dematerialisation of share certificates has resulted in relatively few investors holding paper certificates. When they do, the Companies Act 1985 provides that the certificate is *prima facie* evidence of the title of the shareholder to the shares.[35] It is not conclusive evidence as that issue turns ultimately on who is entitled to have their name entered in the share register. Individual numbering of shares is also a practice that has died out.[36] Therefore, within a particular class, shares are a fungible form of property, meaning that any one is the equivalent of another.

Dematerialisation of share certificates was made possible by section 207 of the Companies Act 1989, which permits the Treasury to make Regulations 'for enabling title to securities to be evidenced and transferred without a written instrument'. The relevant regulations are the Uncertificated Securities Regulations 2001,[37] which set out the principles for dematerialised transfers

---

[32] See ss 352 and 361 Companies Act 1985.

[33] See 4.4.3 below.

[34] In these circumstances art 24 of the Uncertificated Securities Regulations 2001 states that entry of a person's name in the issuer register shall not be treated as showing that person to be a member unless (a) that register shows him as holding shares in certificated form; (b) the Operator register shows him as holding shares in uncertificated form; or (c) he is deemed to be a member of the company by art 32(6)(b) of the Uncertificated Securities Regulations 2001. See below for an explanation of transfer procedures.

[35] Companies Act 1985 s 186. In Scotland, a share certificate is sufficient evidence of legal title unless the contrary is shown.

[36] The authority to dispense with individual numbering of shares is provided, subject to certain conditions, by s 182(2) of the Companies Act 1985. In particular, the shares must be fully paid and rank *pari passu* (equally) for all purposes with all shares of the same class for the time being issued and fully paid up.

[37] SI 2001/3755. These regulations superseded the 1995 Regulations of the same name (SI 1995/3272).

and establish the CREST computer system through which transfers are made. CREST is not a compulsory system as the consent of CRESTCo (the operator), the issuer and the shareholder are required for transfers to be made through CREST. In particular, a shareholder can choose to retain shares in certificated form although this will generally lead to higher transaction costs. It may also affect a shareholder's relationship with an issuer as a small shareholder will generally have little option but to hold the shares in a nominee account run by the purchasing broker.[38]

4.4.3 Transfer

Before considering the law relating to how shares are transferred, it is necessary to consider possible limitations on transferability. In principle, a shareholder has a right to transfer shares and, unless expressly authorised by the articles of association, the directors of a company have no power to refuse to register a transfer.[39] In the case of public listed companies, no restriction is possible because it is a condition for listing that the shares be freely transferable. In the case of non-listed public companies or private companies, it is possible for the articles of association to limit transfer. This occurs most often in the case of private companies whose articles frequently provide that a member may not sell shares without first offering them to existing members at a price determined by an independent valuation (a pre-emption provision).[40] Transfers which do not comply with such a provision in the articles can be set aside so that a transferor is required to make a pre-emptive offer in accordance with the articles.[41]

An agreement to transfer shares, whether made within or outside a regulated market, has no immediate effect on the ownership of the shares. It is necessary for the name of the buyer to be inserted in the company's share register for legal ownership of shares to be transferred. This normally occurs some time after the making of the agreement to transfer ('dealing'). A company can only register a transfer if:

---

[38] The alternatives of becoming a sponsored or full member of CREST are generally not realistic options for small investors.

[39] *Re Smith & Fawcett Ltd* [1942] Ch 304.

[40] This right of pre-emption, which is contractual in nature, should be distinguished from the statutory rights of pre-emption provided by ss 89–95 of the Companies Act 1985, which do not limit the transfer rights of shareholders (see Ch 7.2.3). There cannot be restrictions on transfers of shares in public listed companies as the Listing Rules require such shares to be freely transferable.

[41] See J Birds (ed) *Boyle & Birds' Company Law*, 5th edn (Bristol, Jordans, 2004) para 9.2.2.

(a) A proper instrument of transfer has been delivered to it. The Stock Transfer Act 1963 provides a standard form of stock transfer for registered shares[42] but does not prevent the use of other forms of instrument.

(b) The transfer is made in accordance with the regulations made under s 207 of the Companies Act 1989.[43]

The legal process by which a transferee becomes a member of a company is novation. This is a general principle of contract law that allows a new creditor to be substituted for the existing creditor. The agreement of the debtor (company), existing creditor (seller) and new creditor (buyer) is necessary for novation to take place. The process differs from assignment in that the new creditor does not succeed to the rights of the old creditor but enters a new contractual relationship with the debtor.[44] The terms of the (new) contract are contained in the memorandum and articles of the company, which together form the 'statutory contract'. The agreement of the debtor (issuing company) to the process of novation is shown by it entering the name of the new shareholder (buyer) on the register and removing the name of the previous shareholder (seller).[45]

Transfer of shares held in dematerialised form is effected by an instruction to the company (or the registrar acting for it) to make a change in its share register. In principle, only the operator of the transfer system (CRESTCo) can give such an instruction, although there are some exceptional circumstances (such as a court order) in which instructions from other parties are binding. The company is generally obliged to register a transfer instruction given by the operator and must confirm to the operator that the transfer has occurred. The Regulations contain provisions[46] governing liability for fraudulent or unauthorised instructions but they do not cover such acts emanating from a computer that is part of the system. This reflects the general approach of the Regulations, which is to require that system participants should be able to rely on properly authenticated dematerialised instructions sent by other system participants.[47] The potential risk faced by investors arising from fraudulent or unauthorised instructions emanating from within the system are dealt with by the inclusion of sending dematerialised instructions on behalf of others within

---

[42] The standard form can also be used for gilts and units in unit trusts—see s 1(4).

[43] This is a reference to the Uncertificated Securities Regulations 2001 (SI 2001/3755).

[44] Strictly speaking therefore, novation is not transfer. Novation does not bind a new shareholder to a shareholders' agreement, which is an agreement made by the shareholders outside the memorandum and articles.

[45] There may be circumstances in which the issuer can, according to its articles, refuse to register a transfer but these will be comparatively rare.

[46] Art 36.

[47] Art 35.

the categories of regulated activities for the purposes of FSMA 2000.[48] This means that persons sending such instructions fall within the rule-making and disciplinary powers of the FSA and could potentially face restitutionary claims as well as financial penalties.[49]

Shares in companies (including public companies) that are not listed or admitted to trading on a regulated market are not held in dematerialised form. Transfers of such shares take place outside regulated markets and do not fall within the standard clearing and settlement procedures that apply to listed securities. The transfer procedure for unlisted securities involves the seller providing a completed transfer form and certificate to the buyer in return for the price. The buyer then sends these documents to the company secretary, who, assuming everything is in order, will enter the buyer on the shareholders' register (in place of the seller) and issue a new certificate to the buyer.[50]

4.5 Debt instruments

This category of specified investment[51] refers to loans that are raised by organ-isations other than the government or public sector bodies. Companies frequently raise loans to finance their business in addition to share capital.[52] Such loans can take the following forms:

Debentures. This term has no technical legal meaning but is used in the UK to refer to long-term secured loans.
Loan stock. This refers to long-term unsecured loans.
Bonds. This is a generic term referring to any form of long-term loan.
Commercial paper. This refers to short-term loans of up to one year.

An investor holding any of these instruments is in a better position than a shareholder (ordinary or preference) in the event of liquidation because his claim to the assets of the company ranks ahead of shareholders. This results from the nature of the relationship between the holder of loan capital and the issuer, which is that of debtor(issuer)/creditor(holder). An investor who makes a loan to a company is a creditor in respect of the loan whereas a shareholder is not a creditor of the company for his share capital although he has a contractual and statutory right to share in surplus assets (after payment of creditors) on a winding-up.

---

[48] See art 45 of the RAO.
[49] See Ch 3 regarding the powers of the FSA.
[50] For more detail see Birds (ed) (above n 41) para 9.3.2.
[51] See art 77 of the RAO.
[52] See generally Ch 7.

4.5.1 Definition and categorisation

The term 'debenture' is not in itself a legal term of art and its broad scope is reflected by the most widely-quoted judicial definition:[53]

> In my opinion a debenture means a document which either creates a debt or acknowledges it, and any document which fulfils either of these conditions is a 'debenture'. I cannot find any precise legal definition of the term, it is not either in law or commerce a strictly technical term, or what is called a term of art.

It is clear from this definition that the legal term 'debenture' can be applied to any form of loan made to a company irrespective of the terminology applied to the loan by commercial practice. Debentures can take a variety of forms. They can have a redemption date that is fixed or dependent on a future contingency or they can be perpetual (irredeemable).[54] Interest payable on the loan can be fixed or variable ('floating') by reference to a specified benchmark such as LIBOR.[55] They can be secured on the company's assets or unsecured.[56] They can be listed and traded on a stock exchange or unlisted. They may or may not carry the right to vote at company meetings. Some debentures carry special privileges in addition to the right to interest.[57]

Debentures can be in the form of a loan made by a single lender or (as is more often the case) can comprise a fund lent by a group of lenders ('debenture stock'). In the latter case it is common for trustees to be appointed to represent the collective interest of lenders in dealing with the company.[58] In principle, the duties of trustees include taking charge of documents of title to property on which the debt is secured, safeguarding the interests of debenture stockholders (eg in relation to compliance with the company's obligations under the loan agreement) and enforcing the security.[59] There are, however, no specific provisions in company law relating to the duties of trustees for debenture holders, with the result that the general law relating to trustees is applicable. Company law does, however, make any exclusion of the liability of trustees for debenture holders void.[60]

---

[53] *Levy v Abercorris Slate and Slab Co* (1887) 37 Ch D 260, per Chitty J at 264.

[54] Companies Act 1985 s 193. As Pennington (above n 22) observes (p 564), the term 'irredeemable' is not entirely accurate as perpetual debentures can be redeemed by the holder on the default of the borrower.

[55] The London Interbank Offered Rate, which is the rate at which banks can borrow in the wholesale money market.

[56] Commercial practice in the UK generally refers to secured loans as 'debentures' and unsecured loans as either 'loan-stock' or 'loan notes' depending on the duration of the loan. See Ch 7 for a description of security interests granted by companies.

[57] eg those relating to sporting venues such as Wimbledon and Murrayfield.

[58] See J Benjamin, *Interests in Securities* (Oxford, OUP, 2000) p 13.

[59] Pennington (above n 22 at p 577) notes that in practice trustees rarely fulfil the second and third functions.

[60] Companies Act 1985 s 192(1).

Debentures can be issued in registered or bearer form. Unlike the position in relation to shares, there is no legal obligation to maintain a register of debenture holders. There are, however, two reasons for companies to do so. First, it will normally be required by a trust deed creating debenture stock in registered form. Second, a company is required to open and maintain such a register as a condition for dematerialisation and settlement by electronic transfer within the CREST settlement system.[61] As discussed below, the function of the register of debenture holders differs from the register of members.

When debentures are issued in bearer form the company has no ownership record or manner of identifying the holder. Such debentures may or may not be negotiable instruments. They are if they are promissory notes within the meaning of the Bills of Exchange Act 1882.[62] A single debenture or series of debentures could fall within this definition but debenture stock issued in bearer form cannot fall within the definition as the promise to pay the debt is made to the trustees rather than directly to holders (bearers) of the debentures. Whether or not a debenture issued in bearer form is a negotiable instrument has implications for the rights of a transferee (see below).

Some bonds are convertible into ordinary shares on the basis of a formula that typically allows x bonds to be converted to y shares. This provides investors with a security which has both debt and equity characteristics. The fixed interest rate attached to a bond provides a guaranteed return and the option to convert allows the holder to benefit from a rise in the value of the ordinary shares into which conversion is possible. A variant of the convertible bond is a bond with warrants attached, entitling the holder to subscribe for a fixed number of ordinary shares at an agreed price at some point in the future. Some issues allow for such warrants to become detached from the securities and to be sold or transferred independently.

Holders of convertible bonds are not protected by law from the negative impact of changes in the share capital of the issuer. For example, suppose that five bonds can be converted into three ordinary shares after five years. Assume the company increases its share capital by 25 per cent through a (one-for-four) rights issue in the third year. As a result of this issue the five-for-three conversion option is less valuable because the three represents a smaller proportion of the issuer's ordinary shares. A contract term will not be implied into a convertible or warrant issue that adjusts the conversion or subscription formula to

---

[61] Uncertificated Securities Regulations (SI 2001/3755), arts 18(2), 19(2) and 19(3).

[62] Section 83 provides that

A promissory note is an unconditional promise in writing made by one person to another signed by the maker, engaging to pay, on demand or at a fixed or determinable future time, a sum certain in money, to, or to the order of, a specified person or to bearer.

The most common example is a bank note.

reflect the change in the issuer's share capital.[63] However, in the case of listed convertible securities, holders are protected by a requirement that certain adjustments to the share capital of the issuer are only possible if a proportionate adjustment is made in the conversion rights of the convertible security holders.[64]

Eurobonds are a form of corporate bond that have particular characteristics. They are bearer bonds issued in a currency other than that of the domicile of the issuer (eg bonds issued in US dollars by a UK company). They may be secured or unsecured. The United Kingdom Listing Authority (UKLA) Listing Rules require that a trustee be appointed to safeguard the interests of bondholders.[65] The 'Euro' designation reflects the historic origin of the market, which developed as a means to invest large bank deposits that were built up in European financial centres as a result of the oil price boom in the 1970s and the introduction by the US of withholding taxes on foreign bank deposits. These deposits were available to lend to companies who were willing to borrow in a foreign currency. The market in Eurobonds is not limited to European issuers, lenders or currencies.[66]

The Eurobond market is an 'over-the counter' market, meaning that it has no central location or organisation and each transaction is conducted on an *ad hoc* basis. The 'market' itself is not regulated under FSMA 2000 but market participants are regulated as they are normally dealing in investments in the course of a business. Transfer of Eurobonds (as with other forms of bearer bond) was in the past effected simply by delivery of the instrument to the transferee. Following dematerialisation of Eurobond issues, the standard practice is now for a global bond to be issued to a depositary institution[67], which records the acquisition of a given number of bonds by an investor in its register. Below this level, there may also be a custodian who 'holds' the bonds on behalf of an investor.[68]

---

[63] *Forsayth Oil and Gas NL v Livia Pty Ltd* [1985] Butterworths Company Law Cases 378.

[64] Listing rules Ch 13 para 13.10 and app 2 para 4 (a).

[65] Listing rules Ch 13 para 13.12. Some Eurobond issues are exempt from the rule. It has been observed that the nature of the trust and the role of trustees in respect of Eurobond issues is considerably more complex than in standard trusts as the trust 'property' is the contractual obligation to pay interest to the trustee. While there is no expectation that this will occur, the bond documentation (loan agreement) makes clear that payment to the bondholder discharges any obligation to make payment to the trustee. See P Wood, *Law and Practice of International Finance* (London, Sweet & Maxwell, 1995) p 168.

[66] Many Eurobond issues are raised simply because the cost of borrowing is lowest in that currency and are later swapped into the currency in which the issuer really wants to have the money.

[67] See Ch 10.3.4 regarding the nature of securities depositaries. The depositary institutions are normally Cedel or Euroclear, based in Luxembourg and Brussels respectively.

[68] See Ch 10.3.3 regarding custody of securities.

'Junk bonds' is a generic term for bonds that are below 'investment grade'. This is determined by the rating attached to a bond by rating agencies.[69] A rating below 'BBB' generally results in a bond not being eligible for inclusion in investment portfolios of institutional investors. To attract investors and offset the risk of default, such bonds have to offer interest rates considerably higher than those of investment grade bonds.

4.5.2 Transfers

A debt in any of the forms discussed above is, from the perspective of property law, a legal chose in action (in Scotland incorporeal moveable property) and can therefore in principle be transferred by assignment. Even if a company maintains a register of debenture holders in respect of an issue of debentures, it does not have the status of the register of members. Entry in the register of members is necessary to become a member (shareholder), but it is possible to be a debenture holder without being entered in a register of debenture holders (eg if a company does not have such a register). In other words, ownership of debentures is not based on registration, whereas ownership of ordinary shares is. The result is that the legal process for the transfer of debentures is assignment (in Scotland assignation), which is the standard legal process for the transfer of debt.

The provisions of the Companies Act 1985 and the Uncertificated Securities Regulations 2001 relating to transfers of shares (above) apply equally to debentures in registered form, assuming that the debentures take the form of debenture stock and not a single mortgage or charge over the company's property. However, as registered debentures are transferred by assignment (assignation), the assignee (buyer) in principle takes subject to any defects in the title of the assignor (seller). The law is based on the principle that an assignee of a debt (as opposed to a negotiable instrument) cannot acquire a better title than the assignor.[70] A defect could exist, for example, if the issue of the debenture was induced by misrepresentation and the contract is therefore voidable.[71]

Debentures issued in bearer form are transferred simply by delivery. The rights of a transferee depend on whether the debenture is or is not a negotiable

---

[69] Rating agencies are private sector bodies that grade bonds. The three most prominent agencies are Moody's Investors Services Inc, Standard & Poor's Ratings Services and Fitch Investors Service Inc, all based in the USA. For a general discussion of the role of rating agencies in financial markets, see S Schwarcz, 'Private Ordering of Public Markets: The Rating Agency Paradox' 2002(1) *University of Illinios Law Review* 1. See also Ch 10.

[70] The Latin maxim *assignatus utitur jure auctoris* encapsulates the principle.

[71] See eg *Stoddart v Union Trust Ltd* [1912] 1 KB 181.

instrument,[72] which is a form of debt that occupies a privileged position for the purposes of transfer. If it is, a holder in due course[73] takes free from any defect in the title of a transferor. If it is not (as is generally the case for debenture stock) a transferee takes subject to any defects in title of a transferor. It is, however, possible (and common) for debentures to be issued by a company on the basis that a holder takes the debenture free from any claim of the company against an original or intermediate holder. This frees a holder from the potential risk arising from the common law rule that an assignee takes only the rights of an assignor.[74] Unaltered, that rule would have the effect that any claim of the company against an original holder would be passed down the chain of assignees (debentureholders).

4.6 Depositary receipts

Depositary receipts are specified investments for the purposes of FSMA 2000.[75] They facilitate indirect investment in foreign securities and serve the needs of investors in a variety of circumstances.[76] Examples are where there is a restriction on foreign ownership of investment or where dealing in such investments is administratively complex and costly.[77] Depositary receipts (DRs) are in essence receipts issued by a legal owner of securities to investors specifying that the depositary holds the securities as trustee for the depositary receipt holders.[78] The process can be undertaken either with ('sponsored') or

[72] That issue is dependent on the debenture falling within the definition of a promissory note in s 83 of the Bills of Exchange Act 1882. The provisions of that Act relating to bills of exchange (such as their negotiable character) apply equally to promissory notes (see s 89(1)). A debenture in bearer form would, in principle, fall within this definition but see n 73 below.

[73] See s 29 of the Bills of Exchange Act 1882. An essential element of the definition is that a holder in due course takes a bill in good faith without notice of any defect in the title of the person from whom he took it. See the Financial Markets Law Committee, 'Property Interests in Investment Securities' (July 2004 at www.fmlc.org (10 Nov 2004)) para 6.8, suggesting that investors in bonds, legal title to which is held by an intermediary (eg custodian), are not holders in due course.

[74] See P Davies, *Gower and Davies' Principles of Modern Company Law,* 7th edn (London, Sweet & Maxwell, 2003) p 812.

[75] See art 80 of the RAO.

[76] Although they share the characteristic of indirect investment with collective investment funds, they are not categorised as such under FSMA 2000.

[77] For details of the American Depositary Receipt programmes of FTSE 100 companies, see RC Nolan, 'Indirect Investors: A Greater Say in the Company?' (2003) 1 *Journal of Corporate Law Studies* 73.

[78] The term 'depositary receipt' and references to a 'depositary' in this context should be distinguished from the use of the term 'depositary' in the context of the immobilisation of securities. Securities in respect of which depositary receipts are issued may or may not be immobilised. If they are immobilised, there is the additional complication that the 'depositary' who has issued

without ('unsponsored') the co-operation of the issuer of the underlying shares. In the former case, it is common for a specific issue of shares to be made to the depositary whereas in the latter case the shares have to be bought by the depositary in the market.

The terms on which a depositary holds the underlying shares for the DR holders will be set out in a deposit agreement. This will cover matters such as voting rights in respect of the underlying shares, the payment of dividends and the procedure for transfer of the DRs. In common with many other instances of investment, the rights held by the DR holder are interests in securities derived from the depositary and not direct legal ownership of the underlying securities. Transfers of DRs are arranged through movements between accounts held by investors (or their custodians) with the depositary who is always the legal owner of the security (assuming immobilisation of legal title).

4.7 Warrants

A warrant is a contractual entitlement to acquire securities at an agreed price at a future date. Warrants are generally issued by companies in conjunction with new securities with the objective of attracting investors who will be able either to exercise the warrants (thereby acquiring additional shares in the company) or sell the warrants in the market. They are specified investments for the purpose of FSMA 2000.[79] From a financial perspective, they can be regarded either as a discount applied to the price of the issue of securities with which they are associated or as a form of dilution of future earnings (as exercise of the warrants will increase the number of shares in issue and thereby reduce earnings per share). From either perspective, it is clear that an issue of warrants represents a cost to the company as it dilutes the capital raised from the relevant issue of securities.

Warrants can generally be traded in the secondary market and transfer occurs in accordance with the principles outlined above in respect of debt securities. This remains so even if the warrants relate to registered securities such as ordinary shares because a warrant itself is not a registered security and is therefore transferred through the process of assignment.

Covered warrants are a relatively new development. A covered warrant is issued by a financial institution and gives the holder the right, but not the obligation, to buy or sell an underlying asset, at a specified price, on or before

---

the receipt is not the registered owner of the securities but has an interest (proprietary) in securities that are immobilised in the depositary which is the legal owner.

[79] See art 80 of the RAO.

a predetermined date. It resembles an option in the sense that there is no obligation to buy or sell and the maximum loss that can be suffered by an investor is the premium paid for the warrant. The term 'covered' denotes the fact that when issuers sell a warrant to an investor, they will 'cover' (hedge) their exposure by buying the underlying securities in the market. In the UK, covered warrants are available on a wide range of UK and international blue chip and midcap shares and indices. Covered warrants have on average a life of 6 to 12 months, although some have a lifespan of up to 5 years.

4.8 Derivatives

4.8.1 Nature and typology

Financial derivatives are instruments whose value is derived from other (underlying) investments.[80] The essence of a derivative is that it can have no independent existence because it is based on and its value is quantified by reference to the underlying investment.

Historically, futures contracts were the first form of derivative and were developed in relation to commodities rather than investments.[81] Futures are commitments to buy or sell a given quantity of an underlying product in the future at an agreed price. For example a grain merchant might want to avoid the risk of fluctuations in the price of grain by fixing in advance the price at which he will buy from farmers. The contract cannot be abandoned and the potential gain or loss for each party is unlimited because it is dependent on the movement in the price of the underlying product. The gains and losses on futures contracts are symmetrical in that any deviation in the future spot price of a commodity or financial instrument from the contract price will generate a profit for one party that is the same as the loss for the other.[82] A market in these contracts developed so as to allow merchants to adjust their requirements for commodities on an on-going basis. This allowed one merchant to transfer the contract to another, while at the same time preserving the fundamental characteristics of the contract—that it cannot be abandoned before

---

[80] See generally A Hudson, *The Law on Financial Derivatives*, 3rd edn (London, Sweet & Maxwell, 2002).

[81] See generally E Swann, *The Regulation of Derivatives* (London, Cavendish, 1995). The terms 'future' and 'forward' are often used interchangeably. Hudson (above n 80, p 41) reserves the term 'future' for derivatives traded on an exchange while others (OTC derivatives) are termed 'forwards'. See Pilbeam (above n 8) pp 275–77 for a comparison between currency forwards and futures.

[82] See Pilbeam (above n 8) p 277 for a worked example.

expiry and that gain or loss is in principle unlimited. The use of futures in the context of modern financial markets can be envisaged by substituting financial securities and market indices for grain in this example.

Options differ from futures in that the buyer has an option rather than an obligation to buy (call) or sell (put) the underlying investment. The price paid for an option is in the form of a premium paid by the buyer to the writer of the option. The maximum loss that can be suffered by the buyer of an option is the premium paid to the writer.[83] If the price of the underlying investment moves so as to make exercise of the option economically unattractive[84], the buyer can simply abandon the option. In the case of a simple share option, the buyer pays a premium to the writer of the option for the right to buy or sell shares at an agreed price during a certain period of time. In most cases the contract is settled (performed) by cash transfers between the option holder and the writer by reference to the value of the option at the time of exercise rather than by transfers of the underlying investment. For example, the exercise of an option to buy 1,000 shares in company x on 4 July at 100p when the price is 150p is normally settled by payment of £500 to the holder, rather than the writer delivering 1,000 shares to the holder for purchase at 100p.

In principle, all derivatives contracts are structured from combinations of features derived from the basic options and futures contracts just described. Basic forms of options and futures, as well as more exotic derivatives based on them, are now available in respect of many underlying investments, commodities and market indices. They are attractive to companies and investors for a variety of reasons. For companies raising finance, derivatives offer the opportunity of repackaging obligations so as to gain access to funding on more attractive terms. Swaps are a good example.[85] They became popular in the era of exchange controls because they allowed corporate borrowers to evade exchange controls and raise finance in more attractive jurisdictions. The essence of swaps is that the manner in which companies want to borrow money is not always the manner that is most economically efficient for them. Some may be able to raise a fixed-rate loan on better terms than a floating rate loan or may be better able to borrow in euros than in sterling. The swaps market allows a company to exchange cash flows with another borrower (or a bank) so as to achieve a lower cost of funding. For example, A plc borrows

---

[83] Therefore, unlike futures, the profit/loss profile of an option contract is not symmetrical as between the writer and the holder of the option. (See Pilbeam, above n 8, p 316 for a worked example of the different profit/loss profiles that result from hedging currency risk through futures and options respectively.)

[84] In market parlance, an 'out-of-the-money' option.

[85] See the definition of an interest rate swap given by Woolf LJ in *Hazell v Hammersmith & Fulham LBC* [1991] 1 All ER 545 at 550.

£20m from B bank at a floating rate of 'LIBOR + 100 basis points'.[86] It then agrees with C bank that the latter will pay this interest to B in return for A paying a fixed rate of 6 per cent to C. A has now fixed its borrowing cost and will make a profit if 'LIBOR + 100 basis points' exceeds 6 per cent (ie if the floating rate it would have had to pay before arranging the swap exceeds the fixed rate it now has to pay).[87] The rationale for C's involvement in the transaction is that it believes that the interest rate represented by 'LIBOR + 100 basis points' will remain less than 6 per cent, the margin between the two being C's profit.

From the perspective of investors, derivatives are attractive as a means of speculation and for managing risk. Derivatives are a geared form of investment in the sense that movements in the underlying investment cause a proportionately greater movement in the value of the derivative. It is therefore possible to use derivatives to speculate on relatively small movements in the price of underlying investments. The role of derivatives in managing or reducing risk within a portfolio is less well appreciated, but derivatives can be used for a variety of purposes in this context. They can reduce or increase the overall risk profile, introduce diversification by sector, currency or country, or replicate transactions in assets in which it is difficult to deal. For example, a portfolio manager in the United States could gain exposure to the UK equity market by buying FTSE 100 options rather than by buying the underlying investments, or could use a currency derivative to hedge the risk of a fall in the value of sterling if investments are already held in the UK.

4.8.2 OTC and exchange-traded derivatives

Derivative contracts can be arranged on an *ad hoc* basis between two parties or they can be bought in a standardised form on exchanges. The former are referred to as over-the-counter (OTC) and the latter as exchange-traded. The term 'OTC' is slightly misleading because it gives the impression that there is some form of market infrastructure. In reality there is none, as such contracts are arranged on an *ad hoc* basis between parties, one of which is normally a bank acting as a principal. There is, however, considerable standardisation in the terms of OTC derivative contracts as most are structured around the standard terms set by the International Swaps and Derivatives Association (ISDA).[88] It is common for collateral (typically in the form of a security inter-

---

[86] LIBOR is the London Interbank Offered Rate, the rate charged by banks for loans among themselves. Each whole number of an interest rate is broken down into 100 basis points for the purposes of financial market transactions.

[87] This example is adapted from Hudson (above n 80) p 46.

[88] See www.isda.org (10 Nov 2004).

est or trust) to be given by one or both sides to an OTC derivative transaction. This offers some protection against the default of the other side to the transaction.[89]

The OTC market is mainly one in which large companies and banks are involved. It has grown rapidly in the last 20 years and is considerably larger than the exchange-traded market.[90] The attraction for companies is that OTC derivatives offer a mechanism to re-structure obligations in a manner which better suits a company than the form in which the obligation currently exists. The OTC market is not an organised market and is therefore not regulated in the same manner as organised markets such as the London Stock Exchange.[91] The absence of any market infrastructure, organisation or rules means that the OTC market cannot be regulated in this way.

However, OTC derivative contracts may be 'specified investments'[92] for the purposes of FSMA 2000, with the result that persons engaging in specified activities[93] fall within the scope of FSA regulation. Banks involved in the OTC derivatives market are already subject to prudential supervision and capital adequacy requirements in respect of their mainstream banking business. Non-bank parties to OTC derivative contracts do not normally fall within the FSMA 2000 system of regulation. Their involvement in the market is in principle unregulated but subject to disclosure obligations set by company law, listing rules and accounting standards.[94]

Exchange-traded derivatives are a more recent development. They offer standard contracts to investors over a wide range of commodities, investments and market indices. Contracts relating to investments are generally settled by payment of money rather than by delivery of the underlying investment. The comments made above in relation to OTC derivatives falling within the

---

[89] As is the case with any security interest, the basic objective is to provide a real right in respect of property should a counterparty fail to perform the obligations contained in the derivative contract. Hudson, above n 80, notes that the practice of each party taking collateral allows derivatives to be treated by each as secured, with the result that less regulatory capital is required for banks to engage in such activity.

[90] See the *Annual Report of the Bank for International Settlements* (March 1999).

[91] See Ch 9 for a description of the regulation of recognised investment exchanges in the UK.

[92] See arts 83, 84 and 85 of the Regulated Activities Order (SI 2001/544, discussed in Ch 3.4). They include within their ambit futures, options and contracts for differences. As noted earlier, all derivatives can, in principle, be regarded as combinations of options and futures, with the result that even exotic derivatives can be considered to fall within the RAO. Futures contracts made for commercial rather than investment purposes (eg an oil company using futures to hedge the price of oil) are excluded from the RAO.

[93] Specified activities falling within the scope of FSMA 2000 are discussed in Ch 3.

[94] This issue has come to the fore since the collapse of ENRON, which had engaged in extensive derivatives trading that was disclosed in a limited form to investors. See the Powers Report (WC Powers *et al, Report of Investigation by the Special Investigative Committee of the Board of Directors of Enron Corp* 2003, available at http://news.findlaw.com/hdocs/docs/enron/sicreport/sicreport020102.pdf (10 Nov 2004)).

definition of 'specified investments' for the purposes of FSMA 2000 apply equally to exchange-traded derivatives. Trading is subject to rules set by the relevant exchange. These rules normally provide for the payment of margin on futures contracts, which is intended to ensure that each party meets their obligations under the contract.[95] 'Initial margin' is normally set by the exchange at the level of the expected maximum daily movement in the relevant instrument. Once it has been paid, 'variation margin' becomes payable by one party to the other based on the daily profits/losses arsing from the instrument.[96] This means that when the holder sells a derivative through the exchange, profits/losses arising from that instrument have already been settled between the holder and issuer through the margining process. The comments made above in relation to participants in the OTC derivatives market are equally applicable to participants in the exchange-traded market. The exchanges on which trading occurs can choose to become 'recognised' for the purposes of FSMA 2000.[97]

Exchange-traded derivatives are normally 'cleared' by a clearing-house prior to settlement. The benefit of this procedure is that the clearing-house acts as a central counterparty, thereby guaranteeing the performance of obligations of its clearing members. As part of this function, the clearing-house is responsible for the collection of margin, which acts as a form of performance bond, providing assets to the clearing-house in the event of default. Some, but not all, OTC contracts are cleared through a clearing-house.

4.9 Investment funds

4.9.1 Nature and typology

Investment funds can be defined as arrangements under which individuals contribute to a common fund managed on their behalf by a professional investment manager. They are attractive to both institutional and private investors for a number of reasons. They offer a degree of diversification that would often be difficult to replicate through direct investments, such as when an investor wants exposure to an overseas market. They also offer economies of scale in respect of dealing, custody and transfer as the fund benefits from operating on a larger scale than its contributors. Finally, a fund may be able to

---

[95] For a more detailed discussion of margin, see the London Clearing House publication, *Market Protection* pp 18–25.

[96] This is sometimes referred to as the process of 'marking-to-market'.

[97] See Ch 9 for an explanation of the process of 'recognition'.

offer improved market access for investors by having access to some investments that are offered only to institutional investors.[98]

The most basic distinction is between open- and closed-end funds. Closed-end funds take the form of investment companies, which are public companies whose business is the investing of its funds in securities.[99] The capital of such a company can only be increased or reduced by following the normal rules of company law that apply in this situation. Investment trusts are the main example of closed-end funds. In most respects, they are similar to any other listed company. The main difference is that they do not engage directly in trade. Rather, their assets are investments and their business is to manage these investments on behalf of their shareholders. The main disadvantage of closed-end funds is that they cannot vary their capital on an on-going basis.[100] This means that investors in closed-end funds can only buy or sell a participation in the fund (in the form of shares) in the market, in the same way as they would in respect of any other listed (trading) company. Moreover, there is often a disparity between the price of the shares in investment trusts and the value of the underlying portfolio of investments.[101]

Open-end funds differ in that they have a variable capital structure. This means that they can adjust their capital according to the demand for investment in the fund. They do this by creating and redeeming participations in the fund on a continuous basis. New units are created when a new investor wants to participate in the fund and existing units are cancelled when an investor wants to withdraw. This process is managed internally by the operator of the fund on a continuous basis, with the result that an investor always has liquidity in relation to his holding. Moreover, the pricing of units on issue or redemption is, as a result of the relevant regulatory rules, directly related to the value of the underlying portfolio. This means that, by comparison with closed-end funds, the investor avoids the risk of the value of his (indirect) investment deviating from the underlying investments to which it is linked.

Open-end funds exist in two main forms. Unit trusts, as the name suggests, are organised on the basis of a trust deed. As they are not companies, they were able to avoid the historic prohibition on companies having a variable capital structure. They have a relatively long history dating back to the late 1800s.[102]

---

[98] This would include in some circumstances depositary receipts and new issues offered only to a limited circle of institutional investors.

[99] Companies Act 1985 s 266.

[100] As limited companies, they are subject to the normal company law rules on changes to capital. These rules were developed to protect creditors and limit the extent to which a company can make changes to its capital.

[101] This is commonly referred to by saying that investment trusts trade at a discount to their underlying net asset value. It is not clear why this should be so. The discount has varied considerably over time and some trusts have even traded at a premium.

[102] See *Gower's Principles of Modern Company Law*, 4th edn (London, Sweet & Maxwell, 1979) pp 266–72 for an historical account of the unit trust.

Investment funds that are organised as companies with variable capital (referred to as 'mutual funds' in the USA) are a relatively recent innovation in the United Kingdom, made possible by a relaxation of the historic prohibition against such companies. Such open-ended investment companies (OEICs) have now become the preferred method of organising investment funds as they are more familiar to investors in jurisdictions in which the unit trust is not recognised.

A distinction can also be drawn between regulated and unregulated investment funds. Regulated schemes are referred to as 'collective investment schemes' or 'authorised schemes' by FSMA 2000.[103] A collective investment scheme is defined by FSMA 2000 as follows:[104]

> any arrangements with respect to property of any description, including money, the purpose or effect of which is to enable persons taking part in the arrangements (whether by becoming owners of the property or any part of it or otherwise) to participate in or receive profits or income arising from the acquisition, holding, management or disposal of the property or sums paid out of such profits or income.

The main examples of collective investment schemes are unit trusts and investment companies with variable capital (ICVCs).[105] Investment trusts do not fall within the scope of collective investment schemes as the term excludes funds organised as companies, other then OEICs.[106] The benefit of being constituted as an authorised scheme is that an investment fund can then be promoted to the public. Unauthorised investment funds can be established but they suffer from the drawback that they cannot be promoted to the public under the regulations applicable to collective investment schemes.

Collective investment schemes that qualify as UCITS schemes can be marketed throughout the European Union on the basis of an authorisation granted by the home state. The UCITS Directive[107], adopted by the EC in 1985, was the first example of the operation of the system of 'single licence' and 'home country control' that has since been extended to the remainder of the financial sector.[108] The UCITS Directive was quite restrictive as to the type of

---

[103] See ss 235–37 FSMA 2000 and the FSMA 2000 (Collective Investment Schemes) Order 2001, SI 2001/1062.

[104] FSMA 2000 s 235. The definition does not require that the contributors be the legal owners of the assets in the fund.

[105] While the term OEIC is used generically to refer to any open-ended investment company, ICVC refers to a UK-authorised OEIC. FSMA 2000 sch 5.1(3) provides that an authorised open-ended investment company is an authorised person.

[106] See SI 2001/1062 art 21.

[107] Dir 85/611/EEC on the Co-ordination of Laws, Regulations and Administrative Provisions relating to Undertakings for Collective Investment in Transferable Securities (UCITS) OJ 1985 L375/3.

[108] See Ch 2.5.2 regarding the European system of regulation.

investment that could be held by a qualifying fund, but a new Directive has extended the range of permissible investments.[109]

Two common types of unauthorised investment fund are hedge funds and venture capital funds formed as general partnerships. The term 'hedge fund', while widely used, has no precise meaning but is generally taken to refer to funds with a number of distinct characteristics.[110] Usually, hedge funds:

- are organised as private investment partnerships or offshore investment corporations;
- use a wide variety of trading strategies involving position-taking in a range of markets;
- employ an assortment of trading techniques and instruments, often including short-selling, derivatives and leverage;
- pay performance fees to their managers; and
- have an investor base comprising wealthy individuals and institutions and a relatively high minimum investment limit (set at US$100,000 or higher for most funds).

Hedge funds can be marketed in the UK to intermediate customers and market counterparties.[111] At present, they cannot generally be freely offered to private customers in the UK as they are classified as unregulated collective investment schemes. However, the FSA Handbook does permit marketing to private customers in certain circumstances, such as when a firm takes reasonable steps to ensure that the fund is suitable.[112]

Venture capital (or 'private equity') funds are created for the purpose of investing on a pooled basis in relatively new business ventures. They typically invest at various stages in the development of new ventures with a view to selling their investment at a later date (either to another venture capitalist or through a public offering when the company is 'floated' on the stockmarket). Such funds are normally constituted as limited partnerships under the Limited Partnership Act 1907 and generally comprise a general partner (the venture capitalist) and a number of limited partners. The general partner bears unlimited liability whereas the liability of the limited partners is limited to their capital contribution to the partnership. The partnership will normally have a

---

[109] See Dir 2001/108/EC, OJ 2002 L41/35, commonly referred to as the 'Product Directive'. It is implemented in the UK by changes to the Collective Investment Schemes Sourcebook (CIS) (part of the FSA Handbook of Rules and Guidance).

[110] See FSA Discussion Paper (DP) 16 *Hedge Funds and the FSA* (2002) for a more detailed explanation of the operation of hedge funds. The FSA did canvass a relaxation of the rule relating to the marketing of hedge funds in the UK (see DP 16) but concluded that it was not appropriate on the basis that the current regime provides the right balance of consumer protection and access.

[111] See Ch 10 for an explanation of customer categorisation under FSMA 2000.

[112] FSA Handbook COB 3.11 R and Annex 5.

fixed duration and will often make provision for the proceeds of disposals of investments to be distributed before the end of that period. The distribution of profits is a matter for agreement between the partners, but the higher risk assumed by the general partner is normally associated with a right to a higher proportion of profits than the limited partners.

4.9.2 Unit trusts

Unit trusts can be traced back to the second half of the 19th century but, in their modern form, they originated in the United States in the 1930s.[113] Unlike some of the older forms of unit trust, such as the fixed trust based on a fixed portfolio with a fixed duration, the modern form of unit trust offers unit-holders transferability and liquidity. The manager and trustee are required to issue and redeem units on a continuous basis, so that the unit-holder always has a two-way market available in the units. The issue and redemption process is undertaken by reference to the value of the underlying investments, with the result that, from an investment perspective, the unit-holder is in the same position as if he were the direct owner of the underlying investments, which he is not.

The legal structure combines elements of contract and trust. The parties involved are the manager (also known as the operator), the trustee and the unit-holder. The trust is executed by the manager and trustee, neither of whom can be considered to be in the position of a settlor of a private trust, because the trust makes no provision in respect of their own property. The trust deed instead provides for the safekeeping and investment of sums paid by unit-holders, who are the benficiaries of the trust. The trust is, in effect, the con-tractually agreed mechanism under which the manager and trustee deal with the unit-holder's money. The manager and trustee of a unit trust must each be an incorporated body, be independent of each other, be authorised under FSMA 2000 and have permission to act as manager or trustee respectively.[114] It is not possible for the manager or trustee to exclude liability for any failure to exercise due care and diligence in the discharge of their functions in respect of a unit trust scheme.[115]

Under the unit-trust form of organisation, the ownership interest of a contributor is in the units that are allocated to him by the operator. The con-tributor has no legal ownership in respect of the assets (investments) held

---

[113] See regarding the history of unit trusts Kam Fan Sin, *The Legal Nature of the Unit Trust* (Oxford, OUP, 1997) ch 1 pp 7–44.

[114] See ss 237 and 243 FSMA 2000 and FSA Handbook AUTH Annex 2G T7.

[115] FSMA 2000 s 253.

within the fund.[116] The legal owner of the investments is the trustee who holds the investments on behalf of the contributors (beneficiaries). This is reflected in the regulatory requirement that a unit trust deed must include a declaration that the scheme property is held on trust for the unit-holders.[117] In contractual terms, the investor's stake can be expressed as an entitlement to a proportionate share of the profits (capital gains as well as income) in any period of account.

The operation of the unit trust is controlled by regulatory rules (the Collective Investment Schemes (CIS) Sourcebook[118]), the trust deed and the scheme particulars. As authorisation is dependent on compliance with the regulatory rules, they take priority. A trust deed cannot contain a provision inconsistent with these regulations, but can impose more restrictive rules on the trustee and manager (eg in respect of investment powers). The trustee is in a fiduciary relationship with the unit-holder and therefore must act at all times in the best interests of the untit-holders. While this duty arises from the common law, the CIS Sourcebook incorporates many of the specific instances of fiduciary duty that arise under the common law such as monitoring the manager to ensure that the fund is managed in accordance with the trust deed and the CIS Sourcebook.

The function of the manager, according to the trust deed, is to invest the fund according to the terms of the trust. The precise powers of investment will depend on the type of trust in question and the regulatory rules (CIS Sourcebook) that apply to that particular type of trust. The more problematic issue is whether the manager is or is not to be considered a trustee. Arguments have been made for and against considering the manager to be a trustee.[119] The significance of the issue lies in the potential liability of the manager arising from breach of the investment powers contained in the trust deed. If the manager is a trustee, there is potentially increased liability arising from the

---

[116] In England, a contributor is the beneficial owner of the underlying assets. The legal position of a holder of units in a unit trust in England can be described as that of a person with an indirect and unallocated interest in a changeable pool of securities that is owned beneficially by all unitholders. In Scotland, a contributor does not have ownership of the underlying assets because trust law in Scotland does not recognise division of ownership. A contributor in Scotland is a beneficiary of the trust.

[117] FSA Handbook CIS 2.2.6R.

[118] See FSA Handbook, Collective Investment Schemes (CIS) Sourcebook.

[119] Kam Fan Sin (above n 113) argues against the manager being considered a trustee on the basis that the trust fund is owned by the trustee and that there can be no trust (on the part of the manager) without property. A Hudson, *Law of Investment Entities* (London, Sweet & Maxwell, 2000) argues at p 207 that the manager is a trustee on the basis that the trust deed expressly allocates investment powers to the manager and therefore the manager is functionally in the position of a trustee. On this view, the trustee function in a unit trust is split between the manager and trustee.

high standard of conduct expected by the law from a trustee and a wider range of remedies available to the unit-holders.[120]

The scheme particulars (or prospectus[121]) contain details regarding the operation of the unit trust and represent a contract between the unit-holders and the manager.[122] The authorised fund manager is subject to a general duty to disclose in scheme particulars information required by the CIS Sourcebook.[123] That information covers matters such as the investment objectives of the fund, borrowing policy, arrangements for distribution of income, the remuneration of the fund manager and arrangements for sale and redemption of units. The manager of an authorised unit trust must not effect a sale of units to a person in the UK until it has offered that person free of charge a copy of the scheme particulars.[124]

A fundamental characteristic of the unit trust is that unit-holders are able to realise their investment at a price related to the net asset value of the fund.[125] While the net asset value of the fund is subject to changes in the value of the underlying portfolio, there is no market pricing of the units held by a unit-holder. Pricing of units in a unit trust is undertaken internally by the manager of the trust, subject to regulatory rules set by the FSA. This distinguishes the unit trust from an investment trust, in which a shareholder does not have this guarantee and will often find that the investment can be sold only at a discount to the underlying value of the portfolio. In the case of the unit trust, the pricing mechanism is located within the manager of the fund and is regulated by the CIS Sourcebook.

Historically, UK unit trusts used a 'dual-pricing' system, which involves the manager making an 'offer price' at which customer can buy and a (lower) 'bid price' at which customers can sell. The bid/offer 'spread' includes dealing costs,

---

[120] For example, if the manager is a considered a trustee, it could be required to make good any deficiency in the trust fund arising from a breach of investment powers and duties. While contractual remedies are also available to unit-holders against the manager, it is more difficult to judge whether, in financial terms, they would be functionally equivalent to remedies for breach of trust.

[121] The CIS sourcebook uses the term 'prospectus' to refer both to the scheme particulars of an authorised unit trust and the prospectus of an OEIC.

[122] See Kam Fan Sin (above n 113) at p 81, citing the Australian case *Graham Australia Pty Ltd v Corporate West Management Pty Ltd* (1990) 1 ACSR 682 at 687.

[123] FSA Handbook CIS 3.3.1R.

[124] FSA Handbook CIS 3.2.2R. Scheme particulars must be kept up-to-date on an ongoing basis.

[125] This is a requirement for all collective investment schemes under the UCITS Directive (85/611/EEC). FSMA s 24(3)(10) provides that:

> The participants must be entitled to have their units redeemed in accordance with the scheme at a price related to the net asset value of the property to which the units relate and determined in accordance with the scheme.

CIS 4.4.4R requires the operator to redeem units at all times during the dealing day.

fiscal duties and other front-end charges associated with the fund. More recently, the 'single-pricing' system, which is generally used in continental Europe, has become common in the UK.[126] It involves the manager quoting a single price to buyers and sellers of units, with front-end management charges being shown separately. Managers of authorised unit trusts can choose between single and dual pricing, whereas managers of OEICs are required to use single pricing. From the investor's perspective neither system is inherently superior. The regulatory approach to any pricing system must be based on three objectives: transparency; fairness as between incoming, outgoing and continuing investors; and competitiveness.[127] While both systems are capable of meeting these objectives, it seems likely that single pricing will become the dominant model for the future.[128]

The provisions of the CIS Sourcebook regulating the investment powers of authorised unit trusts have two objectives. First, they limit the proportion of unlisted investments that can be held, on the basis that such investments invariably have lower liquidity and are more difficult to value than listed securities.[129] Second, they require funds to comply with a number of rules that promote risk diversification. Different categories of fund have different investment powers.[130] While some form of exposure to derivatives is permitted for all types of authorised unit trusts, their gearing (borrowing) is restricted by a borrowing limit of 10 per cent of their assets.[131]

4.9.3 Investment companies with variable capital

Investment companies with variable capital (ICVCs) are UK-authorised open-ended investment companies (OEICs).[132] As is the case with a unit trust, there is no requirement for an OEIC to become authorised but an unauthorised scheme cannot be promoted to the general public.[133] OEICs were not, historically, used as a form of collective investment in the UK. The catalyst for change

[126] In Discussion Paper (DP) 8, *Single Pricing of Collective Investment Schemes: A Review* (Oct 2003), the FSA said (at p 13) that it expected close to 40% of authorised unit trust and OEIC funds under management to be single-priced by the end of 2001.

[127] See FSA DP 8 (above n 126), para 7.2.

[128] See DP 8 (above n 12) and FSA Policy Statement *Single Pricing of Collective Investment Schemes* (July 2002) for further discussion regarding the possibility of compulsory single-pricing for authorised unit trusts.

[129] For an explanation of 'listed' securities, see Ch 7.

[130] See FSA Handbook, CIS 5.1.5G for a summary.

[131] See FSA Handbook, CIS 5.15.4R.

[132] See s 236 FSMA for the statutory definition, which requires that an investor be able to realise his investment on a basis that reflects the value of the underlying investments. This rules out the possibility of shares in OEICs being issued or redeemed at a discount to the underlying net asset value.

[133] FSMA 2000 s 238.

was the introduction of the UCITS Directive[134] in 1985, which made possible
the cross-border marketing of funds within the EU. A problem for UK funds
was that the trust form of organisation was not used or well understood in continental Europe and therefore the ICVC structure was a more appropriate
structure for funds that wanted to qualify as UCITS funds. The UK introduced
Regulations[135] permitting the formation of OEICS in 1996 and these have now
been replaced by the 2001 Regulations.[136] These regulations are concerned
mainly with the organisational structure of ICVCs, while the CIS Sourcebook
controls other matters such as investment powers, dealing and pricing of
shares. Although a form of limited liability company, ICVCs are not subject to
the Companies Act 1985.[137] They are constituted by an instrument of incorporation, which must comply with the OEIC Regulations.[138]

Under the company form of organisation represented by an ICVC, the ownership rights of an investor are similar to those of a shareholder in a limited
company incorporated under the Companies Act 1985.[139] The main difference
is that, in common with a unit-holder in a unit trust, a shareholder in an ICVC
is entitled to redeem his shares on an on-going basis by reference to the net
asset value of the underlying portfolio.[140] The redemption process is managed
internally by the ICVC, rather than occurring in the market (as is the case for
shares held in an investment trust). ICVCs are permitted to use only single
pricing[141] when creating or redeeming shares.

Responsibility for the operation of an ICVC is split between an authorised
corporate director (ACD), other directors (if there are any) and the depositary.
The ACD must be a body corporate which is authorised for the purposes of
FSMA 2000 and has permission to act as a director of an ICVC. It is the ACD
which has effective power of management of the ICVC,[142] although where
there are other directors they have a role in monitoring the performance by the
ACD of its allocated functions. The depositary is responsible for custody of the
assets of the ICVC (which are owned by the company) and also has a duty to

---

[134] Dir 85/611/EC [1985] OJ L375/1.

[135] The Open-Ended Investment Companies (Investment Companies with Variable Capital)
Regulations 1996, SI 1996/2827.

[136] The Open-Ended Investment Companies Regulations 2001, SI 2001/1228.

[137] CA 1985 s 735 provides that it applies only to companies formed and registered under the
Act.

[138] See art 14 (conditions for authorisation) and sch 2 (instrument of incorporation).

[139] For a complete definition of a shareholder's rights in a particular ICVC, it is necessary to
examine the instrument of incorporation. This will be the case in particular when there are different classes of share. The OEIC Regulations (sch 2 para 4(1)(e)) permit different classes of
share. See CIS 2.4.2 for the different classes of share that can be issued.

[140] See art 15 of the OEIC Regs 2001 (requirements for authorisation).

[141] See n 127 above and accompanying text.

[142] See CIS 7.3.1R (Functions of the ACD). In this sense, the role of the ACD is similar to that
of a manager of a unit trust.

ensure that the scheme is managed in accordance with the CIS Sourcebook.[143] The directors (including the ACD) and the depositary can retain the services of others (eg a professional custodian) to assist with their duties.

The provisions of the CIS Sourcebook relating to investment and borrowing powers apply to both unit trusts and ICVCs. Therefore, the comments made above in respect of unit trusts can be applied equally to ICVCs. The requirement that an up-to-date prospectus must be maintained and provided to any person free of charge prior to a sale of units also applies to ICVCs.[144] An ACD or authorised unit trust manager is liable for loss caused to investors as a result of errors or omissions in a prospectus.[145]

4.9.4 Investment trusts

Investment trusts are not trusts. They are public limited companies whose business is the management of a portfolio of investments. To become an investment trust a company normally passes through two regulatory hurdles. First, it becomes an investment company for the purposes of section 266 of the Companies Act 1985. This provides that the company should have given notice to the Registrar of Companies of its intention to carry on business as an investment company and that it complies with the requirements of section 266(2), which imposes restrictions on the manner in which the company operates.[146] The benefit of 'investment company' status is that the company becomes subject to the favourable rules on dividend distributions contained in section 265 of the Companies Act 1985. An investment company must then comply with section 842 of the Income and Corporation Taxes Act 1988 (ICTA 1988) in

---

[143] Hudson, *Law of Investment Entities* (above n 119 at p 219) argues that a depositary might be considered a fiduciary in respect of the fund. Even if that were the case, it is not clear that it would result in a material expansion in a depositary's potential liability under contract, tort and regulatory rules.

[144] See FSA Handbook, CIS 3.2.2.

[145] See CIS 3.3.1. The formulation of this liability is similar to the liability for errors or omissions in a prospectus relating to a public offer of securities—see Ch 7.

[146] The requirements are:

(a) that the business of the company consists of investing its funds mainly in securities, with the aim of spreading investment risk and giving members of the company the benefit of the results of the management of its funds;

(b) that none of the company's holdings in companies (other than those which are for the time being investment companies) represents more than 15% by value of the investing company's investments;

(c) that subject to subsection 2A distribution of the company's capital profits is prohibited by it memorandum or articles of association;

(d) that the company has not retained, otherwise than in compliance with this Part, in respect of any accounting reference period more than 15% of the income it derives from securities.

order to qualify as an investment trust.[147] The main benefit of investment trust status is that the fund itself (but not shareholders) is exempt from capital gains tax. Shareholders pay capital gains tax in the normal way on gains in the value of their investment trust shares.

The portfolio of an investment trust is created initially by raising capital through issuing shares in the company to investors. As the capital and number of shares is fixed, an investment trust is a 'closed-end' fund. It is possible for the capital to be varied in accordance with the normal procedure applicable to companies generally,[148] but that procedure does not lend itself to a process of continuous issue and redemption of shares such as occurs in the case of units in unit trusts and shares in OEICs. Thus, while investment trusts are functionally similar to other investment funds in that they offer a diversified form of pooled investment, the mechanism through which an investor participates (ie the share) is indistinguishable from that which is used in ordinary trading companies.

The reference to 'trust' survives from the late nineteenth century when investment companies were commonly established by a 'deed of settlement', which was a form of trust.[149] Investment trusts are listed in the UK and admitted to trading on the London Stock Exchange. Their internal organisation and the rights of their shareholders are, like any other listed company, controlled by three main legal sources: company law; their articles of association; and the Listing Rules. A company that is an investment trust is (like any other company) a separate legal person and owns the investments that comprise the fund. Shareholders have no direct claim to the underlying investments.

Investment trusts are sometimes described as 'unregulated'. This is true in the sense that they are not 'collective investment schemes' for the purposes of FSMA 2000 and therefore do not fall under the regulations applicable to such schemes. They are, however, subject to the UKLA Listing Rules, which apply to all listed companies. One of the requirements for 'investment trust' status under s 842 ICTA 1988 is that the entire ordinary share capital of the company must be listed. The Listing Rules allow up to 20 per cent of gross assets to be invested in the securities of one company or group and do not limit borrowing.[150]

---

[147] ICTA 1988 s 842 is similar in its terms to s 266 of the Companies Act 1985. It is possible, although unusual, to gain 'investment trust' status without being an investment company under s 266.

[148] See Ch 7.

[149] See Kam Fan Sin (above n 113) pp 13–19; and *Gower's Principles of Modern Company Law*, 4th edn (London, Sweet & Maxwell, 1979) pp 266–72.

[150] See Ch 21 of the Listing Rules for modifications and additions to the standard listing rules applicable to investment companies. The disparity between the 20 per cent investment limit found in the Listing Rules and the 15 per cent limit in s 266 of the Companies Act 1985 and s 842 ICTA 1988 reflects the possibility that a listed investment company may not fall within either of those provisions. See the definition of an investment company in para 21.1(f) of the Listing Rules.

Investment managers who manage the assets of investment trusts must be authorised under FSMA 2000 and private customers who are advised on investment trusts are protected by the FSA's Conduct of Business Rules.[151]

Purchase and sale of shares in an investment trust differs from unit trusts and OEICs in two significant ways. First, in the case of the unit trusts and OEICs, the issue/redemption process is managed internally (by the manager or ACD respectively) whereas the sale or purchase of shares in an investment trust occurs in the (public) secondary market for shares. Second, the price at which units/shares in unit trusts and OEICs are issued and redeemed is related to the net asset value of the fund and is regulated by the FSA. In the case of investment trust shares, there is no necessary link between the price at which the shares are transferred between investors and the net asset value of the fund. The price of an investment trust share is determined in the open market just like any other share. Hence, investment trust shares can and often do trade at either a discount or premium to their net asset value.[152]

A split capital investment trust is an investment trust with a fixed life span.[153] Unlike a conventional investment trust, which has no fixed life, a split capital trust is wound up on a pre-determined date. 'Split capital' refers to the existence of different classes of share with different rights. The objective of a split capital structure is to target different types of investor, some of whom require income and others who are more concerned with long-term capital appreciation. Split capital trusts, especially those with more complex structures, involve structural gearing because the return on any one class of share is determined not only by the entitlement of that class but also by that of others. This can be distinguished from financial gearing that arises when an investment trust borrows money to increase the size of the fund available for investment.

The early forms of split capital trust issued income and capital shares. The former were entitled to the entire income from the fund while the latter were entitled to the capital. Over time, more complex structures were introduced. They often included:[154]

Zero dividend preference shares. These are preference shares that have no entitlement to income. They have a predetermined capital return that is not guaranteed and is dependent on sufficient assets being available at wind-up.

---

[151] See Ch 6 for more detail.

[152] While this explains how discounts/premiums can arise, it does not adequately explain why they do. That remains something of a mystery in the sense that the general principles of finance would predict that a basket of shares should have the same value as the aggregate of its components.

[153] See generally FSA Discussion Paper 10, *Split Capital Closed End Funds* (Dec 2001).

[154] This is an overview of typical share classes. Each split capital trust has a unique pattern of entitlement and order of priority on winding-up.

Income shares. These shares vary in their entitlement as to capital and income.

Ordinary income shares. These shares offer potential for a rising income. They have no predetermined capital value but on winding up are entitled to all surplus assets after prior ranking charges (which usually include zero dividend preference shares).

Capital shares. These shares are entitled to all surplus assets after prior ranking charges. The prior ranking charges may include some or all of the share classes above.

The split capital investment trust sector expanded rapidly during the 1990s,[155] driven largely by the rising equity market. However, the collapse in the equity market from 1999 onwards resulted in fundamental problems in the sector being exposed. The two main problems were high levels of borrowing (gearing) and investment in other split investment trusts (cross-holdings). These two characteristics meant that many trusts faced severe financial difficulties as a result of the fall in the equity market. Illustrative figures produced by the FSA show the effect of the fall in the market over the period March 1999 to March 2002. While the FTSE 100 Index fell by 16.2 per cent over that period, a typical split capital investment trust with no cross holdings fell by 39.1 per cent while one with cross-holding representing between 41 per cent and 70 per cent of its portfolio fell by 98 per cent.[156] Many investors suffered heavy losses, exacerbated by the fact that the insolvency of an investment trust is not an event in respect of which a claim can be made under the Financial Services Compensation Scheme.[157]

Following its investigation of the split capital debacle, the FSA introduced changes to the listing rules applicable to investment trusts and to the conduct of business rules applicable to transactions in the securities issued by them.[158] The changes address a number of important issues as follows:

Cross-holdings. There is a new listing rule (in the form of a condition for admission to listing and a continuing obligation) that limits to 10% in aggregate, the value of the gross assets that may be invested in other listed investment companies. The rule does not apply if the relevant investment company has a stated investment policy to invest no more than 15 per cent of their gross assets in other listed investment companies.

---

[155] FSA Policy Statement, *Split Capital Investment Trusts* (May 2002) notes that 55 were launched between 1990 and 1999 and 34 between 1999 and 2001.

[156] See FSA Policy Statement, *Split Capital Investment Trusts* (May 2002) p 6.

[157] See Ch 6.5. Other potential remedies for private investors, such as a complaint to the Financial Ombudsman or an action for damages arsing from breach of a regulatory rule are considered in Ch 6.

[158] The changes are contained in the Investment Entities (Listing Rules and Conduct of Business) Instrument 2003, made under a variety of powers contained in FSMA 2000. On the background and rationale for the changes see FSA Consultation Paper 164 *Investment Companies (including Investment Trusts) Proposed Changes to the Listing Rules and Conduct of Business Rules* (Jan 2003).

Risk warnings. There is a new listing rule to the effect that listing particulars or a prospectus[159] relating to an investment company must draw attention specifically to the investment policy of the company and the risks associated with investing in the securities to be listed. Changes have also been made to the Conduct of Business (COB) Sourcebook to ensure that investors buying investment trust shares in the secondary market are made aware of the risks associated with the investment.[160]

The Board of Directors. The split capital debacle showed that the requirement of the listing rules that the board must be able to demonstrate that it will act independently of any investment manager was often not borne out in practice. The result was that the role of the board of directors in promoting the interests of shareholders and monitoring the performance of the manager was often compromised. To remedy this, the listing rules have been altered so as to cast a wider net over persons who will not be considered to be independent of the manager.[161]

4.9.5 Exchange traded funds (ETF)

Exchange traded funds are open-ended funds that are structured as listed companies. They are relatively new to the UK, having been launched in April 2000, but are well established in other countries such as the USA and Canada. The ETF sector in the UK is composed entirely of index-tracking funds and is able to avoid stamp duty (normally 0.5 per cent of the purchase cost of securities) by being based in Dublin (where, confusingly from the UK perspective, they are classified as mutual funds). They are therefore capable of offering exposure to a diversified portfolio at lower cost than other forms of pooled investment fund.

In financial terms, the process of issue/redemption of ETF shares is in principle similar to that for OEICs and unit trusts in that there is a direct link between the price and the net asset value of the fund. ETFs are not, however, 'collective investment schemes' for the purposes of FSMA 2000, with the result that their regulatory position is more similar to investment trusts. As entities, ETFs are regulated primarily by the listing rules (in respect of admission to listing, financial reporting and continuing obligations) while transactions in ETF shares are regulated by the COB Sourcebook.

---

[159] See Ch 7 for more detail on prospectuses.
[160] See COB 3.8.9G.
[161] These rules are in addition to the requirements of the Combined Code, which are applicable to investment trusts. See Ch 8.

4.10 Investment-related life assurance

In its early forms, life assurance provided financial protection only against premature death. It still performs this function but has also taken on the characteristics of an investment. This occurred for a number of reasons. One was that the traditional manner in which life assurance was organised was similar in character to investment funds and therefore life offices had the organisational and contractual mechanisms in place to enable them to change their focus from protection to investment. Another reason was that life assurance made investment accessible to lower income groups who lacked the wealth to invest directly in company shares or indirectly in unit trusts. This was particularly so in the case of 'industrial' life assurance, which developed as a system of regular collection of relatively small premiums from policyholders' homes. Another influence was the use of life assurance as a mechanism to repay a mortgage from the proceeds of a life policy. This greatly expanded the market for investment-related life assurance in the 1980s, but that process went into reverse in the 1990s as interest rates fell and regulators became concerned that such products had been sold in inappropriate circumstances.

4.10.1 The with-profits system

Although its use has declined in recent years, the 'with-profits' mechanism has been the traditional method by which life assurance companies have allocated the investment returns (both income and capital gains) arising from the fund representing premiums paid by 'with-profits' policyholders (the 'with-profits' fund). The mechanism works by allocating bonuses to individual policies. In order for bonuses to be allocated, the value of the life office's assets must exceed the present value of it future liabilities, which are mainly sums owed to policyholders. In this situation the life office has an actuarial surplus, which is in principle available for distribution to policyholders in the form of bonuses.[162]

The normal practice has been for life offices to declare two types of bonus, annual (or reversionary) and final (or terminal). Annual bonuses are contractually guaranteed additions to the policy which become payable when the policy matures and are normally made at a conservative level as the life offices must include them in the calculation of liabilities. Terminal bonuses are allocated and paid when a policy matures and are intended to increase the value of the policy to a level which reflects the actual investment return

[162] The articles of association govern the distribution of surplus. In a shareholder-owned company they normally provide for the surplus to be split 90 : 10 between policyholders and shareholders, whereas in a mutual company they normally provide for the entire surplus to be distributed to policyholders.

achieved by the with-profits fund rather than the generally lower return assumed in calculating annual bonuses.

The overall objective of bonus allocation in respect of with-profits policies is that the value of the benefits should equate to the policyholder's notional 'asset-share' in the with-profit fund, that is, the notional part of the total fund that has been created over time by the investment of the premiums paid by an individual policyholder. The attraction of the system is that it provides a mechanism that allows the policyholder to participate in the growth of the with-profits fund while at the same time having some protection against sharp fluctuations in the value of investments (through contractually guaranteed annual bonuses). This is generally referred to as 'smoothing' of investment returns. From the perspective of the life office the with-profits mechanism provides very broad powers for distributing actuarial surplus among policyholders in a manner that is equitable to different generations of policyholders who have participated in the fund through periods in which different investment returns have been achieved. It is also attractive to the life office in that no specific investment return is normally guaranteed to the policyholder when the policy is issued, the understanding being that the policyholder accepts, through the bonus allocation process, whatever investment return is achieved by the with-profits fund.

It has always been accepted that annual and final bonus rates could change from year to year and could be set at different levels for different generations of policyholders. Prior to the *Equitable Life* case,[163] however, it remained unclear whether the discretion enjoyed by a life office in respect of the bonus allocation process could be employed so as to eliminate or reduce contractual obligations to policyholders. Following that case, the first in which the operation of the with-profits system had been subjected to judicial scrutiny, it seems clear that in most instances life companies will not be able to act in that manner. While the facts of that case are not universally applicable, it is indicative of judicial resistance to the use of discretionary powers to override contractual rights.[164]

4.10.2 Unit-linked contracts

Unit-linked contracts were developed to provide a more transparent form of investment than was provided by the 'with-profits' system. Although the life

---

[163] *Equitable Life v Hyman* [2000] 2 All ER 331; [2002] 1 AC 408 (HL). See I MacNeil, 'When is a Guarantee Not a Guarantee?' [2000] *Company Financial and Insolvency Law Review* 154 and 'Contract, Discretion and the With-Profits Mechanism' [2000] *Company Financial and Insolvency Law Review* 354.

[164] The House of Lords implied into the society's articles of association (under which the directors were empowered to declare bonuses) a prohibition on linking bonuses to the manner in which policyholders chose to exercise contractual rights under their policies. See MacNeil articles on *Equitable Life* (above n 163).

fund in which premiums are invested may invest in a similar fashion to a with-profits fund, the manner in which the policyholder participates in the fund differs. A unit-linked policyholder is allocated units in the fund, which are priced on a daily basis by reference to the underlying investments.[165] In contrast to a 'with-profits' contract, the value of the policy is evident on a continuous basis. Charges levied from the policyholder are also explicit (usually expressed as a percentage of the value of units) rather than being hidden (and encompassed in the bonus calculation) in the case of with-profits contracts. In addition to its investment value, a unit-linked contract normally carries a minimum guaranteed payment on death.

4.10.3 Regulatory considerations

All contracts of life assurance are specified investments for the purposes of FSMA 2000.[166] Insurers therefore require authorisation and permission from the FSA and are subject to prudential supervision so as to safeguard the interests of policyholders. However, the FSA does not (and cannot) regulate the terms of life assurance contracts.

Considerable regulatory attention has been focused in recent years on the operation of the 'with-profits' system. The following issues in particular have given rise to concern:

1 the manner in which life offices exercise their discretion, particularly as regards the allocation of bonuses to policies;
2 the manner in which the 'inherited estate' accumulated by many life offices should be used;
3 the feasibility of making the with profits system simpler and more transparent for policyholders.

All three issues are relevant to the nature of a with-profits policy as an investment and are therefore discussed below.

Discretion is an inherent feature of with-profits policies because they are based on the principle that a policyholder will share in the (smoothed) investment returns of the with-profits fund. Its presence, however, poses risks for policyholders in that they may encounter during the term of their policy, instances of the exercise of discretion that are unexpected or perhaps even unfair. Unfairness in this sense could mean different treatment for different generations of policyholders or the favouring of the interests of shareholders

---

[165] This distinguishes a unit-linked policy from a 'unitised with-profits' policy, which, although it allocates units to the policyholder, preserves the life office's discretion in allocating units and hence 'smoothing' of investment returns. See FSA document, *A Description and Classification of With-Profits Policies* (Oct 2000) for more detail.
[166] FSMA 2000 s 22(2) and sch 2 paragraph 20; RAO art 75.

over policyholders. Legal controls over the exercise of discretion comprise primarily the FSA's Principles for Businesses[167] and the regulations applicable to all contract terms.[168] The FSA's concern arises from the wide nature of the discretion typically given to insurers by 'with-profits' policies, which could potentially be considered unfair under the Unfair Terms in Consumer Contract Regulations 1999.[169] Disclosure of the principles and practices applicable to the exercise of discretion is the solution favoured by the FSA to make with-profit contracts compliant with these legal and regulatory obligations. This would have the effect of improving policyholders' understanding of the role of discretion and the manner in which it is likely to be exercised.

The 'inherited estate' (sometimes referred to as 'orphan assets') refers to the assets that have been accumulated over time by a with-profits fund that are not required to meet policyholders' reasonable expectations.[170] The latter expression refers to how a policyholder could reasonably expect a life office to use its discretion, particularly as regards bonus policy. An 'inherited estate' arises as a result of the discretion given to a life office in distributing investment returns in a with-profits fund to policyholders. In some instances, life offices have exercised that discretion with caution and have accumulated assets over and above those required to satisfy policyholders' reasonable expectations.

Two issues give rise to regulatory concern. The first is the attribution of ownership of the inherited estate as between shareholders and policyholders. This has been largely settled by the 1995 Ministerial Statement, which has the effect in most cases of attributing it 90 : 10 as between policyholders and shareholders.[171] The second is the re-attribution of an inherited estate to shareholders, or put another way, a buy-out by shareholders of policyholders' interests in the inherited estate. There are two main regulatory concerns that arise in respect of both attribution and re-attribution exercises.[172] The first is that they are commercial negotiations between shareholders and current policyholders in which policyholders have no explicit and distinct negotiator

---

[167] Principle 6, which states that 'A firm must pay due regard to the interests of its customers and treat them fairly'.

[168] In particular, the Unfair Terms in Consumer Contract Regulations 1999, SI 1999/2083.

[169] See paras 22–26 of the FSA document, *With-Profits Review: Issues Paper 4 Discretion and Fairness in With-Profits Policies*.

[170] Policyholders' reasonable expectations are referred to in the Ministerial Statement on 'Orphan Estates' issued by the DTI on 24 February 1995 and the term has since been regularly used by the FSA. Although widely used in the actuarial profession, it does not have a technical legal meaning and is not referred to by FSMA 2000.

[171] See above n 170. This follows the same ratio applied to the distribution of actuarial surplus. The logic is that the inherited estate could potentially form part of surplus. In mutual companies, the inherited estate belongs to the policyholders.

[172] See para 23 of FSA document, *With Profits Review: Issues Paper 1 Process for Dealing with Attribution of Inherited Estates* (October 2001) and FSA Consultation Paper 207, *Treating With-Profits Policyholders Fairly* (Dec 2003).

to act on their behalf. The second is that both attribution and re-attribution are complex exercises that are difficult for policyholders to understand.[173] The FSA's proposals for the appointment of a policyholder advocate are intended to result in more active representation of policyholders' interests in the process than is currently the case.[174]

The feasibility of making the with-profits system simpler and more transparent for policyholders has come to the fore largely as a result of the recommendations of the Sandler Report.[175] It found that the opaque nature of with-profits policies inhibits effective competition and creates inherent conflicts of interest in shareholder-owned companies, particularly over the selection of investment opportunities.[176] The Sandler Report made extensive recommendations for improving the with-profits system. Two points in particular are worthy of note. First, it proposed restructuring with-profits funds so as to separate the interests of shareholders and policyholders and limit the potential for conflicts of interest. Second, it proposed a clearer definition of policyholders' rights and improved disclosure to policyholders.

The FSA has responded to these concerns in three ways. First, it has established a new framework under which firms must disclose the manner in which their with-profits business is being run. This requires firms carrying on a with-profits business to establish and maintain Principles and Practices of Financial Management (PPFM).[177] The Principles are enduring statements describing the standards the firms adopt in managing with-profits business and the business model used by the firm in meeting its duties to policyholders and in responding to longer-term changes in the business and economic environment. The Practices must describe the manner in which the with-profits fund is managed and contain sufficient detail to enable a knowledgeable observer to understand the material risks and rewards arising from maintaining a with-

---

[173] See FSA Consultation Paper 207, (above n 172) at p 28 for an overview of the legal framework relevant to 're-attribution'.

[174] See Ch 5 of FSA Consultation Paper 207 (above n 173).

[175] *Medium & Long Term Retail Savings in the UK—A Review, July 2002.* The Government commissioned this review in June 2001 to 'identify the competitive forces and incentives that drive the industries concerned, in particular their approaches to investment, and, where necessary, to suggest policy responses to ensure that consumers are well served'. It was prompted by the Myners Report (*Institutional Investment in the United Kingdom: A Review*, 2001, available from www.hm-treasury.gov.uk (8 Nov 2004)) which was concerned that investment decision-making was sub-optimal as a result of the structure and operation of the retail investment market. Its focus on industry efficiency, value for money and effectiveness of investment decision-making distinguishes it from the FSA's review of with-profits business, which, as a result of the FSA's statutory objectives, focused more on consumer protection and consumer understanding.

[176] Sandler Report paras 60–61.

[177] The requirement is contained in the FSA Handbook COB 6.10.5R. For background see FSA CP167 *With Profits Governance, the Role of Actuaries in Life Insurers and Certification of Insurance Returns* (Jan 2003).

profits policy with the firm. The PPFM must also cover the firm's management of any inherited estate and the uses to which the firm may put that inherited estate. Firms are required to report to policyholders each year stating whether they have complied with the obligations relating to PPFM.[178]

The FSA also proposes to take action to underline the responsibility of a firm's directors for the valuation of policyholder liabilities, which is of fundamental importance to the financial condition of life insurers.[179] This recognises that there has in the past been a tendency to rely, without adequate scrutiny, on the advice of the appointed actuary on this matter. It is proposed that directors will be required to satisfy themselves (having taken advice) on the adequacy of the liabilities and that this matter should be brought within the scope of audit, from which it is currently excluded. It is also proposed that the role of actuaries within life insurers should be restructured. The main feature of the FSA's proposals is that, for firms writing with-profits business, the role of appointed actuary[180] should be abolished and replaced by two roles; that of with-profits actuary and the actuarial function. This proposal is based primarily on the premise that the appointed actuary currently represents the interests of both the policyholders and the firm and that this inevitably involves a conflict of interest. The identification of two separate roles (although they will be capable of being performed by the same person) is intended to separate the interests of the firm from those of the with-profits policyholders and in particular to ensure that firms comply with their obligation to treat customers fairly when exercising their discretion in the operation of with-profits business.

The third strand of the FSA's response is to create new sections of the COB Sourcebook dealing specifically with treating with-profits policyholders fairly and the attribution of inherited estates.[181] These provisions are regarded by the FSA as a codification of good practice rather than new rules that are being imposed on insurers.

4.10.4 Transfer of rights

Rights under a life assurance contract are a form of incorporeal moveable property (in England choses in action) and are in principle capable of being assigned

---

[178] FSA Handbook, COB 6.11.9R. There must be some independent judgment in the assessment of compliance with PPFM (COB 6.11.5G). One way of providing such independent judgment is through the creation of a with-profits committee with external members to advise on the interests of policyholders (see FSA Consultation Paper 167, above n 177, part 5 'Governance arrangements for with-profits business').

[179] See generally FSA Consultation Paper 167 (above n 177) and FSA Policy Statement, *With-Profits Governance and the Role of Actuaries in Life insurers* (June 2003).

[180] See FSA Handbook, SUP 4.3.13R for a statement of the current role of the appointed actuary.

[181] See FSA Consultation Paper 207 (above n 172).

to a third party. It is possible for a policy to prohibit assignment, but that is unusual as many policies are taken out on the basis that the right to payment will be assigned, for example in connection with the repayment of a mortgage.[182] Assignment is only effective if written notice[183] is given to the insurer, but there is no requirement to obtain the insurer's consent. An assignee takes the policy subject to equities (in Scotland subject to the principle *assignatus utitur jure auctoris*), meaning that any defence that is available to the insurer against the original policyholder is also available against an assignee.[184]

4.11 Pensions

A pension can be defined in simple terms as an arrangement through which a person makes provision for an income in retirement. In the UK, there are two main ways in which such arrangements can be structured in the private sector.[185] The first is possible when contributions are paid into a scheme run by an employer (an occupational pension scheme). Such schemes can be structured so that employees receive a pension that is related to their salary at retirement. From the employee's perspective this offers certainty and predictability of retirement income but from the employer's perspective it results in some uncertainty and risk as regards costs. This arises mainly from the possibility that growth in the accumulated fund of pension contributions will not match liabilities (present and future pension payments), which rise in line with the growth in earnings, leaving the employer with the obligation to make good any shortfall. The 'final salary' structure (under which an employee's pension represented a proportion of salary at retirement) was popular for many years but its use has declined in recent years as a result of employers' concerns over risk and cost.

---

[182] In this case the life assured remains the same, but the policy is transferred in security to the mortgagee, who is entitled to the proceeds to the extent necessary to repay the loan advanced to the mortgagor. Another reason for assignment is that there is now a market in 'second-hand' with-profits life policies, which may offer a policyholder a higher price than the surrender value offered by the life office.

[183] This is a requirement of the Policies of Assurance Act 1867, which governs assignment of life polices in England and Scotland. It is also a requirement of the Law of Property Act 1925, which provides an alternative basis for assignment in English law.

[184] See generally M Clarke, *The Law of Insurance Contracts*, 2nd edn (Lloyd's of London Press Ltd, 1994) pp 176–79.

[185] The state provides a basic pension on a universal basis, but the payments have over time been eroded by inflation and are widely regarded as inadequate to support a decent standard of living. The state scheme is unfunded, meaning that payments are made from current taxation rather than an accumulated fund. Increasing longevity and a resulting increase in the proportion of the population represented by pensioners poses a problem for both state and private sector schemes.

The second type of structure is based on the principle that an individual pays contributions into a plan managed by an organisation independent from his employer (eg an insurer) and then uses the proceeds of that plan to purchase an annuity, which is a contract under which an insurer agrees to pay an income for life in return for a capital sum. The second system is referred to as a 'money purchase' system as the fund available to buy an annuity at retirement is dependent mainly on the market value of the fund at retirement. It results in some uncertainty for employees as regards their retirement income but can be more attractive for employers as they are able to fix and predict their costs more easily than in the case of final salary schemes.

Occupational pensions are organised by employers on behalf of employees and are open only to employees. In general, there is no obligation imposed on an employer to provide an occupational pension scheme for employees. When they are provided, they can be organised either as 'final salary' or 'money purchase' schemes.[186] Rights in such schemes are not investments for the purposes of the FSMA 2000. This may appear anomalous in view of the fact that, for many people, pensions represent their largest investment (in the economic sense of the word), but the legal categorisation of such rights can be justified on two grounds. First, occupational pension schemes are subject to a special regulatory regime. The legal regime applicable to occupational pension schemes is that of trust and the regulatory regime is that created by the Pensions Act 1995.[187] Occupational pension schemes are in essence a trust in which the settlor (trustee) is the employer and the beneficiaries the employees.[188] Trustees (often directors of the employer) are responsible for the operation of the trust and beneficiaries' interests are protected in the normal manner by the application of the law of trusts. The Occupational Pensions Regulatory Authority (OPRA) was created by the Pensions Act 1995 and has an oversight role in respect of occupational pensions. It reports on an annual basis to the Secretary of State and has powers to remove trustees, prohibit persons from acting as trustees of a particular scheme and suspend persons from acting as trustees of a scheme.[189]

Second, although not stated explicitly in the Act, the FSMA regulatory regime is focused on transferable investments and occupational pensions do

---

[186] Recent years have seen a significant decline in the number of final salary schemes and growth in money purchase schemes.

[187] The 1995 Act was a response to the Goode Report (*Pension Law Reform: the report of the Pension Law Reform Review Committee*, London, HMSO, 1993) which was prompted mainly by the Maxwell pensions scandal, which involved the removal of assets from the Mirror Group pension fund.

[188] This is the conventional view. Hudson (above n 119) p 148 takes the view that the employees should also be considered settlers when they provide capital for the trust fund through contributions.

[189] See ss 3 and 4 of the Pensions Act 1995.

not fall into this category. While rights arising from an occupational pension scheme can be considered 'property' in the legal sense,[190] assignment is prohibited by statute[191] and therefore the 'investment' represented by those rights is not transferable.

Alternatives to occupational pension schemes have existed for a long time in the form of self-employed pensions and the State Earnings Related Pension Scheme (SERPS). However, the market for such alternatives expanded rapidly as a result of legislation introduced in the late 1980s that created 'personal pensions'. The policy underlying their introduction was that of promoting greater personal responsibility for retirement planning so as to reduce the role of the state in funding retirement income. The new personal pensions were categorised as investments for the purposes of FSA 1986.[192] That approach has continued under FSMA 2000,[193] with the result that providers of such pensions are subject to authorisation and conduct of business rules.[194]

For regulatory purposes, a personal pension scheme[195] is defined as a scheme of investment in accordance with s 630 Income and Corporation Taxes Act 1988.[196] It is a money-purchase contract, which means that it provides a mechanism through which a person can accumulate a fund with which to purchase an annuity.[197] The annuity can be purchased either from the provider of the personal pension or from another provider of annuities. Alternative methods of accumulating a fund can be considered, but the attraction of a personal pension is that it offers considerable tax advantages by comparison with other forms of investment (eg unit trusts) that might be used for the same purpose.

Rights under personal pension schemes are property in the legal sense and can, in principle, be transferred by way of assignment.[198] However, assignment

---

[190] See *Re Landau* [1988] Ch 223.

[191] Pensions Act 1995, s 91.

[192] They were considered to be long-term insurance contracts under sch 1 para 10 FSA 1986. For a discussion of the insurance characteristic of a personal pension, see J McMeel, 'The Consumer Dimension of Financial Services Law: Lessons from the Pension Mis-Selling Scandal' [1999] *Company Financial and Insolvency Law Review* 29, 31.

[193] See RAO arts 75, 3 and sch 1, pt 2. 'Group' personal pensions, which form an alternative to occupational pension schemes are also specified investments.

[194] Insurers, who are the main providers of personal pensions, are also subject to prudential supervision.

[195] The Glossary to the FSA Handbook distinguishes two types of scheme: personal pension policies sold by insurers; and personal pension contracts sold by collective investment schemes.

[196] See the Glossary to the FSA Handbook. This requirement gives considerable regulatory control to the Treasury, which ultimately controls the tax regulations with which personal pension schemes must comply in order to attract tax concessions.

[197] Use of the fund for other purposes is constrained by tax law.

[198] Applying the reasoning of *Re Landau* (above n 190) by way of analogy to personal pensions. The effect of that decision (holding that rights under a personal pension policy formed part of a bankrupt's estate) has been reversed by s 11 of the Welfare Reform and Pensions Act 1999.

is prohibited as a condition of approval of a personal pension scheme for tax relief.[199] This means that, for practical purposes, rights under personal pensions schemes are not transferable. This distinguishes them from rights under a life assurance policy, which are generally transferable, and limits their use as collateral in connection with mortgages and other forms of lending.[200]

The Welfare Reform and Pensions Act 1999 introduced a new form of low-cost pension, the 'stakeholder pension', aimed primarily at those who do not have access to an occupational pension scheme. Underlying this development was a recognition that state pension provision (whether in the basic or earnings-related form) could not provide a financially secure basis for retirement and that the take-up of a private sector 'second pension' should therefore be encouraged. Stakeholder schemes are organised as trusts, are open to employees of different employers and are required to meet a number of conditions set by the Act. Among the conditions are that the scheme must be structured on a 'money-purchase' basis [201] and that annual charges are limited to 1 per cent of the value of the fund per annum. Employers are required to provide employees with access to a stakeholder pension scheme unless they are exempt.[202]

---

[199] Income and Corporation Taxes Act 1988 ss 620, 634 and 635.

[200] For example, while a lender can require assignment of a life policy as security against repayment of a loan, it is not possible to assign rights under a personal pension policy as security for repayment of a loan.

[201] s 1(4).

[202] An employer is exempt if it has fewer than five employees or offers an occupational pension scheme to employees within one year of their starting work.

5

Institutional Investment

While the nature of investments has changed over time, there has probably been an even more significant change in the nature of investors. Private individuals were the dominant type of investor in the nineteenth century, although insurance companies had begun to build up substantial holdings of government bonds in the early part of the century and had accumulated significant equity investments by the end of that century.[1] The post-second-world-war period witnessed a transformation in the ownership distribution of financial securities as institutional ownership of investments grew to become much more significant than individual ownership. Several factors lay behind this trend. One was the growth of collective investment schemes and in particular the flexible form of unit trust imported from the USA in the 1930s. This provided risk diversification for private investors and also lower transaction costs by comparison with individual ownership of securities. Another was the development of insurance as an investment through products such as with-profits endowments and later unit-linked life assurance. The growth in pension provision was another factor, resulting in pension funds reaching a position where they matched the importance of insurance companies as institutional investors.

The purpose of this chapter is to examine the legal principles and regulatory rules that apply to institutional investment. The manner in which institutional investors operate is controlled primarily by trust and contract law. Trust law is relevant because two of the most important forms of institutional investment (pensions and unit trusts) are structured as trusts.[2] Contract is important because institutional investors manage investment funds on behalf of their clients (the 'ultimate investors') under agreements made with clients. The FSMA 2000 regulatory system also plays a part, primarily by requiring institutional

---

[1] R Michie, *The London Stock Exchange: A History* (Oxford, OUP, 1999) observes (at p 73) that the assets of British life assurance companies rose almost fivefold between 1870 and 1930, while their holdings of stocks and shares rose tenfold.

[2] Trusts are also an important legal structure for private investors. The general principles of trust law were developed in the context of family trusts. The use of trusts for institutional investment was a later development.

investors to be authorised (licensed) but also by setting standards that limit and control the risks to which 'ultimate investors' are exposed. Self-regulation is also an important factor in determining how institutional investment is conducted in the UK. Each of these matters is discussed below in more detail. There then follows an analysis of distinct characteristics of the legal framework applicable to the main types of institutional investor.

5.1 Trust

Several forms of institutional investment are conducted under the legal structure of trust. Unit trusts and pension funds each represent a form of trust with a specific purpose and a specific regulatory regime that is not applicable to other trusts, such as family or charitable trusts. However, subject to the provisions of their special regulatory regime, unit trusts and pension trusts remain subject to the basic principles of the general law of trusts.[3] They are, however, expressly excluded from the scope of most of the provisions of the Trustee Act 2000, which is discussed below.[4]

The general law of trusts (ie excluding the special regulatory regime for unit trusts and pensions) developed originally from equitable and common-law principles but over time was also influenced by a number of statutory provisions. There are some differences in the nature and statutory regulation of trusts as between Scotland and England but these differences do not carry much significance for the exercise of investment powers of trustees.[5] In England, the beneficiary of a trust enjoys beneficial ownership of the trust property whereas in Scotland the rights of a beneficiary have been characterised as being personal (*in personam*), meaning that they are more analogous to contractual rights than they are to property rights.[6] Moreover, trusts in England are subject to the provisions of the Trustee Act 2000, which updates the statutory regulation of investment powers contained in the Trustee Investment Act 1961 (TIA 1961).[7] The 2000 Act does not, however, apply to Scotland where statutory regulation of trustees' investment powers remains based on the TIA 1961.

[3] *Cowan v Scargill* [1984] 2 All ER 750, 763 per Sir Robert Megarry VC. See generally G Moffat, 'Pension Funds: A Fragmentation of Trust Law' (1993) 56 *MLR* 471.

[4] See ss 36 and 37 of the Trustee Act 2000.

[5] See below for more detail on investment powers.

[6] See G Moffat, *Trusts Law Text and Materials*, 3rd edn (London, Butterworths, 1999), ch 1 on England and W Wilson and A Duncan, *Trusts, Trustees and Executors* (Edinburgh, W Green, 1995) ch 1 on Scotland. See Ch 1 for an explanation of the differences between real and personal rights in the law of property.

[7] See s 40 of and sch 2 to the Trustee Act 2000 for details of changes made by the Act to the TIA 1961 in England and Wales.

Trustees have to consider the implications of the FSMA 2000 for their activities. In principle, they could be regarded as falling within a number of regulated activities such as dealing in investments as principal (as they are the legal owners of the investments held in trust), arranging deals in investments, managing investments and safeguarding and administering investments. However, as the scope of FSMA 2000 extends only to regulated activity carried on by way of business, the Regulated Activities Order (RAO)[8] makes clear that trustees who do not carry on these activities by way of business do not require authorisation, provided that they are not paid for these activities in addition to any payments received as trustee.[9] It follows that trustees who provide and charge for services such as fund management or dealing cannot be exempt from authorisation whereas trustees who act only as trustees are exempt even if they do from time to time engage in activity falling within the scope of FSMA 2000.

Professional trustees who are authorised under FSMA 2000 also need to consider the implications of regulatory rules made under the Act. This issue arises when services additional to trusteeship are provided to the trust. In these circumstances, an authorised firm will be required to categorise the trust as either an intermediate or private customer, thereby triggering the application of the relevant Conduct of Business Rules (COBs). This relationship between authorised firm and customer provides an additional layer of protection to the beneficiaries but is probably best viewed as providing little in the way of substantive protection for the beneficiaries that is not already provided by the fiduciary duty owed by the trustee. In the case of professional trustees who are exempt from authorisation as members of a recognised professional body,[10] the FSA's COBs are not applicable, but there are usually professional rules relating to such services.

The starting point for determining the investment powers of trustees is the trust deed. The statutory provisions relating to investment powers[11] are default provisions, meaning that they take effect subject to any contrary provision in the trust deed (eg restricting or expanding the statutory investment powers) or relevant legislation. Most trust deeds make express provision regarding the investment powers of trustees with the result that the statutory default provisions apply to a relatively small number of trusts, such as those that arise on intestacy.[12] Nevertheless, as these statutory powers form the backdrop against which express powers evolved, it is worthwhile considering them.

---

[8] The RAO (SI 2001/544) defines the scope of the FSMA 2000 system of regulation by reference to 'specified activities' and 'specified investments'. See generally Ch 3.

[9] Art 66 of the RAO.

[10] See Ch 3.3.3 for an explanation of the authorisation regime applicable to the professions.

[11] Those contained in the Trustee Act 2000 and (in Scotland) the Trustee Investment Act 1961.

[12] See G Moffat (above n 6 p 369) for an example of a model investment clause.

5.1.1 Statutory powers of investment

In England, the default provisions contained in the Trustee Act 2000 have relaxed the restrictions that previously applied under the Trustee Investment Act 1961 (TIA 1961) considerably. The rationale for this relaxation is mainly the change in perception of investment risk that has resulted from the application of modern portfolio theory. The common law and the Trustee Act 1925 had taken a cautious approach to the investment powers of trustees by defining a range of 'authorised investments' which excluded equity investments. Underlying this approach was a perception that the interests of beneficiaries were best served by requiring trustees to invest in fixed interest securities and by prohibiting speculation in equities.

Two main factors contributed to a change in approach, leading to the authorisation of equity investment by the TIA 1961. One was the realisation that beneficiaries holding fixed interest securities were under threat from inflation and that they could be protected from this risk by holding equities. Another factor was the realisation that a diversified equity portfolio considerably reduced the risk associated with holding individual shares.[13] The upshot was that the TIA 1961 authorised equity investment for the first time but did so in a manner that initially restricted it to 50 per cent of the fund, a limit that was later increased to 75 per cent.[14]

The central provision of the Trustee Act 2000 is that a trustee can make any kind of investment that he could make if he were absolutely entitled to the assets of the trust.[15] This is referred to as 'the general power of investment'. It can be expanded or restricted by specific provisions in the trust deed. In exercising any investment power, a trustee must have regard to the standard investment criteria contained in the Act. They are:

- the suitability to the trust of investment of the same kind as any particular investment proposed to be made or retained and of that particular investment as an investment of that kind, and
- the need for diversification of the trust, so far as is appropriate to the circumstances of the trust.

Before exercising any investment power a trustee must normally take professional advice, other than in circumstances in which the trustee concludes that in all the circumstances it is unnecessary or inappropriate to do so. These

---

[13] See Ch 1.1 regarding risk and diversification.

[14] The Trustee Investments (Division of Trust Fund) Order 1996, SI 1996/845, made under s 13 of the TIA 1961.

[15] s 3. A similar provision is contained in s 34(1) of the Pensions Act 1995.

provisions apply to trusts whether created before or after commencement of the Act. The effect is to apply the new powers to all trusts except those containing express restrictions or those excluded from the relevant provision (eg pension trusts).

In Scotland, the default provisions are still those contained in the TIA 1961. This Act divides investments into three categories, according to risk:

(a) Narrower-range investments not requiring advice. This comprises deposits and various government-backed bonds.

(b) Narrower-range investments requiring advice. This comprises primarily UK government fixed interest securities, company debentures, local authority loans and mortgages.

(c) Wider range investments (requiring advice). This comprises mainly shares in UK companies and units in unit trusts. Company shares are eligible for investment only if the following conditions are met:[16]
   (i)   the company is incorporated in the UK
   (ii)   the shares are listed on a recognised stock exchange
   (iii) the shares are fully paid up or required to be fully paid up within nine months of issue
   (iv)   the company must have total paid up and issued capital of not less than £1 million
   (v)   the company must have paid a dividend on all ranking shares in each of the preceding five years.

Excluded from the list of authorised investments under the Act are land and buildings and life assurance policies.

It is only possible to invest in wider range investments under the TIA if the fund is first split into two parts. The Act originally required the split to be into two equal parts but that was changed in 1996 when the Treasury exercised its power to increase the proportion of the fund available for wider range investments to 75 per cent.[17] This has the effect that a split of the fund is now required to be in the proportion 75 : 25 rather than the 50 : 50 split originally required by the Act. The TIA stipulated that a fund could only be split once, but a further split is permitted to take advantage of the higher proportion of wider-range investments permitted by the Treasury order. Following division of the fund, there is no requirement that the wider-range part of the fund be invested in wider-range investments: division simply opens up this option and leaves the trustees free to invest the wider-range fund in narrow-range investments (but not vice versa).

---

[16] s 1 and sch 1 pts III and IV TIA 1961.
[17] SI 1996/845 (above n 14).

The result of the 'once and for all' approach to division of the trust fund into narrow- and-wider range investment components is that differences in investment performance over time may result in substantial changes in the relative value of each part of the fund. No provision is made for adjustment after such changes in relative values. Accruals to the investments held in the fund (such as dividend or interest or bonus shares) belong to the part of the fund in which the relevant investment is held. Additions to the trust fund (eg from the trustee/settlor) must be divided according to the proportions in which the fund is split (ie 50 : 50 or 75 : 25).

5.1.2 Express investment clauses

Most trust deeds provide trustees with express investment powers that are wider than the default statutory powers discussed above. The main issue that arises in these circumstances is to determine the meaning and scope of the relevant clause(s) in the trust deed. An important issue is the meaning of 'investment' for the purposes of such clauses, especially when the trust deed does not specify the type of investment that it permitted. Where it does specify an investment, there can be no question of the power being interpreted so as to exclude that type of investment. Where it does not, it has been observed that the term 'invest' implies an income yield, thus ruling out non-income producing property (eg derivatives, zero dividend preference shares).[18]

In the nineteenth century the Chancery court in England adopted a restrictive approach by developing the concept of 'authorised investments' to which trustees were restricted.[19] In 1882, for example, a clause authorising trustees to invest 'on such securities as they might think fit' was taken merely to give discretion to select from such authorised investments.[20] However, a more liberal approach was developed in the twentieth century as the courts gave effect to clauses which clearly intended that trustees should enjoy investment powers extending beyond authorised investments. For example in *Re Wragg*, investment in land was approved under a clause which did not expressly authorise investment in land but clearly intended the trustees to have absolute

---

[18] See *Re Power* [1947] Ch 572, holding that an express power in a will trust to invest in any manner that the trustee thought fit as if he were the beneficial owner did not authorise the purchase of a house for the testator's widow to live in. The rationale was that such as purchase was for some other purpose than the receipt of income. The decision was criticised by the Law Commissions (below n 26 p 134) on the basis that a beneficiary's possession or occupation is equivalent to receipt of rental income.

[19] See Moffat (above n 6 at p 366). This approach was later adopted in the statutory provisions relating to trustees' investment powers.

[20] See *Re Braithwaite* (1852) 21 Ch 121.

discretion.[21] Moreover, although the general rule is that express provisions in trust deeds that expand trustees' powers of investment beyond those author- ised by law will be strictly construed, it has been recognised that this does not require a court to take an unduly restrictive approach to particular investment clasues.[22]

There may be circumstances in which both express investment powers and the statutory powers apply to a trust. This could arise for example where a trustee is expressly authorised to invest a specific proportion of the fund in land or shares in private companies (which are not authorised investments under the TIA 1961). In Scotland, where the TIA 1961 is still in force, the bal- ance of the fund not subject to the special power would have to be invested according to the TIA. Property subject to special powers such as the express power referred to above, is 'special range property' under the TIA 1961 and must be carried to a separate part of the fund.[23] In England, the balance of the fund would be invested according to the 'general investment power' of the Trustee Act 2000 (above), with the result that trustees have greater freedom than in Scotland.

5.1.3 Delegation of investment powers

Trustees must determine whether and to what extent they can delegate their powers. This is normally dealt with by the express terms of the trust deed. If it is not, there is a power to delegate asset management functions in England under the Trustee Act 2000.[24] This power is subject to the requirement that the trustees prepare a policy statement relating to the exercise of those powers and that the agent agrees to comply with this statement.[25] When delegation occurs under this power it may relate to any or all of the trustees' investment powers and the 'duty of care' required by section 1 of the Act applies to the selection of the agent. The terms on which a trustee in England may delegate investment management functions are governed by the Trustee Act 2000. Unless it is reasonably necessary for them to do so,[26] such terms cannot allow a term

---

[21] [1919] 2 Ch 58. The clause permitted investments

    of whatever nature and wheresoever as his trustees should in their absolute and uncon- trolled discretion think fit to the intent that they should have the same full and unrestricted powers of investing as if they were absolutely entitled to the trust money beneficially.

[22] *Re Peczenik's Settlement, Cole and Another v Ingram and Others* [1964] 2 All ER 339.

[23] s 3(3) and sch 2 TIA 1961. See Wilson and Duncan (above n 5) pp 416–18.

[24] s 11.

[25] Trustee Act 2000, s 15.

[26] The Law Commissions' Report (no 260, Scottish Law Commission no 172) *Trustees' Powers and Duties* noted (at p 32) that it would often be necessary for this to occur when asset manage- ment is delegated to a discretionary fund manager as the standard terms of business of fund managers commonly permit delegation.

(a) permitting the agent to appoint a substitute, (b) restricting the liability of the agent or (c) permitting the agent to act in circumstances capable of giving rise to a conflict of interest.[27]

The Trustee Act 2000 power does not extend to Scotland, where delegation, in the absence of an express power, must fall within the default statutory power contained in the Trusts (Sc) Act 1921[28] or the common-law principle permitting delegation in certain circumstances. While it is clear that the Trustee Act 2000 authorises delegation of the trustees' discretion in making investment decisions, it is not entirely clear that that the statutory or common law rules in Scotland have this effect. The general principle in Scots law is that a trustee is entitled to delegate duties entrusted to him in circumstances in which a person of reasonable prudence dealing with his own affairs would do so.[29] Moreover, there is authority for the proposition that trustees must employ suitable agents when they themselves lack the appropriate skills or qualifications.[30] As a matter of good practice it is nevertheless preferable to assume that this form of delegation must be expressly authorised in Scotland.[31]

The liability of trustees for the acts of an agent is governed in England by the Trustee Act 2000 and Trustee Act 1925 and in Scotland by the common law.[32] A distinction can be made between the selection and supervision of an agent. In England, the 'general duty of care' mentioned above applies to selection of an agent by a trustee. In Scotland, the common law imposes a similar requirement.[33] As regards supervision of the agent, the Trustee Act 1925 in England discharges the trustee from liability other than in cases where loss arises from the wilful default of the trustee. This provision does not apply to Scotland, where supervision of agents is subject to the same common law duty of care as applies to selection of agents.[34] This means that in Scotland a trustee can be liable for careless selection of an agent (eg an investment manager) and/or careless supervision.

---

[27] Trustee Act 2000 s 14.

[28] s 4(1)(f) of the Act authorises trustees to appoint factors and law agents and to pay them suitable remuneration. On the meaning of 'factors' see *Mills v Brown's Trs* (1900) 2 F 1035.

[29] *Hay v Binny* (1861) 23 D 594.

[30] See D Walker, *Principles of Scottish Private Law*, 4th edn (Oxford, OUP, 1988–89) vol IV pp 44–45.

[31] As suggested at p 369 of Wilson and Duncan (above n 6).

[32] In each case, the rules differ to those found in the context of delegation by an agent who is not a trustee, where the agent assumes full responsibility for the actions of the sub-agent. See generally *Fridman's Law of Agency*, 7th edn (London, Butterworths, 1996) and, in respect of Scotland, F Davidson and L MacGregor, *Commercial Law in Scotland* (Edinburgh, W Green, 2003) ch 2.

[33] *Carruthers v Carruthers* (1896) 23 R (HL) 55.

[34] See *Carruthers, ibid*.

5.1.4 Trustees' powers to employ nominees and custodians

The position in England prior to the Trustee Act 2000 was that, in the absence of an express power in the trust instrument or an express statutory exception, trustees could neither vest trust property in nominees[35] nor place trust documents in the custody of a custodian—to do so would result in a breach of trust.[36] Two statutory exceptions were relevant:

(a) Section 21 of the Trustee Act 1925 empowers trustees to deposit any documents held by them relating to the trust, or to the trust property, with any banker or banking company, or any other company whose business includes the undertaking of the safe custody of documents.

(b) Under section 7(1) of the same Act, trustees have a statutory duty to deposit bearer securities with a banker or banking company for the purposes of safe custody and the collection of income. There is no similar statutory duty in respect of any other form of trust property.

The Law Commissions regarded these rules as being unduly restrictive for trustees. In particular, they did not allow for legal title to assets to be vested in a nominee unless there was an express power to do so. The default rule was that legal title had to be held in joint names so that the consent of all trustees was required for transfer. This posed particular problems following the dematerialisation of title to securities traded through the CREST system (as well as similar overseas systems) because that system was designed on the basis that nominees would normally hold legal title on behalf of investors.[37]

The result was that the Law Commissions recommended that the law be changed. In so doing, they recognised that the use of nominees and custodians posed risks in respect of fraud and loss of shareholders' rights. The fraud risk arises from the loss of (legal) ownership and control of trust assets on the part of trustees while the loss of shareholders' rights arises from the principle that rights (eg to vote at company meetings or receive dividends) follow legal ownership.[38] The Trustee Act 2000 introduced default powers enabling trustees to appoint nominees and custodians.[39] Unlike the position in respect of delegation of investment powers to fund managers, there is no requirement that the

---

[35] Nominees are trustees whose only function is to hold legal title to assets.

[36] See Law Commission Report No 260 (above n 26) at p 160, citing *Browne v Butter* (1857) 24 Beav 159, 161, 162; 53 ER 317, 318, *per* Romilly MR. The rationale underlying the law is that trustees are bound to preserve the trust fund under their own control.

[37] On dematerialisation and the CREST system, see Chs 4 and 9.

[38] Under s 22 of the Companies Act 1985, it is the registered holder of a share who is *prima facie* entitled to exercise the rights of a member (shareholder) of the company. See, regarding the rights of investors when shares are registered in the name of a nominee, R Nolan, 'Indirect Investors: A Greater Say in the Company' (2003) 3 *Journal of Corporate Law Studies* 73.

[39] ss 16 and 17.

nominee or custodian be authorised to conduct investment business under FSMA 2000. The rationale for this is that the FSMA system of regulation does not extend to all cases in which it would be appropriate for trustees to employ nominees and custodians.[40]

The position in Scotland regarding the employment of nominees and custodians is less clear as the Law Commissions' recommendations have not been implemented.[41] The analysis presented above in respect of delegation of investment powers is equally applicable here, with the result that it is preferable for the power to employ nominees and custodians to be granted expressly by the trust deed.

5.1.5 Investment strategy and selection

When there has been no delegation of the asset management function, the trustees must take account of the relevant law relating to the manner in which they should determine investment strategy and make individual investment decisions. Depending on the terms of the trust[42], the relevant law can be the common law or the statutory powers of investment contained in the Trustee Act 2000 in England or the TIA 1961 in Scotland. The same law will be relevant in circumstances in which an agent has been delegated discretionary investment powers by trustees, as in these circumstances, the agent stands in the shoes of the trustee.

In principle, a distinction can be made between investment strategy (or asset allocation) and selection of individual investments.[43] Investment strategy (sometimes referred to as asset allocation) involves making decisions as to what type of assets to hold. It involves choices between different types of security (eg equities vs fixed interest securities), different currencies in which securities are denominated and different types of business risk (eg across different business sectors). In principle it is a separate process from the selection of individual investments within the parameters set by the investment strategy. Both strategy and selection may be limited by trustees' powers of investment, but even within relatively narrow powers it is possible for the distinction to remain meaningful as the trustees may choose to ignore a permitted category

---

[40] An example would be a nominee who holds land, which does not fall within the scope of FSMA 2000.

[41] The leading text on trusts in Scotland (Wilson and Duncan, above n 65) makes no reference to the possibility of legal title being held other than jointly by the trustees (see pp 21 and 359).

[42] See above re express and default (statutory) powers of investment.

[43] See generally the Myners Report (*Institutional Investment in the United Kingdom: A Review*, 2001, available at www.hm-treasury.gov.uk (8 Nov 2004)) ch 13, 'Investment Decision-Making by Trustees'.

of investment. It is likely in most circumstances that both strategy and selection will have a material influence on the performance of the fund.[44]

The legal principles encompass both aspects of investment management, although the focus has been much more on selection than on strategy. The legal principles derive from the duty of care owed by trustees to beneficiaries in exercising their investment powers. The standard of care required to discharge that duty is that of the 'ordinary prudent man of business'. It has been described as follows:[45]

> Business men of ordinary prudence may, and frequently do, select investments which are more or less of a speculative character; but it is the duty of a trustee to confine himself to the class of investments which are permitted by the trust, and likewise to avoid all investments of that class which are attended with hazard.

In *Bartlett v Barclays Bank Trust Co Ltd*[46] it was held that a corporate professional trustee owed a higher standard of care to beneficiaries than did other (ie individual non-corporate) trustees. Such trustees are required to show the skill and experience that they profess to have as professional trust managers. Precisely how this differs from the standard of the 'ordinary prudent man of business' is not entirely clear, nor is it obvious why trustees who are paid professionals (eg a solicitor) are excluded from the ambit of the enhanced duty that applies to trust corporations.[47] The Trustee Act 2000 has modified that principle as far as English law is concerned. It requires trustees acting under its powers to exercise such care and skill as is reasonable in the circumstances, having regard in particular—

> (a) to any special knowledge or experience that he has or holds himself out as having; and (b) if he acts as a trustee in the course of a business or profession, to any special knowledge or experience that it is reasonable to expect of a person acting in the course of that kind of business or profession.[48]

---

[44] See the Sandler Report (*Medium and Long-Term Retail Savings in the UK*, July 2002 available at www.hm-treasury.gov.uk (11 Nov 2004)) p 127.

[45] *Learoyd v Whiteley* (1887) 12 App Cas 727 at 733 per Lord Watson. In that case a mortgage on a freehold brickfield, which was *prima facie* within the investment powers of the trustees, was held to be a breach of trust on the basis that the particular property was a wasting asset and therefore hazardous. A similar approach was adopted in Scotland in the case of *Raes v Meek* (1889) 16 R (HL) 31. See J Chalmers, *Trusts, Cases and Materials* (Edinburgh, W Green, 2002) p 173 for a comparative analysis of the English and Scots law formulations of the standard of care required on the part of trustees.

[46] [1980] 1 All ER 139.

[47] See generally Moffat (above n 6) pp 383–4. The Law Commissions' Report *Trustees' Powers and Duties* (above n 26) regarded the higher standard as being applicable to 'remunerated and professional' trustees (see para 2.15). It also noted that there was some doubt over whether remunerated trustees in Scotland are subject to a higher standard of diligence and knowledge (p 26): see para 9.08 of Chalmers (above n 45) on this point.

[48] s 1.

This clearly brings paid professionals other than trust corporations within the scope of the enhanced duty as regards the exercise of the Trustee Act 2000 powers but the common law (above) remains applicable to the exercise of express powers.

An element of the basic duty of care owed by any trustee to beneficiaries is to take advice in appropriate circumstances.[49] This duty arises under both statutory powers and the common law. The common law requires a trustee to take advice on matters that the trustee does not understand, to consider the advice and act on it in accordance with the standard of the 'ordinary prudent man of business'.[50] This involves the exercise of judgment. A trustee (or an agent exercising the powers of a trustee) cannot hide behind advice as a means of avoiding consideration of whether a particular course of action is in the best interests of the beneficiaries. In England, the Trustee Act 2000 follows this approach, requiring trustees to take advice except where they conclude that in all the circumstances it is not necessary.[51] In Scotland, the TIA 1961 requires trustees to take advice in respect of narrower-range investments requiring advice and wider-range investments.

When exercising any power of investment, trustees are required to have regard to the 'standard investment criteria' established by the Trustee Act 2000.[52] They are that the investments should be suitable for the trust and should be diversified. The suitability obligation requires trustees to consider characteristics of investments such as risk, duration and liquidity, by reference to the trust purposes. A trustee will be liable for breach of trust in the event that unsuitable investments are selected and cause loss to the trust.[53]

The purpose of diversification is to reduce the overall risk associated with the fund.[54] Risk can be categorised for investment purposes as being either market risk or specific risk. Market risk describes the risk arising from movements in the general level of the market in a particular class of investment. Specific risk describes the risk arising from a particular investment, such as the risk of insolvency making a share worthless. While in the main market risk cannot be avoided, specific risk can be reduced through diversification, which,

---

[49] The Law Commissions' Report *Trustees' Powers and Duties* (above n 26 at p 23) noted that 'appropriate circumstances' would depend upon a number of variables, including the size, nature and purpose of the particular trust, the composition of its investment portfolio and the skills and experience of the trustees. The report also notes that modern trust deeds do not generally oblige a trustee to take advice before exercising an express power of investment, however wide (p 24).

[50] *Cowan v Scargill* [1984] 2 All ER 750 at 752 per Megarry V-C.

[51] s 5.

[52] s 4. In Scotland, these criteria are contained in s 6(1) of the TIA 1961, which applies to all trustees.

[53] *Target Holdings v Redferns* [1996] 1 AC 421.

[54] See Ch 1 regarding risk.

by spreading risk across a number of holdings limits the effect of specific risk on the fund as a whole.

The importance of diversification is recognised by statutory requirements in both England and Scotland that extend to any exercise of investment powers, whether under express powers or statutory default powers. In Scotland, the TIA 1961 provides that a trustee exercising any investment power must consider the need for diversification in so far as it is appropriate to the circumstances of the trust. In England, the TA 2000 requires diversification in the same manner as part of the standard investment criteria that apply when a trustee is exercising any investment power.

Diversification gives rise to a further problem. It is the issue of the liability of trustees who have diversified the fund but have fallen short of the growth that could have been achieved had the fund been invested in different proportions in the relevant asset classes. In other words, are trustees liable for a short-fall in relative performance against comparable funds[55], and if so for what are they liable? The matter was considered in *Nestlé v National Westminster Bank plc.*[56] The plaintiff alleged that a combination of failure on part of the trustees to understand their investment powers and to review the performance of the fund led to the beneficiary suffering a loss in excess of the value of the fund. The plaintiff was unable to prove the loss and therefore the case failed. The case suggests that it will be very difficult to attach liability to a trustee in circumstances in which relative performance falls short of comparable funds in the absence of some other failing, such as failing to take advice or to conduct periodic reviews. The following extracts from the judgments in that case contribute to this conclusion:

> Of course it is not a breach of trust to invest a trust fund in such a manner that its real value is not maintained. At times that will be impossible, at others it will require extraordinary skill or luck.[57]

> The trustees' performance must not be judged with hindsight: after the event even a fool is wise, as a poet said 3000 years ago.[58]

> The starting point must, in my judgment, be that as the plaintiff is claiming compensation, the onus remains on her to prove that she has suffered loss because from 1922 to 1960 the equities in the annuity fund were not diversified.[59]

[55] This issue becomes particularly relevant when a fund manager has a mandate to manage on the basis of a 'peer group total fund benchmark'. In this situation the manager is responsible for both strategy and selection and his performance is measured against what is believed to be a relevant peer group (normally other funds managed under a similar mandate). See generally the Myners Report (above n 43) ch 2, 'Pension Funds: the Context for Investment Decision-Making'.

[56] The first instance decision was handed down in June 1988 but only belatedly reported in (1996) 10 *Trust Law International* 112. The Court of Appeal decision is reported at [1993] 1 WLR 1260.

[57] Staughton LJ at 1275.

[58] Staughton LJ at 1276.

[59] Dillon LJ at 1269.

Another important issue for trustees is the extent to which they can take account of considerations other than financial return when exercising their investment powers. This issue arises mainly when ethical or political considerations influence investment decisions. In *Cowan v Scargill*,[60] the issue was whether the trustees of a pension scheme for mineworkers could exercise their power of investment so as to prohibit future investment overseas, require the sale of existing overseas investment and prohibit investment in energies in direct competition with coal. The court held that the trustees could not act in that way as it was inconsistent with their fiduciary duty to act in the best interests of the beneficiaries, which was normally their best financial interest. It was recognised that there could be cases[61] where other considerations could coincide with the best financial interest of the beneficiaries, but they could not take priority to that interest. A similar approach was adopted in *Martin v City of Edinburgh District Council*,[62] a case involving sale by trustees of shares with a South African interest following the adoption of an anti-apartheid policy by Edinburgh District Council. It was held that the members of the council as trustees had not applied their minds separately and specifically to the question whether the changes in investments would be in the best interests of the beneficiaries of the trusts.

In *Harries v The Church Commissioners for England*[63] the court was required to review the investment policy of trustees (the commissioners) in respect of South Africa as well as the compatibility of that policy with basic Christian values. It was held that the trustees were entitled to follow an ethical policy that precluded investment in South African companies or other companies with more than a small part of their business in South Africa. It was stressed, however, that financial return must be the main criterion for trustee investments and that 'the circumstances in which trustees are bound or entitled to make a financially disadvantageous investment decision for ethical reasons are extremely limited.'[64] It is, of course, a different matter when trustees are specifically authorised to take account of non-financial considerations, as occurs when trust funds are established on an 'ethical' basis.[65]

---

[60] [1984] 2 All ER 750.

[61] The court referred to the US case of *Withers v Teachers' Retirement System of the City of New York* 447 F Supp 1248 (1978), where a pension fund bought bonds issued by the City of New York as part of a strategy of ensuring continuation of the City's contributions to the (unfunded) pension scheme.

[62] 1988 SLT 329.

[63] [1992] 1 WLR 1241.

[64] *Ibid* at 1250.

[65] See generally on ethical funds, N Kreander, 'An Analysis of European Ethical Funds' Association of Chartered Certified Accountants publication ACCA/ORP 33/001.

5.1.6 Exclusion of trustees' liability

If trustees have failed to discharge the duties outlined above, they are in breach of trust and will be liable in damages to the beneficiaries for loss resulting from the breach. However, it may be that the trust deed exempts the trustees from liability in defined circumstances. The common law in both Scotland and England allows a trust deed to do this. The authorities were recently reviewed in England in the case of *Armitage v Nurse*,[66] in which a widely drawn clause exempted the trustees from liability other than in cases involving 'actual fraud'. It was argued that such a clause could not be given effect because it was contrary to public policy to allow such a wide exemption in the context of a relationship of trust. This argument was rejected in favour of an approach analogous to that in contract, with the result that any exemption clause other than in respect of fraud is acceptable and the role of the court is essentially to determine the meaning of the exemption. The position was explained as follows:[67]

> In my judgment clause 15 exempts the trustee from liability for loss or damage to the trust property no matter how indolent, imprudent, lacking in diligence, negligent or wilful he may have been, so long as he has not acted dishonestly.

It was also noted in this case that the Scottish authorities supported a similar conclusion in respect of the scope and validity of exemption clauses under Scots law.[68]

The Trustee Act 2000 does not alter the position in respect of exclusion of trustees' liability as the duty of care created by the Act is not a mandatory rule. The possibility of exclusion of the duty in whole or part is referred to expressly in the Act.[69] The position differs in respect of trustees of occupational pension schemes,[70] trustees of issues of debentures[71] and trustees of unit trusts,[72] all of whom are subject to statutory limitations in respect of the validity of exclusion clauses.

---

[66] [1998] Ch 241.

[67] Millet J at 251.

[68] Reference was made to *Knox v Mackinnon* (1888) 13 AC 753 and *Raes v Meek* (1889) 16 R (HL) 33. The Scottish Law Commission, however, are of the view that it is not possible under Scots law to exclude the liability of trustees in respect of gross negligence (*culpa lata*): see para 3.16 of the Scottish Law Commission Discussion Paper No 123, *Discussion Paper on Breach of Trust* (2003).

[69] See s 1 and sch 1 para 7.

[70] See s 33 of the Pensions Act 1995.

[71] Companies Act 1985 s 192(1). See Ch 4 for an explanation of debentures.

[72] FSMA 2000 s 253. See Ch 4 for an explanation of unit trusts.

5.2 Contract

Many institutional investors manage funds under management contracts, even when the legal structure under which the investment fund is structured is that of trust. For example, a fund manager who is awarded a mandate to manage a pension fund for a certain period will normally enter into a management contract with the trustees. Subject to the general law of contract, restrictions arising under trust law and obligations arising from the FSA's regulatory rules, the parties to such an agreement are free to agree whatever terms they wish.[73]

Contracts may also have implications for the manner in which ownership rights, and particularly the right to vote, are exercised. In many instances, legal title to investments such as shares is held by an investment manager rather than by the ultimate investor. This results in the investment manager having the right to vote on resolutions at a company meeting. It is possible, however, for voting rights to be passed down to the ultimate (or indirect) investor by contractual agreement.[74] This can take the form of an agreement between the investment manager and ultimate investor that the former will appoint the latter as proxy in respect of the shares, with discretion as to how the votes attached to the shares should be cast.[75]

The impact of the general law of contract and trusts on investment management agreements depends on the parties to the contract. Each of the three main types of contractual relationship found in institutional investment can be considered separately.

5.2.1 Trustees and investment managers[76]

This is the type of relationship under which the larger pension funds are normally managed. In principle, trustees are free to make whatever bargain they wish with investment managers, subject to the limitations mentioned above in respect of delegation of investment powers and contract terms that

---

[73] The general law of contract contains some restrictions on freedom of contract (eg contracts to commit a crime are unenforceable) but none are directly relevant to investment management agreements.

[74] See J Nolan, 'Indirect Investors: A Greater Say in the Company' (2003) 3 *Journal of Corporate Law Studies* 73.

[75] As a registered shareholder always has a right to appoint a proxy under s 372 of the Companies Act 1985, such an agreement provides an on-going mechanism for votes to be passed down to the ultimate investor. The position becomes more complicated when there is a chain of indirect ownership, but the same mechanism can be employed within the extended chain.

[76] This category includes pension fund trustees, and the trustees of unit trusts.

exclude liability on the part of trustees. Neither the Unfair Contract Terms Act 1977 nor the Unfair Terms in Consumer Contracts Regulations 1999, which apply mainly to contracts between a business and a private individual, regulate the terms of such contracts. Over time, the standard terms of these contracts have changed.[77] In the 1980s most funds were managed on a 'balanced' basis. This type of contract involved a single fund-manager being given responsibility for the entire portfolio of a pension fund, including both asset allocation and stock selection. Contracts would specify an objective of outperforming or being in the top quartile of a peer group of funds ('peer group benchmarking') and provision would be made for performance to be evaluated by independent consultants. By the mid 1990s balanced mandates were seen to have produced disappointing results and the focus shifted to employing specialist managers for asset allocation and different asset classes.

5.2.2 Insurers and policyholders

The contractual relationship between an insurer and a policyholder is not, strictly speaking, an investment management agreement but a contract of long-term insurance. However, it is appropriate to consider it here as it is the mechanism under which insurers hold the funds that they manage. Such contracts are not subject to the Unfair Contract Terms Act 1977 but may be subject to the Unfair Terms in Consumer Contracts Regulations 1999.[78] Insurers are also subject to Principle 6 of the FSA's Principles for Businesses, which requires that an authorised person treat customers fairly. This is particularly important in contracts (such as with-profits insurance) in which considerable discretion is given to the insurer.[79]

5.2.3 Unit trusts and investment companies with variable capital (ICVCs)

The contractual arrangements under which the investments of unit trusts and ICVCs are managed reflects their legal structure and in particular the legal ownership of the investments. In the case of unit trusts, legal ownership rests with the trustees and they are entitled to delegate responsibility for investment management. In principle they are free to make whatever arrangements they

---

[77] See the Myners Report (above n 43) p 75.

[78] The manner in which the regulations apply to insurance is complex: they do not apply to the main terms of the contract (often referred to as the core terms) or to the price (premium) but may apply to the remainder of the contract. See N Legh-Jones (ed) *MacGillivray on Insurance Law* (London, Sweet & Maxwell, 2003) para 10.18.

[79] See Ch 4.10 for a discussion of this issue.

consider appropriate subject to the limitations imposed by trust law in respect of delegation (5.1.3 above) and exclusion clauses (5.1.6 above). Investments held by an ICVC are owned by the company, which is a separate entity from its shareholders. The legal structure of an ICVC makes provision for the management of investments, which is the responsibility of the authorised corporate director, with the result that there is no need for a separate investment management agreement with an external manager. In the case of both unit trusts and ICVCs, investment management is also subject to a substantial body of regulatory rules contained in the Collective Investment Scheme (CIS) part of the FSA Handbook.[80] These regulatory rules take precedence over contractual arrangements and cannot be excluded by contract.

5.3 Self-regulation

There are a number of organisations through which institutional shareholders can co-ordinate their activity and promote their interests as shareholders. The members of the Institutional Shareholders' Committee are particularly influential. They are:

The Association of British Insurers (ABI)

The ABI is a trade body which represents the interests of its members, who are engaged in all forms of insurance business. As insurance, and in particular life assurance, involves holding and investing substantial funds accumulated from premiums (as well as shareholders' capital), insurers occupy an important position as investors in bonds and equities.[81]

The National Association of Pension Funds (NAPF)

The National Association of Pension Funds is the principal UK body representing the interests of the employer-sponsored pensions movement. Among its members are both large and small companies, local authority and public sector bodies.[82] NAPF members also include the leading businesses providing professional services to pension funds, such as consultancy, actuarial, legal, trustee, administration, IT and investment services.

The Investment Management Association (IMA)

The Investment Management Association represents the UK unit trust and investment management industry. It acts as a trade body to promote its

---

[80] See generally Ch 4.9.

[81] See the Myners Report (above n 43 p 27) for a table showing the ownership distribution of UK equities.

[82] Together they provide pensions for over 10 million employees and 5 million people in retirement, and account for more than £600 billion of pension fund assets.

members' interests to government and regulators and to promote the general principle of investing through collective funds to the general public. The IMA was formed on 1 February 2002 when the Association of Unit Trusts and Investment Funds (AUTIF) and the Fund Managers Association (FMA) merged to establish a new association.

The Association of Investment Trust Companies (AITC)
The AITC is the non-profit making trade body of the investment trust industry and was formed in 1932. It represents investment trust companies and their shareholders but also works closely with the management groups that administer the companies. The individual trusts provide funding for AITC, and its activities are focused on providing value to them and their shareholders (eg by promoting the benefits of investment trusts to the public).

An example of the work of the Institutional Shareholders' Committee is the Statement of Principles dealing with the responsibilities of institutional shareholders and agents, which provides a framework within which institutional shareholders will carry out their responsibilities within investee companies.[83] The purpose of the Statement is to ensure that institutional investors act in the best interests of ultimate investors (whose money they manage) in the manner in which they deal with investee companies.

The ABI and NAPF are particularly active in producing specific guidance for members on issues relating to institutional investment. They have for example formulated guidelines on share options and executive remuneration, shareholders' pre-emption rights and voting policy.[84] The dominant role of institutions in the ownership of investments in the UK means that these self-regulatory measures have *de facto* a similar status to formal legal measures. Institutional investors also play an important role in developing and enforcing the self-regulatory measures adopted in the fields of corporate governance and takeovers.

5.4 The FSMA 2000 regulatory system

Reference was made at the beginning of this chapter to the role of the FSMA 2000 system of regulation in controlling risks to which investors are exposed. Those risks are primarily management risk (arising from incompetent or fraudulent management) and investment risk (the assumption of risk beyond

---

[83] Document available from the ABI website—www.abi.org.uk (11 Nov 2004).
[84] See Chs 7 and 8 for more detail on these matters.

that which is appropriate for a particular fund).[85] The role of FSMA 2000 in controlling exposure to such risk is apparent both at the point of entry into regulated activity (permission and authorisation) and during the conduct of the activity.

While, for the purposes of this chapter, institutional investors are all regarded as being engaged in the activity of managing investments, which is itself an activity that requires permission under FSMA 2000, the reality is that the nature of the arrangements under which institutional investors become responsible for investment funds differs widely. For example, insurers manage investments primarily as a result of engaging in the business of insurance and require separate permission to engage in that activity. Banks may make investments as a way of earning a return on money that they hold as a result of engaging in the regulated activity of taking deposits. Both banks and insurers differ in this respect from professional fund managers who manage investments under agreements entered into with third parties who are the legal owners of the investments (eg pension fund trustees). The point here is that for the purposes of authorisation under the FSMA system of regulation, what is routinely termed 'institutional investment' in the financial literature comprises a range of separate and quite distinct activities. This aspect is developed further in section 5.5 below, in which the legal basis for different forms of institutional investment is discussed in more detail.

Once authorised, all forms of 'institutional investor' become subject to parts of the FSA Handbook that in principle extend to all forms of regulated activity. Of particular importance are the senior management arrangements, systems and controls[86] and the approved persons regime[87]. There are, however, parts of the FSA Handbook that apply only to particular types of institutional investor. For example, in the case of life assurance, the FSA's solvency rules have the effect of limiting the manner in which the life fund can be invested but these rules are not applicable to investment funds, which have their own rules. Thus, the regulatory position in respect of institutional investors is complex and is best approached from the perspective of the specific activity concerned.

---

[85] This follows the classification adopted by O Loistl and R Petrag in *Asset Management Standards* (Basingstoke, Palgrave MacMillan, 2003).

[86] See Ch 3

[87] See Ch 3.

5.5 Institutional investors by type

5.5.1 Insurance companies

The funds available for investment by insurance companies are derived from three main sources. First life funds, which comprise the premiums paid by policyholders and are available to meet claims on life policies. These funds can be organised on the with-profit or unit-linked basis.[88] Second, claims reserves relating to non-life policies. These are funds derived from premiums paid under non-life policies that have been allocated to the payment of claims. Third, in the case of shareholder-owned companies, shareholders' capital and reserves is available for investment. Mutual companies do not have shareholders and hence no shareholders' capital is available for investment, but there will normally be accumulated reserves. The policyholders of insurance companies (whether life or non-life) have no direct ownership interest in the investment funds of the insurer. This is true both of insurers organised as registered companies and as mutual organisations.[89] The claims of policyholders are entirely contractual. Policyholders who are members (ie shareholders in registered companies or members of mutual organisations) have no ownership rights in investment funds because the assets held in the fund are owned by the insurer, which is a separate legal person.[90]

Insurers are not subject to direct controls over their investments but there are indirect controls arising from the prudential supervision sourcebook applicable to insurers.[91] The Interim Prudential Sourcebook for Insurers (IPRU (INS)) requires insurers to secure that:[92]

    (a) liabilities under contracts of insurance are covered by assets of appropriate safety, yield and marketability having regard to the class of business carried on; and

    (b) investments are appropriately diversified and adequately spread so that excessive reliance is not placed on investments of any particular category or description.

---

[88] See Ch 4.10 for an explanation of these terms.

[89] See Ch 7 n 10 regarding the nature of mutual organisations.

[90] See re the legal personality point *Salomon v Salomon & Co Ltd* [1897] AC 22 and more generally on ownership and control rights GP Stapledon, *Institutional Shareholders and Corporate Governance* (Oxford, Clarendon Press, 1996).

[91] See generally H Patel, 'Financial Supervision', Ch 4 in J Young (ed) *A Practitioner's Guide to the FSA Regulation of Insurance* (Old Woking, City & Financial Publishing, 2002). For an historical account of the development of the regulation of insurance companies see ch 15 of *The Equitable Life Inquiry* (Penrose Report) available at www.hm-treasury.gov.uk (11 Nov 2004).

[92] FSA Handbook, IPRU (INS) rule 2.3.

It is a fundamental part of the approach to prudential regulation for insurers that the rules limit the assets which are 'admissible' for solvency purposes and prescribe the methods of valuation. The valuation rules adopt a cautious approach, focusing on realisable value in the short term. The admissibility rules have the effect of limiting over-exposure to particular types of asset or particular counterparties. They achieve this result by excluding from the solvency calculation any assets which do not satisfy the admissibility rules.

The collapse of Equitable Life during the 1990s prompted a re-appraisal of the effectiveness of the system of prudential supervision in protecting policyholders and meeting their reasonable expectations.[93] While the business and regulatory circumstances surrounding the collapse of Equitable Life are complex,[94] two points are of central significance. First, the financial failure arose from a mismatch between the returns promised by Equitable to policyholders on some products (in particular guaranteed annuities) and the returns that it was able to earn within the life fund in which the relevant premiums were invested.[95] That mismatch was built up over a considerable period of time and was exacerbated by falling interest rates in the mid-1990s following the United Kingdom's exit from the European exchange rate mechanism. Second, the regulatory arrangements for the supervision of life assurance companies underwent considerable change during the 1990s with responsibility for prudential supervision being transferred first from the Department of Trade and Industry (DTI) to the Treasury and then to the FSA. Moreover, during that time the Government Actuary's Department (GAD), whose responsibility was primarily the monitoring of the solvency of life assurance companies through scrutiny of the regulatory returns that are required to be submitted on an annual basis, operated separately from the prudential supervisors at the DTI and Treasury.[96]

The independent report[97] commissioned by the FSA into its role in the regulation of Equitable Life concluded that there were a number of matters in respect of which the Authority's performance could have been better, but the crucial finding was that by the time the FSA assumed responsibility for the prudential supervision of insurance (1 January 1999) the 'die was cast' and

[93] See Ch 4 for a discussion of the nature of life assurance contracts and the concept of policyholders' reasonable expectations.

[94] See Ch 19 paras 3–82 of the Penrose Report (*The Equitable Life Inquiry*, available at www.hm-treasury.gov.uk (11 Nov 2004)) for more details.

[95] In other words, the income from invested premiums did not match contractual liabilities to policyholders.

[96] The GAD was integrated into the FSA in April 2001.

[97] The Baird Report (*Report of the Financial Services Authority on the Review of the Regulation of the Equitable Life Assurance Society from 1 January 1999 to 8 December 2000, which Her Majesty's Government is submitting as Evidence to the Inquiry Conducted by Lord Penrose, House of Commons* no 244, 16 October 2001). The reporting team was led by the FSA's director of internal audit, Ronnie Baird.

there was nothing that the FSA could have done thereafter which would have mitigated, in any material way, the impact of the court case[98] or made any material beneficial difference to the final outcome. However, it soon became clear that the failure of Equitable Life would lead to a strengthening of the system of prudential supervision. This was made clear by the FSA in its report[99] to the Treasury regarding implementation of the recommendations contained in the Baird Report. The FSA promised that 'the insurance industry will be subject to more proactive and challenging regulation than it has experienced up to now'.[100] This was followed in August 2003 by proposals to strengthen the capital requirements for life insurers.[101] The focus of these proposals is on the realistic valuation of liabilities, which are the present value of future payouts to policyholders. This process is central to the assessment of the solvency of life insurers but it poses particular difficulties in respect of 'with-profits' contracts, which allow the insurer discretion in allocating investment returns to contracts through the process of bonus allocation.[102]

5.5.2 Occupational pension schemes

Occupational pension schemes (OPS) are normally organised as trusts. They are governed by both the general law of trusts[103] and various statutory provisions, the most comprehensive being the Pensions Act 1995, which establishes a regulatory framework for the operation of occupational pension schemes.[104] The Act was introduced following recommendations made by the Pensions Law Reform Committee,[105] which was set up following the Maxwell pensions funds scandal in the early 1990s. Smaller pension funds are organised either as an insured scheme or as pooled funds. The former is in effect simply an insurance policy, with the result that beneficial ownership of the assets rests with the insurer and the insured has a contractual claim similar to other insurance policies (ie they form part of the overall life fund). The funds from such

---

[98] As regards the crucial House of Lords decision which sealed Equitable's fate (*Equitable Life v Hyman* [2002] 1 AC 408) see I MacNeil, 'When is a Guarantee not a Guarantee?' (*Equitable Life v Hyman*) (2000) 4 *Company Financial and Insolvency Law Review* 154 and 'Contract, Discretion and the With-Profits Mechanism' (2000) *Company Financial and Insolvency Law Review* 212.

[99] *The Future Regulation of Insurance* (Nov 2001).

[100] *Ibid* p 3.

[101] FSA Consultation Paper 195, *Enhanced Capital Requirements and Individual Capital Assessments for Life Insurers.*

[102] See Ch 4 for a discussion of the 'with-profits' system.

[103] See *Cowan v Scargill* [1984] 2 All ER 750, 763.

[104] Occupational pension schemes are not 'specified investments' for the purposes of FSMA 2000 but managing the investments of an OPS is a 'specified activity': see generally Ch 3.4. Implementation of the EC Occupational Pensions Directive (2003/41/EC [2003] OJ L235/10) will result in changes to the regulatory structure established by the Pensions Act 1995.

[105] See *Pension Law Reform* (The Goode Report) Cm 2342, 1993.

schemes are treated similarly to those from other policies. Pooled funds differ only in that the funds from a number of pension schemes are aggregated into a single fund that is distinct from the general life fund. Ownership and control of the investments comprising this fund also lie with the insurer. The only asset held by the trustees of insured or pooled pension funds is the insurance policy (ie a contractual rather than a proprietary claim).

The trustees of an occupational pension fund act on behalf of the beneficiaries, who are the employees covered by the scheme. Members of a scheme have a right to nominate one-third of the trustees.[106] The main function of trustees is to invest (or, as is more often the case, enter into arrangements for the investment of) the contributions of the employer and employees so as to provide a fund that can pay pensions to employees on retirement.[107] Decisions of the trustees of an occupational pension scheme may, unless the scheme provides otherwise, be taken by agreement of the majority of trustees. The investment powers of trustees are *prima facie* determined by the trust deed that creates the scheme. If no provision is made in the trust deed, the default provision in the Pensions Act 1995 applies, with the result that the trustees are free to make investments as if they themselves were the beneficial owners of the assets.[108] It is possible for the trustees to delegate their investment powers internally to a subcommittee of two or more trustees, although the trustees collectively remain responsible for the acts of the subcommittee.[109]

The larger pension schemes are directly invested, meaning that the scheme controls its own investments. Such schemes can use an 'in-house' investment manager or, as is more common, an external manager.[110] Irrespective of how the investment is organised the employees covered by the scheme remain the beneficial owners of the investments. However, voting and information rights associated with shares are likely to be held by other parties. While under trust law, the exercise of voting rights is a matter for the trustees, it is likely that these rights will be delegated to an external fund manager when the investment management function is delegated by the trustees. It is also possible that the registered owner of the shares will be a nominee (eg a custodian) who under company law has voting rights.[111] However, as a nominee holds the shares as trustee, equity (and usually also a contract between the pension fund trustees

---

[106] Pensions Act 1995 s 16.

[107] See Ch 3 as regards the authorisation requirements for trustees.

[108] Pensions Act 1995 s 34(1).

[109] Pensions Act 1995 s 34(5).

[110] Delegation of the investment powers of pension fund trustees is permitted by s 34(2) of the Pensions Act 1995, including delegation to a fund manager operating outside the United Kingdom as regards overseas investment business. See the Myners Report (above n 43) for a description of the differing types of mandate typically given to external fund managers.

[111] Companies Act 1985 s 370(1) and (2); Table A, art 38. See *Re Perkins, ex p Mexican Santa Barbera Mining Co* [1890] QB 613.

and the custodian) requires that he follow the voting instructions of the trustee or investment manager. The beneficial interest of the trustees in shares cannot be recorded on the shareholders' register of an English company and they have no direct right against the company.[112]

The discretion given to trustees (or fund managers when delegation has occurred) in making investments means that, in principle, any form of investment (in the broad sense of the word and not its narrower regulatory sense) is eligible for inclusion in the fund. There are, however, a number of safeguards. When choosing investments, the trustees or fund manager must have regard to (a) the need for diversification, so far as this is appropriate to the circumstances of the scheme, and (b) the suitability of proposed investments.[113] Trustees who have retained responsibility for selecting investments are required to take proper advice before making investment decisions, other than in respect of 'narrow-range investments not requiring advice' under the TIA 1961. This means that, in the case of advice that is a regulated activity under FSMA 2000, trustees should be advised by an authorised person, and in other cases (eg direct property investment) by a person believed by the trustees to have appropriate expertise. The trustees or fund manager must exercise their powers of investment in accordance with the statement of investment principles (SIP) which the trustees are required to prepare and maintain. The SIP must include:[114]

(i)   The policy regarding diversification of investments as required by s 36 of the Pensions Act 1995;
(ii) The policy for complying with the Minimum Funding Requirement;[115]
(iii) The principles for the investment of the fund, including types of investment risk and expected return; and
(iv) The trustees' policy on socially responsible investment and their policy on voting their shares.

There are also safeguards relating to employer-related assets and the extent to which non-financial considerations can be taken into account by trustees. Investment in employer-related assets gives rise to concern because of the potential risk posed by failure of the employer's business. A substantial investment in the employer's business might result in employees losing their jobs and a substantial part of their pension entitlement simultaneously. Reflecting

---

[112] See s 360 Companies Act 1985. The prohibition does not apply to Scotland and it is common for the existence of a trust to be recorded in the shareholders' register of Scottish companies.

[113] Pensions Act 1995 s 36(2). A suitability obligation also applies to a firm managing the assets of an OPS under FSA Handbook COB 5.3.1R.

[114] Pensions Act 1995 s 35(2).

[115] The Minimum Funding Requirement sets a minimum level of funding (contributions) for occupational pension schemes. See ss 56–61 of the Pensions Act 1995.

this concern, the general rule is that occupational pension schemes cannot invest more than five per cent of their assets in employer-related investments.[116] Additionally the investment must be in line with the SIP and be capable of justification in financial terms by comparison with other similar investments.

Pension fund trustees are unlikely to incur personal liability if they follow the procedures outlined above. If the trustees retain the power to select investments they are required to take advice and any negligent advice will give rise to legal liability on the part of the adviser.[117] If the trustees have delegated responsibility for making investments to a fund manager, they are not liable for the acts or defaults of the fund manager in the exercise of discretion where the trustees have taken all such steps as are reasonable to satisfy themselves that the fund manager has appropriate knowledge and experience for managing the investments of the scheme and that he is carrying out his work competently and in compliance with the provisions of the Pensions Act 1995 regarding the selection of investments.[118] It is not, however, possible for a trustee (where there has been no delegation) or an investment manager to whom the investment function has been delegated, to exclude liability for breach of an obligation under any rule of law to take care or exercise skill in the performance of any investment functions.[119] There are also regulatory sanctions available to the Occupational Pensions Regulatory Authority to fine or disqualify trustees who fail to adhere to the conditions attached to their power to delegate their investment functions.[120]

5.5.3 Unit trust and ICVC managers

In the case of unit trusts and investment companies with variable capital (ICVCs), the investment powers of the manager are determined by both the instrument constituting the scheme and the regulatory rules contained in the CIS Sourcebook.[121] The regulatory rules set limits for investment in different types of asset but these limits can be further restricted for a particular scheme by the instrument under which it is constituted. The general approach of the regulatory rules is to protect consumers by setting minimum standards for the type of investments that can be held and the spreading of risk.

---

[116] Pensions Act 1995 s 40(1) and art 5 of the Occupational Pensions Schemes (Investment) Regulations 1996 (SI 1996/3127).

[117] Under the general principles of the law of negligence. See G McCormack 'Liability of Trustees for Negligent Investment Decisions' (1997) 13 *Professional Negligence* 45–52.

[118] Pensions Act 1995 s 34(4).

[119] Pensions Act 1995 s 33.

[120] Pensions Act 1995 ss 3, 10.

[121] See Ch 4 regarding the nature and legal structure of these entities.

The CIS Sourcebook requires a number of basic principles to be observed by all authorised unit trusts and ICVC managers when exercising their powers of investment. They include:

- a requirement that the assets provide a prudent spread of risk, taking account of the objectives of the fund
- a prohibition on holding non-voting shares
- a prohibition on holding more than 10 per cent of the shares or debt securities of an issuer
- a prohibition on holding more than 10 per cent of the units in a unit trust or ICVC
- a requirement that the investments of the fund are traded on eligible markets
- a prohibition on holding funds in cash, other than in schemes designed for that purpose or to meet operating requirements.

In addition to these general rules there are more detailed investment rules that apply to different types of fund. There is also a general power to borrow up to 10 per cent of the value of the fund. This allows the fund manager to use 'gearing' as a technique to improve returns in rising markets, but also involves greater exposure to loss in falling markets. There is a prohibition on lending money and assets from the funds, but stocklending is permitted.[122]

The registered owner of the investments of unit trusts is either the trustee or a custodian. Beneficial ownership rests with the unit-holders. Voting rights attached to property of an authorised unit trust scheme must be exercised or not exercised as directed by the manager.[123]

Unit trust and ICVC managers are also subject to prudential standards, which mainly take the form of what are termed 'financial resources rules'. The objective of these rules is to set minimum capital and other risk management standards, thereby mitigating the possibility that firms will be unable to meet their liabilities and commitments to consumers and counterparties. The rules (set out in the IPRU(INV) part of the FSA Handbook) distinguish between firms that carry out different activities as those carrying out limited activities (eg when a firm acts only as a trustee of a unit trust or is not permitted to hold customers' monies or assets) pose only limited risks to consumers. The two

---

[122] Stocklending is a form of loan of securities. The lender is usually an institutional investor and the borrower a market-maker or proprietary trader with a short position who borrows to meet settlement obligations.

[123] FSA Handbook, CIS 7.8.1R(3). The rule can be justified on the basis that, even if the manager is not the legal owner, she is likely to be better informed about the company's position than a trustee, custodian or unit-holder and has an incentive to exercise the vote so as to maximise value. The rule does not apply to the exercise of voting rights in scheme property that comprises units in collective investment schemes or shares in an investment trust managed by the same manager. In these circumstances the trustees are entitled to vote after consulting the manager. This limits conflicts of interest on the part of the manager.

main techniques that are employed are to require firms to hold either minimum 'own funds'[124] or a 'liquid capital requirement'[125] (or both).

5.5.4 Investment companies

The investment powers of an investment company (including an investment
trust[126]) are determined by its articles of association and will reflect the purpose for which it was established. Unlike the position in respect of authorised
unit trusts and ICVCs, the FSA has no regulatory remit in respect of investment trusts and there is therefore no regulatory control of their investment
powers. Responsibility for investment of the company's assets is usually
delegated to a fund management firm.[127]

The registered owner of the company's investments can be the company
itself or a custodian, who holds the shares on trust for the company (which is
the beneficial owner). Shareholders in an investment company have no ownership interest in the portfolio of investments held by the company, as the
company is a separate legal entity that owns its own property.

---

[124] This comprises primarily shareholders' capital and reserves. See FSA Handbook
IPRU(INV) 5.2.2(1) R.

[125] The liquid capital requirement comprises a proportion of the firm's annual expenditure
plus various measures of the risk inherent in the firm's business (position risk, counterparty risk
and foreign exchange risk). See IPRU(INV) 5.2.3(4)(a) R.

[126] See Ch 4 for the distinction between an investment company and investment trust.

[127] The fund management firm itself will be subject to the prudential rules outlined above that
apply to unit trust and ICVC managers. The difference lies in the fact that, as an entity, investment trusts are not directly regulated by the FSA but unit trusts and ICVCs are.

6

Private Investors and the Retail Financial Market

This chapter considers the way in which the FSMA 2000 system of regulation and the common law deal with private investors. The 'retail' investment market is the market for investment products and services that are sold to private individuals. While almost all investments are available to private individuals, there are some, such as life assurance, personal pensions and collective investment schemes, that have been designed specifically for the private rather than the professional or institutional investor. Moreover, while investment services such as portfolio management are available to both institutional and private investors, the nature of the services and their regulatory treatment differ. It is therefore useful to distinguish the 'retail' investment market from the 'wholesale' investment market in which professionals and institutions are active. The distinction is based on the participants in each market and their different regulatory treatment.

6.1 Market structure and regulatory framework

The structure of the retail investment market and the products and services available to private investors reflect a number of influences. First, there is considerable diversity among private investors in terms of the type of investment they want and the degree of risk they are prepared to assume. There is also considerable diversity in terms of how much money private investors are able to invest. The market can therefore be characterised as encompassing a spectrum ranging from risk-averse investors with very little money available for investment to wealthy individuals with a substantial appetite for risk. The products and services offered in the retail market reflect this diversity. Second, the structure of the retail market reflects the constraints imposed by the regulatory system on the manner in which investments can be sold to private customers. In particular, the rules relating to the status of different types of seller and the provision of financial advice have had a major influence on the structure of the market. Third, long-standing resistance on the part of private investors to pay for financial advice in respect of most financial products has influenced the development of remuneration patterns, which have been a major concern of the regulatory system since the introduction of the FSA 1986.[1]

In common with the investment market generally, the basic regulatory structure of the retail market is built around the authorisation and financial promotion regime. The authorisation regime creates a perimeter within which, broadly speaking, all providers of investments and advisers on investments are regulated by the FSA.[2] The financial promotion regime controls the promotion of investments by unauthorised persons and the manner in which promotion is undertaken by authorised persons. Broadly speaking, it prohibits unauthorised persons approaching customers with a view to entering into an agreement to buy an investment or to provide investment services.[3]

Central to the regulatory regime for the retail market is the definition of a 'packaged product' and a 'private customer' as the regulatory regime for the retail market is largely concerned with sales of 'packaged products' to 'private customers'.[4] The concept of a packaged product is that it is a product that has been assembled from underlying financial instruments in a manner that makes it suitable for the retail market.[5] The regulatory definition of a packaged product is:[6]

(a) a life policy;
(b) a unit in a regulated collective investment scheme;
(c) an interest in an investment trust savings scheme;
(d) a stakeholder pension scheme;

whether or not (in the case of (a), (b) or (c)) held within a Personal Equity Plan or an Individual Savings Account.[7]

---

[1] See FSA Occasional Paper 6, *Price of Retail Investing in the UK* (2000).

[2] See Ch 3 for a more detailed discussion of the scope of the regulatory regime and the requirement for authorisation.

[3] See Ch 3 for a more detailed analysis.

[4] The 'retail' market is not itself a formal regulatory concept although the term is commonly used in the market and in regulatory circles. It will become clear later in this chapter that not all products sold in the retail market are packaged products.

[5] As noted in Ch 1, the creation of a packaged product generally involves transformation of the maturity and risk characteristics of the underlying financial instruments. A unit trust, for example, offers a degree of diversification in equity investment that would not normally be available to a private investor of modest means.

[6] See the glossary to the FSA Handbook of Rules and Guidance. See Ch 4 for a discussion of the nature of the underlying investments to which the definition refers.

[7] Personal Equity Plans and Individual Savings Accounts offer tax advantages to investors who hold qualifying investments in designated accounts.

The definition of a private customer is also of central significance because many of the FSA's rules are limited in their operation to private customers. This issue is developed in more detail in 6.2 below.

There are a number of different ways in which investments are sold in the retail market. This is a function not just of long-established market practices but also of regulatory rules. In particular, the polarisation regime introduced under the Financial Services Act 1986 had a fundamental impact on the structure of the retail market by creating a strict regulatory division between different types of person selling and advising on investments. The different ways of selling and their respective regulatory regimes are discussed below.

6.1.1 Direct selling

Direct selling occurs when a financial institution sells one of its products to a customer without the involvement of an intermediary. The sale is normally made through a representative who is an employee of the company and a contract is concluded directly between the product company and the customer. It is a sales method that is particularly common in the life assurance and pensions market.[8] There is no fiduciary duty owed by the seller to the buyer, with the result that, under the common law, the buyer is expected to look after his own interests (the principle of *caveat emptor*).

The disregard of the common law for the relatively weak position of the retail buyer of investments has been remedied to a considerable extent by the protection extended to private investors by the Conduct of Business Rules (COBS) made by the FSA. In particular, the COBs relating to product information, suitability and best advice (discussed below) improve the position of the private investor considerably.

'Direct offers' differ from direct sales in that they are offers made to the public (often with conditions attached) that can result in a binding contract being made if an offeree accepts the offer and meets the conditions.[9] Unlike the position in respect of direct sales, there is no opportunity for the seller to assess the suitability of the product for the buyer or to engage in the giving of advice (irrespective of how limited or conflicted it might be). The polarisation regime

---

[8] See Ch 4 of the Sandler Report (*Medium and Long-Term Retail Savings in the UK: A Review*, July 2002 available at www.hm-treasury.gov.uk (11 Nov 2004)) for an analysis of distribution methods in the retail market. Sandler notes that the numbers of sales representatives employed by life offices fell from 190,000 in 1991 to 20,000 in 2001. The decline is attributed to a failure to appeal to high-income customers, high staff turnover and high compliance costs. Over the same period, the share of the life assurance market taken by independent financial advisers rose sharply, reaching 55% (by value of sales) in 2000.

[9] A common example is a direct offer of life assurance made in a newspaper or magazine, usually subject to satisfying some basic conditions as regards health. See FSA Handbook COB 3.9.

(discussed below) does not apply to such direct offers as they are made without advice (in any form) being given to the customer.[10]

6.1.2 Intermediaries and financial advice

Intermediaries have always been important in the retail financial market because many private investors lack the information, expertise or judgment required to make fully informed investment decisions. However, the nature of intermediaries and the type of service that they can and do offer has historically been a matter of some confusion for private investors.

Prior to the Financial Services Act 1986, the provision of investment advice was not regulated in terms of the status of the adviser or the substance of the advice. It was therefore primarily controlled by the common law of agency.[11] Under the common law, it is possible for an agent to offer a limited range of services to a principal because the nature of the service to be provided is a matter for private agreement. Before the FSA 1986 took effect, it was common for agents to offer advice to private investors based on a limited product range. The rationale for this practice was that it was often considered uneconomic for agents to act for a large number of product providers and that most customers' needs could be met from the products provided by a limited range of companies.

The position changed with the introduction of the FSA 1986. The polarisation rule made by the Securities and Investment Board required anyone selling packaged products to be either a company representative or an independent financial adviser. The former was restricted to selling products of his marketing group[12] and the latter was required to advise the customer by reference to the entire market for the relevant product. The result was that the market for financial advice became 'polarised' between these two extremes. The rule was intended to address two perceived deficiencies of the existing legal regime for financial advice. The first was information asymmetry as between an adviser and a private customer regarding the nature of the advice being given. The

---

[10] See FSA Handbook COB 5.1.2G.

[11] See generally G McMeel and J Virgo, *Financial Advice and Financial Products: Law and Liability* (Oxford, OUP, 2001) ch 12.

[12] A marketing group is defined by the FSA glossary as a group of persons who:

   (a) are allied together (either formally or informally) for purposes of marketing packaged products of the marketing group; and

   (b) each of which, if it holds itself out in the United Kingdom as marketing packaged products to private customers, does so only as an investment manager or in relation to packaged products of the marketing group.

The reference to acting as an investment manager reflects the fact that the polarisation rule is disapplied when a firm acts as a discretionary investment manager. In those circumstances, polarisation is not relevant as the nature of the service requires advice on a wide range of investment options.

polarisation rule was intended to remove any doubts as to the nature of the advice by indicating the status of the adviser clearly to the customer. It was also intended to deal with conflicts of interest in the advisory process such as agents that were ostensibly independent favouring the products of a particular company so as to earn higher remuneration.[13]

Despite the Office of Fair Trading concluding that it had anti-competitve effects,[14] the polarisation rule was carried over to the regulatory regime established under FSMA 2000 and is still, for the time being, in force.[15] However, its value for private investors has increasingly been questioned both within the FSA and externally.[16] The potential benefits of reforming or ending polarisation are primarily that consumers are likely to be offered a wider range of advice options, greater variety and higher quality of financial products and that there is likely to be a greater degree of competition between direct-selling providers.[17] In recognition of these benefits the FSA has now concluded that the polarisation rule (as well as some related rules) should be repealed.[18]

'Appointed representatives' (also known as 'tied agents') were a creation of the FSA 1986 regulatory system that has been carried over to the FSMA 2000 system. They are persons (often legal persons such as companies) who enter into agreements with an authorised person to act (eg by advising or selling) on behalf of that authorised person (the principal). In respect of designated investment business[19] with private customers, an appointed representative is permitted to have only one principal, but in respect of other business (eg non-investment insurance) there is no restriction.[20] The limitation to one principal in the former case is based on making clear the status of the appointed representative, whereas the freedom granted in the latter case

---

[13] See Ch 2 of FSA Consultation Paper 121 *Reforming Polarisation: Making the Market Work for Consumers.*

[14] See *The Rules on the Polarisation of Investment Advice* (Aug 1999) available from www.oft.gov.uk/News/Publications (11 Nov 2004).

[15] See FSA Handbook COB 5.1. Note that the rule applies only when advice is given, with the result that products outside that of the marketing group may be sold on an 'execution-only' basis. See below 6.1.4.

[16] The FSA has commissioned several reports by external consultants on the operation and effects of the polarisation regime. See FSA CP 121 (above n 13) for details. As noted at p 27 of CP 121, no other country uses the concept of polarisation.

[17] For a discussion of the background to these conclusions see generally FSA CP 121 (above n 13) and FSA CP 166, *Reforming Polarisation: Removing the Barriers to Choice* (Jan 2003).

[18] That change is likely to take place at some point during 2005. See FSA CP 04/3, *Reforming Polarisation: A Menu for Being Open with Consumers* for details of the regulatory rules that will replace polarisation. They will be structured around an Initial Disclosure Document that will make clear the nature of the advice being offered (entire market, limited range, single provider) and a Menu that sets out details of the services offered and their likely cost (on a comparative basis against market averages).

[19] See below n 49.

[20] COB 12.5.6AR, effective 30 June 2004.

reflects a judgment that this is necessary to prevent disruption to existing distribution systems and business models.[21]

Appointed representatives differ from company representatives in that their business is separate from that of the principal (they are engaged under a contract for services rather than an employment contract). However, they are similar to company representatives in that the principal is required to accept responsibility for the actions of the appointed representative.[22] An appointed representative is exempt from FSMA 2000, meaning that it does not have to seek authorisation and is not directly subject to the FSA rulebook. However, many rules do apply to appointed representatives and the principal takes responsibility for compliance.

Advice on investments provided by members of the professions is also an important part of the retail market. Members of a designated profession can provide such advice without authorisation provided it represents 'incidental business'.[23] The relevant professional bodies regulate their own members in respect of this activity. If the activity does not fall within the 'incidental business' category but is carried on as a separate activity in its own right, the member (or firm) will require authorisation and will be regulated in the normal manner by the FSA.

As a matter of market practice, intermediaries selling packaged products are normally remunerated by the product provider rather than by the customer. This remains the case even when a product is sold to a customer by a person considered by the law to be the agent of the customer (eg an independent financial adviser). Remuneration generally takes the form of a commission based on the sum to be invested. This practice carries with it considerable risks to the interests of the customer. It can quite easily lead to a situation in which an intermediary's advice is focused more on earning commission than taking care of the best interests of the customer. This will be the case in particular if the customer is not aware of the scale of the intermediary's remuneration and the potential impact it is likely to have on investment returns.

Prior to the entry into force of the FSA 1986, the remuneration of agents was controlled by the common law. While it focuses primarily on the more common situation in which an agent is remunerated by the principal, it does not

---

[21] See FSA Policy Statement, *Appointed Representatives—Extending the Current Regime* (Sept 2003).

[22] Under s 39 FSMA 2000. This provision creates a statutory form of vicarious liability on the part of the principal in respect of the actions of the appointed representative 'for which he has accepted responsibility'. As to the meaning of this statutory provision see *Emmanuel v DBS Management plc* [1999] Lloyd's Rep PN 593, where it was observed that a principal is not responsible for the theft of money by its appointed representative if the latter is acting in a different capacity. The case is discussed in ch 12 of McMeel and Virgo (above n 11).

[23] See Ch 3 for more detail on the authorisation regime for members of the professions.

forbid the agent being remunerated by a third party (such as a product provider). Moreover, even if it were not expressly agreed between a customer and an agent that the agent would be remunerated by the product provider, it would be possible to imply such a term into an agency agreement as a result of the widespread practice of commission payments.[24] The common law allows the principal to require the agent to disclose any payments from a third party but there is no obligation imposed on an agent to volunteer this information.

The confusion and lack of transparency resulting from the common-law approach to commission payments resulted in the introduction of conduct of business rules under the FSA 1986 regime that required the disclosure of commission paid to intermediaries. These rules were carried over into the FSMA 2000 system of regulation and are discussed in more detail in 6.2 below.

Intermediaries operating in the retail financial market ('personal investment firms' for the purposes of the FSA Handbook) are subject to financial resources (also known as 'capital adequacy') rules that operate in principle in a similar manner to those in the 'wholesale' market.[25] The financial resources that a firm is required to maintain depend on the business conducted by the firm, the principal distinction being between those that carry on 'core services' within the meaning of the Investment Services Directive[26] and those that do not. The latter benefit from lower financial resources requirements, reflecting the limited risk posed for investors in the event of their failure. There are three different tests that must be met by personal investment firms.[27] For large firms the most significant requirements are likely to be those that that require financial resources to represent a proportion of annual expenditure or alternatively a fixed amount per adviser.

6.1.3 Execution-only business

Execution-only business refers to transactions executed by a firm upon the specific instructions of a client where the firm does not give advice on investments relating to the merits of the transaction.[28] A common example is 'execution-only' dealing services provided by 'discount' stockbrokers. The consequence of business being transacted on this basis is that the conduct of business rules relating to 'suitability' and 'best advice' (see 6.2.2 below) do not apply and the client is required to take personal responsibility for the selection

---

[24] It could be considered to be part of the usual or customary authority of such an agent. See generally *Fridman's Law of Agency*, 7th edn (London, Butterworths, 1996) pp 69 and 76.

[25] See Ch 10.1.5.

[26] Directive 93/22/EEC, [1993] OJ L141/27.

[27] See FSA Handbook, IPRU(INV) pt 13.

[28] This is the definition given in the Glossary to the *FSA Handbook of Rules and Guidance*.

of investments.[29] A transaction can be considered to be execution-only (a) when a client agreement provides that all transactions for a client fall into that category or (b) when a client agreement provides for an advisory service but stipulates that failure to follow the advice given will result in the transaction being categorised as 'execution-only'. However, the fact that only limited advice on investments is given to a private client in respect of a particular transaction is not enough to make it 'execution-only'.[30]

6.1.4 Regulation of products

Regulation of financial products does not, in the main, form part of the regulatory approach adopted under FSMA 2000, which favours regulation of the process of investment and in particular the process whereby advice (in whatever form) is provided to a client.[31] However, a limited form of product regulation has been developed in recent years as a means of creating simpler and less costly financial products for the retail sector that are likely to appeal in particular to those on lower incomes.[32] Two techniques have been adopted. The first is the concept of 'CAT-marked' products and the second is the so-called 'stakeholder' suite of products.

'CAT' standards, short for 'comparability, access and terms', are voluntary benchmarks of quality and charges for retail financial products.[33] They were first introduced with Individual Savings Accounts (ISAs) in April 1999 then extended to residential mortgages. The Cruickshank Report[34] recommended that they be extended to credit cards and basic bank accounts. The objective of CAT standards is to help consumers identify suitable products and to permit lighter regulation of the sales process (and thereby lower charges) in appropriate cases. There is no requirement for any product to become CAT-marked, the objective being that consumer demand would lead providers to offer CAT-marked products.

[29] Nor is the firm required to carry out any investigation into the customer's personal and financial circumstances: COB 5.2.2G.

[30] COB 5.2.3G. See also *Loosemore v Financial Concepts* [2001] 1 Lloyd's Rep PN 235.

[31] Quite apart from its likely effect on innovation and competitiveness (see pp 23–24 of HM Treasury document, *Standards for Retail Financial Products*), product regulation would put the United Kingdom in breach of its obligations under article 34 of the EC Consolidated Directive on Life Assurance (2002/83/EC [2002] OJ L345/1).

[32] Interestingly, this initiative has been developed by the Treasury and not the FSA. It has not been based on any of the statutory powers given to the Treasury by FSMA 2000. It is based on the policy that the government should act as an 'intelligent sponsor' of the financial services industry: see HM Treasury document, *Proposed Product Specifications for Sandler 'Stakeholder' Products* (Feb 2003).

[33] See generally Treasury document, *Standards for Retail Financial Products*.

[34] *Competition in UK Banking* (2001), available from www.hm-treasury.gov.uk (11 Nov 2004).

The concept of a 'stakeholder suite' of simplified financial products was first put forward in the *Sandler Report*[35], which concluded that low to middle income consumers were being driven out of the market because the heavy costs of compliance were making it uneconomic for providers and intermediaries to sell products to them. The review proposed that a simplified suite of products should be developed in which risk and charges would be controlled.[36] This was seen as a means of limiting the need for regulation of the sales process, thereby cutting compliance costs and ultimately charges to the consumer. The review proposed that there should be three products in the suite (a mutual fund[37] or unit-linked life fund, a with-profits fund and a pension) and that the annual charge should be limited to 1 per cent. The product suite has now been expanded and the annual charge for the investment and pension products capped at 1.5 per cent for the first year and 1 per cent thereafter.[38] The new products became available in April 2005 and are sold through a 'basic advice' process that has been developed by the FSA.

To the extent that both developments offer the possibility of improving access to financial products with modest charges, these developments can hardly be criticised. The potential problem, however, is that they add to rather than remove the complexity associated with buying financial products, as consumers will have the choice not only of the type of financial product they want but also the type of regulatory regime under which the product is sold (CAT, stakeholder or mainstream FSA regulation). It is difficult to avoid the conclusion that CAT and 'stakeholder' products are 'bolt-on' solutions that do not address the fundamental problems of cost[39] and complexity[40] in the regulation of sales of financial products.

---

[35] *Medium and Long-Term Retail Savings in the UK* (2002), available from www.hm-treasury.gov.uk (11 Nov 2004).

[36] Paragraph 10.14 of the review states 'Product regulation provides an embedded means of protection that does not rely on advice and so minimises the fixed cost element of interacting with customers.'

[37] This is the generic term used in the United States to describe pooled investment funds (see Ch 4.9).

[38] See HM Treasury press release of 17 June 2004. The increase in the permissible charge reflected industry concerns that a 1% cap would not generate a return sufficient to attract providers into this market as well as an independent study of the effects of different price caps.

[39] See the *Financial Times* reports of 3 July 2004: 'Sandler renews call for study into regulatory costs of FSA' and 'Sandler backs 1.5% compromise on fees'.

[40] See J Gray 'Personal Finance and Corporate Governance: The Missing Link: Product Regulation and Policy Conflicts' (2004) 4 *Journal of Corporate Law Studies* 187, stating at p 215 that CAT standards 're-design and re-price the product'.

6.2 Regulatory rules

The principle that the regulatory system ought to treat investors acting in a private capacity differently from those acting in a professional capacity was recognised in the Financial Services Act 1986 and this approach has been continued under FSMA 2000. Section 156(1) of FSMA 2000 provides that:

> Rules made by the Authority may make different provision for different cases and may, in particular, make different provision in respect of different descriptions of authorised person, activity or investment.

This provision forms the basis of the system of customer classification created by the FSMA regulatory system, which distinguishes between private customers, intermediate customers and markets counterparties. A private customer is a client who is not a market counterparty or an intermediate customer.[41] The term applies most obviously to individuals acting in a private capacity but also includes regulated collective investment schemes, partnerships with net assets below £5m, trustees of trusts with assets below £10m and trustees of small occupational pension schemes.[42] The general approach of the FSA is that private customers require more protection than do intermediate customers or market counterparties. The rationale is that private investors suffer most from the information asymmetry problem that forms the basis for regulation.[43] They have problems acquiring information, processing it and using it to make appropriate decisions.

The policy of protecting the private investor is given effect largely through conduct of business rules that regulate the manner in which transactions are conducted.[44] The conduct of business rules distinguish between different types of customer through a process of rules being 'switched on' or 'switched off' in respect of different categories of customer. For example, most of the conduct of business rules do not apply to market counterparties.[45] This chapter deals only with conduct of business rules applicable to private customers. Generally applicable conduct of business rules are dealt with in Chapter 10.[46]

---

[41] For definition of these terms see Ch 10.

[42] See The Financial Services Glossary (part of the FSA Handbook) definitions of customer for more details.

[43] See Ch 2 regarding information asymmetry.

[44] Many of the particular rules protecting the private customer have been carried over from the FSA 1986 regime and there is therefore no significant change from the previous position as regards the formulation of the rules.

[45] See Ch 10 for more detail.

[46] Note that client asset and client money rules are dealt with in Ch 10 under generally applicable regulatory rules.

As a result of mortgages and general insurance becoming regulated activities, two new conduct of business sourcebooks have taken effect: the Mortgage Conduct of Business Sourcebook (MCOB) effective from 31 October 2004; and the Insurance Conduct of Business Sourcebook (ICOB) effective from 14 January 2005. Extensive changes to the COBs already in force have resulted from implementation of the EC Distance Marketing Directive[47], which provides rights to consumers of financial services that are already available to consumers of other products under the EC Distance Selling Directive.[48]

The common law, in contrast to the regulatory system, has not developed special rules that take account of the weak position of private investors. They are, in most respects, treated similarly to professional and institutional investors. There are remedies available, such as for misrepresentation, negligence or breach of contract, but they deal with problems after they have occurred and, at least from the private investor's perspective, the cost of litigation is high and the outcome often unpredictable. Nevertheless, as will be seen later, the common law offers the potential to develop effective and far reaching remedies for private investors.

6.2.1 Accepting customers

A firm is required to classify the persons with or for whom it intends to carry on designated investment business.[49] The purpose of classification is to achieve appropriate application of the conduct of business rules, bearing in mind that the rules apply in different ways to different customers. A client who would otherwise be classified as a private customer can be classified as an intermediate customer if he has sufficient experience and understanding.[50] The result is that he loses some of the safeguards provided by the regulatory system and therefore the client's informed consent is necessary for this to occur. Similarly, a client who would otherwise be an intermediate customer can be classified as a market counterparty if certain conditions are met (mainly

---

[47] Dir 2002/65/EC [2002] OJ L271/16, implemented in respect of FSA regulated activities by the Distance Marketing Directive Instrument 2004 (FSA 2004/39) with effect from 9 October 2004 (and 31 October 2004 and 14 January 2005 for MCOB and ICOB respectively). See FSA CP 196, *Implementation of the Distance Marketing Directive's Proposed Rules and Guidance* and FSA Policy Statement 04/11 *Implementation of the Distance Marketing Directive.*

[48] Dir 97/7/EC [1997] OJ L144/19.

[49] See COB 4.1. 'Designated Investment Business' (see the glossary to the FSA Handbook) is business relating to a sub-set of 'specified activities' (see Ch 3). The definition serves the purpose of distinguishing 'mainstream' investment business from the other activities (such as banking) that are included within the scope of regulation of FSMA 2000. It corresponds to what was termed 'investment business' under the FSA 1986 (see FSA CP 45a, *The Conduct of Business Sourcebook,* Feb 2000).

[50] COB 4.1.9R.

relating to the size of the organisation). It is also possible for clients who would otherwise be classified as intermediate customers or market counterparties to be classified as private customers.

COB 4.2.5R deals with terms of business:

Requirement to provide terms of business to a customer

(1) A firm must provide a customer with its terms of business, setting out the basis on which designated investment business is to be conducted with or for the customer within the period specified in (2) or (3).

(2) A firm must, before conducting any designated investment business with or for a specific private customer, provide him with its terms of business, unless the customer has made an oral offer to enter into an investment agreement relating to an ISA, or a stakeholder pension scheme, that relates to a designated investment, in which case the terms of business must be provided to him within five days of the offer.

(3) If the customer is an intermediate customer, the firm must provide its terms of business within a reasonable period of the firm beginning to conduct designated investment business with or for the customer.

In relation to some forms of designated investment business[51] with or for a private client (eg managing investments on a discretionary basis) the terms of business must take the form of a client agreement, which is terms of business signed by the client or to which the client has assented.[52]

The requirement to provide terms of business or enter into a client agreement does not apply in relation to some common forms of designated investment business. They include:[53]

- execution only transactions (in which no advice is given to the client)
- direct offer financial promotions (eg offers published in newspapers)
- the issue of a life policy by an insurer
- acting as trustee of a unit trust or depositary of an ICVC.[54]

6.2.2 Advising and selling

The rules in this section form the core of the regulatory obligations that govern the advisory and sales process through which private customers make investments.

---

[51] See above n 49.

[52] Although the regulatory objective is to ensure that private customers agree to the terms on which an authorised firm is to act for it, it is unlikely that the distinction between terms of business and a client agreement carries any significance for the purposes of contract law, as it would be assumed that a client who acts on the terms supplied by a firm consents to those terms.

[53] See COB 4.2.9R.

[54] See Ch 4.9 for an explanation of these terms.

Know your customer

The purpose of this requirement is to require a firm to have sufficient information about a private customer to enable it to give suitable advice in accordance with Principle 9 (see below). The rule is contained in COB 5.2.5R:

> Before a firm gives a personal recommendation concerning a designated investment to a private customer, or acts as an investment manager for a private customer, it must take reasonable steps to ensure that it is in possession of sufficient personal and financial information about that customer relevant to the services that the firm has agreed to provide.

This requirement is normally implemented by a 'fact-find', although there is no specific regulatory requirement in respect of the manner of implementation. A firm that arranges an execution-only transaction for a private customer is not generally required to obtain any personal or financial information about that customer (other than in respect of requirements arising from the money laundering regulations). The rationale for this limitation in the scope of the 'know your customer' rule is that a customer who has chosen an execution-only service has accepted that the firm will not provide advice and this will no doubt be reflected in the firm's remuneration.

Suitability

The suitability rule is expressed at a general level by Principle 9 of the Principles for Business as follows:

> A firm must take reasonable care to ensure the suitability of its advice and discretionary decisions for any customer who is entitled to rely upon its judgment.

It is expressed in more detail by COB 5.3.5R as follows:

> Requirement for suitability generally:
>
> (1) A firm must take reasonable steps to ensure that it does not in the course of designated investment business:
>   (a) make any personal recommendation to a private customer to buy or sell a designated investment; or
>   (b) effect a discretionary transaction for a private customer (except as in (3)) unless the recommendation or transaction is suitable for the private customer having regard to the facts disclosed by him and other relevant facts about the private customer of which the firm is, or reasonably should be, aware.
> (2) A firm which acts as an investment manager for a private customer must take reasonable steps to ensure that the private customer's portfolio or account remains suitable, having regard to the facts disclosed by the private customer and other relevant facts about the private customer of which the firm is or reasonably should be aware.

(3) Where, with the agreement of the private customer, a firm has pooled his funds with those of others with a view to taking discretionary management decisions, the firm must take reasonable steps to ensure that a discretionary transaction is suitable for the fund, having regard to the stated investment objectives of the fund.

The suitability requirement is linked to the 'know your customer' rule in that the information obtained through the 'fact-find' undertaken when accepting a customer is relevant when considering what constitutes a suitable recommendation. Each part of the rule refers to 'reasonable steps', with the result that the liability of the firm is based on fault and is not a strict liability. The reference to 'reasonable steps' presumably includes those arising directly or indirectly from regulatory requirements. It is not entirely clear, however, whether and if so to what extent a firm is expected to go beyond express regulatory requirements in taking 'reasonable steps'.

There is now included in the COB suitability rules the principle that was in the past (misleadingly) referred to as 'best advice'. The rules distinguish the content of the suitability requirement for sales of packaged products[55] according to whether a firm is a provider (a principal) or an independent intermediary. A provider must ensure that a recommended packaged product is the most suitable that it can provide and if no suitable product can be provided no recommendation should be made. This requirement also applies when a provider sells through an appointed representative rather than its own employees. An independent intermediary, however, must select the most appropriate packaged product from the whole of the relevant market. It cannot recommend a packaged product from a connected provider[56] if there is another product available that would satisfy the needs of the customer just as well.[57] In some circumstances,[58] a firm is required to issue a suitability letter. The purpose of the suitability letter is to make clear why the firm has concluded that the transaction is suitable for the customer and the main consequences and any possible disadvantages of the transaction. While the fact that the suitability letter is issued after the transaction has occurred would tend to suggest that it is of limited value to a customer, it should be borne in mind that cancellation rights apply to several of the circumstances in which a suitability letter must be issued. In these circumstances the suitability letter must

---

[55] See 6.1 (above) for a definition.

[56] A connected provider is defined in COB 5.3.10R: examples are being in the same group of companies or the same marketing group.

[57] When the content of the suitability obligation was in the past referred to as 'best advice', this requirement was referred to as the 'better than best' requirement, meaning that a connected firm's product could only be recommended if it were better than one which could be recommended as satisfying the 'best advice' requirement.

[58] See COB 5.3.14 R. See also COB 5.3.19 for exclusions from the requirement to issue a suitability letter.

be issued no later than the issue of the post-sale notice of the customer's right to cancel. Where there are no cancellation rights, the suitability letter must be issued as soon as possible after the transaction is effected.

6.2.3 Customers' understanding of risk

The relevant conduct of business rules are derived from Principle 7, which provides:

> A firm must pay due regard to the information needs of its clients and communicate information to them in a way which is clear fair and not misleading.

The central requirement is contained in COB 5.4.3R:

Requirement for risk warnings

A firm must not:
(1) make a personal recommendation of a transaction; or
(2) act as a discretionary investment manager; or
(3) arrange (bring about) or execute a deal in a warrant or derivative; or
(4) engage in stock lending activity,
with or for a private customer unless it has taken reasonable steps to ensure that the private customer understands the nature of the risks involved.

The need for customers to understand the risk that they are running in making an investment is central to the system of regulation because no amount of information can compensate for a failure to appreciate this aspect of an investment. Failure to understand risk lies at the root of many disputes, involving both professional investors and private customers. There are many aspects of risk that can go unrecognised or be misunderstood. The following are typical examples:

(a) Failure to distinguish market risk from the specific risk attaching to a particular investment (eg even 'blue chip' investments will tend to decline in value when economic fundamentals deteriorate).[59]
(b) Failure to understand risks in the underlying business of the entity in which the investment is made.
(c) Failure to understand risks arising from the complexity of the investment (eg derivatives or split capital investment trusts).
(d) Failure to understand risks arising from the different underlying bases of competing investments (eg in relation to pension opt-outs, the difference between 'defined benefits' and 'money purchase' schemes).

---

[59] See Ch 1 for a discussion of risk.

Special risk notices are required in respect of warrants and derivatives in recognition of the particular risks faced by private customers in this area.

6.2.4 Excessive charges

The relevant conduct of business rules are derived from Principle 6, which provides that:

> A firm must pay due regard to the interests of its customers and treat them fairly.

COB 5.6.3R provides:

> A firm must ensure that its charges to a private customer made in connection with the conduct of designated investment business are not excessive.

COB 5.6.4G provides:

> When determining whether a charge is excessive, a firm should consider:
>
> (1) the amount of its charges for the services or product in question compared with charges for similar services or products in the market;
> (2) the degree to which the charges are an abuse of the trust that the customer has placed in the firm; and
> (3) the nature and extent of the disclosure of the charges to the private customer.

6.2.5 Inducements and soft commissions

The conduct of business rules covering inducements and soft commissions are designed to limit the extent to which payments (in whatever form) give rise to conflicts of interest that prejudice the interests of consumers.[60] They give effect to Principles 1 and 6 of the FSA Principles for Business, which require respectively the firm to conduct its business with integrity and treat customers fairly. It is prohibited to offer, solicit, give or take such an inducement.[61] Detailed guidance is included in the FSA Handbook as to what falls within the scope of this rule.[62] In particular, there is a substantial list of 'indirect benefits' that may be made to independent intermediaries by firms without breaching the rule on inducements.[63]

The conduct of business rules limit the extent to which soft-commission agreements can be used.[64] This refers to an agreement in any form under

---

[60] An obvious example would be gifts or lavish entertainment provided to an adviser as an inducement to select an investment that is clearly not the best for the client.

[61] COB 2.2.3R.

[62] See COB 2.2.6G.

[63] As regards the implications of such payments for the comparability of disclosure of remuneration as between different types of adviser (ie IFA or company representative) see below n 67.

[64] COB 2.2.8R.

which a firm receives goods or services in return for designated investment business put through or in the way of another person. The most obvious example is the provision of investment research 'free of charge' by a broker to a fund manager in return for an agreed volume of business. The risk posed by such agreements is that they may not work in the best interests of the fund manager's customer (who ultimately pays for the research through dealing charges). For this reason, the COBs control the use of such agreements by requiring them to be structured in a manner that limits the possibility of the interests of the customer being prejudiced.

6.2.6 Disclosure of charges, remuneration and commission

The relevant conduct of business rules are derived from Principle 7, shown in 6.2.3 above.

The central principle is stated in COB 5.7.3R:

> Before a firm conducts designated investment business with or for a private customer, the firm must disclose in writing to that private customer the basis or amount of its charges for conducting that business and the nature or amount of any other income receivable by it or, to its knowledge, by its associate and attributable to that business.

A similar approach had been adopted under the Conduct of Business Rules made under the FSA 1986. The rationale for this form of disclosure is that customers were in the past often unaware of the fact that an adviser was being paid a commission or (more likely) the scale of the commission and the effect it would have on the overall return from the investment. The common law rules of agency do not appear to require a financial adviser to disclose remuneration from a third party unless the information is requested by the customer.[65]

A firm may make the required disclosure in its terms of business, in a client agreement or in a separate written statement. The disclosure should include any product-related charges that are deducted from the private customer's investment. If the product is a packaged product, charges and expenses will be

---

[65] The underlying legal basis of such an approach is not entirely clear. *Prima facie*, it would be a breach of fiduciary duty for an independent adviser to accept (at least without declaring it and securing the client's approval) a payment from a third party that created a conflict with the interests of the client. It may be that non-disclosure of commission payments in such transactions could be regarded as an implied contract term between the adviser and client (based on trade custom) that modified the content of fiduciary duty. However, as it was not entirely clear until the House of Lords decision in *Kelly v Cooper* [1993] AC 205 that fiduciary duty could be modified in this way, it seems unlikely that the common law relating to disclosure of commission could have taken this form. It may have been that there was simply a failure to recognise the relevance of fiduciary duty in this context and that may have been the result of a large proportion of sales being conducted as direct sales, in which fiduciary duty is not relevant.

disclosed in the key features document or in the minimum information that the firm is required to provide to the private customer (see below).

The conduct of business rules require that in respect of a packaged product, remuneration or commission paid to the person selling the product to a private customer must be disclosed in cash terms before the transaction is concluded.[66] This requirement applies to both sales effected by independent intermediaries and direct sales from a product company. An independent intermediary must disclose remuneration or commission receivable in connection with the transaction. In the case of direct sales, remuneration payable to employees or agents must be disclosed. In determining the amount to be disclosed as remuneration a firm must put a proper value on the cash payments, benefits and services provided to its employees and agents in connection with the transaction that could not be provided to another firm which is subject to the 'indirect benefits' rule.[67] This approach is intended to ensure consistency in the disclosure of remuneration as between independent financial advisers and company representatives.

The disclosure requirement for packaged products does not apply if:

• the firm is acting as an investment manager; or
• the transaction is effected for a private customer who is habitually resident overseas; or
• the packaged product is a life policy and the private customer is not present in the United Kingdom at the time the application is made.

6.2.7 Product particulars, withdrawal and cancellation rights

The product disclosure requirements are derived from Principle 7, shown in 6.2.3 above. They have two main purposes. First, they allow a customer who is considering purchasing a packaged product to identify the main features of the product so as to determine if that type of product meets his needs. Second, they are intended to allow a customer to make a comparison between different products, all of which may meet his basic needs but with differences in design, risk and charges.

The central requirement is that a product provider must produce 'key features' for each packaged product which it offers.[68] The rule applies not only

---

[66] See COB 5.7.5R. The rule is stated differently in respect of life policies and other packaged products, but the effect is similar.

[67] This is the rule contained in COB 2.2.3R (prohibition of inducements) and COB 2.2.6G (packaged products—guidance on indirect benefits). It limits the benefits that can be paid to an independent intermediary and which the latter would therefore have to fund from 'disclosable' commission.

[68] COB 6.1.4R.

to packaged products sold to private customers but also to those sold to trustees of an occupational pension scheme or the trustee or operator of a stakeholder pension scheme.[69] However, the rule is subject to a number of exceptions. A product provider need not provide 'key features' when a life policy is sold through an independent intermediary.[70] Nor need they be provided when a private customer is habitually resident in an EEA state other than the UK[71] or a non-EEA state and is not present in the UK. There are also exceptions relating to scheme holdings:[72]

- when purchased by a private customer on an execution-only basis;
- when purchased on behalf of a private customer by an investment manager exercising discretion;
- when a private customer is adding to a holding in a scheme that has not changed and in respect of which he has already received key features.

Key features must include an assessment of the risk relating to the product and detailed guidance is provided by the FSA Handbook as to factors that might be relevant.[73] A projection must be included in some cases such as the purchase of a life policy or an annuity and calculated according to the conduct of business rules. When a life policy has a surrender value, 'key features' must include an indication of the likely value in the early years of the policy. The objective is to make clear to customers that life policies typically have low surrender values in the early years as a result of costs associated with the sale. If a life policy has no surrender value (eg term assurance) this must be drawn to the customer's attention. For most but not all life policies, there is a requirement to include information relating to 'reduction in yield'. This is a statement of the effect which deductions (charges, commission, remuneration, expenses, surrender penalties and other adjustments) will have on the total return available from the investment.[74] A similar statement is required in relation to investment in unit trusts. Reference must also be made to commission and remuneration associated with the sale of the product. For direct sales, the cash amount must be disclosed and for sales through independent intermediaries there must be a statement that the intermediary will provide the relevant details.

---

[69] This would arise for example if the trustees of a pension scheme arranged life assurance for members of the scheme.

[70] COB 6.2.9R.

[71] In which case the law governing the contract and the conduct of business rules applicable to the sale will normally be that of the country in which the private customer is habitually resident.

[72] Mainly units in collective investment schemes and investment trust savings schemes.

[73] See COB 6.5.14G.

[74] See COB 6.5.27R. One of the possible formulations of 'reduction in yield' is 'Putting it another way, if the growth rate were to be x%, which is in no way guaranteed, this would have the effect of reducing it to y% a year'.

The purpose of withdrawal and cancellation rights is to give a customer the opportunity to reconsider a proposed investment. Withdrawal rights arise before a contract has been concluded. They require that an offer made by the customer to enter into an agreement cannot be accepted within a defined period. Cancellation rights arise after a contract has been concluded and permit the customer to cancel the contract within a defined period. Both rights modify the common law of contract, which would otherwise permit the customer's offer (to enter into an investment agreement on the terms proposed by the product provider) to be accepted at any time before it is withdrawn and would not allow the customer to cancel the contract except on grounds applicable to contracts generally (eg misrepresentation, undue influence).

The rules relating to withdrawal and cancellation rights are complex.[75] The first issue that must be determined is whether the particular investment agreement carries with it a right to withdraw or cancel.[76] Some agreements carry only one right, but others carry both. The second issue that must be determined is the period of reflection available to the customer. A minimum period of 14 days is specified for the exercise of cancellation rights but this can be varied upwards by agreement between the customer and firm.[77] A minimum period of 7 days is specified for the exercise of the right of withdrawal.

Customers must be given notice of the right to cancel when it is available.[78] They can exercise the right to cancel by serving notice upon the firm. A notice is valid when it is served on the firm, its appointed representative or an agent with appropriate authority. A notice is treated as being served on the day it is posted. In most cases, exercise of the right of cancellation has the effect that the customer withdraws from the entire agreement. The process is in effect rescission of the contract as the conduct of business rules make clear that *restitutio in integrum*[79] must follow exercise of the right. This means that the firm must return any sums paid in connection with the agreement and the customer must return any property transferred to him under the agreement (eg units in a unit trust) and any money paid by the firm. Special provisions apply in circumstances in which the market falls during the cancellation period: their effect is that the customer bears the loss.[80]

---

[75] The rules are contained in COB 6.7.

[76] See the table at COB 6.7.5E.

[77] See COB 6.7.10R and COB 6.7.11R. The 14 day period is mandated by the EC Consolidated Life Assurance Directive (above n 31).

[78] See COB 6.7.30R.

[79] This is a general principle of contract law that requires the parties to be returned to their pre-contractual position if rescission is to be permitted.

[80] See COB 6.7.54R for the rule described as 'shortfall'.

In the case of with-profits life assurance, the Principles and Practices of Financial Management (PPFM) adopted by the firm must also be made available to customers.[81]

6.2.8 Dealing and managing

Many of the conduct of business rules relating to dealing and managing (COB 7) apply equally to non-private customers and are considered in Chapter 10. Some parts of COB 7, however, apply only to private customers and are outlined below.

It is common for firms such as stockbrokers to include in their terms of business a power to sell assets of the customer if the customer does not have funds available to settle her obligations. This reflects the fact that firms may be subject to additional costs as a result of the operation of the financial resources rules relating to transactions that have not settled by the due date.[82] The conduct of business rules require a firm that proposes to realise a private customer's assets either to have given notice of such a power in its terms of business or client agreement or to give three days' notice of the intention to exercise this contractual right.[83]

Firms that lend money to private customers to finance investment transactions are required to make and record an assessment of the customer's standing and ensure that the loan is suitable for the proposed investment.[84]

Firms that execute transactions for private customers in instruments (eg derivatives) that require the payment of margin[85] must obtain such payments from customers. Before entering into such a transaction, the firm must notify the customer of the circumstances in which margin is payable and the consequences of the customer failing to provide the required margin.

A firm that deals for private customers in securities that are not traded on a regulated market (eg Eurobonds) and holds itself out as a market-maker in that security is subject to an obligation to repurchase the security within a three-month period. The customer must be given notice of this right and of the fact that sale after the three-month period may be difficult as a result of the nature of the security and its liquidity. The purpose of the rule is to ensure that a firm deals fairly with private customers in relation to non-exchange traded securities.

---

[81] COB 6.10.8R, effective from 1 May 2004. See Ch 4.10 for more detail on the nature and content of the PPFM.

[82] See Ch 9.6 'clearing and settlement'.

[83] COB 7.8.3R. If the right to do this is not included in terms of business or a client agreement it is not clear how a firm could have the right to act in the manner suggested by the second option (the giving of three days notice).

[84] COB 7.9.3R.

[85] See Ch 4.8.

6.3 The common law

Since the FSA 1986 came into effect, the role of the common law in developing investor protection standards has become marginalised.[86] The main developments, in terms of both setting standards and enforcing them, have occurred within the regulatory system. However, there are now indications that the common law may have a more active role to play. As discussed below, the courts have begun to apply common law agency and tort principles in situations where regulatory rules apply.

6.3.1 Agency

As noted earlier, private customers often buy investments through agents rather than directly from the representatives of product providers. They do so primarily to take advantage of the knowledge and experience of the agent in dealing with the type of transaction they propose to enter. While prior to FSA 1986 the term 'agent' was capable of being understood in different ways, there are only two types of agent[87] that are recognised by FSMA 2000 (which continues the approach established by FSA 1986). An independent intermediary (or a member of a 'recognised' profession) is the agent of the client. An authorised representative is the agent of the company for which it acts. There can be no confusion between these two categories because the regulatory system requires that any person selling investments must choose between being one or the other and must identify themselves as falling into one category or the other. The result is that, for the purposes of applying the common-law rules of agency, the regulatory system effectively removes any doubt regarding the issue of whom an agent represents.

The regulatory system, however, operates without prejudice to the common-law rules of agency. These rules remain important because they determine:

- the extent of the authority of an agent;
- the circumstances in which an agent can bind the principal to a contract;

---

[86] Of course, to the extent that the introduction of statutory regulation reflected the perceived failure of the common law to apply effective controls to investment, it can be argued that the common law had in the past contributed little to investor protection. See generally A Page and R Ferguson, *Investor Protection* (London, Weidenfeld and Nicolson, 1992) ch 2.

[87] The reference to 'agent' is to a person (natural or legal) that is independent of the product provider—it does not therefore refer to a company representative who is an employee of the adviser. A true agent (as defined) is governed by the law of agency, while the acts of an employee fall under employment law.

- the circumstances in which the principal can be liable in tort (delict) for the actions of the agent;
- the liability of the agent.

These aspects will now be examined in more detail. The starting point is that it is a basic principle of agency law that a principal is only bound by acts of the agent that are within the authority of the agent. Provided that an agent acts within his authority, he can bind his principal to a contract with a third party. Similarly, a principal can be liable in tort (delict) for acts done or omitted by an agent acting within his authority. A significant difference between the regulatory system and the common-law rules of agency is that the latter do not use the regulatory concept of a 'private customer'. In principle, agency law applies in the same manner to private customers as it does to other types of customer. However, agency law responds to the context in which it operates and is therefore able to take account of the needs of private investors. A clear example is the case of *Martin v Britannia Life Ltd*, discussed below.

The authority of an agent can be express, implied or ostensible. Express authority arises where the principal expressly authorises the agent to undertake a particular task (eg an instruction given by a client to a stockbroker to sell 1,000 shares in company A at a minimum price of 150p during the next week). Implied authority arises where no express authority has been given but it can be implied from the circumstances in which the express authority was given that the parties intended that the agent should have that authority. Ostensible (or apparent) authority arises where the principal[88] has represented to a third party (by word or action) that the agent has the necessary authority for a particular transaction.

These principles were considered in the context of the regulatory regime established by FSA 1986 in the case of *Martin v Britannia Life Ltd*.[89] The case concerned financial advice given by an appointed representative of the defendant company. As is the case under FSMA 2000, a principal was required under FSA 1986 to assume responsibility for anything said or done or omitted by an appointed representative in carrying out the investment business for which the principal has accepted responsibility.[90] At issue in this case was the extent of the authority of the appointed representative in acting on behalf of Britannia Life Ltd. The issue was of significance because the advice given to the plaintiff had included advice relating to a remortgage provided by another company, which was not classified as an 'investment' under FSA 1986 and therefore did

---

[88] It is clear from *The Ocean Frost* case (*Armagas Ltd v Mundogas* [1986] AC 717) that the representation must be made by the principal. Ostensible authority cannot be created by a false representation as to authority made by an agent to a third party.

[89] [2000] Lloyd's Rep PN 412.

[90] s 44 of FSA 1986 and s 39 of FSMA 2000.

not fall within the scope of the Act or its regulatory rules. It was contended by the defendant that the authority of the appointed representative could not extend beyond 'investment' advice as defined by FSA 1986 and that its responsibility was similarly limited.

The court rejected this contention and chose to define the actual authority of the appointed representative very broadly. The rationale for this approach was stated as follows by Jonathan Parker J:[91]

> In my judgement, advice as to the 'merits' of buying or surrendering an 'investment' cannot sensibly be treated as confined to a consideration of the advantages or disadvantages of a particular 'investment' as a product, without reference to the wider financial context in which the advice is tendered.

This was despite a limitation in the contract between the appointed representative and Britannia Life Ltd, which provided that the former was engaged solely to advise, market and sell the products of the latter. The reasoning of the court was that the statutory agency created by section 44(6) FSA 1986 overrode the express contractual limitation and had to be understood as referring to the broad concept of 'investment advice' indicated above. It followed that the appointed representative had actual authority to advise on the remortgage. Moreover, even if there were no actual authority, there was ostensible authority arising from the description of the appointed representative as a 'financial adviser' on the business card supplied to him by the defendant. The court's view was that this description represented that the appointed representative had authority to engage in transactions ancillary to or associated with insurance.

Applying the rationale of this case to FSMA 2000 points to the following conclusions. First, contractual limitations on the authority of an appointed representative are unlikely to have much effect in protecting a principal. They are likely to be overriden by a broad view of the statutory agency created by section 39 FSMA 2000 (the successor to section 44 FSA 1986). Second, appointed representatives who engage in activities outside the 'permission' of their principal are still likely to be considered as acting within their actual authority, at least as far as associated transactions are concerned. Third, even when authorised representatives engage in unregulated activity, they can in principle be considered to be acting within their authority, at least as far as associated transactions are concerned.

---

[91] [2000] Lloyd's Rep PN 412 at p 431.

6.3.2 Liability in tort

Liability in tort (delict in Scotland) is based on the existence of a duty of care. To establish liability, it is necessary to show that breach of a duty of care caused loss to the person to whom the duty is owed. There are no special rules of tort relating to 'private customers' but as in the case of agency, the common-law rules respond to context and are capable of accommodating the special needs of 'private customers'. This is made clear by the decision in *Gorham v British Telecommunications plc*.[92]

This case involved financial advice given by a company representative of the Standard Life Assurance Company in 1991 in connection with the pension arrangements of an employee of British Telecom plc. Following that advice, the plaintiff took out a personal pension plan. He was under the misapprehension that he was a member of his employer's pension scheme because he had not returned an opt-out form after joining the company. When he realised that he could not have both a personal pension and be a member of his employer's scheme he contacted Standard Life who informed him that he would be better off in the employer's scheme. As a result, he stopped contributing to the personal pension, assuming that he was a member of the employer's scheme. He died shortly thereafter. Had he joined the employer's pension scheme following the advice from Standard Life his family would have been eligible for a lump sum payment but not other pension rights which were payable only after two years' membership. Standard Life admitted that they owed Mr Gorham a duty of care and that their representative had been negligent in failing to advise him about the differences between an occupational scheme and a personal pension, and in selling him the personal pension without being satisfied that he had made an informed choice between the two, but they denied owing the plaintiffs (his wife and children) any duty of care.

The Court of Appeal held that Standard Life owed the plaintiffs a duty of care. The rationale for the existence of this duty was articulated by Pill LJ in the following terms:[93]

> The advice in this case was given in the context in which the interests of the dependants were fundamental to the transaction, to the knowledge of the insurance company representative giving advice as well as to his customer, and a duty of care was owed additionally to the intended beneficiaries.

The implication of this principle is that there may be a duty of care in other contexts in which these circumstances exist. Nor is this process limited by

[92] [2000] 1 WLR 2129.
[93] At p 2142.

FSMA 2000 and its regulatory rules. The relationship between the system of regulation and the common-law principles of tort was explained as follows:[94]

> Had Parliament not intervened, remedies for the abuses which existed in this field would almost certainly have been developed by the courts. The courts now do so in the context, and with the benefit of, rules and codes of practice laid down by those concerned with the maintenance of proper standards. The courts can be expected to attach considerable weight to the content of codes drafted in these circumstances but they are not excluded from making their own assessment of a situation.

The implication is that tort liability exists independently of the regulatory system even if 'considerable weight' is given to it in determining the existence of a duty of care.

Once the existence of a duty of care has been confirmed, it is necessary to establish the standard of care associated with that duty. This addresses the issue of the standard of conduct necessary to discharge the duty of care. In *Gorham v BT*, it was said that the standard of care expected from Standard Life was a duty to the dependants not to give negligent advice to the customer which adversely affected their interests as he (the customer) intended them to be. It was also said that:[95]

> The restrictions imposed by statute on what products the adviser can recommend do not have the effect of relieving him of the duty not to recommend his principal's products unless they are suitable.

This reference to a suitability requirement was to one imposed by the common law and not by the regulatory system. The implication is that there is both a regulatory and a common law suitability requirement and that they are not necessarily co-extensive.[96]

6.4 Complaints and redress

This part considers the options available to a private investor when there has been a contravention of any applicable regulatory rules. A major achievement of the regulatory system has been to improve the scope for redress on the part of the private investor, at low cost and without having to resort to litigation.

---

[94] At p 2141.
[95] Schiemann J at p 2144.
[96] On suitability obligations generally see L Lowenfels and A Bromberg, 'Suitability in Securities Transactions' (1999) 54 *Business Law* 1577.

6.4.1 Complaints

The most obvious starting point for a dissatisfied private customer is to complain to the authorised firm with which he has dealt. Resolution of any dispute at this stage will result in the costs associated with a reference to the Financial Services Ombudsman, a complaint to the FSA or a lawsuit being avoided. In recognition of this and of the FSA's statutory objective to promote consumer protection,[97] the FSA Handbook requires firms[98] to have in place effective written procedures for dealing with complaints from eligible customers. Customers fall within this category if they are eligible to refer a complaint to the Financial Ombudsman Service (FOS)[99] and the FSA Handbook provides that only private customers are eligible to make such complaints.

A firm's internal complaint handling procedure must make provision for:

1 complaints to be investigated by an employee of sufficient competence who, where appropriate, was not directly involved in the matter which is the subject of the complaint;
2 the person charged with responding to complaints to have the authority to settle complaints (including the offering of redress where appropriate) or to have ready access to someone who has the necessary authority;
3 responses to complaints to address adequately the subject matter of the complaint and, where a complaint is upheld, to offer appropriate redress.

Appropriate redress may take the form of an apology, but is most likely to involve fair compensation.

The FSA Handbook sets a time limit of five business days for the acknowledgement of a complaint and eight weeks for a final response.[100] The final response must inform the complainant of the right to refer the matter to the FOS within six months and enclose a copy of the FOS explanatory leaflet. Firms are required to keep records of complaints in different categories and to report to the FSA twice a year on this.[101]

[97] See FSA CP 4, *Consumer Complaints*, pt III.

[98] Recognised investment exchanges and clearing houses, while 'exempt' from FSMA 2000, are required by the recognition requirements to have effective arrangements for the investigation and resolution of complaints: see FSMA 2000 (Recognition Requirements for Investment Exchanges and Clearing Houses) Regulations 2001, SI 2001/995, sch 1 para 9 and sch 2 para 23.

[99] FSA Handbook DISP 1.2.1R and 1.2.2G. DISP is the Dispute Resolution part of the FSA Handbook.

[100] FSA Handbook DISP 1.4.1R and 1.4.5R.

[101] These records reveal that 90% of upheld complaints are made against 'tied' advisers. See the figures quoted in 'Tied Advisers at Root of Mis-Selling gripes' *Financial Times* (6 Aug 2003).

6.4.2 The Financial Services Ombudsman

Before the FSMA 2000 came into effect, there were eight different Ombudsman schemes in place. Some operated on a voluntary basis (eg the Insurance and Banking Ombudsmen) while the jurisdiction of others was based on statute (the Building Societies Ombudsman) or a regulatory requirement (the Personal Investment Authority Ombudsman). The Financial Ombudsman Scheme (FOS) replaces all of these with a single scheme. It is operated by a company established by the FSA, Financial Ombudsman Service Ltd.[102] This company is required to have operational independence[103] from the FSA but the FSA nevertheless exerts a strong influence over the working of the FOS through appointment of the chairman and members of the board, approval of the FOS annual budget and the making of rules governing the compulsory jurisdiction of the FOS.[104] The costs of the FOS are borne by authorised firms.

The jurisdiction of the FOS, split between compulsory and voluntary categories, reflects the varied background from which it evolved. The compulsory jurisdiction covers many but not all regulated activities as well as some unregulated activities. Compulsory refers to the obligation imposed on a regulated firm to submit to the procedure and comply with the decision of the Ombudsman; no such obligation is imposed on the complainant. As the name implies, there is no obligation imposed on regulated firms to submit to the voluntary jurisdiction of the FOS.

The FSA Handbook limits both the type of complaint that can be referred to the FOS and the type of customer who is entitled to refer. The following are not eligible customers:

(a) an individual, business, charity or trustee who was an intermediate customer or market counterparty in relation to the firm in question at the time of the act or omission, and in respect of the activity, which is the subject of the complaint;
(b) a firm whose complaint relates in any way to an activity which the firm itself has permission to carry on and which is subject to the compulsory or voluntary jurisdiction of the FOS.

A person referring a complaint must also be an eligible complainant. The following are included in this category:

---

[102] See www.financialombudsman.org.uk (11 Nov 2004).

[103] FSMA 2000 s 225(4) and sch 17 para 3(4).

[104] See E Ferran, 'Dispute Resolution Mechanisms in the UK Financial Sector' (http://ssrn.com/abstract=298176)(11 Nov 2004), who comments at p 15: 'The powerful controls enjoyed by the FSA make it possible to question whether the FOS can actually achieve operational independence.'

(a) a private individual;
(b) a business which has a group annual turnover of less than £1million at the time the complainant refers the complaint to the firm;
(c) a charity which has an annual income of less than £1million at the time the complainant refers the complaint to the firm;
(d) the trustee of a trust which has a net asset value of less than £1million at the time the complainant refers the complaint to the firm.

A potential customer falling into one of the above categories is also an eligible complainant. This allows the FOS to consider issues arising from the act or omission of a firm in circumstances in which no transaction has been concluded (eg loss suffered as a result of a failure to act according to the FSA's rules). Complaints must refer to a matter that an authorised firm has failed to resolve satisfactorily within eight weeks of receiving (the time limit for making a final response to complaints).

There are also circumstances in which indirect complaints allow a person to be an eligible complainant. They arise when a person falling within categories (a) to (d) above who is not a customer of a firm either has a certain type of relationship with the firm or the complaint derives from another person in certain circumstances. The relevant relationships are:

1 the complainant has given the firm a guarantee or security for a mortgage or loan;
2 the complainant has relied in the course of his business on a cheque guarantee card issued by the firm; or
3 the complainant is the true owner or the person entitled to immediate possession of a cheque, or to the funds it represents, collected by the firm for someone else's account; or
4 the complainant is the recipient of a bankers' reference given by the firm; or
5 the complainant is the holder of units in a collective investment scheme and the firm is the operator or depositary of the scheme.

The circumstances in which a complaint derived from another person allows a complainant to become eligible are:

1 that the complainant is a beneficiary under a trust or estate of which the firm is trustee or personal representative; or
2 that the complainant is a person for whose benefit a contract of insurance was taken out or was intended to be taken out; or
3 that the complainant is a person on whom the legal right to benefit from a claim under a contract of insurance has been devolved by contract, statute or subrogation.

Categories 2 and 3 of complaints derived from another person include employees covered by a group permanent health policy taken out by an employer which provides in the insurance contract that the policy was taken out for the benefit of the employees. A complaint can also be brought on behalf of an eligible complainant, or a deceased person who would have been an eligible complainant, by a person authorised by the eligible complainant or authorised by law.

All authorised firms are subject to the compulsory jurisdiction of the FOS. It covers the following types of activity:

1 regulated activities;
2 lending money secured by a charge on land (ie mortgage lending);
3 lending money (other than restricted credit);
4 paying money by a plastic card (other than a store card);
5 the provision of ancillary banking services,

or activities ancillary to them (for example advice provided by a firm in connection with these activities). Activity is understood to include a failure to act and encompasses activity for which a firm is responsible, such as the activity of an authorised representative. Complaints relating to 'non-mainstream regulated activity' undertaken by a professional firm that can be handled by a designated professional body are excluded from the FOS.[105]

The FOS Voluntary Jurisdiction is a service open to unauthorised firms and authorised firms in respect of complaints not covered by the compulsory jurisdiction. There is no requirement to join but if a firm does join it becomes bound by the standard terms governing the voluntary jurisdiction.[106] The rules for determining eligible complainants are the same as for the compulsory jurisdiction (above). However, the type of complaint that can be considered is different. First, a complaint can only be made under the voluntary jurisdiction if it is not covered by the compulsory jurisdiction. Second, the complaint must relate to one or more of the following activities:

1 lending money secured by a charge over land (ie mortgages);
2 activities previously covered by an ombudsman scheme before 1 December 2001 ('commencement day', the in-force day for the section 19 FSMA 2000 general prohibition),

or an activity ancillary to it.

Category 2 relates only to acts or omissions arising after commencement day. Acts or omissions occurring before commencement day and falling within a previous ombudsman scheme now fall within the compulsory jurisdiction of the FOS.[107] However, the ombudsman has the power to consider complaints

---

[105] See Ch 3 for an account of the regulatory regime for professional firms.
[106] See DISP 4.
[107] See DISP 2.6.10G, 2.2.2G and the FSMA 2000 (Transitional Provisions) (Ombudsman Scheme and Complaints Scheme) Order 2001 (SI 2001/2326).

even if the act or omission occurred before the voluntary jurisdiction participant joined the scheme or occurred before commencement day either:

1 if the complaint could have been dealt with under a former scheme; or
2 as a consequence of the agreement of the voluntary jurisdiction participant.[108]

The first condition provides a mechanism for dealing with complaints that were not made to a relevant previous scheme. The second condition relates to the consent required from a voluntary jurisdiction participant as part of the standard terms of the scheme. It effectively gives the ombudsman an alternative basis to the first condition on which to deal with such complaints.

The territorial scope of the FOS service covers complaints about the activities of firms carried on from an establishment in the UK. It therefore covers firms operating from a permanent place of business including EEA firms and Treaty firms.[109] Complaints about business conducted by branches of UK-authorised firms outside the UK or EEA firms operating in the UK on a 'services' basis are excluded from both the compulsory and voluntary jurisdiction of the FOS.[110]

The Ombudsman is entitled to deal with complaints on the basis of written submissions made by the parties but also has the option of inviting the parties to attend a hearing. The parties are entitled to request a hearing but ultimately this is a matter for the Ombudsman, who is required to have regard to the provisions of the European Convention on Human Rights.[111] They must however be informed of their right to make representations before the Ombudsman makes a determination. A complaint can be dismissed without consideration of its merits for a number of reasons. They include the following:

1 the complainant has not suffered loss;
2 the firm has already made an offer of compensation which is fair and reasonable;
3 the matter has been previously considered or excluded under the FOS or a previous scheme;
4 the complaint is the subject of current court proceedings unless proceedings are stayed or sisted so that the matter may be considered by the FOS;
5 the complaint relates to investment performance.[112]

---

[108] DISP 2.6.12R.
[109] See Ch 2 for the meaning of these terms.
[110] See Ch 2.5.2 for an explanation of business conducted on a 'services' basis.
[111] This is relevant to the manner in which the hearing is held.
[112] See DISP 3.3.1R for more detail.

Complaints are determined according to what is fair and reasonable in all the circumstances of the case.[113] In considering what is fair and reasonable in all the circumstances of the case, the Ombudsman will take into account the relevant law, regulations, regulators' rules and guidance and standards, relevant codes of practice[114] and where appropriate what he considers to have been good industry practice at the time. When a complaint has been determined[115] the Ombudsman must give both the complainant and the firm a written statement of the determination, stating reasons for it. The statement will invite the complainant to notify the Ombudsman in writing before the date specified in the statement whether he accepts or rejects the determination. If the complainant accepts the determination within the time limit set by the Ombudsman, it is final and binding on both the complainant and the firm. If not, the firm is not bound by the determination and both sides are free to pursue legal remedies in court.

If a complaint is determined in favour of the complainant, the determination may include:

- a money award subject to a maximum of £100,000; or
- a direction that the firm take such steps in relation to the complainant as the Ombudsman considers just and appropriate; or
- both of these.

In the case of a money award, the Ombudsman may decide to award compensation for the following kinds of loss or damage (in addition to or instead of compensation for financial loss):

- pain and suffering; or
- damage to reputation; or
- distress or inconvenience.

---

[113] In the case of the compulsory jurisdiction, s 228(2) FSMA 2000 provides a statutory basis for this approach. In the case of the voluntary jurisdiction, FSA Handbook DISP 3.8.1R provides a contractual basis for the Ombudsman to determine a complaint in this manner.

[114] See, in this regard, *Norwich and Peterborough Building Society v The Financial Services Ombudsman Service* [2002] EWHC 2379. This was a judicial review of an award made by the FOS in respect of a complaint relating to 'downgrading' (the practice of offering new customers better terms than existing customers). In making its award, the FOS (in accordance with the Building Societies Act 1986, sch 12, Pt II para 4c) had regard to the Banking Code. It also based its decision on a standard, developed in previous decisions, which it called 'relative onerousness', which involved comparing the terms of accounts with their relative interest rates. The court held that while interpretation of the Banking Code was ultimately a matter for the court, the FOS's power to decide what was fair was not limited to compliance with legal obligations. The approach based on 'relative onerousness' was therefore upheld. For a discussion of the case see R Nobles, 'Rules, Principles and Ombudsmen: *Norwich and Peterborough Building Society v The Financial Services Ombudsman Service*' (2003) 66 *MLR* 781.

[115] As to the procedure see Annex B to FSA Consultation Paper 04/12, *FSMA 2 Year Review: Financial Ombudsman Service*. A provisional decision, which gives both parties an opportunity to comment, is issued before the final decision.

The limit on the maximum money award has no bearing on any direction that the Ombudsman may make as part of a determination. The result is that the complainant can receive benefits in excess of the monetary limit of £100,000 in circumstances in which a direction has a financial benefit for the complainant (eg a direction that a person be re-admitted to a pension fund). Where the Ombudsman finds in a complainant's favour, he may also award an amount which covers some or all of the costs which were reasonably incurred by the complainant in respect of the complaint. A money award under the compulsory jurisdiction is enforceable through the courts in the same way as money awards made by the lower courts.[116]

No appeal to the courts is possible from a determination made by the Ombudsman. The rationale for excluding a right of appeal from FSMA 2000 was that it would be inconsistent with the objective of resolving disputes quickly and with minimum formality.[117] In principle judicial review is available but this provides only a limited basis on which to mount a challenge.

The FSMA 2 Year Review[118] has recently focused attention on the respective roles and relationship between the FSA and FOS.[119] Concern has been voiced by some authorised persons that the involvement of the FOS in 'wider implication cases' has resulted in the FOS setting standards rather than resolving individual disputes.[120] The argument is that the FOS may make a decision in an individual case that has wide implications for firms and consumers because it concerns issues that arise in a large number of similar cases and is likely to be followed in those cases. The FSA and FOS have agreed a memorandum of understanding governing 'wider implication cases', which is intended to ensure that both the FOS and FSA can carry out their respective functions. In the case of the FSA, the relevant action may involve disciplinary proceedings, issuing or amending rules or guidance and taking action to secure redress for consumers.

6.4.3 Redress required or initiated by the FSA

A complaint from a private customer may lead the FSA to take disciplinary proceedings against a firm or individual. If the FSA imposes a sanction for a

---

[116] FSMA 2000 sch 17 para 16.

[117] See FSA Consultation Paper 04/12, (above n 115) p 27. The possibility of establishing a right of appeal (which would require amendment of s 228(5) FSMA 2000) was canvassed by the FSA in that paper, which noted that there was considerable support among authorised persons for a right of appeal but that consumer groups were generally content with the existing arrangements.

[118] See generally Ch 3.1.

[119] See FSA Consultation Paper 4/12 (above n 115).

[120] An example of such a case is split capital investment trusts, which are discussed in Ch 4.9.4.

contravention of the Act or rules made under it, this may carry no direct benefit for the complainant. This will be the case if the sanction is a fine (payable to the FSA) or a public censure. However, it is also open to the FSA to order restitution in cases:

(a) where a person has accrued profits as a result of a contravention of a relevant requirement or a person has suffered loss as a result of the contravention; or

(b) in market abuse cases when a contravention has resulted in the making of a profit for the person concerned in it or a loss for another person.[121] The amount of the restitution is the amount of the profit gained or the loss suffered, respectively, from the contravention. FSA action is not intended to duplicate the functions of the Financial Ombudsman Service, but there may be cases, such as where many persons have suffered loss, in which it is deemed appropriate.[122]

Another possibility, which is relevant when an authorised person is experiencing financial difficulty, is for the FSA to initiate or intervene in insolvency procedures. The relevant powers[123] enable the FSA to take action to safeguard the interests of consumers of financial services. When insolvency is looming or has occurred, consumers of financial services may face considerable difficulty in taking independent action to safeguard their interests: the possibility of FSA action therefore promotes market confidence and discourages financial crime.

It is also open to the FSA to act in its capacity as a 'qualifying body' under the Unfair Terms in Consumer Contracts Regulations 1999.[124] The objective of the regulations is to prevent the use of unfair terms in contracts concluded between a business and a consumer. In its capacity as a qualifying body the FSA is able to consider the fairness of contact terms on its own initiative or following the making of a complaint by a consumer.[125] The FSA's policy is to talk constructively with firms to deal with unfair terms,[126] but if that fails it is able

---

[121] FSMA 2000 s 384. Restitution can be ordered in favour of any person, not just private customers. It can be exercised against any person, whether authorised or not. There was no parallel power under FSA 1986, with the result that the FSA (and previous regulators) had to apply to court for restitution orders.

[122] See ENF 9.6.

[123] See Part XXIV of FSMA 2000 as amended by the Enterprise Act 2002.

[124] SI 1999/2083. The FSA has agreed with the Office of Fair Trading that the FSA will take lead responsibility for contracts in the areas of investments, pensions, life and general insurances, mortgages and banking. Contracts covered by the Consumer Credit Act 1974 remain the responsibility of the OFT.

[125] See generally ENF 20. The FSA Discussion Paper, *Discretion and Fairness in With Profits Policies* (discussed in Ch 4.10) was a product of this review process.

[126] See FSA Consultation Paper, 148 *The FSA's Approach to the Use of its Powers under the Unfair Terms in Consumer Contracts Regulations 1999* para 4.11.

to apply for an injunction to prevent the use of the term.[127] The Regulations do not authorise the FSA to make a financial award or otherwise compensate consumers, but it remains open in principle to a consumer to refer the case to the Financial Ombudsman Service or for the FSA to require restitution if the use of an unfair contract term also amounts to a breach of FSA rules.

6.4.4 Legal action

The availability of the FOS removes much of the need for litigation on the part of private customers. However, there may be circumstances in which litigation is deemed appropriate, such as:

1 where the loss suffered by an investor exceeds the £100,000 limit set by the FOS;
2 where a private customer has 'opted-up' to the status of an intermediate customer for the purposes of the relevant transaction and is thereby excluded from the FOS;
3 where it is likely that a court would take a view more favourable to the complainant in relation to the common law duties of an authorised person than would the FOS Ombudsman (eg because the relevant law is in a state of flux or development).

The first option that should be considered is an action for breach of statutory duty. Several different sections provide for this action to be available to an investor, the most wide-ranging being section 150 FSMA 2000.[128] This provides that a contravention by an authorised person of a rule[129] is actionable at the suit of a private person[130] who suffers loss as a result of the contravention, subject to the defences and other incidents applying to actions for breach of statutory duty.[131] It is also open to the FSA to prescribe circumstances in which this remedy is available to a non-private person.[132]

---

[127] An injunction as to future use does not affect the validity of unfair terms in existing contracts. Only a court could apply the provision (art 8 of SI 1999/2083) that provides for an unfair term to have no binding effect on a consumer.

[128] The others are ss 20(3), 85(5), and 202(2).

[129] Listing rules and financial resources rules are not rules for the purposes of this section: see s 150(4).

[130] Private person is defined by art 3 of the FSMA 2000 (Rights of Action) Regulations 2001, SI 2001/2256.

[131] This includes contributory negligence as a partial defence. See *Morgan Stanley UK Group v Puglisi Consentino* [1998] CLC 481, a case brought under s 62(1) FSA 1986 in respect of breach of the rules of the Securities Association (a 'self-regulating organisation' under FSA 1986) in connection with the sale of currency derivatives.

[132] It is available to institutional investors in respect of contraventions of rules that relate to dealing on the basis of unpublished price-sensitive information: see SI 2001/2256 art 6.

The section 150 remedy (and its predecessor, section 62 of the FSA 1986) has not been popular with investors for two main reasons. First, its restriction to private persons means that it is generally not available to those institutional investors who might be more inclined to pursue litigation. Second, the plaintiff in a section 150 case is required to show not only a breach of the relevant rule but a casual link between the breach and the loss.[133]

The availability of the section 150 remedy does not exclude the possibility of legal action based on the common law. The most obvious options are the law relating to negligence, breach of trust, fiduciary duty, duties of skill and care or confidentiality. While much of the substance of the common-law rules in these fields are reflected in regulatory rules, they are not co-extensive, a point made clear by the Court of Appeal in *Gorham v BT*.[134] The approach taken in that case suggests that it may be better in some circumstances to ground a case on basic common-law principles such as negligence rather than attempting to establish a rule breach and its causal link with loss under section 150 FSMA 2000.

It is also possible for the FSA to take legal action on behalf of investors. The purpose of such action is to require persons who have contravened rules or been knowingly concerned[135] in such a contravention to make restitution.[136] The FSA will normally consider using its administrative powers[137] to require restitution before applying to the court for a restitution order.[138] The court can order these persons to pay to the FSA such sum as appears just having regard to the profits appearing to have accrued to them or the loss suffered by others as a result of the contravention. Any amount paid to the authority in pursuance of such a restitution order must be paid by it to such qualifying person or distributed by it among such qualifying persons as the court may direct.

6.5 The Financial Services Compensation Scheme

The purpose of compensation schemes is to provide some reassurance to investors that their investment or other assets will be secure in the event that an authorised firm becomes insolvent. The rationale for establishing such

---

[133] As to the difficulties involved in so doing, see I MacNeil, 'FSA 1986: Does s 62 Provide an Effective Remedy for Breaches of Conduct of Business Rules?' (1994) 15 *Company Lawyer* 172.

[134] See 6.3 (above).

[135] See *SIB v Pantell SA (No 2)* [1993] 1 All ER 134.

[136] FSMA 2000 s 382.

[137] See 6.4.3 above.

[138] See ENF 9.7.2G.

schemes and their role in a regulatory system is made clear by FSA Consultation Paper 5, *Consumer Compensation*:[139]

> The justification for establishing compensation schemes is that individual investors, depositors and policyholders are not generally in a position to make an informed assessment of the risk that the firm to which his or her funds are entrusted may fail. As well as providing protection in the last resort for consumers, the existence of compensation schemes also helps to reduce the systemic risk that a single failure of a financial firm may trigger a wider loss of confidence in the rest of the financial sector concerned (eg through a run on deposit-taking institutions).

A new system of compensation following the failure of a regulated firm has been established under FSMA 2000.[140] It rationalises the previous arrangements for compensating customers of failed firms and reflects the provisions of the two relevant European Directives, the Deposit Guarantee Directive[141] and the Investor Compensation Directive.[142] Before the new system took effect, there were different arrangements in place for banking (The Deposit Protection Scheme) insurance (The Policyholders' Protection Scheme and The Friendly Societies Protection Scheme), and investment (The Investors' Compensation Scheme). Each of these schemes had different rules for eligible claimants, the maximum amount payable and the claims procedure. The new scheme replaces these schemes and is run by a new body established for that purpose, the Financial Services Compensation Scheme Ltd,[143] which is operationally independent from the FSA but accountable to it.[144]

A claimant must meet several criteria to make a claim against the Financial Services Compensation Scheme (FSCS). A claimant must:

- be an *eligible complainant*;
- have a *protected claim*;
- be claiming against a *relevant person*; and
- the relevant person must be in *default*.

A claimant must also, when required by the FSCS, agree to assign legal rights in the claim to the FSCS. Each of these aspects is now considered.

Eligible complainants are defined as any person who does not fall within a long list of excluded persons.[145] The effect of the exclusions is to limit access to the FSCS on the part of persons other than private individuals and small businesses.

---

[139] Para 11.
[140] See generally M Blair (ed) *Butterworths Annotated Guide to the Financial Services and Markets Act 2000* (London, Lexis-Nexis, 2003) Pt XV.
[141] Dir 94/19/EC [1994] OJ L135/5.
[142] Dir 97/9/EC [1997] OJ L84/22.
[143] See www.fscs.org.uk (11 Nov 2004).
[144] See ss 212 and 218 FSMA 2000.
[145] See COMP 4.2.1R and 4.2.2R.

A protected claim can be a claim for a protected deposit, a claim under a protected contract of insurance or a claim in connection with protected investment business. The definitions of each category are complex, largely as a result of their giving effect to the principle that 'passporting firms' (whether incoming or outgoing) are not required to join the compensation scheme of the host state in which they engage in 'passported' activities.[146] In European law, the compensation schemes that Member States must maintain for the protection of depositors and investors in securities markets operate on a home country basis. This means that 'passporting firms' operating in the UK are not required to join the FSCS, although they have the option to do so. If such firms undertake regulated activities in the UK not covered by their EU passport they are required to join the FSCS. The definition of protected contracts of insurance includes contracts that, under the choice of law rules of the EC consolidated life insurance directive[147] are governed by UK law, irrespective of whether they are underwritten by a firm exercising passport rights. This avoids the potential problems that would arise if contracts subject to UK insurance law were to become subject to the compensation scheme of a Member State whose insurance law differs materially from the UK.

Relevant persons against whom claims can be made are participant firms[148] and appointed representatives of such firms. Such relevant persons are considered to be in default whenever the FSA determines that this is the case or (if earlier) a judicial authority has made a ruling that has the effect of suspending the ability of eligible claimants to bring claims against the participant firm (eg the making of an administration order). The FSA can make such a determination when a relevant person (natural or legal) is subject to specified insolvency proceedings.

The FSCS may make an offer of compensation conditional on the assignment of rights to it by a claimant. The result will be that any sum payable in relation to the rights so assigned will be payable to the FSCS and not the claimant. This is subject to the proviso that any recovery that exceeds the compensation payable to the claimant must be returned to the claimant and that the FSCS must endeavour to ensure that a claimant must not suffer disadvantage resulting from prompt acceptance of the FSCS offer of compensation.[149]

The amount of compensation payable by the FSCS reflects the principle that claimants should not have their claims met in their entirety. The rationale for

---

[146] See Ch 2.5.2 for an explanation of the concept of 'passporting'.

[147] Above n 31.

[148] Excluded from the definition are, inter alia, EEA banks and investment firms 'passporting' into the United Kingdom, authorised professional firms that are subject to the rules of the Law Society (England and Wales) or the Law Society of Scotland and Investment Companies with Variable Capital. See COMP 6.2.1R.

[149] See the example at COMP 7.2.6G.

requiring claimants to bear part of the loss lies in the concept of moral hazard, which predicts that the behaviour of parties may change after the making of a contract or the provision of a guarantee (eg by not taking precautions they would otherwise take). The FSA explained its approach as follows:[150]

> It would be possible to structure compensation arrangements as a complete safety net for all consumers. Such a provision would be more in the nature of an indemnity for consumers, providing total protection for anything that goes wrong. It could undermine the encouragement which we would otherwise wish to give to individuals to enter into transactions in financial services only after proper consideration, to the best of their ability, of the balance of risk and reward.

The amount payable also reflects the different reasons for consumers using different types of financial services. In the case of insurance for example, the main concern is to avoid risk and therefore a high level of protection against failure of the firm underwriting the business can be justified.

The maximum payable in respect of a protected deposit is £31,700.[151] There is no limit to the amount payable in respect of a protected claim under a relevant general insurance contract and in the case of long-term insurance contracts there is a minimum but no maximum limit set.[152] In the case of protected investment business there is a limit of £48,000.[153] These limits apply to the aggregate amount of claims in respect of each category of protected claim that an eligible claimant has against the relevant person.[154] Payment of compensation must normally be made to a claimant within three months of the FSCS (a) being satisfied that a claim meets the requirements of the scheme and (b) calculating the amount of compensation to be paid.

There are no statutory or FSA Handbook provisions dealing with appeal against decisions made by the FSCS. It seems clear, however, that such decisions can, in principle, be the subject of judicial review.[155]

---

[150] FSA Consultation Paper 5, *Consumer Compensation* (1997) p 6.

[151] This comprises 100% of the first £2,000 and 90% of the next £33,000.

[152] The minimum is 100% of the first £2,000 and at least 90% of the remaining value of the policy.

[153] This comprises 100% of the first £30,000 and 90% of the next £20,000.

[154] See COMP 10.2.2G for an example of the operation of this principle.

[155] See *R v Investors Compensation Scheme Ltd, ex p Bowden* [1996] AC 261. Although this case was an unsuccessful attempt to challenge the discretion given to the operator of the compensation scheme established under s 54 of the Financial Services Act 1986, it did establish that compensation decisions are open to judicial review.

Part 3

Finance and Governance

7

Corporate Finance—The Legal Framework

Financing refers to the way in which enterprises fund the projects that form their business. It is inevitably linked with investment because large-scale enterprises generally rely on finance raised through the process of investment. Put another way, financing is the process that leads to the creation of the set of legal claims (comprising an investment) that are issued to an investor who contributes money (capital) to an enterprise. The nature of those claims is linked to the manner in which an enterprise chooses (or is able) to finance its activity. For example, the choice of a perpetual form of finance (without a fixed duration) that does not guarantee a return to the investor leads to the creation of equity-type investments. Similarly, the willingness of some investors to provide funds only on the basis that they have a fixed return and that the investment is for a fixed duration leads to the creation of fixed interest investments. In each instance the nature of the investment reflects the financing requirement that it is intended to meet.

The legal regime governing financing is relevant to investors because it has the capacity to affect the legal claims that comprise an investment. For example, the legal regime governing the issue of new shares in a company is clearly a matter that is of interest to existing shareholders because it may affect their relative power within the company. The process of investment is also influenced by the legal regime governing financing. The law relating to prospectuses issued by a company in connection with a new share issue, for example, is of considerable relevance to investors because they rely on its accuracy in making investment decisions.

This chapter aims to provide an introduction to the basic principles of the law relating to corporate finance. Its focus is primarily on those issues that are of direct relevance to portfolio investors and the process of investment.

7.1 Corporate finance: overview

7.1.1 Internal and external finance

A business can finance investment either from funds generated by the business itself (internally) or from funds raised externally. Internal funds are principally profits that are retained within a company (as reserves) rather than distributed to shareholders. The extent to which internal funds can finance investment varies greatly and depends inter alia on the nature of the business, its cash flow pattern, the extent to which it is capital-intensive and the dividend policy pursued by the company. External funds include the proceeds of issues of shares and bonds as well as bank loans. In aggregate, it is clear that internal finance is a more important source of funds for investment for UK companies than external finance. This means that companies typically finance their investment in productive capacity from internal resources rather than from external finance.[1]

The balance between internal and external finance is ultimately controlled by shareholders in a company. There are two ways in which this occurs. First, shareholders set dividend policy. This is crucial because dividend policy determines the balance between the proportion of profits that are distributed as dividends to shareholders and the proportion that is retained within the company. Retained profits are generally the most significant source of internal finance available to a company. Second, shareholders' approval is normally required for a substantial issue of new shares. There is generally greater freedom given to companies to raise loan capital and shareholder approval is not normally required. However, it is common for a company's constitution to limit borrowing and there are self-regulatory restraints imposed by institutional investors in the case of listed companies.[2]

7.1.2 Equity and debt finance

When a company's investment plans require external finance, a choice has to be made between equity and debt financing. Equity financing refers to financing through the issue of share capital, the most common form being ordinary share capital. It has the benefit of making finance available to the company on the basis that returns paid to the shareholders (in the form of dividends) are discretionary. Reliance on equity funding, however, carries the disadvantage

---

[1] See generally E Ferran, *Company Law and Corporate Finance* (Oxford, OUP, 1999) p 70.
[2] See below n 50.

that equity finance may not be available (whether from existing or new share-holders) on a scale that is capable of financing the growth of a company.

Debt financing refers to financing through loans under which a company enters into a debtor/creditor relationship with a lender. Some of the character-istics of debt financing are variable, such as the duration of the loan, whether or not it is secured on the company's property and the obligations undertaken by the company in the loan agreement concluded with the lender. All forms of debt finance, however, share some common features. First, unlike equity, debt finance provides a contractually guaranteed return to the lender in the form of interest, which may be at a fixed or floating rate (eg by reference to a bench-mark). Second, lenders are entitled to repayment on a pre-determined date (maturity of the loan). Equity investors (shareholders) have no such right as they provide in effect a perpetual form of financing to the company, although they can 'withdraw'[3] their investment by selling their shares to another investor. Third, lenders assume less risk than shareholders as, in the event of the company's insolvency, they take priority over shareholders in claiming the remaining assets of the company. Linked with their lower level of risk is the absence of profit-sharing on the part of lenders. They are entitled only to con-tractual interest and repayment and have no claim to share in either the profits of the company or any rise in value in the company's assets.

Some forms of finance are described as hybrid in that they combine both equity and debt characteristics. These include preference shares, convertible bonds and bonds with warrants attached.[4] The attraction of these instruments for investors is that they offer the security and fixed income of debt instru-ments combined with some of the profit-sharing features of equity investment.

The choice between equity and debt finance is influenced by a number of factors. Cost of capital, control rights and gearing are particularly important. In the case of debt finance, the cost of capital is the interest payable (and, in the case of convertibles or attached warrants, the earnings dilution[5] resulting from the exercise of the relevant rights). In the case of an equity issue, the cost is the dividend payable on the shares (the dividend yield). The higher the price at which shares can be issued, the lower is the cost of equity capital. Taxation also plays a role in comparing the cost of equity and debt because interest on loans is paid from pre-tax profits and dividends are paid from profits after tax. Another element of cost, in the case of debt, is the credit rating[6] of the bor-rower, which is itself influenced by the existing level of debt and the company's

---

[3] Withdrawal in this sense has no effect on the capital of the company as an investor transfers her share in the capital to another person.

[4] See Ch 4 for an explanation of the legal nature of these instruments.

[5] Earnings dilution arises as a result of aggregate earnings being divided among a larger num-ber of shares in issue following exercise of the relevant rights.

[6] See Ch 10 re credit-rating agencies.

historic record of servicing its debt. Risk is another important factor in judging the appropriate balance between debt and equity and attitudes towards risk may vary considerably between different companies and their shareholders.

Another factor to be considered is control. From the perspective of the existing shareholders, a new issue of equity capital to outsiders dilutes their influence (through voting) whereas loan capital has the potential to provide additional capital without any loss of control. However, while it is unusual for control rights in the form of votes to be allocated to anyone other than company members (shareholders), lenders often require a company to accept loan covenants which limit the freedom of action of the company (and therefore also the control rights of the members) during the currency of a loan.[7]

Debt financing introduces gearing (or leverage) into the financial returns of shareholders, with the result that changes in the financial performance of the company have a greater effect on shareholders than if the company is financed entirely by equity capital. This is because debt financing carries a fixed cost whereas dividends paid to shareholders are discretionary and are paid only after interest on debt capital has been paid. Gearing increases risk, delivering benefits when times are good and, at least at high levels, posing the threat of substantial losses or insolvency when times are bad.

7.1.3 Legal structure and financing

There exists a close relationship between the legal structure of a business and its financial structure because the legal structure governs the type of financing that is available to a business.[8] For this reason, legal structure is central to the initial establishment of a business and to its subsequent development.

The most basic distinction in terms of legal structure is between incorporated and unincorporated businesses. The main example in the former category is a company formed by registration under the Companies Act 1985. Unincorporated businesses are either sole traders or partnerships. Neither of these forms of unincorporated business organisation was developed for the purpose of facilitating investment by outsiders who are not involved in running the business, although it is possible for a partnership to be structured in a way that achieves this purpose. It follows that, from the perspective of portfolio investment, unincorporated businesses do not generally provide investment opportunities.

---

[7] Loan covenants are discussed below at 7.3.

[8] It is possible also to regard the relationship as working in the opposite direction. From this perspective the law is regarded as facilitating different forms of financing by creating financial instruments that meet different financing needs.

A further distinction can be drawn between businesses that have a financing structure involving share (equity) capital and those that do not. The main example in the former category is companies limited by shares. The extent to which such companies are able to attract investment depends to some extent on whether they are private or public companies, an issue considered further below. Companies that do not have a share capital include companies limited by guarantee, in which the members agree to contribute a certain sum in the event of insolvency and their liability is limited to that amount. Included in this category are some 'mutual' companies.[9]

The legal distinction between public and private companies is important in considering the extent to which there can be 'investment' in a company. Only public companies are permitted to offer their shares to the general public and to have their shares traded on a regulated market. Therefore, companies that want access to institutional investment and liquid markets for their securities must be public companies. Such companies must be designated as such by their memorandum of association, have a minimum authorised share capital of £50,000 (of which at least £12,500 must be paid up) and must include 'plc' in their name.[10] Any other company is a private company.[11] The vast majority of companies are private companies, and almost all companies start out as private companies. Conversion to public company status is possible at a later date. Only a relatively small proportion of public companies have a stock-market listing.[12]

---

[9] The concept of 'mutuality' is not an essentially legal one: the law does not and probably could not provide a definition of a mutual organisation that is capable of encompassing the wide range of organisations which operate on the basis of mutual principles. There are, however, two features which are common to mutual organisations: first, the members are both the customers and providers of capital for the organisation; and second, the organisation is run on the basis that all members have equal voting rights irrespective of their capital investment.

[10] See ss 1(3), 11, 25 and 118 of the Companies Act 1985.

[11] In the past, private companies were required to impose restrictions on the transfer of their shares. Although that is no longer a statutory requirement, it is common for the articles of private companies to restrict transfer. The result is to create a closed shareholding structure that is similar to a partnership. In contrast, listed company shares must be freely transferable.

[12] See the figures quoted in the Company Law Review Steering Group (CLRSG) document *Modern Company Law for a Competitive Economy, Final Report* at p 23. As at March 2000 there were over 1.3m private limited companies and 12,400 public companies. Of these public companies, 2,415 had a full stockmarket listing and 460 had an Alternative Investment Market (AIM) listing (see London Stock Exchange, *Primary Market Factsheet* at www.londonstockexchange.com (19 Nov 2004).

7.2 Raising new equity capital

At the time of its formation (through incorporation) a new limited company is required to have a share capital. It may or may not require further share capital during its lifetime. Whether it does so will depend on a number of factors: these include its cash-flow, profitability, dividend policy and ability to borrow money. All these factors influence the extent to which a company can remain self-financing.

A decision to issue new shares is likely to be made at one of the following stages in the life of a company. These are:

(a) when it is still a private company;
(b) when it has become a public company but before its shares are listed;
(c) at the time of listing;
(d) subsequent to listing.

Other than at stage (a) the issue of new shares is likely to involve a public offer. This process will trigger the application of the legal provisions relevant to public offers and possibly also listing. These issues are considered in 7.4 below. In this section, the focus is on the relevant provisions of company law that must logically be considered before any decision regarding a public offer or listing can be made. A number of issues are relevant. First, what is the relevance of the company's capital structure to its ability to issue new shares? Second, who can authorise the issue of new shares and in what circumstances? Third, to whom can new shares be issued? Fourth, what controls are imposed over the price at which new shares can be issued? Each of these issues is now considered.

7.2.1 Capital structure and share issues

Company law requires every company to state its authorised share capital in its memorandum of association.[13] This is the maximum share capital a company can have in issue at any given time. The issued share capital is the proportion of the authorised share capital that has been issued at any given time. The memorandum of association will also specify the nominal (or par) value of each share: this is simply the result of dividing the authorised share capital by the authorised number of shares and serves the purpose of apportioning a fixed participation in the entire share capital to each share.[14]

---

[13] Companies Act 1985 s 2(5)(a).

[14] It is now generally agreed that there is no need for par values in respect of shares and some countries operate without them. There is, however, a need for some alternative mechanism to determine the extent of the (typically limited) liability of members in a company if par values are

Shares may be issued on a fully paid, partly paid or nil paid basis. This means that, in each case, an investor pays the full price, a proportion of the price or nothing when shares are issued. In the case of a public company at least 25% of the nominal value, plus the whole of any premium, must be paid when shares are allotted.[15] When an issue is made other than on a fully paid basis, shareholders are liable to pay the balance and payment dates may be set by the articles or left to the discretion of the directors. The paid-up share capital of a company refers to that part of the issued capital that has been paid up and the called-up share capital refers to paid-up capital plus amounts due in respect of calls (for payment) made on shares that are not fully paid.[16]

So long as the issued share capital is less than the authorised share capital, a company can, in principle, issue new shares to raise capital. Whether, in reality, it would want to do that will depend on a number of considerations and in particular the availability of buyers for the shares, the price at which an issue can be made and the cost of a comparable issue of loan capital.

7.2.2 Authority for new share issues

A company limited by shares or a company limited by guarantee and having a share capital can issue new shares provided it is authorised to do so by its articles of association.[17] This power can be exercised by the shareholders in general meeting or by the directors if they are so authorised by a shareholders' resolution or by the company's articles. An authorisation given to the directors to issue shares must state the number of shares that can be issued and the expiry date of the authorisation. The authority cannot last for more than five years from (a) in the case of an authority contained in the company's articles at the time of its original incorporation, the date of that incorporation; and (b) in any other case, the date on which the resolution is passed by virtue of which the authority is given.[18] It is common for a resolution granting such authority to be adopted by listed companies each year at their annual general meeting.[19] Such authority can be revoked at any time by ordinary resolution even if this involves a change to the company's articles. Special provisions apply in respect

---

abolished. See R Pennington, *Pennington's Company Law*, 8th edn (London, Butterworths, 2001) p 161 re the history of par values and the CLRSG's comments at para 7.3 of their *Final Report* (above n 13).

[15] Companies Act 1985 s 737.

[16] For public companies the main relevance of called-up share capital is in determining if a distribution (eg a dividend) can be paid to members. See 7.4 below.

[17] Companies Act 1985 s 121. Table A 1985, art 2 provides for such a power.

[18] Companies Act 1985 s 80(4).

[19] For an example of such a resolution see Ferran (above n 1) p 614.

of private companies who are able to give directors authority to allot new shares for any fixed period of time or indefinitely.[20]

In the case of listed companies, institutional investors voting on section 80 resolutions are expected to follow the guidelines adopted by the Investment Committees of the Association of British Insurers (ABI) and the National Association of Pension Funds (NAPF). The guidelines indicate that the number of shares which the directors should be authorised to issue should be the lesser of (a) the unissued ordinary share capital and (b) a sum equal to one third of the issued ordinary share capital.

7.2.3 Pre-emption rights

New issues of shares are controlled by the principle of pre-emption in company law. The objectives of a pre-emption rule are to protect the existing shareholders against two risks that arise from the process of issuing new shares. The first is the risk that the proportion of voting shares held by an existing shareholder may be diluted by an issue of new shares. This can be illustrated by reference to a simple example. Assume that company A has an issued share capital of 1000 ordinary shares. If the company proposes to increase its equity capital by 30 per cent it can in theory do this by offering the new shares either to existing shareholders or to third parties outside the company. If the shares are offered to and taken up by the existing shareholders then the result is that the proportionate shareholding and voting power of each shareholder remains the same. Alternatively, if the shares are issued to outsiders in their entirety, the proportionate shareholding and voting power of existing shareholders will be diluted: in this situation a 15 per cent shareholder would see their shareholding fall to 11.5 per cent. A range of intermediate solutions would also be possible in a situation in which the new shares were taken up by different combinations of existing shareholders and outsiders. It is also possible for dilution to occur in a similar manner when shares are offered only to a select group of shareholders, with the result that the remaining shareholders suffer dilution.[21] Protecting shareholders against the risk of dilution in their voting power does of course assume that they have an interest in exercising their votes, an assumption that is not always supported by empirical evidence.[22]

The second risk against which a pre-emption rule seeks to protect shareholders is that of reduction in the value of their shares resulting from a share issue made to outsiders at a price below the prevailing market price. The

[20] Companies Act 1985, s 379A and s 80A.
[21] See *Shareholders' Remedies, A Consultation Paper* (Law Commission no 142) 1996 paras 9.36–9.38, which discuss this issue from the perspective of s 459 'prejudicial conduct' actions relating to breach of pre-emption rights.
[22] See Ch 8.4.

example already given can also be used to illustrate this point. Assume that Company A makes an issue of 300 new shares to outsiders at a price of 150p at a time when the market price of the shares is 200p. In this situation the new shareholders will have paid less than the market value of the shares and the share price will fall, causing a loss to the existing shareholders.[23]

The absence of a common law rule of pre-emption in the United Kingdom meant that shareholders were not regarded as having the right to control the entry of new members into a company in the way that partners can control entry into a partnership.[24] The adoption of the Second EC Directive on Company Law[25] in 1976 resulted in pre-emption becoming a statutory right, now contained in sections 89–96 of the Companies Act 1985. The right of pre-emption under section 89 of the Companies Act 1985 arises only when a company is proposing to make an allotment of 'equity securities'.[26]

The right of pre-emption is excluded when a company makes a share issue for a cash consideration.[27] It may also be restricted where a company's memorandum or articles contain a provision requiring that an issue of shares of a particular class[28] be offered first on a pre-emptive basis to the holders of that

---

[23] The fall in the share price will reflect the fact that, *ceteris paribus*, the number of shares in issue will have increased to a greater extent than the company's capital and dividend-paying capability. The ABI/NAPF Joint Position Paper (1996) (see www.abi.org.uk (19 Nov 2004)) states, 'any discount [in the price of a new issue relative to existing shares] represents a transfer of wealth from, and therefore a cost to, existing shareholders'. In contrast, a new issue made to existing shareholders at less than the prevailing market price (the typical rights issue in the UK equity market) has no significant effect on an existing shareholder's financial position. The ABI/NAPF Paper goes on to say, 'It makes no difference to an existing shareholder whether new shares issued by way of rights are issued at a deep discount to the market price, at a modest discount or at the market price itself.'

[24] Gower comments that it was odd for company law to have developed in this way given the willingness of the legislature and the courts to adopt partnership principles in other situations (LCB Gower, 'Some Contrasts between British and American Corporation Law' (1955) *Harvard Law Review* 1369 at 1380). The common law in the United States did contain a principle of pre-emption but this was removed by individual state corporation laws: see I MacNeil, 'Shareholders' Pre-Emption Rights' (2002) *JBL* 78.

[25] Dir 77/91/EEC [1977] OJ L26/1.

[26] This term is defined in s 94(2) as being 'a relevant share in the company . . . or a right to subscribe for, or to convert securities into, relevant shares in the company'. Relevant shares are defined in s 94(5) as shares other than (a) shares which are entitled only to a fixed participation in dividends and capital; (b) shares held pursuant to an employees' share scheme. Preference shares may or may not fall into category (a) and therefore there is no simple rule as to whether or not the holders of preference shares have statutory pre-emption rights. Holders of warrants and convertible loan stock do not have statutory pre-emption rights, but may be granted such rights by the terms on which the relevant securities are issued.

[27] Companies Act 1985, s 89(4), replicating Article 17(1) of the Second EC Company Law Directive (above n 26). This means that 'vendor consideration' issues, which are issues in respect of which the consideration for the share issue is either property or share capital (of another company), do not fall within the scope of statutory pre-emption rights.

[28] For this purpose a class of shares is defined as shares to which the same rights are attached as to voting and as to participation, both as respects dividends and as respects capital, in a distribution.

particular class of share. In this situation, the pre-emptive rights of the holders of other classes of shares (to which the general right of pre-emption in section 89(1) relates) apply only to those shares which are not taken up by the holders of the relevant class to whom the offer was required to be made.

In the case of a public company, where the directors have a general authority to allot shares under section 80, pre-emption rights can be excluded or modified by the articles of association[29] or by a special resolution[30]. If the directors are authorised only in relation to a particular allotment, a special resolution is required to disapply pre-emption rights. The disapplication of section 89 in the case of a listed company has no effect on the application of the listing rules. In the case of a private company, pre-emption rights may be excluded entirely or in part by the articles of association.[31]

Although the listing rules do not restrict disapplication of statutory pre-emption rights, self-regulation on the part of institutional investors does. Guidelines drawn up by the Stock Exchange Pre-Emption Group[32] in 1987 limit the size of share issues not involving pre-emption rights that will be approved by ABI/NAPF members when voting on a resolution under section 95 of the Companies Act 1985 and control the price at which such an issue can be made. Such resolutions for an annual disapplication of pre-emptive rights will be approved by ABI/NAPF members provided they do not exceed 5 per cent of the issued ordinary share capital shown in the latest published annual accounts. A cumulative limit is also applied to restrict issues made over a three-year period by a company using its disapplication entitlement (under a section 95 resolution) to 7.5 per cent of issued ordinary share capital shown by the latest published annual accounts. As regards the price of an issue to non-shareholders, the Pre-Emption Guidelines provide that any discount should

---

[29] Table A 1985 does not disapply pre-emption rights. Until relatively recently, rule 9.20 of the Stock Exchange Listing Rules provided that authority to disapply pre-emption rights could last no longer than 15 months from the date of the relevant special resolution. The time limit has been dropped from the current version of rule 9.20 which simply provides that pre-emption rights can be disapplied in accordance with s 95 of the Companies Act 1985.

[30] This requires a 75% majority of members who vote on the resolution. Section 95(5) also provides that such a special resolution cannot be proposed unless it is recommended by the directors and there has been circulated, with the notice of the meeting at which the resolution is proposed, a written statement by the directors setting out the reasons for the recommendation, the amount to be paid in respect of equity securities allotted and the directors' justification of that amount.

[31] Companies Act 1985 s 91. The Second Company Law Directive (above n 26) does not apply to private companies and therefore the application of pre-emption to private companies remains a matter for the Member States of the EC.

[32] The group comprises representatives of institutional investors, investment banks and listed companies.

not exceed 5 per cent and the Stock Exchange monitors this guideline both before and after an issue is made.[33]

A shareholder's financial position will not normally be affected by a decision to take up or decline a share issue made in accordance with pre-emption rights (i.e. a rights issue). This is because it is normally possible to sell in the market the right to buy the new shares at a discount. The principle of pre-emption does not restrict the sale of these rights by a shareholder. The price at which the rights trade in the market will reflect the size of the discount to the prevailing market price at which the rights issue is made. Therefore, a shareholder will be in the same financial position irrespective of whether the rights are sold or exercised.[34]

If shares are issued in contravention of a shareholder's pre-emptive rights, there are two remedies available to the shareholder. First, the company and every officer of it who has knowingly authorised or permitted the contravention are jointly and severally liable to compensate any person to whom an offer should have been made.[35] This requires the shareholder to show that a loss has resulted from the contravention. In the case of a rights isue from which the shareholder was excluded, this would be the value of the 'nil paid rights'.[36] Second, the shareholder could apply to the court to have the company's share register rectified. Failure to observe pre-emption rights does not automatically invalidate an issue, but the court can exercise its power to rectify the share register in such circumstances.[37]

7.2.4 Pricing of new shares

The minimum price at which a company can issue shares is the nominal (or par) value of the shares. If shares are issued at a discount to their nominal value, the allottee and any subsequent holder (other than a holder in due course[38]) is liable to pay the company the amount of the discount in cash.[39]

---

[33] The Pre-Emption Guidelines require companies to complete a form showing the projected discount at which the new shares will be issued and the actual discount at which the shares are issued. The actual discount will reflect market conditions at the time that the pricing decision is made.

[34] See the example in 7.2.4 below.

[35] Companies Act 1985 s 92.

[36] See the example in 7.2.4 below.

[37] Companies Act 1985 s 359. See *Re Thundercrest Ltd* [1995] BCLC 117 for an example of the exercise of this power in the context of a private company.

[38] This refers to a person who is a purchaser for value without actual notice of the issue at a discount at the time of the purchase or he derived title directly or indirectly from such a purchaser: see Companies Act 1985 s 112(1).

[39] Companies Act 1985 s 100(2) and s 112(1) and (3). The statutory provisions give effect to a long-established common-law principle which aimed to ensure that companies did not overstate their capital by issuing shares at a discount to their nominal value. The rationale for the

The actual price at which a company can issue shares is the price that investors (and in particular the existing shareholders) are prepared to subscribe to a new issue, and that may be a determining factor in deciding whether or not to make an issue. Any difference between the nominal price and issue price is referred to as a premium and is treated in much the same way as capital. It is available to finance the company's activity but is not generally available to distribute to shareholders as dividend.[40]

Just as there is no direct relationship between the nominal value of shares and their issue price, there is no direct relationship between the nominal value of shares and the price at which they trade in the secondary market. A company has no involvement in the trading of its shares between investors and is not directly affected by that process because, irrespective of who owns the shares, its share capital remains the same.[41] The value of assets that represent the share capital (such as land, buildings, and plant and machinery) will fluctuate in value according to market movements and the fortunes of the company and will have a direct effect on the market value of a company's shares. However, that process has no effect on the share capital or nominal value of shares, both of which remain fixed unless altered in accordance with the procedure set by company law.

A rights issue is a share issue in which shareholders have a legal right to participate.[42] The size of the issue is measured by reference to the existing issued share capital. For example, in a one-for-three rights issue, the issued share capital is being increased by 33 per cent and shareholders have a right to buy one new share for every three that they already own. It is normal for a rights issue to be made at a discount to the prevailing market price and sometimes at a 'deep-discount'. The only limit on the size of the discount is that shares cannot be issued below their par (nominal) value. While directors who allot shares to outsiders at a discount to market value may be guilty of a breach of duty and liable to pay the premium that could have been obtained as damages,[43] there is no restriction on offering shares at a discount to market value to shareholders.[44] As discussed below, this reflects the fact that any discount in the price at which shares are offered to shareholders (in a rights issue) does not prejudice their financial position.

principle was to protect creditors who relied on the stated capital being available to pay their debts. See *Ooregum Gold Mining Co of India Ltd v Roper* [1892] AC 125.

[40] The legal framework governing the distribution of dividends is considered at 7.5 (below).

[41] A company is indirectly affected in that a new issue of shares will be made by reference to the price at which the company's shares trade in the market.

[42] The right is that of pre-emption, considered at 7.2.3 (above).

[43] *Lowry v Consolidated African Selection Trust Ltd* [1940] AC 648 at 679 per Lord Wright. For an analysis of this and other cases dealing with the price at which new shares are issued see MacNeil (above n 24).

[44] *Mutual Life Insurance Co of New York v Rank Organisation Ltd* [1985] BCLC 11.

In principle, the size of the discount is neutral for the financial position of an individual shareholder, irrespective of whether she takes up the offer or sells her entitlement to the offer in the market (in the form of 'nil paid rights'). However, as the size of the discount acts as a measure of shareholders' demand for the company's shares and the attractiveness of the project that the issue is to fund, 'deep-discount' issues are regarded by many companies and investors as less attractive than those priced close to the prevailing market price.[45]

The effect of a (discounted) rights issue on the position of a shareholder can be analysed by calculating the 'theoretical ex-rights price' price of the shares. This is an estimate of the price at which the share should trade in the market after the rights issue. It is only an estimate as it ignores factors such as the expected return earned by the company on the funds raised by the issue, which in reality will have an important influence on the market's response to a rights issue.

Assume that company A's shares trade at 150p. It announces a 'one for five' rights issue at 100p. The position of a shareholder with 20 shares who takes up the offer is as follows:

20 'old' shares @ 150p	£30.00
4 'new' shares @ 100p	£ 4.00
24 shares in total	£34.00
Each share is worth	142p

In this example, the 'theoretical ex-rights' price is 142p and this is the price at which the shares could be expected to trade in the market after the rights issue. The value of the 'rights' is the difference between the 'theoretical ex-rights' and the subscription price payable to the company, in this case $142 - 100 = 42$p. A shareholder can sell the rights in the market as 'nil paid rights' at this price, giving the buyer the rights to buy the shares at 100p. If the shareholder in this example were to do this as opposed to taking up the offer, her position would be:

20 shares @ 142p	£28.40
sale of 'nil paid rights' over 4 'new' shares	£ 1.68
Combined total	£30.08

This can be compared with the position after taking up the rights, which is that the shareholder has a shareholding of 24 shares worth £34.08 but has paid £4 for the new shares. Adjusting for the £4 paid for the new shares, the position is the same irrespective of whether the shareholder takes up the rights offer or

---

[45] Companies also face the problem that they may not be able to maintain the same level of dividend on the increased share capital. However, as it is normal for earnings and dividends to be adjusted (downwards) for a rights issue, this is essentially a problem of investor expectations rather than an inherent defect in the deep-discount financing technique.

not. This remains true irrespective of the fraction of the share capital represented by the rights issue or the size of the discount.

A capitalisation issue of shares (also referred to as a bonus or scrip issue), unlike a rights issue, does not involve the raising of new capital by a company. It is a mechanism by which a company can use retained profits[46] to pay up unissued shares in the company which are then issued to existing shareholders pro rata to their existing shareholding.[47] The result is that the number of shares in issue is increased but shareholders' funds (net assets) remain the same. The result is that the market price will fall to reflect the new issue[48] and a shareholder's financial position remains the same. Companies make such issues for a variety of reasons, one being that it is sometimes believed that the liquidity of shares (and hence their value) may benefit from a lower price per share.

7.3 Raising new loan capital

7.3.1 Borrowing powers and procedures

Companies generally have greater freedom to issue loans than share capital. A company formed to carry on a trade or business has an implied power to borrow and give security for loans made to it, but it is normal for express powers to be included in a company's constitution. In the absence of any restriction in its constitution, the amount of money a company can borrow is unlimited. The directors' authority to issue loan capital is also in principle unlimited unless limitations are imposed by the constitution.[49]

In the United Kingdom, the term 'debenture' is associated with secured long-term loans, although that usage runs counter to the legal meaning of the term and to its meaning in the United States.[50] Unsecured long-term loans are typically referred to as loan stock[51], while short- or medium-term unsecured loans are often termed 'loan notes'. Short- and medium-term loans of up to

---

[46] It is also possible for such an issue to be funded by a transfer from the share premium account (Companies Act 1985 s 130(2)) or the capital redemption reserve (Companies Act 1985 s 170(4)).

[47] This definition is contained in s 280(2) Companies Act 1985.

[48] Eg a bonus issue of 1 new share for every 5 held will result in a 20% fall in the share price but as a shareholder will have 20% more shares the overall impact is neutral.

[49] See Pennington (above n 14) p 234 for historic restrictions requiring shareholders' approval for loans above a certain threshold. In the case of listed companies, the ABI generally expects borrowing to be limited to twice capital and reserves and such a limitation can be included in the articles of association. (See Ferran, above n 1 p 256.)

[50] See Ch 4.5 for an explanation of the legal nature of debentures.

[51] If unsecured loan stock is listed it must be referred to as 'unsecured': Listing Rules chapter 13 app 2, para 11.

seven years' duration, which comprise mainly fixed-term bank loans and over-drafts, are generally excluded from the term 'loan capital'.[52] Such loans include money-market instruments, which are short-term debt instruments (with less than a year's maturity) used by treasury departments to manage the short-term financing needs of companies. Eurobonds are a special type of loan issued by companies.[53]

Debentures and loans are frequently issued in the form of 'stock'. Old forms of debenture were issued to a single lender, but over time the process of issuing debentures adapted to the need to raise loan capital from large numbers of investors. The modern procedure is for the loan to be made to trustees who are the creditors of the company for the whole amount of the loan plus interest. This offers the benefit that the company does not have to deal directly with large numbers of small creditors. The individual subscribers are issued with 'debenture stock', which evidences their share in the loan but does not make them creditors of the company. The debenture stockholders' rights are primarily against the trustees who act on their behalf. The trust deed normally provides that the debenture stockholders rank *pari passu* (equally) as regards their rights, thereby avoiding the possibility that any one holder can gain a preference or priority over the others.

Like shares, instruments representing loan capital have a nominal value, which is the sum repayable to the lender on maturity. Unlike shares, they can be and are issued at a discount to their nominal value. This has the effect that the amount of the discount repayable at maturity is capital rather than income, which may give rise to tax benefits.[54] It also allows the contractual rate of interest for loan capital to be set well in advance of the issue date, as the issue price can be fixed closer to the issue date so as to make the redemption yield on the issue attractive in relation to comparable securities.

Redemption of debentures can occur in a variety of ways, according to the loan agreement. It is unusual for repayment of the entire loan to be made at a fixed date. More commonly, repayment is made by instalments over a period of between two and five years before the final date for repayment. The loan agreement can provide for repayments to be distributed pro rata across all holders, or alternatively it can provide for lots to be drawn to determine which debentures shall be repaid from each instalment. It is possible for a premium to be payable by the company on redemption of debentures. This can be provided for by the loan agreement (eg if the company wants to pay the loan before maturity) or can be agreed at the time of repayment.[55]

---

[52] Short-term loans of up to one year's duration are generally referred to as commercial paper.
[53] See Ch 4.5.
[54] See Pennington (above n 14) p 235.
[55] As to potential problems arising from the restriction that a premium may impose on the 'equity of redemption' see Pennington (above n 14) p 566.

7.3.2 Loan agreements and security interests

In principle, loans to companies can be made on any terms.[56] The terms of a
loan agreement, including the rate of interest, will reflect the creditworthiness
of the borrowing company. In the case of loan capital that is to be listed and
offered to the public, it is common for the borrower to arrange for a credit-
rating to be attached to the loan by a credit rating agency.[57] The purpose of a
credit-rating is to provide independent verification of the ability of a borrower
to meet its loan obligations. The better the credit rating, the better the terms
on which a company can borrow.

Lenders generally adopt three techniques to protect against the risks inherent in lending to companies. First, loan agreements generally guarantee the
accuracy of the information on which a lender has made a lending decision.
This is achieved through representations and warranties in loan agreements.
Second, covenants in loan agreements protect lenders against the risk of a
debtor acting in a manner that prejudices the interests of the lender. Third,
lenders often take a security interest so as to ensure that, in the event of a borrower defaulting, assets will be available from which the debt can be repaid.
Each technique is now considered in turn.

The purpose of representations and warranties in a loan agreement is to
guarantee the accuracy of the information on which a lending decision is
based. Factors relevant to that decision include the financial position of a company; the legal capacity of the company and the authority given to directors to
enter into loan agreements; litigation pending against the company, pre-
existing loans and security interests; and compliance with relevant laws and
regulations. A loan agreement will normally specify that an incorrect representation or warranty is an act of default, giving the lender the right to call for
repayment of the loan. This avoids the technical arguments which would otherwise arise as a result of the different implications in contract law arising from
a breach of a warranty and a misrepresentation.[58]

Covenants in loan agreements vary according to the bargaining position of
the lender and the nature of the loan. They are intended to ensure that a borrower remains able to fulfil its loan obligations, which are the repayment of both

---

[56] Controls over interest rates do not apply (as they potentially do to consumer credit under
s 137 of the Consumer Credit Act 1974), nor do the controls over contract terms contained in the
Unfair Contract Terms Act 1977 or the Unfair Terms in Consumer Contracts Regulations 1999,
SI 1999/2083.

[57] See Ch 10.

[58] These terms have a specific meaning in the law of contract in England: see GH Treitel, *The
Law of Contract*, 11th edn (London, Sweet & Maxwell, 2003) pp 330 and 790. While they may be
used in loan agreements subject to Scots law, they do not have the same meaning in that context:
see W McBryde, *Contract*, 2nd edn (Edinburgh, W Green, 2001) p 372.

interest and capital. The most common forms of covenant are those relating to the financial position of the company. They can include minimum requirements as to a company's level of working capital and net assets or prohibitions on dividend distributions above a certain level or substantial asset disposals. They can also include reporting covenants, which require the debtor to provide the lender with on-going financial information, in addition to that which is publicly available.[59] It is also possible to prevent or restrict the creation of new security interests during the term of a loan, through the insertion of a 'negative pledge' clause. Breach of a covenant is normally an act of default under the loan agreement, giving the lender the right to demand repayment of the loan.

The floating charge is the most common technique used by lenders to take security from companies.[60] It offers the benefit that it can cover any or all of the company's property and the company can continue to deal (buy and sell) in the property subject to the charge. Under a fixed charge[61] relating to specific property, by way of contrast, it is not possible for the company to sell the relevant property. The 'floating' characteristic reflects the fact that, prior to enforcement, property subject to the charge is constantly changing.

The Companies Act requires details of floating charges to be made available to the Registrar of Companies within 21 days of their creation, for the purposes of registration. The purpose of registration is to publicise the existence of the security interest, as it may affect the likelihood of other creditors (in particular ordinary trade creditors) recovering their debts in the event of the company's insolvency.[62] Information held by the Registrar of Companies is available to the general public.[63] Details of the charge must also be entered in the register of charges maintained by the company at its registered office.[64] If a floating charge is not registered within the statutory period, the holder loses her priority as against other secured creditors.[65]

---

[59] In this situation, it is possible for a lender of loan capital to be better informed than a shareholder. However, in the case of listed loan capital, lenders need to exercise caution in the use of inside information. See Ch 9 for a discussion of legal controls over the use of such information.

[60] The floating charge was recognised under the common law in England but was not recognised in Scotland until 1961. The floating charge is an exception to the general rule in Scotland that transfer of possession to the creditor is necessary to create a valid security interest over property.

[61] eg a mortgage in England or a standard security in Scotland.

[62] As to the limitations of the Companies Register in providing an up-to-date record of charges granted by a company see Ferran (above n 1) p 538.

[63] There is a Registrar of Companies for companies incorporated in England in Bristol and for companies incorporated in Scotland in Edinburgh.

[64] This register can be inspected freely by members and creditors and by the public on payment of a small charge.

[65] Companies Act 1985 s 395 in England and s 410 in Scotland. The substance of the provisions is the same but the separate system of property law and security interests in Scotland led to separate provisions in the Companies Act 1985. The precise meaning of these provisions is a matter of some debate: see Ferran (above n 1 at p 543) and (in respect of Scotland) G Grettton 'Registration of Company Charges' (2002) 6 *Edinburgh Law Review* 146.

When certain events occur, the floating charge is said to 'crystallise' or 'attach' to the relevant property. When the charge relates (as is commonly the case) to 'all the property and undertaking of the company', all the assets owned[66] by the company at that point in time become subject to the charge and cannot be sold. The effect of attachment is that the floating charge becomes a fixed charge, an event which has important consequences for the priority of the holder as against other creditors of the company.

The events that can result in attachment of a floating charge differ between England and Scotland and represent different approaches to the manner in which creditors are treated on the insolvency of a company. In England, it is possible for the instrument creating a floating charge to specify which events will give rise to crystallisation, without any action being necessary on the part of the creditor ('automatic crystallisation').[67] In the absence of express provision, the instrument will be assumed to create implied terms providing for crystallisation in three circumstances. These are the appointment of a receiver by the holder of the floating charge, the commencement of the winding up of the company and the cessation of its business.

In Scotland, a more restrictive approach is adopted. A floating charge only attaches to the relevant property when a company goes into liquidation or on the appointment of a receiver.[68] It is not possible to have an 'automatic crystallisation' provision (as occurs in England). This restriction reflects the potential prejudice that could be created for other creditors as a result of the occurrence of 'automatic crystallisation' events of which they are not aware. Liquidation and receivership, by way of contrast, are events that attract publicity and are therefore likely to put creditors on notice that they face problems in recovering debts from the relevant company.

Following the changes introduced by the Enterprise Act 2002, it will in future be more common for an administrator rather than a receiver to be appointed to a company that is in financial distress. The role of an administrator is essentially to ensure the continued survival of the company as a going concern. If that is not possible, administration will normally be followed by liquidation. In those circumstances, the floating charge holder is entitled to repayment only after payment of, inter alia, holders of fixed charges[69] that rank ahead of the floating charge and preferential creditors. Fixed charges that have been created in accordance with relevant legal requirements[70] before a floating

---

[66] Assets held by a company as trustee or as agent are not owned by the company and do not become subject to the charge. As regards the status of property in respect of which a contract of sale has been agreed but no transfer has taken place, see *Sharp v Thomson* 1997 SLT 636.

[67] See *Re Brightlife Ltd* [1987] Ch 200 and *Re Permanent Houses (Holdings) Ltd* (1989) 5 BCC 151.

[68] Companies Act 1985 s 463(1) and Insolvency Act 1986 s 53(7).

[69] Such as a mortgage in England or standard security in Scotland.

[70] eg as to registration.

charge becomes a fixed charge (on attachment) take priority to the floating charge.[71]

The statutory priority in which a company's debts are to be repaid in receivership or liquidation can be varied by contract.[72] This process is referred to as subordination and the relevant debt as subordinated. Secured debt can be subordinated by the making of a ranking agreement among the relevant creditors. Unsecured debt can be subordinated if the relevant creditor agrees to accept that her claim ranks behind other creditors.[73] The purpose of subordination is generally to allow a company to borrow in a manner that does not threaten the interests of existing creditors. The subordination agreement can be enforced either by the company[74] against the relevant debenture holders or by a creditor[75] who is intended to benefit from the subordination.

7.3.3 Loan capital and listing

Loans raised by companies in the form of debt securities (such as debentures) that are listed or offered to the public are subject to the listing and public offers regime discussed below, unless they benefit from exemption or a special regulatory regime. There are two main types of loan security that benefit from some form of exemption in respect of the listing and public offers regime: Eurobonds and money-market instruments.[76] Eurobonds are categorised as 'specialist securities' by the Listing Rules.[77] This is because their nature is such that they are normally bought and traded by a limited number of investors who are particularly knowledgeable in investment matters. They are not traded on regulated markets but are traded on an 'OTC' basis between banks.[78] Although Eurobond issuers are required to produce listing particulars, they benefit from a lighter regulatory regime as a result of the disapplication of many of the listing rules. All money-market instruments are exempt from the

---

[71] The priority given to holders of fixed charges created before the floating charge crystallises (or attaches) means that it is important for lenders taking security in this form to ensure that there are no pre-existing fixed charges and that none is created while the charge remains 'floating'. This can be achieved through the use of a 'negative pledge' clause.

[72] As noted by Ferran (above n 1 at p 550), this is not an attempt to place a debt outside the liquidation procedure, in which the *pari passu* principle applies, meaning that creditors are in principle treated equally unless they hold preferential rights.

[73] As there can be no question of the rights of other creditors being prejudiced in these circumstances, their consent is not required.

[74] *Beswick v Beswick* [1968] AC 58.

[75] In England, under the Contracts (Rights of Third Parties) Act 1999, s 1(1)–(3) and in Scotland under the common law based on the *ius quaesitum tertio* (the right of a third party).

[76] See Ch 4 for an explanation of the nature of these instruments.

[77] Ch 23.

[78] See Ch 9 for discussion of the over-the-counter (OTC) market.

requirement to produce a prospectus at the time of an offer.[79] Unlike loan capital or equity securities, which are capable of meeting the needs of long-term investors, they are not appropriate instruments for listing and trading on recognised investment exchanges.

7.4 Listing and public offers of securities

7.4.1 Background

Listing is a regulatory process through which the securities of a public company can become eligible to be traded in a regulated market.[80] The attraction of listing for investors is that the liquidity of their holding is improved. Listed securities generally have a higher degree of transferability and liquidity than unlisted securities, for which there may be no real market or one with only very limited liquidity. The attraction of liquidity (in essence the ability to buy or sell) for issuers of securities is that it is likely to increase the price at which a company can issue securities, as investors will generally pay a premium for liquidity.

There are three broad approaches to the regulation of listing. 'Merit-based' regulation involves a regulator reviewing the merits of securities in respect of which an application for listing has been made.[81] The objective is to restrict listing to securities that are regarded, on objective criteria, as sound investments. 'Mandatory disclosure' is an alternative approach which assumes that investors can be left to make their own decisions provided full disclosure is made by issuers.[82] In the UK, the latter approach has generally prevailed, although there have always been conditions for listing, which have had the

---

[79] They can become exempt either under art 3(1) of the Public Offers of Securities Regulations (SI 1995/1536) in the case of debentures having a maturity of less than one year from their date of issue, or art 7(2) in the case of securities that are offered only to investment professionals.

[80] See Ch 9.1 for the meaning of a regulated market.

[81] Merit-based regulation was adopted by most states of the USA prior to the introduction of the federal securities laws in the 1930s. It was referred to as 'blue sky' law because it was claimed that many securities salesmen were so dishonest that they would sell 'buildings in the blue sky' to investors. See, for background and history, P Mahoney, 'The Origins of the Blue Sky Laws: A Test of Competing Hypotheses' at http://papers.ssrn.com/abstract=296344 (19 Nov 2004).

[82] It is derived from the Efficient Market Hypothesis, which, in its semi-strong form, predicts that the prices of securities will reflect all publicly available information (ie there will be no pricing anomalies in respect of that information). For a discussion of the role of disclosure in modern securities markets see S Schwarcz, 'Rethinking the Disclosure Paradigm in a World of Complexity' (2004) 1 *University of Illinois Law Review* 1.

effect of excluding some types of company from listing.[83] The main concern of the law and regulatory rules relating to listing in the UK is to ensure that, following listing of a company's securities, there will be a proper market, meaning one in which investors are able, at any point in time, to make fully informed investment decisions (eg to buy or sell). Finally, although not generally favoured, it would in principle be possible to leave disclosure to be determined by market forces. This could result in either disclosure requirements being set on an individual basis or (more likely) some form of self-regulation being agreed between issuers and (professional) investors.[84]

A public offer of securities is an invitation to the general public to buy securities.[85] A public offer can be made in respect of listed or unlisted securities and in practice it is common for a public offer to be made of securities that are to be listed. The focus of the law relating to public offers runs parallel to that relating to listing in that it aims to ensure that adequate disclosure is made in respect of the securities offered for sale. However, as a public offer will not always involve securities that are to be traded on an organised market, the law relating to public offers is more directly concerned with the fairness of the particular sale transaction involved in the public offer, whereas the law relating to listing has a broader focus on the fairness of the operation of the market as a whole.

The regulatory framework governing listing and public offers in the UK is built around the concept of 'official listing'. This refers to the 'official list' maintained by the regulatory authority responsible for listing (the United Kingdom Listing Authority or UKLA). The purpose of the 'official list' has historically been to provide a regulated market for the trading of company securities. Securities that are not admitted to the official list are not 'listed' for this purpose even if they are admitted to trading on a market such as the Alternative Investment Market (AIM). The essential distinction for the investor is that 'official listing' imposes more onerous regulatory obligations on companies than exist in respect of 'unlisted' securities.

The legal framework governing listing and public offers is as follows:[86]

1 Securities which are to be admitted to 'official listing' are governed by Part VI of FSMA 2000. This applies also to securities when a public offer is made

---

[83] eg newly formed companies and hedge funds. FSMA 2000 s 74(2) provides that 'The competent authority may admit to the official list such securities and other things as it considers appropriate' but this has not been viewed as a mandate for the introduction of 'merit-based' regulation.

[84] See BR Cheffins, *Company Law. Theory, Structure and Operation* (Oxford, OUP, 1997) 163–8 and JC Coffee, 'Market Failure and the Economic Case for a Mandatory Disclosure System' (1984) 70 *Virginia Law Review* 717.

[85] This is an explanatory definition. The legal definition (below) is more complex.

[86] See generally J Birds (ed) *Boyle & Birds' Company Law*, 5th edn (Bristol, Jordans, 2004) ch 18.

at the same time as listing (as is often the case when a company 'goes public' or 'floats').

2 First-time public offers of unlisted securities are regulated by the Public Offers of Securities (POS) Regulations 1995[87]. This is relevant when the securities are not to be admitted to 'official listing' (eg when listing is to be on AIM).

3 Offers of securities falling outside both Part VI of FSMA 2000 and the Public Offers of Securities Regulations are subject to the provisions of section 21 of the Financial Services and Markets Act 2000, which regulates the activity described as 'financial promotion'.[88] This has the effect that such offers must be approved by a person authorised under FSMA 2000.

4 Certain matters relating to the allotment of shares and debentures remain subject to the Companies Act 1985.[89]

5 Special rules apply when a company wants to make a simultaneous offer of its securities in two or more Member States of the EU.[90]

7.4.2 The UK listing regime

Admission to listing is controlled by the United Kingdom Listing Authority (UKLA), which is part of the FSA. It is the 'competent authority' for the purposes of the EU directives relating to listing and public offers, which require such an authority to be designated in each Member State.[91] When discharging its responsibilities, the UKLA must have regard to six regulatory principles, which are similar to the principles that must be observed by the FSA when discharging its general functions under the FSMA 2000 as a whole.[92]

The conditions for listing are contained in the Listing Rules of the UKLA, which implement the requirements of the EC Consolidated Admissions and

---

[87] SI 1995/1537.

[88] See Ch 3 regarding financial promotion. In these circumstances the offer must be approved by a person authorised under FSMA 2000.

[89] See *Boyle & Birds' Company Law* (above n 86) para 6.3.

[90] These are contained in art 20 of and sch 4 to the POS Regulations.

[91] In the past, the London Stock Exchange had been the 'competent authority' in the UK. Following its demutualisation and flotation, it was no longer considered appropriate for the LSE to exercise regulatory functions and so these were transferred to the UKLA, which is part of the FSA—see the Official Listing of Securities (Transfer of Competent Authority) Regulations 2000, SI 2000/968. The Treasury has power to transfer (by order) the functions of the competent authority to another person: FSMA 2000 s 72(3) and sch 8.

[92] See Ch 3. Note that the 'general functions' in s 2(4) FSMA 2000 do not apply to the UKLA's role as competent authority (s 72(2) and sch 7 FSMA 2000). The Acts's regulatory objectives (ss 3–6) therefore do not apply to the UKLA as competent authority. This reflects the dominance of EC directives (based primarily on the single market integration objective) in relation to listing and public offers and the obligation of the competent authority to give effect to the EC Directives.

Reporting Directive (CARD).[93] The CARD (as were its predecessors) is a minimum standards directives, meaning that Member States are free to add their own requirements to their listing rules over and above the requirements of the Directive.[94] While this has allowed Member States some flexibility in making listing rules, it has also limited the operation of the principle of mutual recognition because it has limited the possibility of listing particulars being suitable for approval in more than one Member State.

For admission to the official list, the conditions set by the Listing Rules include the following:

1 The market value of the shares to be listed must be at least £700,000[95] (but, in practice, an applicant may have difficulty in finding a broker or issuing house to sponsor[96] the issue and may find the costs involved make an official listing prohibitively expensive unless the value of the securities involved is substantially greater than this).
2 The company must normally have a trading record of at least three years and must have audited accounts for those three years.
3 The company must have carried on an independent business which is supported by its historic revenue-earning record for at least the period covered by the accounts required in (2).
4 The company's directors must collectively have appropriate expertise and experience for the management of its business and must in general be free of conflicts between their duties to the company and their personal interests, or other duties.
5 If the company has a controlling shareholder (i.e. one who can exercise, or control the exercise of, 30 per cent or more of the rights to vote at general meetings or who can control the appointment of directors who are able to exercise the majority of votes at board meetings), the company must be capable at all times of operating and making decisions independently of the controlling shareholder.

---

[93] Dir 2001/34/EC, [2001] OJ L184/1. The CARD consolidated the following directives:

  The Admissions Directive 79/279/EEC, [1979] OJ 66/21;
  The Listing Particulars Directive 80/390/EEC, [1980] OJ L100/1;
  The Interim Reports Directive 82/121/EEC, [1982] OJ L48/26.

Further changes will eventually be introduced by the Transparency Obligations Directive, which is expected to be formally adopted in autumn 2004. See the Financial Markets Law Committee document 'Issue 76—Transparency Obligations Dircetive' (at www.fmlc.org (19 Nov 2004)) for a discussion of potential problems posed by this directive for UK financial markets.

[94] In the UKLA Listing Rules, requirements drawn from EC directives are indicated by a marginal note. Listing rules that are not required by EC directives are referred to as 'super-equivalents' because they exceed the EC minimum standard.

[95] In an application for the admission of debentures the equivalent figure is £200,000.

[96] The Listing Rules (Ch 2) set out the requirement to have a sponsor.

6 At least 25 per cent of the shares must be in the hands of the public after the flotation.[97]

7 The shares must be freely transferable.

Applications for listing must be made to the UKLA, which is required to make a decision on admission within six months.[98] A listing application can only be made by or with the consent of the issuer of the securities concerned.[99] This removes the possibility of a listing application being made by a substantial shareholder who may not be able to satisfy the disclosure obligations imposed by FSMA 2000 and the Listing Rules.[100] An application may be refused if, for a reason relating to the issuer, the competent authority considers that granting it would be detrimental to the interests of investors.[101] If the competent authority decides to refuse an application for listing, the applicant may refer the matter to the Financial Services and Markets Tribunal.[102]

Admission to listing does not in itself result in securities being eligible to be traded on a regulated market. A second regulatory barrier must be overcome, which is admission to trading on a regulated market. In the past, these two regulatory stages were combined as the London Stock Exchange (LSE) was the 'competent authority' for listing and had an effective monopoly over trading in securities. Two developments led to change. The first was the demutualisation of the LSE, resulting in it becoming a company listed on the LSE. The second was the emergence of competitors to the LSE in the form both of recognised investment exchanges and alternative markets.[103] These developments made it inappropriate for the LSE to continue to act as regulator ('competent authority') and therefore the Treasury exercised its power to transfer responsibility to the FSA (UKLA).[104] The new structure involves a division of regulatory responsibility between the UKLA, which is responsible for compliance with the listing rules, and recognised investment exchanges, which are responsible for compliance with their rules relating to trading (eg trade reporting, execution of transactions).[105]

The CARD is concerned only with admission to the Official List. There are currently no EU or UK statutory conditions for admission of securities

---

[97] This ensures that there will be a market for the shares.

[98] FSMA 2000 s 76.

[99] FSMA 2000 s 75(2).

[100] No such restriction applies to listing on AIM.

[101] FSMA 2000 s 75(5). It is virtually unknown for this provision to be used as a basis for rejecting an application and it does not form the basis for a 'merit-based' approach to regulating listing and public issues (see n 81 above).

[102] FSMA 2000 s 76(6).

[103] See Ch 9.1 for a discussion of this issue.

[104] See n 91 above.

[105] See Ch 9 regarding the regulatory regime for recognised investment exchanges.

without an official listing to trading on markets. This is regulated contractually by individual markets (eg AIM in the UK).

For admission to the Alternative Investment Market (AIM) the conditions are less onerous than the Official List, reflecting the objective that AIM should provide a market for relatively new companies.[106] They include the following:

(1) The company must be duly incorporated or otherwise validly established according to the laws of its place of incorporation or establishment.
(2) The company must be permitted by its national law to offer its securities to the public. In the UK this means that it must be a public limited company.
(3) The securities to be traded on the market must be freely transferable.
(4) The company must appoint and retain a nominated adviser and a nominated broker.
(5) The company must state that it has sufficient working capital for its present requirements.
(6) The company must accept continuing obligations with regard to such matters as preparation of accounts, completion of transfers of securities and dealings in securities by directors and employees.

The Financial Services and Markets Act 2000, implementing a requirement of the CARD, imposes a general duty of disclosure in respect of listing particulars.[107] The listing particulars must contain all such information as investors and their professional advisers would reasonably require, and reasonably expect to find there, for the purposes of making an informed assessment of—

• the assets and liabilities, financial position, profits and losses, and prospects of the issuer of the securities; and
• the rights attaching to the securities.

The listing rules spell out in considerable detail information which must be disclosed but the general duty of disclosure is in addition to any information required by the listing rules or the competent authority as a condition of admission to listing.

The disclosure obligation in respect of listing particulars can be enforced in three different ways. First, a person who knowingly or recklessly gives false or misleading information to the UKLA commits an offence.[108] Second, where there is a contravention of the listing rules on the part of an applicant for listing (a company), the FSA may impose a financial penalty on the applicant.[109] The FSA can take similar action against a director of the applicant who is

---

[106] See www.londonstockexchange.com for more detail.
[107] FSMA 2000 s 80.
[108] FSMA 2000 s 398.
[109] FSMA 2000 s 91.

knowingly concerned in the contravention. Third, a person responsible for listing particulars is liable to pay compensation to a person who has acquired securities and suffered loss as a result of any untrue or misleading statement in the particulars or the omission from the particulars of any matter required to be included by the general duty of disclosure.[110] The following persons are responsible for listing particulars:[111]

- the issuer (of the securities to be listed)
- directors of the issuer, when it is a body corporate
- persons who have agreed to become directors of an issuer which is a body corporate
- each person who accepts, and is stated in the particulars as accepting responsibility for the particulars[112]
- each person not falling within any of the foregoing sub-paragraphs who has authorised the contents of the particulars.

The most obvious category of claimant in respect of a breach of the duty of disclosure is a person who buys from the company (or its adviser in the case of an offer for sale) in reliance on false information contained in a prospectus. However, the relevant provision extends to market purchasers and also to anyone who contracts to acquire an interest (such as an option) in them.[113]

Finally, there are a number of common-law remedies applicable to false or misleading information in listing particulars.[114] These are rescission for misrepresentation, damages for breach of a duty of care or damages for deceit. In the main, these remedies pose greater difficulties in pursuing a successful claim than does the statutory remedy, with the result that most claimants would probably choose the statutory route.[115]

Disclosure remains a central principle of the listing regimes for companies after they have been admitted to listing. The rationale for such disclosure is that it is necessary for the proper functioning of the market as it enables investors to make informed decisions.[116] The relevant obligations are referred to in the Listing Rules as 'continuing obligations'[117], which can be categorised

---

[110] FSMA 2000 s 90. The section applies also to prospectuses: see FSMA 2000 s 86.

[111] The FSMA 2000 (Official Listing of Securities) Regulations 2001 (SI 2001/2956) art 6. In the case of a prospectus relating to listed securities governed by Pt VI of FSMA 2000, the offeror, along with those listed, is responsible. The offeror will often but need not be the issuer (eg the offeror could be an institutional investor selling a large holding).

[112] It is customary for auditors, valuers and financial advisers (investment banks) to accept responsibility for parts of listing particulars and prospectuses.

[113] See FSMA 2000 s 90 and para 6.30 of *Boyle & Birds' Company Law* (above n 86).

[114] The common-law remedies are preserved by s 90(6) FSMA 2000.

[115] See Ferran (above n 1 pp 593–605) for a discussion of the relative merits of the various remedies.

[116] See generally N Moloney, *EC Securities Regulation* (Oxford, OUP, 2002) pp 118–28.

[117] See Ch 9 of the Listing Rules.

as periodic disclosure obligations and on-going disclosure obligations. The main example of periodic disclosure is the requirements relating to the public-ation of financial information on a regular basis.[118] On-going disclosure requires particular types of information to be publicised whenever they occur. The most wide-ranging obligation of this type requires listed companies to disclose material developments in their business and changes in their financial position which are not public and are likely to have a significant effect on their share price.[119] This is intended to ensure that there is a proper market in the relevant securities, that is, one in which investors are making fully informed decisions and in which 'insiders' are not able to take advantage of delays in reporting significant changes in the financial position of a company.[120]

The manner in which information is disseminated to the market has recently been changed at the initiative of the FSA. In the past, information was submitted by listed companies to the Regulatory News Service, operated by the FSA and funded in part by fees paid to the FSA by listed companies. The FSA was concerned about the monopoly position enjoyed by the Regulatory News Service in carrying out this function and decided, following consultation, to open that function to competition.[121] In order to provide this service an organisation must now be approved by the FSA and thereby become a desig-nated Primary Information Provider (PIP).[122]

7.4.3 Public offers of securities

Public offers of securities are often made in conjunction with a listing[123] but there is no necessary link between the two.[124] Securities can be listed without a public offering (through an introduction to listing) and a public company can make an offer of securities to the public without the shares being listed. Public offers are essentially substantial sales of securities outside regulated markets. Listing provides liquidity by making those securities eligible to be traded on a regulated market.

The regulatory regime reflects this distinction. A public offer of secur-ities requires the publication of a prospectus. The information that must be

---

[118] See Ch 12 of the Listing Rules.

[119] See the Listing Rules paras 9.1–9.7.

[120] For a discussion of the legal and regulatory regime relating to 'insiders' see Ch 9.

[121] See FSA Policy Statement, *Proposed Changes to the UK Mechanism for Disseminating Regulatory Information by Listed Companies* (Nov 2001).

[122] See sch 12 to the Listing Rules for details of designated PIPs.

[123] In these circumstances, the offer is of securities that are to be listed and the offer is condi-tional on, inter alia, the securities being admitted to listing.

[124] The link will often arise from the requirement that at least 25% of shares to be listed must be in public hands. For some companies, the simplest way to comply will be by making a public offer in conjunction with listing.

contained in a prospectus is very similar to that which is required in listing particulars. The 'mandatory disclosure' philosophy is applied to both listing and public offers in the UK. The main difference is that a prospectus contains information relating to the terms on which securities are offered for sale, whereas listing particulars do not contain this information as they are not compiled for the purpose of selling securities.

EU regulation of public offers takes the form of the Public Offers Directive (POD)[125]. It applies to offers of securities to the public in the UK for the first time.[126] Its provisions are implemented in the UK by Part VI of FSMA 2000 in respect of offers of listed securities (or securities to be listed following a public offer). Public offers of unlisted securities are governed by the Public Offers of Securities Regulations 1995[127]. A 'non-listing' prospectus cannot be governed by the UKLA's Listing Rules (as is the case for a 'listing' prospectus) because there is no application for listing: hence the need for a separate set of regulations.

A prospectus must be published before 'new securities' are admitted to listing.[128] 'New securities' means securities that are to be offered to the public in the UK for the first time before admission to listing. Any subsequent offer of the same issue[129] of securities does not require a prospectus. To determine if a prospectus is required for a new issue, it is necessary to consider the meaning of a public offer in the UK. The 'public' dimension is satisfied if an offer is made to the public, including any section of the public, and the offer is not an exempt offer.[130] There are a substantial number of exempt offers.[131] They include:

Professionals. This exemption applies to offers made to persons whose ordinary business involves them holding or managing investments (as principal or agent).

Limited numbers of investors. This exemption applies when the securities are offered to no more than fifty persons.

Restricted circle of informed investors. This exemption applies if the securities are offered to a restricted circle of persons whom the offeror reasonably believes to be sufficiently knowledgeable to understand the risks involved in accepting the offer.

---

[125] Dir 89/298/EC, [1989] OJ L124/8.

[126] Sometimes referred to as an 'initial public offering' (IPO), the US equivalent of the UK market term 'flotation'. Neither are technical legal terms.

[127] SI 1995/1537.

[128] FSMA 2000 s 84.

[129] eg by a substantial shareholder. Such an offer is possible as, unlike listing, the consent of the issuer is not required for a public offer.

[130] FSMA 2000 s 103(6) and sch 11(for listed securities) and art 6 of the POS Regulations for unlisted securities.

[131] Offers are exempt if they satisfy the conditions in sch 11 to FSMA 2000 or art 7 of the POS Regulations.

Specified consideration or denomination. This exemption applies where (i) the total consideration payable for the securities does not exceed 40,000 euros; (ii) the minimum payable by any person acquiring securities is 40,000 euros; and (iii) the securities are denominated in amounts of at least 40,000 euros.[132]

Takeover offers. Offers made in connection with a takeover are exempt.[133]

It is possible for some of the exemptions, but not all, to be aggregated.[134] This means that it is possible for one part of an offer to fall under one exemption and another part of the offer to fall under a different exemption.

Public offers of securities can take different legal forms. An offer for subscription invites the public to subscribe for shares that have not yet been issued. It therefore involves the raising of new capital by the company. An offer for sale is an offer made by shareholders to sell shares to the public: it does not in itself involve the raising of new capital. An investment bank can make this type of offer as agent for the shareholders or as principal, following acquisition of the shares by the bank. In the latter case, the bank will expect to sell the shares to the public at a profit. A public offer can be a combination of an offer for subscription and an offer for sale.

Other than when an investment bank acts as principal, the company (in the case of an offer for subscription) and selling shareholders (in the case of an offer for sale) face the risk that the offer may not be taken up. This may present serious problems, such as creating uncertainty over the funds available to the company for its future development. A solution is available in the form of underwriting. This involves an underwriter (or more likely a group of underwriters and sub-underwriters) agreeing to take up the offer to the extent that it is not taken up by public subscription. In return, the underwriters are paid a fee expressed as a percentage of the value of the issue.

A placing is another form of public offering, in the sense that new shareholders are introduced to the company. It involves an offer being made to a limited number of investors and is therefore exempt from the requirement for the publication of a prospectus. The rationale for this exemption is that the investors involved in a placing are likely to be professional investors who are able to determine their own information requirements and do not need a statutory disclosure obligation.[135]

---

[132] The first exemption can be justified by reference to the small amount of capital being raised, the second and third by reference to the likelihood that most private investors are unlikely to take up such offers.

[133] The reference is to takeovers as defined in Pt XIIIA of the Companies Act 1985. The rationale is presumably that takeovers are regulated by the Takeover Code and (to a lesser extent) by the Companies Act 1985.

[134] FSMA 2000 sch 11 para 2.

[135] See H Jackson and E Pan, 'Regulatory Competition in International Securities Markets: Evidence from Europe in 1999—Part 1' (2001) 56 *Business Law* 653.

A rights issue involves a company making an offer to existing investors pro rata to their existing shareholding.[136] Such an issue falls within the definition of an offer to the public as the public includes a section of the public selected as members of a company.[137] As they involve a new issue of shares, rights issues normally require the publication of a prospectus.[138] It is possible for a very small rights issue (raising less than 10 per cent of the existing capitalisation) to be exempted[139] from the requirement to produce a prospectus but companies generally raise greater amounts in rights issues. It is also possible for companies quoted on AIM to be exempt from the requirement to produce a prospectus in certain circumstances.[140]

Although it contains some specific provisions relating to prospectuses, the general approach of FSMA 2000 is to treat a prospectus in the same way as listing particulars.[141] The result is that the general disclosure obligation and the provisions relating to enforcement of that obligation (above) apply equally to a prospectus. In effect, listing particulars and a prospectus are treated as equivalent documents that relate to different circumstances.

While the POS Regulations set specific disclosure requirements for 'non-listing' prospectuses, they share two important features with the FSMA provisions. First, the POS Regulations contain a general duty of disclosure in similar terms to that discussed above in the context of listing.[142] Second, the POS Regulations provide for the possibility of compensation to be paid for loss caused by false information, misleading information or an omission in a prospectus.[143]

7.4.4 EC regulation

A feature of the regulatory regime for both listing and public offers is that they incorporate measures designed to facilitate the operation of the single market in the EC. As has been the case elsewhere in the financial sector, the EC's approach has been based on the principles of minimum harmonisation and mutual recognition. To this end it has set minimum regulatory requirements

---

[136] See 7.1 (above).

[137] FSMA 2000 sch 11 para 1.

[138] Specific disclosure requirements for a rights issue prospectus are contained in Ch 5 of the Listing Rules and the POS Regulations.

[139] The UKLA can grant such an exemption under Ch 5 para 5.27(e) of the Listing Rules.

[140] Art 8(5) of the POS Regulations.

[141] FSMA 2000 s 86 provides that Pt VI of the Act applies equally to prospectuses.

[142] Art 9. There are some differences between the FSMA 2000 disclosure obligation (for offers of listed securities) and the POS Regulations disclosure obligation: see Ferran (above n 1) p 590.

[143] Art 14.

for listing[144] and public offers[145]. While this has resulted in a common core of minimum requirements in Member States, it has left in place a separate system of regulation in each Member State. The mutual recognition provisions in the Directives are intended to counteract the negative effect of state-by-state regulation of listing and public offers on the operation of the single financial market.

Several of the provisions of the EC Consolidated Admissions and Reporting Directive[146] give effect to these objectives. The first applies when an application for listing is made for securities that have been listed in another Member State less than six months previously. In these circumstances, the competent authority to whom application is made should contact the competent authority which has already admitted the securities to official listing, and should, as far as possible, exempt the issuer from the preparation of new listing particulars, subject to any need for updating, translation or the issue of supplements in accordance with the individual requirements of the Member State concerned.[147] The second is that when the shares of the issuer have been officially listed in another Member State for at least three years before application is sought for listing in another state, the competent authority may exempt the issuer from the obligation to produce listing particulars. For this to occur, the issuer must have complied fully with all listing obligations and must publish information that falls short of that required by the listing particulars.[148] The third is that when an application for the listing is made and the securities have been the subject of a public-offer prospectus under POD in the three months preceding the application, the prospectus shall *prima facie* be treated as listing particulars in the Member State in which listing is sought.[149] This is subject to the translation of the document into the appropriate language and the right of the competent authority considering the application to require information specific to the market of the country of admission to be included.

As far as public offers are concerned, the POD provides that a prospectus approved by a competent authority in one Member State must, subject to translation, be recognised as complying with the laws of the other Member States in which the same securities are offered to the public simultaneously, or within a short interval of one another, without being subject to any form of

---

[144] In the CARD (above n 93).

[145] In the POD (above n 125). A new prospectus directive (2003/71/EC, [2003] OJ L345/64), replacing the POD, will take effect from 1 July 2005: see FSA Discussion Paper 14, *Review of the Listing Regime* (July 2002) and the Financial Markets Law Committee document 'Issue 89—Prospectus Directive: Choice of Home Member State' (at www.fmlc.org (19 Nov 2004)).

[146] The 'CARD', above n 93.

[147] Art 40(2) of the CARD. Note however, that the option is left to a host state to impose its own requirements.

[148] Art 23(4) of the CARD.

[149] Art 39 of the CARD.

approval and without those states being able to require that additional information be included in the prospectus.[150] Those Member States may, however, require that the prospectus include information specific to the market of the country in which the public offer is made concerning in particular the income tax system, the financial organisations retained to act as paying agents for the issuer in that country, and the way in which notices to investors are published.

While these provisions had the potential to facilitate cross-border listing and public issues in the EC, the reality is that they have been used very little. There are three main reasons. One is that the competent authorities in the Member States have been reluctant to cede their role in monitoring listing particulars and prospectuses to authorities in other Member States. Another factor is that the necessity for cross-border listing has declined as securities have become more widely traded on different European exchanges and investors have been prepared to trade on exchanges in other countries. This has removed the need to list in other countries to gain access to local investors. Third, the time period of three months during which a prospectus can be used to make an offer in more than one country is so short that it has proven to be of little practical use.

An alternative solution has been devised in the capital markets to facilitate cross-border listing and public offers within the EU. It is referred to as an 'international-style offering' and takes the form of a regulated public offer in one state (typically one such as the UK with a well-developed capital market) and 'exempt' offers in other Member States. The exemption is based on one or more of those provided by the POD, such as the exemption relating to a restricted group of informed investors. Such an offer is capable of being taken up by the public at large in the first state and by professional investors in other Member States. It thereby provides a mechanism through which a large pool of capital can be tapped through a prospectus that is regulated by only one country.[151]

7.4.5 Overseas listing

Overseas listing refers to a company listing its securities in a country other than the one in which it is incorporated.[152] It can take the form of a 'primary' or 'secondary' overseas listing. A primary overseas listing occurs when a company which has no listing in its country of incorporation obtains a listing in another country.[153] A secondary listing occurs when a company incorporated and

---

[150] Art 21 of the POD.

[151] See generally Jackson and Pan (above n 135).

[152] See generally I MacNeil and A Lau, 'International Corporate Regulation: Listing Rules and Overseas Companies' (2001) 50 *ICLQ* 787.

[153] For UK incorporated companies this is a relatively rare occurrence.

listed in its home country obtains a listing in another country.[154] From the regulatory perspective a company with a primary overseas listing is treated no differently to other listed companies, meaning that they are subject to the full requirements applicable to listing in that country. In the case of a secondary listing some concessions from the standard requirements for listing are permitted.[155]

It is possible for companies seeking an overseas listing to list securities that have been 'repackaged' specifically for that purpose. This occurs frequently in the case of depositary receipts[156], which are attractive to companies because of the less onerous regulatory obligations applicable to them by comparison with listing the underlying securities. The rationale for the lower regulatory burden is that the relevant securities cannot be sold freely to the public in the secondary listing jurisdiction and therefore the information asymmetry basis for regulation is not as strong as if that were possible.[157]

There are several reasons why primary overseas listings occur. One is that the country in which a company is incorporated does not have the scale of capital market that is appropriate to the company's requirements. This can arise in a number of different circumstances. First, a limited shareholder based in the country of incorporation may restrict the ability to raise capital. Second, there may be limited trading opportunities in the company's shares in the stockmarket of the country of incorporation (eg as a result of poor liquidity). Third, a deliberate choice may be made to incorporate the company in a jurisdiction without a developed capital market in the knowledge that it will seek an overseas listing in the jurisdiction in which the company has most of its business operations.[158] There may also be taxation advantages to be gained through overseas incorporation.

The rationale for a secondary listing differs from a primary listing because in this situation a company will already have a listing and therefore the issue becomes one of whether there are advantages in having a second listing on a different market. Research suggests that, for London, the following factors are of broadly similar significance: the large investor base in the United Kingdom, the liquidity of the London stockmarket and the possibility of raising new

---

[154] New York and London are the two main destinations for companies seeking an overseas listing.

[155] For an assessment of the concessions made by the UKLA and Hong Kong listing rules see MacNeil and Lau (n 152 above).

[156] See Ch 4 for a discussion of the nature of depositary receipts.

[157] See, regarding the form and regulation of secondary listing in the United States JC Coffee, 'Competition among Securities Markets: A Path Dependent Perspective' Columbia Law School, The Center for Law and Economic Studies, Working Paper No 192, available at http://papers.ssrn.com/abstract=283822 (19 Nov 2004).

[158] This is a common occurrence in Hong Kong: see S Chan, I MacNeil and A Lau, 'Lawyers' Perceptions of Overseas Incorporated Companies Listed in Hong Kong' 16 (2001) *Managerial Auditing Journal* 290–96.

capital.[159] London is the world's largest centre for the trading of international securities and this position clearly makes it attractive for overseas companies who wish to extend their shareholder base and to ensure the level of liquidity in the trading of their shares that will be required by large institutional investors. Other factors may also be relevant, such as the ability to issue shares to investors within the secondary listing jurisdiction to finance a take-over and the facilitation of share ownership by local employees.

The 'bonding' explanation for overseas listings predicts that high standards of regulation in one country will attract listings from countries with lower standards of regulation.[160] This results not from any desire to be more heavily regulated per se, but from the expectation that a company which 'bonds' to a higher regulatory standard (particularly as regards the quantity and quality of information made available to investors) will benefit from a higher share price. The result of regulatory competition according to the 'bonding' hypothesis is therefore that there will be a general movement towards higher regulatory standards in listing rules as a result of competition between jurisdictions.

7.5 Dividends

Dividends are central to equity investment yet shareholders have no legal right to be paid a dividend. The apparent conundrum implicit in this statement is explained by the very nature of equity investment. It is a form of risk-taking under which an investor agrees to provide capital in return for a residual[161] claim to all the profits and surplus assets of a company. Dividends are essentially a mechanism through which investors are able to assert their residual claim during the time that a company is a going concern.

Historically, the payment of dividends has been subject to the rules of company law dealing with distributions made to shareholders. Those rules aim to protect a company's creditors by ensuring that a company's capital (a matter of public record open to scrutiny by creditors) remains available on an on-going basis as a fund to meet the claims of creditors.[162] A dividend can only be paid if 'distributable profits' are available for this purpose. They are defined as a company's

---

[159] See MacNeil and Lau (n 152 above).

[160] See I MacNeil, 'Competition and Convergence in Corporate Regulation: The Case of Overseas Listed Companies' (2001) at http://ssrn.com/abstract=278508 (19 Nov 2004).

[161] The residual nature of the claim is reflected in the priority given to creditors' claims in the event of insolvency.

[162] See, regarding the principle of maintenance of capital *Boyle & Birds' Company Law* (n 86 above) ch 7. The principle was regarded as fundamental in the case law of the late nineteenth century: see eg *Trevor v Whitworth* (1887) 12 AC 409 at 423–42.

accumulated, realised profits, so far as not previously utilised by distribution or capitalisation, less its accumulated, realised losses, so far as not previously written off in a reduction or reorganisation of capital duly made.[163]

Realised capital gains are included within this definition, but not unrealised gains, which are treated as non-distributable reserves. The availability of distributable profits is determined by reference to a company's relevant accounts, which may be either the last audited annual accounts or interim accounts.[164]

Public companies are subject to a further constraint in paying dividends: a dividend can only be paid if (a) at that time the amount of the company's net assets is not less than the aggregate of its called-up share capital and undistributable reserves; and (b) if, and to the extent that, the distribution does not reduce the amount of those assets to less than that aggregate.[165] The purpose of this provision is to attempt to ensure that share capital and undistributable reserves (which are regarded as equivalent to capital) are represented by assets. This can never be guaranteed as assets are always open to erosion from trading losses, but at least it prevents such an outcome being the result of the payment of dividends to the shareholders.

The Companies Act specifically provides that a payment of dividend in circumstances where there are no distributable profits (an unlawful distribution) must be repaid by the recipient.[166] However, that provision is made subject to the requirement that the recipient must know or have reasonable grounds for knowing that the distribution is unlawful. If that requirement is not satisfied, the statutory liability to repay the dividend does not apply.[167] However, the statutory liability is without prejudice to any other obligation to repay. This might arise, for example if the recipient was considered to be a constructive trustee of the payment. For this to occur, it must be shown that the payment was made by the directors in breach of their fiduciary duty and that the recipient was aware of the factual circumstances, though not necessarily the illegality of the payment.[168]

The procedure for declaring dividends is not mandated by the Companies Act and is therefore determined by a company's articles. They normally provide that decisions on dividend payments should be made by ordinary resolution of the company in general meting and that no payment greater than that

---

[163] Companies Act 1985 s 263.

[164] Companies Act 1985 s 270.

[165] Companies Act 1985 s 264.

[166] Companies Act 1985 s 277.

[167] As occurred for example in *Precision Dippings Ltd v Precision Dippings Marketing Ltd* [1986] Ch 447.

[168] See *Re Cleveland Trust plc* [1991] Butterworths Company Law Cases 424. Regarding the possibility of illegal dividend payments being traced in the hands of shareholders and the payments being recovered from directors, see Ferran (above n 1) p 425.

recommended by the directors may be paid.[169] Provision is also made for the directors to declare an interim dividend without the approval of share-holders.[170]

Dividends can be paid in the form of assets, in cash or in the form of scrip dividends. Most dividends are paid in the form of cash. Under the common law, dividend payments were calculated by reference to the nominal value of shares,[171] but it is now common for the articles to provide that payments will be calculated by reference to the amounts paid-up on shares.[172] The purpose of such a provision is to link the amount paid by way of dividend to the capital contributed to the company by a member (shareholder) rather than to the number of shares held.

Some companies are authorised by their articles to pay 'scrip dividends'. This allows shareholders to elect to receive new shares as an alternative to the payment of a cash dividend. The attraction for companies is that scrip dividends retain cash within the company that would otherwise have been paid out in the form of dividends. In this sense, scrip dividends are the economic equivalent of re-investment in the company as shareholders are in effect re-investing their dividend in the company.[173] For shareholders, the main attraction is that they can increase their holding in the company without incurring transaction costs.

Transfers of shares raise the issue of the person to whom dividends should be paid. The common-law rule is that the dividend is paid to the registered owner at the date of declaration of the dividend.[174] Companies and stock exchanges have overcome the potential uncertainty resulting from the application of this rule by adopting a device that makes clear who is entitled to a dividend. Shares are quoted either *cum* (with) or *ex* (without) dividend on either side of a date (the record date) fixed by the company (as authorised by its articles) for payment of dividends to shareholders. The matter really only assumes significance around the time of the record date as for the remainder of the year shares are traded *cum* dividend. The process of going 'ex-dividend' is in principle associated with a fall in the value of the shares equal to the div-idend payment, as a buyer will not have the right to that payment.[175]

---

[169] Table A, Art 102. It is very unusual for the directors' recommendation regarding dividend payment to be rejected by the shareholders.

[170] Table A, Art 103.

[171] *Oakbank Oil Company Ltd v Crum* (1882) 8 App Cas 65 (HL).

[172] This is compulsory in the case of listed companies: Listing Rules, Ch 13 app 1 para 16.

[173] For further discussion of the character and accounting treatment of scrip dividends see Ferran (above n 1), p 422.

[174] *Re Wakley, Wakley v Vachell* [1920] 2 Ch 205.

[175] Expectations relating to the next dividend payment will, in principle, be reflected in the share price over the period that the shares are traded *cum* dividend before the next dividend payment.

7.6 Share buy-backs

From the corporate finance perspective, share buybacks offer a mechanism by which companies can return surplus capital to shareholders.[176] The purpose of such an exercise is generally to boost those financial ratios (such as earnings and assets) that are commonly measured on a per share basis. Those ratios will be boosted because there will be a lower number of shares as the divisor of total earnings or assets. Put another way, a share buyback should in principle boost the share price because the number of shares with a right to participate in the profits of the company will be reduced. The same principle can be applied if shares are bought back from the proceeds of a loan raised for that purpose. The effect is to replace equity with debt and if the financing cost (interest) of the debt is lower than the cost of paying dividends on the equity, earnings per share will improve.

Historically, the law has viewed share buybacks with suspicion.[177] The common law prohibited a company purchasing its own shares on the basis that it represented a mechanism by which a company could return capital to its members.[178] The common-law rule is restated in the Companies Act 1985.[179] Contravention of the prohibition makes the company liable to a fine and the officers of the company liable to a fine or imprisonment or both. A purported acquisition of shares contrary to the prohibition is void.

The prohibition is, however, disapplied in respect of a purchase or redemption of shares made in compliance with the provisions of the Act.[180] As a result of its potential to damage the interests of creditors, the process is strictly controlled but is nevertheless commonly used by listed companies. The relevant provisions of company law vary according to whether the purchase is a 'market purchase' or an 'off-market purchase'. The latter is a purchase other than on a recognised investment exchange (RIE) or on an RIE in circumstances in which the shares are not subject to a marketing arrangement on that RIE.[181] A marketing arrangement exists if shares are listed or the RIE provides on-going facilities for dealing in the shares (such as on AIM). 'Market purchases' are those made on a RIE other than off-market purchases. The stricter

---

[176] In the case of private companies or public companies in which there is no active market, share buybacks also provide a mechanism for shareholders to 'exit' the company: see Ferran (above n 1) p 431.

[177] It was only in 1981 that the law was amended to permit share re-purchases. On the prior law and the debate surrounding its amendment, see Ferran (above n 1) pp 435–36.

[178] *Trevor v Whitworth* (1887) 12 AC 409.

[179] Companies Act 1985 s 143.

[180] See Companies Act 1985 s 143 and s 162. A company must be authorised by its articles of association to purchase its own shares (see art 85, Table A).

[181] See Ch 9 for a discussion of recognised investment exchanges.

regulation of 'off-market' purchases reflects the fact that such purchases are not subject to a valuation determined (by market forces) in a regulated market, in which it is expected that the price formation process (in respect of the shares being purchased or redeemed) will be fair and efficient.

In the case of a 'market purchase', the purchase must be authorised by an ordinary resolution of the company.[182] The authorisation must state the maximum number of shares that may be purchased and the maximum and minimum price to be paid.[183] The resolution must state the duration of the authority, which must not exceed 18 months. It is common for such resolutions to provide authority for only 12 months until the next annual general meeting, when a similar resolution will be adopted so as to provide a continuing mandate to repurchase shares.[184] In the case of 'off-market' purchases, authority (for a maximum of 18 months) can be given only by special resolution and the terms of the purchase contract must be approved in advance by the shareholders.[185]

It is also possible for a company to buy its own shares through a contingent purchase contract. This is a contract under which the company may, subject to conditions, become entitled or obliged to purchase shares in itself but there is no immediate obligation.[186] A typical example would be a 'put' contract, under which the company would become obliged to buy shares from a shareholder at an agreed price. Such a contract must be approved by a special resolution and is subject to the same rules as an 'off-market' purchase.[187]

Shares that are to be repurchased must be fully paid and the payment to shareholders must be in the form of cash paid at the time of purchase.[188] A repurchase cannot be made if it would result in only redeemable shares being held by members,[189] the rationale being that a company would then face the eventual prospect of having no members (when the redeemable shares were redeemed).

For a public company, the main source of finance for share buybacks is distributable profits.[190] It is also possible for the proceeds of a fresh issue of shares

---

[182] Companies Act 1985 s 166. In practice, many companies adopt a special resolution, as recommended by the ABI.

[183] The prices may be expressed as a formula so long as it is not reliant on any person's discretion or opinion.

[184] This is the procedure recommended by the ABI: see the ABI IVIS service at www.abi.org.uk (19 Nov 2004).

[185] Companies Act 1985 s 164. The company is obliged to make the contract available for inspection by shareholders.

[186] Companies Act 1985 s 165(1).

[187] Companies Act 1985 s 165(2).

[188] Companies Act 1985 s 159(3). Although there is no explicit statutory requirement for payment in cash, this is the construction favoured by Ferran (above n 1) p 442.

[189] Companies Act 1985 s 162(3).

[190] For a definition of distributable profits see section 7.5 above.

to be used to finance a repurchase but there are restrictions associated with the use of such funds.[191] Private companies benefit from a less restrictive regime governing the sources from which repurchases may be financed. In particular, provision is made for repurchases to be made, in some circumstances and subject to safeguards, from capital.[192] Shares that have been purchased by a company must be cancelled with the result that the issued share capital is reduced by the nominal value of the repurchased shares.[193] In the case of a repurchase funded from distributable profits, this would result in a reduction in the issued share capital of the company and pose a potential risk to creditors.[194] To protect against this risk, a company must, following a purchase funded from distributable profits, transfer to its capital redemption reserve an amount equivalent to the fall in its issued share capital (equivalent to the nominal value of the shares repurchased). The capital redemption reserve is treated as paid-up share capital, except that it can be used to fund an issue of fully paid bonus shares to members of the company. The authorised capital of the company remains unaltered by a purchase.

In addition to the requirements imposed by company law, listed companies must also comply with the requirements of the Listing Rules.[195] Companies are required to notify the market[196] of a decision to seek shareholder approval for purchases (other than a renewal of authority) and of actual purchases when they occur. The content of circulars seeking shareholder approval is controlled by the Listing Rules[197] and in some circumstances (such as a purchase from a related party) prior approval of circulars is required. The price of dealings is also controlled. For purchases of less than 15 per cent of any class of shares a ceiling is set at 5 per cent above the average of the market value of the shares for the five days preceding the purchase. For purchases of more than 15 per cent a tender offer (open to all shareholders) must be made at a stated maximum or fixed price.

Redeemable shares differ from ordinary shares in that they are issued with the intention that they will be redeemed (purchased) by the company at some point in the future. Any company whose articles permit it can issue redeemable shares, but a company cannot only have members holding only redeemable

---

[191] See Companies Act 1985 s 162 and Pennington (above n 14) p 224.

[192] See ss 171–181 Companies Act 1985 and Ferran (above n 1) p 446–47.

[193] It is also now possible for shares to be held in 'treasury' by the company. This provides a mechanism through which a company can manage its equity financing requirements. See *Boyle & Birds' Company Law* (above n 86) para 7.17.2.

[194] A repurchase funded from a new issue of shares does not pose this risk as the new issue will result in the issued capital remaining at the level it stood prior to repurchase and cancellation.

[195] See generally Ch 15 of the Listing Rules. These requirements apply to repurchases of any security, not just shares.

[196] Through a primary information provider—see text at n 122 above.

[197] See para 15.4.

shares.[198] The terms and manner of redemption are a matter to be determined by a company's articles,[199] but only full-paid shares can be redeemed.[200] Authority for redemption is provided on a continuing basis by the articles as opposed to the more limited authorisation provided by a shareholders' resolution for the purchase of non-redeemable shares. When redemption of shares is financed from distributable profits, the same potential problem arises as in the case of purchases (above), and the same solution is adopted by requiring a transfer to be made to the capital redemption reserve equivalent to the nominal value of the shares to be redeemed.[201]

7.7 Takeovers and reconstruction

7.7.1 Takeovers

From the legal perspective, takeovers can be defined as an offer to acquire all the shares, or all the shares of any class, in a company, being an offer on terms which are the same in relation to all the shares to which the offer relates, or, where those shares include shares of different classes, in relation to all the shares of each class.[202] A takeover in this sense involves a transfer of shares from shareholders in the target company to the bidder. If the bidder is a company, the target will become a subsidiary of the bidder when the bidder secures sufficient shares to control the target.[203] Arrangements that are in economic terms equivalent to a takeover, but do not involve a transfer of shares, are not takeovers in the legal sense and are considered later.

From the finance perspective, takeovers have potential attractions for both shareholders in the bidder and the target. The shareholders in the bidder are generally asked to approve the making of a takeover offer on the basis that it will enhance the earnings of the bidder. Such expectations are often based on the

---

[198] See n 190 above and relevant text.

[199] Companies Act 1985 sub-s 160(3). For a discussion of the potential problems associated with the construction of this sub-section and its associated provision in the standard articles (article 3 Table A) see Ferran (above n 1) pp 450–51.

[200] Companies Act 1985 s 159(3).

[201] Companies Act 1985 s 170(1) and (4). This has the effect of maintaining the issued capital at the same level after the redemption has occurred and gives effect to the company law principle of maintenance of capital.

[202] This is the definition adopted for the purposes of the Companies Act 1985 in s 428(1). There are, however, two types of takeover subject to the Takeover Code that do not fall within this definition: partial offers and tender offers: see *Boyle & Birds' Company Law* (above n 87) ch 18.

[203] The terms 'subsidiary' and 'holding company' are defined in s 736 Companies Act 1985. Note that a 'parent company' (defined in s 258) need not be the same as a holding company. The concept of a parent company is relevant for the accounts and audit provisions of Pt VII of the Companies Act 1985.

potential economies of scale resulting from the combination of two enterprises or from the 'synergy' resulting from the different capabilities of bidder and target. While there must be some objective basis for such a claim (under the Takeover Code) it will often be the case that shareholders place their trust in the Board's claim on the basis of past performance. The shareholders in the target company will generally sell their shares to the bidder if it appears that there is no reasonable prospect of the shares trading at the price being offered by the bidder. It may also be the case (in share-for-share offers, considered below) that shareholders in the target would prefer to become shareholders in the bidder.

A takeover offer can be framed in different ways. A general offer follows the above definition without modification. It relies on a sufficient number of shares in the target being sold to the bidder so as to allow the bidder to gain control of the target.[204] Another option is for the offer to be based on a scheme of arrangement under section 425 of the Companies Act 1985. Such schemes are not restricted to takeovers but can be used a means of restructuring the target so as to pass ownership to the bidder. They require approval by three-quarters of the shareholders of the target company.[205] Finally, it is possible for a new company to be formed (typically 'Newco') for the purposes of acquiring the shares in both bidder and target. The acquisition by Newco can take the form of a general offer or a scheme of arrangement under section 425.

Irrespective of their legal form, takeovers are normally financed in one of two ways. The first is a 'share-for-share' offer in which a bidder offers shares in itself as consideration for the acquisition of the entire share capital of the target company. The second is a cash offer, in which a bidder offers cash as the consideration. There are also hybrid forms of takeover that combine elements of both: this normally takes the form of a share-for-share offer with a full or partial cash alternative.

In the case of a 'share-for-share' offer, there is no need for external finance to fund the bid. A company is able to issue shares up to the extent of its authorised share capital and, provided that is sufficiently large, there is in principle no legal limit on the extent to which new shares can be issued to fund a 'share-for-share' offer. For this reason, this type of bid is sometimes said to be financed by the company's own paper (a 'paper' offer). There are two forms of control on this type of offer. The first is the discipline of the market. The following example illustrates the point:

---

[204] Under the Takeover Code, an offer cannot become unconditional (capable of acceptance by the target shareholders so as to create a binding contract) unless the bidder has acquired over 50% of the voting equity capital of the target. This ensures that a takeover offer does in reality represent an offer to the shareholders in the target company that will result in a change of control in the company.

[205] Companies Act 1985 s 425(2). This may be a disadvantage for the bidder by comparison with a general offer, under which control could be gained with a 50% acceptance level from the target's shareholders.

> Company A wants to bid for company B; they are both listed.
>
> Company B has 200 million shares in issue and the current market price is £1, giving a market capitalisation of £200m.
>
> Company A believes that B's shareholders would accept an offer of 120p. The consideration for the takeover would therefore be £240m.
>
> Company A has 100 million shares in issue and they currently trade at £5, giving a market capitalisation of £500m.
>
> At this point the bid will require an issue of 48 million shares in A (ie an issue valued at £240m).
>
> When the bid is announced, A's shares fall to £4.50.
>
> At this point the bid will require an issue of 53.3 million shares in A.

A significant factor for A will be the effect of the proposed acquisition on its earnings and dividend-paying capability. The scenario described above would be consistent with a market expectation that the proposed takeover would have a negative impact on earnings and dividends. The increased cost of capital associated with the increased number of shares required to fund the takeover may have the effect of causing the takeover to be abandoned. Equally, a positive market reaction to the proposed takeover would reduce its cost by lowering the number of shares that A would require to issue to fund the bid. In this sense, market expectations, which relate essentially to the future prospects of the combined entity, largely determine both the cost of a takeover and its outcome.

Another relevant factor is that the bidder's shareholders will have to approve the transaction. Although directors are often authorised to make relatively small share issues, most share issues made to fund takeover offers are likely to fall outside that authorisation and will therefore require approval by shareholders.[206] Listed companies must also comply with the requirements of the Listing Rules regarding transactions.[207] The Listing Rules divide transactions into three types (Class 1, 2 and 3) according to a number of financial thresholds and require details of the transactions to be publicised. It is only in respect of the largest category of transaction, Class 1, that the prior approval of shareholders in general meeting is required.[208] In the case of a share-for-share takeover involving the issue of new shares (to the shareholders in the target) that are to be listed, the normal rules relating to listing (above) will apply.[209]

---

[206] See 7.2 above for the general principles governing the issue of new shares.

[207] See Ch 10 of the Listing Rules.

[208] A Class 1 transaction is one in which ratios relating to assets, profits, turnover and consideration to market capitalisation and gross capital exceed 25%.

[209] A takeover offer is exempt from the Public Offers of Securities Regulations SI 1995/1537 (see art 7(2)(k)) but is likely to fall within the scope of the Takeover Code (see Ch 8.8).

In the case of cash offers, the bidder will need to have cash available from either internal or external sources. Internal resources are primarily retained profits (reserves) while external resources can include the proceeds of loan or share issues made with the intention of having funds available for takeovers. External resources can also be provided by the underwriting of a cash alternative to a share-for-share offer. This involves an underwriter agreeing to provide cash payments to shareholders in the target as an alternative to shares in the bidder. In some cases, such as when a bid is mandatory under the Takeover Code,[210] the bidder must offer cash or a cash alternative to a share-for-share offer. Such arrangements are popular with investors, as they may not want to take shares in the bidder, and can therefore improve the likelihood of a bid succeeding. For the bidder, however, an underwritten cash alternative adds to the cost of a share-for-share offer.

7.7.2 Transfers of undertakings

A transfer of an 'undertaking' means a transfer of the assets and liabilities of one company (A) to another (B). There is no transfer of the shares in A, which remain in the hands of A's shareholders. However, as A no longer has any 'undertaking' it becomes a 'shell' and may have little or no economic value. From B's perspective, however, it has achieved a result similar to a takeover offer in that it has secured control of the undertaking of A.

There are two legal mechanisms that allow for transfers of the undertaking of a company to occur.[211] One is the 'scheme of arrangement' under section 425 of the Companies Act 1985. However, a disadvantage of this by comparison with a takeover offer (for shares) is that it requires the approval of the creditors of the target company and the court. Another option, which is available in the case of an insolvent company, is section 110 of the Insolvency Act 1986. This allows the undertaking of an insolvent company to be sold to another company in its entirety and thereby provides a mechanism which allows a liquidator to realise a higher value for creditors than if the assets of the insolvent company were broken up and sold on a 'piecemeal' basis.

7.7.3 Reconstruction

Corporate reconstruction describes the process by which a company adjusts its legal relationship with its creditors and/or members. One of the main reasons for reconstruction is financial distress and the objective of reconstruction in

---

[210] See Ch 8.8.
[211] See generally ch 18 of *Boyle & Birds' Company Law* (above n 87).

these circumstances is to preserve the company as a going concern. The substance of typical reconstruction arrangements in these circumstances includes:

- creditors agreeing to modify provisions of loan agreements (eg duration, covenants);
- creditors agreeing to forgo their rights under loan agreements in exchange for the issue or transfer to them of shares (debt/equity swaps);
- members (shareholders) agreeing to forgo rights or surrender shares.

Other reasons for reconstruction are to change the legal structure of groups of companies for tax reasons or to align the legal structure more closely with the manner in which a company does business. These issues are likely to be significant for international companies, who have a wide range of choices in determining the legal relationship between business units in other countries and a head office in the UK (or vice versa).

The main legal mechanism for giving effect to reconstruction arrangements is section 425 of the Companies Act 1985. This provision does not regulate the substance of the reconstruction agreement but requires that it be approved by those whose rights are affected and also by the court. A majority of 75 per cent of creditors or members affected by the arrangement must approve the proposal. In both instances the prescribed majority is able to bind the minority to the arrangement.[212]

---

[212] The majorities relate to those who vote on the relevant resolution at a company meeting, meaning that in neither case is the approval of an absolute majority required. Creditors vote according to the value of their debts in the company. For more detail see ch 18 of *Boyle & Birds' Company Law* (above n 87).

8

Corporate Governance

This chapter deals with corporate governance in listed companies. The term 'corporate governance' is used in different ways depending on its context. One definition is that it refers to how companies are directed and controlled.[1] That is a very broad definition that is capable of covering a wide range of issues. Another is that it refers to 'the ways in which suppliers of finance to corporations assure themselves of getting a return on their investment.'[2] That is a more restrictive definition in which governance mechanisms are viewed as being a monitoring device for investors. Yet another definition is that corporate governance refers to the various mechanisms associated with company law that shape the way company managers exercise their discretion.[3] The last definition is the one adopted for the purposes of this chapter. It focuses attention on corporate governance as a system of rules or guidelines that control the exercise of discretion by company managers, and in particular the board of directors.

The law plays a crucial role in defining the sphere within which discretion can be exercised. Company law, for example, determines the respective roles of shareholders and directors in making decisions within a company and determines the powers available to directors in running a company. However, two characteristics of company law in particular help to explain why the formal legal framework has increasingly come to be regarded as an inadequate means to control the exercise by directors of their wide powers. First, legal remedies, such as challenging decisions or actions taken by directors on the basis that they are beyond their powers (ultra vires) or represent an improper use of powers, represent an ex post form of control in that they deal with problems after they have occurred. They are also complicated by the legal rules that

---

[1] This is the definition adopted in the Cadbury Report (*Report of the Committee on the Financial Aspects of Corporate Governance*, Gee & Co Ltd, 1992) para 2.5.

[2] A Shleifer and R Vishny, 'A Survey of Corporate Governance' (1997) 52 *Journal of Finance* 737.

[3] See J Parkinson, 'The Role of "Exit" and "Voice" in Corporate Governance' p 75 in S Sheikh and W Rees (eds) *Corporate Governance and Corporate Control* (London, Cavendish, 1995).

determine who is able to institute legal action on behalf of a company.[4] Second, the power given to shareholders to appoint and remove directors[5] represents a 'nuclear option' and does not necessarily create genuine accountability in respect of decisions or conduct on the part of directors which may be objectionable from the shareholders' perspective but which is not a 'sacking offence'. Corporate governance has emerged as a process for establishing and developing[6] control mechanisms and detailed standards within this sphere. Its main focus is on strategic direction, high-level decision-making, supervision of management and satisfying legitimate expectations for accountability. Corporate governance is relevant for investors because each of these issues is of crucial importance to the long-term relationship between investors and companies and to the valuation of investors' shareholdings.[7]

8.1 Corporate governance, share-ownership and company finance

The structure of share-ownership is relevant for corporate governance because different ownership patterns create different incentives for investors to become involved in corporate governance. This can be illustrated by comparing two hypothetical countries. Assume that in country A ownership of listed companies is typically widely dispersed, meaning that no single investor has a sufficiently large holding to be able to exercise a strong influence through the exercise of votes. By way of contrast, assume that in country B, listed companies typically have a single large shareholder who has sufficient voting power to be able to dominate decision-making. In country A, it is likely that there will be no incentive for a shareholder to become actively involved in corporate governance because that shareholder will have to bear the cost while all other shareholders will share the benefits, if any, that are reflected in the share price. It can therefore be expected that in country A, considerable emphasis will be placed on alternatives to active involvement in corporate governance and in particular the

---

[4] See generally J Birds (ed) *Boyle & Birds' Company Law*, 5th edn (Bristol, Jordans, 2004) ch 17.

[5] The Companies Act 1985 s 303(1) provides that

A company may by ordinary resolution remove a director before the expiration of his period of office, notwithstanding anything in its articles or in any agreement between it and him.

[6] It will become clear from the account of the development of corporate governance in recent years (below) that is regarded as a system that it is undergoing constant development.

[7] See M Maher and T Andersson, 'Corporate Governance: Effects on Firm Performance and Economic Growth' in L Renneboog *et al* (eds) *Convergence and Diversity of Corporate Governance Regimes and Capital Markets* (Oxford, OUP, 2000).

development of mechanisms (such as stock exchanges) that provide an exit mechanism for dissatisfied shareholders who are unwilling to become actively involved in corporate governance. This process has been described as shareholders choosing 'exit' (selling) over 'voice' (active involvement in corporate governance) in respect of poorly performing companies.[8] In country B, it is likely that the single large shareholder will take a more active role in corporate governance for the simple reason that much of the benefit of that action will accrue to that shareholder. Moreover, the emphasis on exercising 'voice' in that country might well be expected to lead to less emphasis on 'exit' and therefore a reduced role for financial markets by comparison with country A.

Institutional investors dominate share-ownership in the United Kingdom.[9] This remains the case even after the phase of popular capitalism during the 1980s in which small private investors were encouraged to buy shares in the privatisations of several large state-owned organisations. Institutional investment takes several forms.[10] Pension funds account for the largest percentage, followed by insurance companies (primarily life assurance funds) and collective investment schemes. Individual investors' direct holdings are relatively small, although it is of course true that, ultimately, all institutional investment is held on behalf of individual investors. In common with the United States, but unlike most other countries, most public companies in the United Kingdom do not have a single dominant shareholder. Shares in UK and US companies are widely dispersed, as even the large institutional shareholders referred to above rarely hold more than 3 per cent of a listed company.[11] Elsewhere, it is common for companies to have a single large shareholder (a concentrated shareholding structure).[12]

Different explanations have been offered as to why there has been such divergence in the historical evolution of the pattern of share-ownership.[13] One is that concentrated shareholding is a mechanism that allows for effective monitoring of company management.[14] On this view, the presence of a large

---

[8] The terminology is derived from A Hirshman, *Exit, Voice and Loyalty, Responses to Decline in Firms, Organizations and States* (Cambridge, Harvard University Press, 1970).

[9] See p 7 of the Myners Report (*Institutional Investment in the United Kingdom: A Review*, 2001 available at www.hm-treasury.gov.uk (19 Nov 2004)) for a table showing the distribution of share ownership in the UK.

[10] See generally Ch 5.

[11] This is the threshold at which the Companies Act 1985 requires disclosure of the identity of a shareholder.

[12] See eg R La Porta, F Lopez-de-Silanes, A Shleifer and R Vishny (hereafter 'LLSV'), 'Corporate Ownership around the World' (1999) 54 *Journal of Finance*, 471

[13] See H Demsetz and K Lehn, 'The Structure of Corporate Ownership: Causes and Consequences' (1985) 93 *Journal of Political Economy* 1155.

[14] See A Shleifer and M Vishny, 'Large Shareholders and Corporate Control' (1986) 94 *Journal of Political Economy*, 461–88 and D Leech and J Leahy, 'Ownership Structure, Control Type, Classification and the Performance of Large British Companies' (1991) 101 *Economic Journal* 1418–437.

shareholder acts as a counterweight to the tendency of boards of directors to have effective control of a company. Another explanation is that widely dispersed shareholding developed in countries in which small shareholders were well protected against self-interested action on the part of boards of directors and majority shareholders.[15]

On this view, the quality of investor protection attracts small shareholders into share-ownership because they feel secure about being treated fairly. Another possible explanation is that political considerations have influenced the evolution of the pattern of share-ownership by discouraging the concentration of industrial power in small groups.[16] This has been an issue in particular in the US where, historically, there has been a stronger emphasis on competitive markets than in Europe and a corresponding distrust of accumulation of industrial and commercial power.

Company finance is relevant for corporate governance because different forms of finance create differing legal rights and expectations regarding involvement in decision-making within companies. This issue has already been examined in Chapter 7 in terms of the differing position of contributors of equity and loan capital to a company. However, the extent to which the corporate sector as a whole relies on different sources of finance is also relevant for corporate governance. In this respect a distinction is typically made between 'bank-centred' systems of corporate governance, in which companies rely more heavily on loan capital and 'market-centred' systems of corporate governance in which companies typically rely more on equity rather than loan capital. Linked with this is the fact that companies in 'bank-centred' systems tend to have controlling shareholders.[17]

Both systems have advantages and disadvantages and this is reflected in the fact that many countries can be described as 'hybrid' in that they do not fall squarely into one category or the other. The market-based system lays considerable emphasis on disclosure of financial information so as to allow shareholders to make informed investment decisions but tends to encourage a short-term focus on performance and exit rather than voice. It is associated primarily with the United States and the United Kingdom. The bank-centred system allows for the development of long-term relationships between companies and providers of (loan and equity) capital but tends to suffer from lower

---

[15] See LLSV, 'Legal Determinants of External Finance' (1997) 52 *Journal of Finance* 1131; 'Law and Finance' (1998) 106 *Journal of Political Economy* 1113; 'Investor Protection and Corporate Governance' at www.ssrn.com (ID 183900 code 99092719.pdf) (19 Nov 2004).

[16] See MJ Roe, 'A Political Theory of American Corporate Finance' (1991) 91 *Columbia Law Review* 10. Roe's account cannot be regarded as a generalised explanation of the evolution of all systems of dispersed ownership. See, with respect to the United Kingdom, B Cheffins, 'Law, Economics and the UK's System of Corporate Governance: Lessons from History' (2001) 1 *Journal of Corporate Law Studies* 71.

[17] See 'LLSV' (above n 12).

standards of disclosure and the appropriation of private benefits by controlling shareholders at the expense of minorities. It is associated primarily with countries such as Germany, Japan and Italy.[18]

8.2 The corporate governance agenda

Four issues underlie the debate on corporate governance. They are discussed in turn below.

8.2.1 Stakeholders and ownership rights

The concept of 'stakeholders' in a company has now become widespread. It refers to the notion that there are different groups who all have a stake in the success of a company. Shareholders and employees are always regarded as stakeholders but customers or suppliers may or may not be regarded as stakeholders depending on their relationship with a company. The nature of a stakeholder's interest in a company differs from a shareholder in two important ways. First, there is no convenient method of *measuring* a stakeholder's interest analogous to the role performed by a company share. Second, unlike shareholders, there are substantial differences in the *legal rights* of different stakeholders.

Stakeholding is relevant to ownership rights in a company because it influences the residual rights of ordinary shareholders. To the extent that legal rights are allocated to other stakeholders, they limit the ownership rights of ordinary shareholders. In other words, the characterisation of shareholders as 'owners' of a company is dependent on the way in which rights are allocated among stakeholders. This allocation can occur in two distinct ways. First, it is possible for internal regulation to allocate rights within a company. For example, employees could be given some form of board representation or, if that is regarded as too radical, directors could simply be required to take account of the interests of employees.[19] Second, it is possible for external regulation to control the manner in which a company interacts with stakeholders and others. Examples are health and safety legislation, environmental regulation and statutory minimum wages. In principle, it is possible for stakeholders' interests to be recognised through either route.

---

[18] See N Dimsdale and M Prevezer, *Capital Markets and Corporate Governance* (Oxford, Clarendon Press, 1994) for an extensive discussion of the relative roles of banks and financial markets in the UK, Germany and Japan.

[19] Section 309 of the Companies Act 1985 requires the latter.

The most contentious issue is to determine who should be recognised as stakeholders and how extensive the rights of the respective groups of stakeholders should be. The following groups all have some claim in this respect.

Shareholders

Shareholders are often described as the 'owners' of companies[20] and this reflects the fact that they ultimately control companies through their voting power. Their ownership is, however, residual, in the sense that shareholders exercise control subject to the rights of other stakeholders. The rationale for allocating control rights to shareholders is that it is necessary to compensate for the unspecified nature of the return provided by equity investment and the indefinite duration of their investment in the company. Put another way, shareholders are not guaranteed a financial return and bear the risk of failure in that creditors' claims are given priority on insolvency: they therefore require control rights as an incentive to engage in equity investment.[21] Indeed, it is difficult to envisage that equity investment could exist without the allocation to shareholders of residual control rights. Even so, it remains the case that the extent of those residual rights is a function of the rights allocated to other stakeholders.

Creditors

The case for creditors to be recognised as stakeholders is based on the significance of their contribution to company financing. The argument is that they have a substantial interest in the success or failure of companies and the process of corporate governance because they have a substantial investment in companies. However, it has not generally been accepted in the UK that creditors' interests should be recognised in decisions made by a board of directors. Two reasons can be suggested for this. First, it is open to creditors to determine contractually the nature of their relationship with a company.[22] Second, the nature of the risks faced by creditors differs from that faced by shareholders in that creditors have an agreed return on their investment and their claims are given priority over shareholders in the event of insolvency. The most recent review of company law in the United Kingdom has followed this approach, concluding that it is not appropriate to require a board of directors to take account of creditors' interests.[23]

[20] See eg para 6.1 of the Cadbury Report (above n 1).

[21] See G Kelly and J Parkinson, 'The Conceptual Foundations of the Company: a Pluralist Approach', ch 6 in J Parkinson, A Gamble and G Kelly (eds) *The Political Economy of the Company* (Oxford, Hart Publishing, 2000).

[22] See Ch 7 for a discussion of this issue.

[23] See the CLRSG document, *Modern Company Law for a Competitive Economy, Developing the Framework* (March 2000) paras 3.72–3.73.

Employees

The claim of employees to be recognised as stakeholders is based on either the simple observation that they are essential to the success of a company or the more complex argument that, like shareholders, they make a firm-specific investment and that, in these circumstances, it is efficient for the corporate sector as a whole to award control rights to employees so as to minimise transaction costs.[24] Inherent in the second argument is the idea that employment contracts are, in essence, incomplete or 'relational' contracts and control rights act as a substitute for more detailed or 'complete' contracts. In some other countries, these arguments have been used to justify representation of employees at board level.[25] In the UK, however, there has been resistance to employee representation at board level. Even the requirement that directors take account of employees' interests[26] is of little direct relevance because it cannot be enforced directly by employees. Recognition of employees' interests in the UK has largely been developed through external regulation such as health and safety regulation and employment law.

Customers/Suppliers

The customers and suppliers of companies are clearly essential to its success, but that observation does not in itself establish a claim to the status of 'stakeholder'. It is possible to apply the 'firm-specific' investment argument (above) to some instances in which companies have a particularly close relationship with specific customers or suppliers, but that would probably be the exception rather than the norm. Reflecting this, customers' interests are largely recognised through external regulation (eg the law relating to sale and product safety) and they are given no status within the internal organisation of companies. Suppliers have traditionally been in the same position,[27] but it is now proposed that directors should take account of all these interests.[28]

---

[24] See Kelly and Parkinson (above n 21).

[25] See CJ Meier-Schatz, 'Corporate Governance and Legal Rules: A Transnational Look at Concepts and Problems of Internal Management Control' (1988) 13 *Journal of Corporation Law* 431.

[26] Companies Act 1985 s 309.

[27] It is possible to argue that suppliers have not been afforded the same degree of protection as customers as they often bear the risks arising from limited liability when a company fails. However, there are legal mechanisms available to suppliers to protect their interests (such as retaining legal title to goods until full payment is made).

[28] See sch 2, para 2 of the draft Companies Bill in the White Paper *Modernising Company Law* (Cm 5553–II). The proposal is that directors should be required to take account of these interests to the extent that they 'promote the success of the company for the benefit of its members as a whole'. The focus, therefore, remains on directors acting ultimately in the interests of shareholders.

Society at large

The idea that society at large can be considered a stakeholder in companies is reflected in the development of the concept of corporate social responsibility. This refers to the idea that companies should be expected (and may indeed have economic incentives) to act in a manner that is regarded as socially responsible.[29] This goes beyond observing the minimum requirements set by the law and includes a company's approach to the environment, equal opportunities and remuneration. In essence it deals with the issue of whether or not a company is viewed in its own right as a responsible citizen. The increasing acceptance of corporate social responsibility as an issue relevant to the monitoring by shareholders of management and to an assessment of a company's prospects is reflected in the proposal made by the Company Law Review Steering Group that all companies of a significant size should be required to prepare an 'operating and financial review' that would encompass corporate social responsibility.[30]

8.2.2 Principal/agent theory

Corporate governance is concerned with the accountability of directors to shareholders. This relationship has been characterised by economists as a principal/agent relationship in which shareholders (the principal) face the problem of how to monitor the conduct and performance of directors (the agent).[31] The main risk faced by shareholders is that directors will act in a self-interested manner rather than in the best interests of the company, thereby imposing 'agency costs' on the shareholders.[32]

One possible way to limit agency costs is for only limited powers to be given to directors. However, this poses a problem for anything other than very small companies since most shareholders do not want to be involved in routine decision-making within companies. The approach taken by company law and (for listed companies) the Listing Rules is that, while the board of directors is given broad authority to conduct the company's affairs, shareholder approval is required for a number of important matters. They include changes to the

---

[29] See generally DTI Publication, *Business and Society, Corporate Social Responsibility Report* (2002).

[30] See *Modern Company Law for a Competitive Economy, Final Report*, vol 1 paras 3.33–3.45 and 8.29–8.71. See the background report on the operating and financial review at www.dti.gov.uk/cld/review.htm (19 Nov 2004).

[31] See MC Jensen and WH Meckling, 'Theory of the Firm: Managerial Behaviour, Agency Costs and Ownership Structure' (1976) 3 *Journal of Financial Economics* 305–60.

[32] The directors are often described in the literature as having a tendency to engage in 'shirking' or securing 'perks' for their own benefit.

constitution under company law and substantial transactions under the Listing Rules. This division of responsibility goes some way towards resolving the agency problem inherent in delegating responsibility to a board of directors, but it cannot remove the risk that directors will exercise their powers in a self-interested fashion rather than in the best interests of the company.

Concern over the potential for such self-interested action has been evident in two aspects of corporate governance. The first has been to ensure that the board of directors contains individuals who are independent of management. The purpose of such independent (non-executive) directors is to ensure that decisions of the Board are based on the interests of the company as a whole and not just the interests of the executive directors who are responsible for running the company. The second has been to ensure that directors are not excessively remunerated at the expense of the shareholders. This poses a difficult problem of balance because incentives (eg in the form of share options) have always been regarded as important in motivating management.

8.2.3 Shareholders' voting

Although not at the forefront of the contemporary debate on corporate governance, the law relating to the manner in which shareholders are able to exercise their votes is fundamental to the framework of corporate governance. This is so because voting rights are central to the 'property' that is owned by a shareholder. Those property rights are derived primarily from the contract that is represented by the company constitution and that contract is widely recognised as being incomplete because it cannot anticipate all future events that will give rise to issues regarding shareholders' rights. A governance structure, in which voting rights play a central part, creates the possibility for investment to be attracted into a company despite the incomplete nature of the rights granted to investors by the company constitution. It follows that the manner in which the law controls the exercise of voting rights is fundamental to the relationship between shareholders and a company as well as to the relationship among shareholders.

The default rule under company law is that each share in a company carries one vote.[33] This rule can be varied by the articles of association to create non-voting shares or to provide enhanced voting rights to certain shares. In the case of listed companies, resistance on the part of institutional investors to non-voting or weighted voting shares has resulted in the default rule becoming the

---

[33] Companies Act 1985 s 370(6). It was not always so: see C Dunlavy in Hopt Kanda *et al*, *Comparative Corporate Governance* and also HG Manne, 'Some Theoretical Aspects of Share Voting' 64 *Columbia Law Review* 1427.

norm. Listed companies that in the past did not adopt the principle of one vote per share have now largely been forced to fall in line.

The person entitled to vote is the registered owner of a share and company law prohibits the interest of any other person being recorded in a company's register of shareholders.[34] While this rules out an indirect investor (eg a person holding through a nominee) being recorded as the legal owner, it does not preclude arrangements that allow indirect investors to exercise voting rights. Such arrangements can be created through contract between an indirect investor and an intermediary (who is the registered holder) supported by changes to a company's constitution (so as to recognise the vote of the indirect investor).[35] Entitlement to vote carries with it no obligation to vote. Most shareholders are passive in the sense that they generally do not vote on resolutions[36] and this is generally attributed to the fact that most regard themselves as having a shareholding too small to exert influence over resolutions.[37] The result is that it is often possible for a relatively small shareholding to give effective control over a company.

At one time, it appeared that the common law might have developed a rule requiring shareholders to vote by reference to interests other than their own. That possibility arose from a line of case-law relating to the exercise of powers by a company. In one case, it was held that the general principle applicable to all instances of the exercise of powers by a company is that the power must be exercised 'bona fide for the benefit of the company as a whole'.[38] This principle has proven difficult to apply to resolutions adopted by a company, in the main because it qualifies the general principle that shareholders, including controlling shareholders, are entitled to vote according to their own interests provided that such action is not illegal or fraudulent or oppressive towards those who oppose it.[39] The clear implication of a requirement to vote bona fide for the benefit of the company as a whole is that a much wider duty would be imposed on shareholders than simply to avoid oppression of a minority.

---

[34] Companies Act 1985 s 360. The prohibition does not apply to companies registered in Scotland.

[35] See R Nolan, 'Indirect Investors: A Greater Say in the Company' (2003) 3 *Journal of Corporate Law Studies* 73, citing the example of BP's enfranchisement of holders of depositary receipts (explained in Ch 4) issued in connection with its takeover of Amoco and ARCO. The Company Law Review Steering Group (set up by the DTI to review company law) recommended that s 360 be amended to enable companies to recognise the rights of persons other than registered shareholders: see *Modern Company Law for a Competitive Economy: Final Report* para 7.4.

[36] See E Ferran, *Company Law and Corporate Finance* (Oxford, OUP, 1999) pp 248–9.

[37] This issue is discussed in more detail in 8.4 below.

[38] *Allen v Gold Reefs of West Africa Ltd* [1900] 1 Ch 656 per Lindley MR at p 671.

[39] *Northwest Transportation Co v Beatty* (1887) 12 AC 589, 593.

Later cases attempted to clarify the meaning of such a duty. On one occasion[40] the court took the view that the determination of whether a resolution was bona fide in the interests of the company was for the shareholders and not the court to decide, subject to the right of the court to intervene if it could not reasonably be regarded as being in the interests of the company. On another,[41] 'bona fide' was taken to mean simply the honest opinion of the particular shareholder casting his vote and 'the company as whole' was taken to be a reference to the interests of an individual hypothetical member. The implication was that a particular shareholder was required, before casting his vote, to consider the position of such a hypothetical shareholder, assuming such a person could be identified. A later case[42] illustrated the difficulty of applying such a test: in that case there were only two shareholders in the company and the interests of a hypothetical shareholder were equated with those of the minority shareholder despite the ostensible application of the approach adopted in *Greenhalgh*. The decision in *Clemens* is of particular interest in that the majority shareholder was prevented from authorising a new issue of shares because the result of the new issue would be to reduce the shareholding of the minority shareholder to below 25 per cent, resulting in the minority shareholder being unable to block a special resolution.

The net result is that, in the absence of special circumstances such as those that applied in *Clemens* (which could not arise in the case of a listed company), shareholders are entitled to vote simply by reference to their own interests. Such control as does exist over voting has developed through two routes. The first is the principle that a majority group of shareholders cannot exercise their votes in a manner that constitutes a 'fraud on the minority', which is considered in the next section. The second type of control over voting is self-regulation on the part of institutional investors.[43] These restrictions are intended to enhance the ownership rights of institutional investors by taking a uniform line on the authorisation of certain action (eg share issues) and cannot be viewed as restrictions in the same way as the common-law rules.

It can be concluded therefore that the law gives shareholders a relatively free hand in exercising their votes. This creates an environment that is, at least at the level of the individual shareholder, conducive to the adoption of an activist stance in respect of corporate governance. The law does not require an activist stance but it does facilitate it. However, as discussed in 8.4 below, there are other factors that work in the opposite direction.

---

[40] *Shuttleworth v Cox Brothers* [1927] 2 KB 9.

[41] *Greenhalgh v Arderne Cinemas* [1950] 2 All ER 1120.

[42] *Clemens v Clemens Bros Ltd* [1976] 2 All ER 268. See also V Joffe, 'Majority Rule Undermined?' (1977) 40 *MLR* 71.

[43] See, for example, the voting restrictions adopted by the ABI/NAPF in respect of the disapplication of pre-emption rights, discussed in Ch 7.2.3.

8.2.4 Minority shareholders' rights

Corporate governance is also concerned with the balance between the legal rights of controlling shareholders and minorities. As noted above, company law in the United Kingdom generally permits majority rule to prevail within companies and allows all shareholders to vote on resolutions in accordance with their own interests.[44] However, there are important protections against the abuse of majority rule. One is the requirement that certain resolutions require more than a simple majority. While most decisions can be taken by ordinary resolution, which requires approval only by a majority of shareholders who vote on the issue, some decisions (eg a change in the company's articles of association[45]) can be made only by special resolution, which requires approval by a three-quarters majority of shareholders who vote. This provides some protection to minorities in respect of important decisions that are made by a company, but still leaves open the possibility of exploitation by the majority.

Two other forms of control do, however, limit the extent to which such exploitation can occur. The first is the remedy provided to minorities by section 459 of the Companies Act 1985 in respect of 'unfairly prejudicial conduct'. It has been viewed as primarily of relevance to shareholders in small (generally private) companies and has not been used to any significant extent by shareholders in listed companies, who often simply prefer to 'exit' by selling in the market rather than engaging in expensive litigation. Section 459 permits a minority shareholder or group of shareholders to petition the court for a remedy in circumstances when a company is being run in a manner that is prejudicial to their interests. This might be because the directors are acting without regard to their fiduciary duties or because controlling shareholders are favouring their own interests at the expense of the minority.[46] The most common remedy sought by shareholders in these circumstances is an order requiring the other shareholders to buy the shares of the minority at a price fixed by an independent valuer.

A second legal mechanism that limits exploitation of a minority is the possibility of the minority bringing a 'derivative' action based on 'fraud on the minority'. The most blatant example of such circumstances is where a majority use their voting power to transfer company assets or opportunities to themselves.[47] The law's approach in these circumstances, broadly stated, is to

---

[44] See generally P Davies, *Gower and Davies' Principles of Modern Company Law*, 6th edn (London, Sweet & Maxwell, 2003) ch 19.

[45] Companies Act 1985 s 9.

[46] For a discussion of the techniques through which this may occur see S Johnson, R Laporta, F Lopez-de-Silanes, and A Shleifer, 'Tunneling' (2000) 90 *American Economic Review* 22–27.

[47] See eg *Prudential Assurance Co Ltd v Newman Industries Ltd (No 2)* [1981] Ch 257.

modify the operation of the principle of majority rule so as to allow an oppressed minority to take action to prevent or remedy the relevant act of the majority.[48]

The relevance of these legal principles for corporate governance in the United Kingdom is that they create an underlying legal framework in which routine exploitation of minority shareholders by a majority is made difficult. The dispersed nature of share ownership in the UK also limits the potential for exploitation of minorities as it results in the absence of controlling shareholders in most listed companies. In this respect the UK differs from many other countries,[49] where concentrated share ownership leads to the corporate governance agenda being framed much more in terms of controlling the appropriation of private benefits by controlling shareholders rather than controlling the exercise of discretion by directors. It is therefore not surprising to find that virtually no attention has been paid to minority rights in the development of corporate governance codes in the UK. They are already entrenched in the law and there was therefore no obvious need to remedy any deficiency by adopting additional provisions in corporate governance codes.

8.3 Evolution of corporate governance in the UK

At the beginning of this chapter, corporate governance was defined as the mechanisms associated with company law that shape the way managers (and in particular the board of directors) exercise their discretion. The sphere within which that discretion can be exercised is largely a function of the distribution of powers between shareholders and directors respectively. The legal framework that determines this distribution is discussed below[50] and attention is then turned to the development of corporate governance codes.

8.3.1 The sphere of discretion

The powers of the board of directors is determined largely by a company's constitution as there are relatively few matters that are required by company law to

---

[48] See generally *Boyle & Birds' Company Law* (above n 4) ch 17.

[49] See eg LLSV (above n 12).

[50] To the extent that much of company law takes the form of default rules, the framework is capable of adaptation and therefore need not be the same for every company. However, the analysis is applicable to whatever distribution applies within a particular company.

be reserved for decision-making by the shareholders in general meeting.[51] It is therefore largely for each company to determine the extent to which powers are delegated to the board of directors. Article 70 of Table A (the standard articles of association) delegates wide-ranging powers to the board of directors as follows:

> Subject to the provisions of the Act, the memorandum and the articles and to any directions given by special resolution, the business of the company shall be managed by the directors who may exercise all the powers of the company. No alteration of the memorandum or articles and no such direction shall invalidate any prior act of the directors which would have been valid if that alteration had not been made or that direction had not been given. The powers given by this regulation shall not be limited by any special power given to the directors by the articles and a meeting of directors at which a quorum is present may exercise all powers exercisable by the directors.

However, Article 70 does not provide a means by which the shareholders in general meeting can invalidate action already taken by directors: it relates solely to the future actions of the board.[52] Moreover, in the case of public companies it is rare for the general meeting to be given the power to give directions to the board in the manner envisaged by the standard article 70. The rationale is that shareholders invest in public companies because they expect a strict separation of ownership and control and therefore it is inappropriate for such companies to have mechanisms that run contrary to that principle.[53] However, this only exacerbates the nature of the principal/agent problem in public companies and gives rise to particular problems when, as is generally the case, directors are permitted to set their own remuneration. It is in this context that the concerns of principal/agent theory regarding the likelihood of directors over-rewarding themselves are particularly evident. Further consideration is given to this issue in 8.5 below.

8.3.2 Corporate governance codes

The development of corporate governance codes in the UK can be viewed largely as a response to the relatively wide sphere of discretion enjoyed by directors in running companies and the limited obligations placed on institutional shareholders in monitoring and controlling companies. The existence of wide discretion in both spheres can be viewed as creating an environment in which problems are likely to emerge. As regards directors' discretion, the main risks are excessive risk taking, manipulation of financial results and excessive

---

[51] See R Pennington, *Pennington's Company Law*, 8th edn (London, Butterworths, 2001) p 696 fn 5 regarding the matters reserved to the shareholders under the Companies Act 1985.

[52] Pennington (above n 51) p 699.

[53] The position will differ in small private companies where there will often be an expectation that shareholders should be directly involved in running the business.

remuneration. From the shareholders' perspective, it is less obvious that discretion in exercising voting rights poses risks, but for the corporate sector as a whole it is likely that the absence of any formal or informal requirement to vote will tend over time to weaken shareholder monitoring.

Developments in corporate governance in the UK over the past decade address both these issues. The specific impetus for change was a number of high-profile corporate failures that highlighted the risks associated with ineffective control of company management.[54] However, the concerns underlying the developments in the 1990s had been evident for a long time.[55] The Cohen Committee, set up in 1945 to review company law, observed that:[56]

> The illusory nature of the control theoretically exercised by shareholders over directors has been accentuated by the dispersion of capital among an increasing number of small shareholders who pay little attention to their investments, so long as satisfactory dividends are forthcoming, who lack sufficient time, money and experience to make full use of their rights as occasions arise and who are, in many cases, too numerous and too widely dispersed to be able to organise themselves.

Later initiatives also recognised problems but the prevailing support for self-regulatory solutions was an important factor in preventing statutory intervention. For example, the Jenkins Committee, which recommended changes in company law in 1962, warned against excessive regulation of the corporate sector.[57] In 1973 the CBI published a report entitled *The Responsibilities of the British Public Company*[58] in which it argued that self-regulation and evolution in corporate governance were preferable to statutory intervention. Many of the principles contained in the current Combined Code of Corporate Governance can be traced back to the *Principles of Corporate Conduct* adopted by the CBI at that time. The tendency to favour self-regulation over statutory intervention has been continued by the recent DTI review of company law on the basis that it provides for a more competitive and effective system of regulation than statutory regulation.[59]

Another factor supporting self-regulation then and now is the activity of the Association of British Insurers (ABI) and the National Association of Pension Funds (NAPF). These bodies represent the collective interests of institutional

---

[54] See B Cheffins, *Company Law, Theory, Structure and Operation* (Oxford, OUP, 1997) pp 612–13.

[55] See generally S Sheikh and S Chatterjee, 'Perspectives on Corporate Governance' ch 1 in S Sheikh and W Rees (eds) *Corporate Governance and Corporate Control* (London, Cavendish, 1995).

[56] Board of Trade, *Report of the Company Law Committee* (1945) Cmnd 6659.

[57] Board of Trade, *Report of the Company Law Committee* (1962) Cmnd 1749, p 3 para 11.

[58] CBI, *The Responsibilities of the British Public Company: Final Report of the Company Affairs Committee* (1973).

[59] See *Modern Company Law for a Competitive Economy* (1998) *Final Report* paras 1.28 and 3.5.

investors in listed companies. While they could no doubt operate effectively whether the sphere of corporate governance were subject to statutory intervention or not, their existence and power makes self-regulation workable. These bodies are able, through the scale of their shareholdings, to ensure that companies comply with codes that they have endorsed. Without such organisations, much of the impetus for developing and implementing codes of corporate governance would be missing. Although they act primarily in their own interests, their activities also bring benefits to other investors.

The self-regulatory approach underpinned the development of corporate governance in the UK during the 1990s. None of the codes have a formal legal status. Nor do they form part of the Listing Rules, with the result that non-compliance cannot threaten a company's listed status. Reliance is instead placed on disclosure of the extent to which a listed company has complied with the relevant code. This opens up the possibility of institutional investors applying pressure on companies who do not comply. On the assumption that the codes have introduced measures that improve governance, it is also likely that disclosure of non-compliance will have a negative influence on a company's share price as the market will assume that such a company operates a sub-optimal governance structure.

The Financial Reporting Council, the London Stock Exchange and the accountancy profession established a Committee on the Financial Aspects of Corporate Governance in May 1991. Its first report (the Cadbury Report) in 1992 represents the most significant landmark in the development of a code of corporate governance in the United Kingdom. It produced a Code of Best Practice that dealt with the structure and role of the board of directors, the role of non-executive directors, directors' remuneration and reporting and controls. This was followed in 1995 by a second report from the Greenbury Committee, whose remit was to set out best practice in determining and accounting for directors' remuneration. The final report of the Committee (the Hampel Report) considered the implementation of the Cadbury and Greenbury Reports and was given the fresh task of examining the roles of directors, shareholders and auditors in corporate governance. Following the final report, the committee produced the Combined Code, which consolidated the recommendations of all three reports. A revised version of the Combined Code was published in 2003 incorporating the 'Turnbull Guidance on Internal Control'[60], the 'Smith Guidance'[61] (on audit committees) and the 'Higgs Suggestions for Good Practice'.[62]

[60] *Internal Control: Guidance for Directors on the Combined Code* produced by the Turnbull Committee and published by the Institute of Chartered Accountants in England and Wales in September 1999.

[61] *Audit Committees: Combined Code Guidance* produced by Sir Robert Smith and published January 2003.

[62] *Review of the Role and Effectiveness of Non-executive Directors* produced by Sir Derek Higgs and published Janaury 2003.

The Combined Code is appended to but does not form part of the Listing Rules. Listed companies are, however, required to state in their annual report and accounts whether they have complied with the Combined Code and to give reasons for any areas of non-compliance.[63] The rationale for this approach is explained in the following terms:

> The 'comply or explain' approach has been in operation for over ten years and the flexibility it offers has been widely welcomed both by company boards and by investors. It is for shareholders and others to evaluate the company's statement.[64]

Some observations can be made about this approach.[65] First, if flexibility is desired because there is no clear link between corporate governance standards and company performance, it can be questioned whether there is any point in having any standards. In other words, if it is not clear that the objective (improved performance) can be achieved by the means proposed (corporate governance standards), the nature of the proposed standards makes little difference. Second, if the pre-occupation with flexibility is instead simply to allow companies to adapt rules to suit their own particular circumstances, so as to avoid a 'one size fits all' approach, it is not clear that that this can only be achieved outside a formal legal framework. For example, the process by which a company can 'tailor' its articles of association from default rules set by company law provides a clear analogy that could be applied to the Combined Code. However, it must be recognised that the speed with which the Combined Code can be and has been updated does offer a significant advantage by comparison with the long delays associated with reform of company law.

8.4 Shareholder activism

The term 'shareholder activism' is used here to refer to the extent to which shareholders become involved in active monitoring and supervision of companies in which they are invested. Shareholders are generally viewed as having two options when there is a liquid market in the relevant securities. The first is that they can engage in monitoring and supervising the company with a view to ensuring that it is operating efficiently and according to their wishes.[66] The

---

[63] The Listing Rules, Ch 12 paras 12.43A, effective for annual reports and accounts for financial periods ending on or after 31 Dec 1998.

[64] Preamble to the Combined Code (2003 version), para 4.

[65] See generally C Riley, 'The Juridification of Corporate Governance' in J de Lacy (ed) *The Reform of United Kingdom Company Law* (London, Cavendish, 2002).

[66] For a discussion of how investors do this, see S Gillan and L Starks, 'Corporate Governance, Corporate Ownership and the Role of Institutional Investors: A Global Perspective' Working Paper 2003–01, John Weinberg Centre for Corporate Governance, University of Delaware, at http://ssrn.com/abstract=439500 (19 Nov 2004).

second is that they do not engage in monitoring and supervision and instead simply sell the securities of companies with which they are dissatisfied. The first option has been characterised as the exercise of 'voice' and the second as 'exit'.[67] The extent to which the exit option is available is dependent on the liquidity of the capital market and the degree to which shareholdings are concentrated. If shareholdings are typically concentrated (as indicated by the presence of controlling shareholders) it will be more difficult to exercise the exit option and therefore there may be no alternative but to exercise the voice option. On the other hand, the conditions under which the exit option is generally available (widely dispersed share-ownership) are such that the exercise of voice in a meaningful manner by a single investor is usually not possible. Exit and voice are therefore not alternatives in all circumstances. The legal framework in the UK surrounding the exercise of voting rights by shareholders supports the 'voice versus exit' analysis. As noted above, shareholders are under no duty to vote and when they do they are entitled to vote as they wish. Moreover, the United Kingom, unlike some other countries,[68] does not generally restrict the ability of shareholders to collaborate over voting on resolutions, thereby making it possible, at least in principle, for some form of collective voice to be exercised.

Shareholders have largely been passive investors in the UK.[69] The Hampel Committee Report commented:[70]

> Typically institutions used not to take much interest in corporate governance. . . . Institutions tended not to vote their shares regularly, and to intervene directly with company managements only in circumstances of crisis.

A number of explanations can be offered for this. One is that there is little incentive for an individual shareholder to engage in costly monitoring of listed companies. Any benefits to the share price resulting from that monitoring have to be shared with other investors whereas the costs have to be borne by the individual shareholder (the 'free rider' problem). While such monitoring might be an attractive proposition for a controlling shareholder, who can retain much of the value derived from monitoring, the relatively widely dispersed nature of share ownership in the UK makes that scenario unlikely. The

---

[67] See n 8 above regarding the origin of this terminology.

[68] See B Black and J Coffee, 'Hail Britannia? Institutional Investor Behaviour under Limited Regulation' (1997) 92 *Michigan Law Review* 1.

[69] See eg A Peacock and G Bannock, *Corporate Takeovers and the Public Interest* (Aberdeen, Aberdeen University Press, 1991), who refer (at p 32) to a 1991 NAPF survey showing that nearly a quarter of pension funds have a policy of never using their shareholders' voting rights, while only 20% have a policy of voting at all times. The 1998 ABI publication 'Statement of Voting Policy and Corporate Governance Good Practice' (p 32) indicates some change: 'ABI members have made an active voting policy a priority and this is reflected in their creditable voting record in recent years.'

[70] para 5.2.

obvious solution might be collective action. However, while institutional investors do engage in collective action in relation to matters which affect their collective interest, monitoring individual companies raises issues of competitive advantage as between institutional investors. Institutional investors are competitors and are unlikely to collaborate in monitoring companies on a routine basis[71] because monitoring is an integral part of investment management. Another explanation is that the nature of retail investment products creates a complex link between the ultimate investor and the investee company and thereby discourages activism on the part of those persons and organisations that together link the company and the ultimate investor.[72]

The system under which a substantial proportion of institutional funds are managed in the UK is another explanation for shareholder passivity. Pension funds in particular tend to be managed under relatively short-term contracts, with the result that there may be little incentive to incur monitoring costs that do not yield an immediate benefit.[73] Potential conflicts of interest may also contribute to passivity. They are likely to arise when there are business links between investors and companies (eg between a bank shareholder and a company that is a customer of the bank) that could be threatened if an active stance were to be adopted. It is also possible that widespread use of nominees and custodians, which results in an 'ownership' chain being interposed between an investor and an issuer, results in either confusion over exactly who is entitled to exercise voting rights or administrative difficulty in passing voting rights down the 'ownership' chain.[74]

The important question is whether shareholder passivity poses a problem for companies and investors. For investors, the main risk arising from a passive stance is that the directors are given too much freedom in setting strategy and running the company. In other words, the sphere within which directors enjoy discretion expands and there may be a need to constrain that discretion through rules and procedures that do not require active engagement by shareholders. There is, however, no risk of any re-balancing of passive shareholders' financial and voting interests in the company by comparison with other (active) shareholders.[75] In principle, therefore, the effect of a passive stance is

---

[71] For examples of collaboration on specific issues see Black and Coffee (above n 68).

[72] See J Gray, 'Personal Finance and Corporate Governance: The Missing Link: Product Regulation and Policy Conflicts' (2004) 4 *Journal of Corporate Law Studies* 187.

[73] J Coffee, 'Liquidity versus Control: The Institutional Investor as Corporate Monitor' (1991) 91 *Columbia Law Review* 1277 at 1325 makes the same point in respect of the United States.

[74] Although it is the registered owner of shares who is entitled to vote, it is possible for voting rights to be passed down an 'ownership' chain through contractual provisions in custody agreements.

[75] See HG Manne, 'Some Theoretical Aspects of Share Voting' (1964) 64 *Columbia Law Review* 1427. The essential point made by Manne is that while a passive stance may lead to a reduction in company value (market capitalisation), the proportionate share of each shareholder remains unaffected.

likely to depend on whether there are other mechanisms through which directors can be held accountable for their actions. If there are (eg as a result of
codes of corporate governance), a passive stance is unlikely to result in
investors being exposed to high levels of agency cost as a result of directors'
self-interested actions. If the mechanisms through which directors are made
accountable are weak, agency costs associated with directors' actions are likely
to be high and the rationale for a more active stance on the part of investors
becomes apparent.

It is doubtful whether corporate governance codes alone can remove shareholder passivity because they do not directly address many of the causes
identified above. Nevertheless, they are important because they offer the
possibility for (institutional) investors to hold directors accountable in a sys-
tematic and consistent manner in respect of the exercise of their discretion. For
codes to operate effectively investors must take an active stance, and that is
recognised by both the Combined Code[76] and the Guidelines adopted by the
Institutional Shareholders' Committee.[77] Whether such recognition actually
results in a significant change in the relatively small number of shares that are
typically voted in the UK remains to be seen. There did not appear to be any
significant change in practice in the years (1993–98) between the Cadbury and
Hampel Reports.[78]

8.5 Board structure and independent directors

In the United Kingdom, the law relating to the structure of boards of directors
is sparse.[79] A minimum number of directors is specified[80] but the law does not
mandate the structure of the board of directors of a company or by whom they
should be appointed. Nor does the law prescribe whether a board of directors
should consist of a single or two tiers,[81] whether any of the directors should be

---

[76] See s 2 'Institutional Shareholders' stating that 'institutional shareholders have a responsibility to make considered use of their votes'.

[77] See Ch 5.3 for more detail relating to the Committee. Its guidelines 'The Responsibilities of
Institutional Shareholders' state (para 3):

It is considered important that institutional shareholders support Boards by a positive use
of their voting rights unless they have good reasons for doing otherwise.

[78] It was noted in the Hampel Report (1998) para 5.7 that the number of shares voted in the
previous five years had risen only marginally and remained at less than 40%.

[79] See CA Riley (above n 65).

[80] The Companies Act 1985 s 282 requires two directors for a public company and one for a
private company.

[81] For a comparative analysis of this issue as between Germany and the UK (following the
introduction of the Combined Code) see P Davies, 'Board Structure in the UK and Germany:
Convergence or Continuing Divergence?' at http://ssrn.com/abstract=262959 (19 Nov 2004).

independent of management or whether any particular tasks should be undertaken by committees of the board.

There are, however, sound reasons why, at least in the context of listed companies, board structure would evolve in a manner whereby shareholders would be able to monitor and control the decisions of directors.[82] The decision-making process in listed companies can be characterised as having four stages: initiation, ratification, implementation and monitoring. Initiation and implementation are usually termed management while ratification and monitoring are usually termed 'decision-control'. In listed companies, agency problems will usually be minimised if there is some separation of these two functions. If there is no separation, shareholders face the risk that directors will act in a self-interested manner. It would therefore seem likely that, even without formal legal intervention, shareholders would establish board structures that minimised this risk. One way of doing this would be to appoint to the board independent directors who have no operational involvement in the company. In the United Kingdom, such directors are referred to as 'non-executive' directors, thereby distinguishing them from executive directors, who have responsibility for managing the company's business.

In principle, independent directors can serve two different purposes. In countries such as the United Kingdom, where listed companies generally do not have a controlling shareholder, they can protect against the possibility of directors engaging in self-interested conduct. This can take a variety of forms since directors are likely to value not just financial rewards but status and power over increased resources.[83] Company law already provides some protection through the fiduciary duties of directors and the statutory provisions requiring disclosure of a personal interest in transactions.[84] Independent directors provide a different type of control over self-interested action in that they should have sufficient experience and involvement in a company's affairs to be able to 'smell trouble' and exert their influence to prevent it.[85] In countries where controlling shareholders are frequently found in listed companies, the presence of independent directors on the Board can serve the different purpose of protecting minority shareholders from the expropriation of private benefits by the controlling shareholder at the expense of other shareholders. This can occur, for example, by awarding contracts to other businesses controlled by that shareholder or selling assets to associates at an undervalue.

---

[82] See E Fama and M Jensen, 'Separation of Ownership and Control' (1983) 26 *Journal of Law and Economics* pp 301–25.

[83] The extent to which such conduct causes a welfare loss to shareholders is sometimes termed the residual loss.

[84] See generally *Boyle & Birds' Company Law* (above n 48) ch 16.

[85] See generally R Gilson and R Kraakman, 'Reinventing the Outside Director: An Agenda for Institutional Investors' (1991) 43 *Stanford Law Review* 863.

The Combined Code is based on the belief that mandating board structure will have a beneficial effect on corporate governance and ultimately on corporate performance. To this end the Code requires that non-executive directors (NEDs) should comprise not less than half of the board.[86] The NEDs should be independent of management and free from any business or other relationships that could materially interfere with the exercise of their independent judgement.[87] The Code also defines a particular role for NEDs by reference to the operation of several board sub-committees that carry out key functions.[88] A nomination committee should be appointed, comprising a majority of non-executive directors, to make recommendations to the board on all new board appointments.[89] A remuneration committee, comprising only non-executive directors, should be established with authority delegated to it by the board to set remuneration for all executive directors and the chairman.[90] Finally, an audit committee comprising only non-executive directors should be established to keep under review the scope and results of the audit and the conduct of the auditors.[91]

It remains to be seen whether the considerable effort devoted to board structure will yield benefits in terms of financial performance. Initial indications based on empirical research are not encouraging. One study based on data drawn from the period 1994 to 1996 concluded that there was at best a weak link between the internal governance structures established by the Cadbury Code and performance.[92] The authors suggested three possible conclusions: first, it simply may not be possible to protect shareholders' interests by mandating board structure; second, the study may reflect inappropriate non-executive appointments; and third, it may not be appropriate to mandate a 'one size fits all' rule applicable to board structure. Another study examined the relationship between board structure and performance in newly listed companies in the period 1990–94.[93] It concluded that there was no evidence of any link between adherence to governance guidelines and enhanced performance in newly listed companies during that period. However, a more recent study did conclude that compliance with the Cadbury recommendations had

---

[86] s 1, para A.3.2.

[87] s 1, para A.3.1.

[88] There has been widespread compliance with the requirement to appoint internal committees of the board: see Pensions Investment Research Consultants (PIRC), *Compliance with the Combined Code*, Sept 1999 (fn 30 in Davies above n 81).

[89] s 1, para A.4.1.

[90] s 1, para B.2.1.

[91] s 1, paras C.3.1 and C.3.2.

[92] See C Weir, D Laing and P McKnight, 'An Empirical Analysis of the Impact of Corporate Governance Mechanisms on the Performance of UK Firms' at http://ssrn.com/abstracts=286440 (19 Nov 2004).

[93] See R Buckland, 'UK IPO Board Structures and Post-Issue Performance' *Aberdeen Papers in Accountancy, Finance & Management Working Paper 01-05.*

a positive impact in limiting the manipulation of accounting information and disciplining senior management.[94]

8.6 Directors' remuneration

Concern over the scale of the remuneration of directors of listed companies has grown considerably in recent years. In the 1980s it was largely prompted by the 'fat cat' allegations that surrounded the large rises in remuneration awarded to directors in the newly privatised utilities. In recent years, concern has focused on the mis-match between remuneration and performance, the perception being that in some cases directors have been rewarded excessively either for failure or mediocre performance.

There is relatively little substantive control exerted by company law over the remuneration of directors. The emphasis is instead on disclosure. The standard articles of association[95] provide that:

> The directors shall be entitled to such remuneration as the company may by ordinary resolution determine and, unless the resolution provides otherwise, the remuneration shall be deemed to accrue from day to day.

This provision relates to payments made to directors (executive or non-executive) in their capacity as directors. It does not relate to payments to executive directors under service (employment) contracts, as such payments are made to directors in their capacity as employees. Neither company law nor the standard articles control the amount that can be paid to executive directors under service contracts. Nor do they limit the power of the board of directors to set their own remuneration under those contracts.[96] Members are, however, entitled to inspect directors' service contracts.[97] In the unlikely event that a director's service contract runs for more than five years and can only be terminated by the company in specified circumstances, shareholders must approve the contract.[98]

The Combined Code introduced some potentially significant changes in the practice of setting directors' remuneration. First, following the earlier

---

[94] See EB Dedman, 'The Cadbury Code Recommendations on Corporate Governance—A Review of Compliance and Performance Impacts' (2002) 4 *International Journal of Management Reviews* 335–52.

[95] Table A, contained in the Companies (Tables A to F) Regulations SI 1985/805, art 82.

[96] This power is derived from art 84 of the standard articles (Table A).

[97] Companies Act 1985 s 318. In the case of listed companies, directors' service contracts are available for inspection by any person and must include specified information: see rule 16.9 of the UKLA Listing Rules.

[98] Companies Act 1985 s 319.

recommendation of the Cadbury Committee,[99] it requires companies to establish a remuneration committee comprised of independent non-executive directors with delegated responsibility for setting the remuneration of executive directors and the chairman.[100] The board itself or, where required by the articles of association the shareholders, should determine the remuneration of the non-executive directors within the limits set by the articles. These procedures are intended to limit the conflicts of interest that inevitably arise if executive directors are responsible for setting their own remuneration.[101] Second, the Combined Code sets companies an objective of limiting or reducing directors' service contracts to a period of one year or less.[102] This has important implications for payments made to directors in cases of early termination. A company has the right to remove (by ordinary resolution) a director before expiration of his period in office and notwithstanding anything in its articles or in any agreement between it and him.[103] Early termination can result in two types of payment being made to a director. One is compensation for loss of office as a director. Another is damages for breach (through early termination) of a service contract. Company law requires that the former type of payment must be disclosed to and approved by shareholders.[104] Damages for breach of a service contract are specifically excluded from this statutory provision.[105] The result is that, according to company law, substantial payments can be made to directors following early termination in respect of damages for remuneration that would have been paid in the unexpired period of their service contracts; and such payments do not require disclosure or approval. Restriction of service contracts to a maximum period of one year in accordance with the Combined Code would limit the potential for such payments to be made. Companies may also consider the advantages of providing explicitly in directors' service contracts for such compensation except in the case of removal by misconduct (in which case it is the director who is in breach of contract and the company has no liability in damages).[106] Linked with this is the recommendation made by the Code that companies should avoid rewarding poor performance when making early termination payments and should take a robust line on a departing director's duty to mitigate loss.[107]

[99] See (Cadbury) Code of Best Practice para 3.3.

[100] Combined Code para B.2.2.

[101] The possibility of non-executive directors being involved in setting their own remuneration poses less risk of conflict of interest in that their expectations are generally much lower, reflecting their limited involvement with the company.

[102] s 1 para B1.6. The Cadbury Code of Best Practice had recommended that directors' service contracts should not exceed three years without shareholders' approval (para 3.1).

[103] Companies Act 1985 s 303.

[104] Companies Act 1985 s 312.

[105] Companies Act 1985 s 316(3).

[106] See s 1 para B.1.9 of the Combined Code (April 2002 version).

[107] s 1 para B.1.10. The duty to mitigate loss following breach is a general principle of contract law.

The Code requires all new long-term incentive schemes (as defined in the Listing Rules[108]) to be approved by shareholders.[109] They include bonuses linked to service and/or performance over periods longer than one financial year. Also relevant in this context are the guidelines on executive remuneration adopted by the ABI/NAPF.[110] These guidelines are concerned with the structure of remuneration, the conditions attaching to share incentive schemes and disclosure to and approval by shareholders of various aspects of remuneration. They recognise a role for both fixed and variable pay and for long-term and short-term incentives. Variable pay should generally take the form of bonuses linked to performance targets that are disclosed in the remuneration report (see below). Transaction bonuses that reward directors for effecting transactions irrespective of their financial consequences (eg takeovers) are discouraged. Pension entitlement and other benefits accruing during a year should also be disclosed. Share incentive schemes are subject to detailed rules. Underlying these rules is a recognition that they involve either the commitment of shareholders' funds (to buy shares for distribution to scheme members) or dilution in shareholders' equity (when options are granted to buy shares at a discount to the market price in the future). A limit of 10 per cent of issued ordinary share capital applies to the capital of a company that can be used for all share incentive schemes over a ten-year period[111]. Individual members of share option schemes should not normally be granted options with a value exceeding four times annual remuneration.[112] Vesting[113] of options should normally be subject to performance conditions that extend over three years or more.[114] Finally, all new share-based incentive schemes and material changes to existing schemes should be subject to approval by shareholders.

As a result of recent amendments to the Companies Act 1985, the requirement for disclosure of remuneration policy (previously in the *Code*[115]) has now become statutory and shareholders have been given a more substantial

---

[108] See the definitions section of the Listing Rules.

[109] para B.2.4 of the Combined Code. The Listing Rules do, however, permit options to be granted without shareholder approval subject to the condition that the exercise price is not below the market price at the time of exercise: see para 13.30 of the Listing Rules. This presumably reflects the fact that there can be no dilution of shareholders' equity in these circumstances and therefore no need for approval.

[110] The most recent guidelines are those adopted following the changes to the Companies Act 1985 described below. See also the ABI documents 'Share Option and Profit Sharing Incentive Schemes' (1995) and 'Long-Term Remuneration for Senior Executives' (1996).

[111] ABI/NAPF, *Guidelines for Share Incentive Schemes* (2002) para 13.1.

[112] ABI Guidance 'Share Option and Profit Sharing Incentive Schemes' (1995) para 4.2.

[113] Vesting refers to the acquisition of a right to exercise the option. The grant of an option does not in itself lead to its exercise as the conditions for its exercise may not be met.

[114] ABI Guidance 'Share Option and Profit Sharing Incentive Schemes' (1995) para 6.

[115] See s 1.B.3 of and sch B to the April 2002 version of the *Code*.

role in voting on remuneration policy.[116] The rationale for this approach is that, while there had been adequate disclosure of directors' remuneration packages (as a result of the requirements of the Listing Rules), there was inadequate compliance with the Greenbury recommendations on the disclosure of remuneration policy.[117] Directors of listed companies are now required to prepare a remuneration report containing specified information.[118] This information is more extensive than previously required by company law[119] or the Listing Rules.[120] Moreover, a listed company must consider at its annual general meeting a resolution approving the remuneration report and the existing directors must ensure that the resolution is put to the vote at that meeting. The vote has been described as 'advisory', meaning that it cannot change contractual agreements relating to remuneration that have already been concluded. A vote does, however, provide a mechanism for shareholders to signal dissatisfaction and require a change in practice.

8.7 Auditors and corporate governance

The significance of audit to the development of corporate governance standards in the UK is made evident by two factors. First, doubts over the reliability of audit reports given in respect of the accounts of failed companies were significant in prompting demands for the introduction of corporate governance standards.[121] Second, the accountancy profession itself recognised this concern and the associated need to bolster the standing of the profession by participating directly in the process of creating standards. The Cadbury

---

[116] The amendments were introduced by the Directors' Remuneration Report Regulations 2002, SI 2002/1986, effective 1 August 2002 in respect of companies' financial years ending on or after 31 December 2002. They apply only to companies officially listed in the UK or EU or admitted to dealing on either the New York Stock Exchange or NASDAQ (National Association of Securities Dealers Automated Quotation System: an exchange that operates as a competitor to the NYSE). The *Combined Code* does not apply to companies without a UK listing even if they are incorporated in the UK.

[117] See DTI Consultative Document, *Directors' Remuneration* (URN 01/1400, December 2001).

[118] The information is contained in the (new) sch 7A of the Companies Act 1985. See generally L Roach, 'The Directors' Remuneration Report Regulations 2002 and the Disclosure of Executive Remuneration' (2004) 25 *Company Lawyer* 141.

[119] See Companies Act 1985 s 232 and sch 6. As a result of the requirement to produce a remuneration report listed companies are now largely exempt from Pt I of sch 6.

[120] The DTI Consultative Document (above n 117 p 10) highlights three differences: the remuneration report has a clearer focus on forward looking disclosure of remuneration policy; there is a requirement for information on performance linkage by comparison with a company's peer group; and there is disclosure of the role of the board and remuneration committee in respect of their consideration of directors' remuneration.

[121] See the preface to the Cadbury Report (above n 1).

Committee was established by the Financial Reporting Council, the London Stock Exchange and the accountancy profession and its remit was essentially to focus on financial reporting and audit.[122]

Cadbury (and later the Combined Code) adopted standards that were built around an existing legal framework that distinguishes the roles of directors and auditors in relation to financial statements. According to company law, directors are responsible for preparing the annual report and accounts of a company.[123] The Combined Code reinforces the responsibility of directors by adopting the principle that 'The board should present a balanced and understandable assessment of the company's position and prospects'.[124] It goes on to say that this responsibility extends to interim and other price-sensitive public reports and reports to regulators. The role of auditors under company law is to state whether the annual accounts have been properly prepared, whether they are consistent with the company's accounting records and whether they provide a 'true and fair' view of the company's financial position.[125]

The Combined Code provisions relating to accountability and audit are based on two guiding principles. The first is that a company should maintain a sound system of internal control.[126] The second is that a company should appoint an audit committee of at least three non-executive directors, all of whom should be independent.[127] The duties of the audit committee should include keeping under review the scope and results of the audit and its cost effectiveness and the independence and objectivity of the auditors. Where the auditors also supply a substantial volume of non-audit services to the company, the committee should keep the nature and extent of such services under review, seeking to balance the maintenance of objectivity and value for money.

---

[122] Hence the reference to the 'financial aspects of corporate governance' in the designation of the Cadbury Committee. See App 1 of the Cadbury Report for a statement of the Committee's remit.

[123] See Companies Act 1985 s 226 and s 233.

[124] s 1. C.1.

[125] Companies Act 1985 s 235. A recent amendment to this section requires auditors to report to a company's members on the auditable part of the directors' remuneration report. See SI 2002/1986, art 4.

[126] para C.2 of the Combined Code. The 'Turnbull Guidance' suggests (but does not mandate) ways in which this principle can be implemented.

[127] para C.3.1 of the Combined Code. The 'Smith Guidance' suggests (but does not mandate) ways in which this principle can be implemented.

8.8 Takeovers

8.8.1 Rationale

The relevance of takeovers to corporate governance is that the threat of takeover can act as disciplining mechanism for the board of directors.[128] A poorly performing company faces the threat of takeover because the shareholders are likely to lose confidence in the exisiting board of directors and may prefer to accept a takeover offer than to hope for a recovery in the share price. Although a change in control resulting from a takeover does not automatically lead to changes in the board of directors, this is likely to occur in most cases as the new shareholders will want to install new directors to give effect to their plans. The threat of removal as a result of a takeover can represent just as serious as threat to a board of directors as any other sanction for poor performance and therefore takeovers can potentially be a significant mechanism in corporate governance. Indeed, takeovers can be regarded as a residual form of control that is available as a last resort when other mechanisms have failed.

Takeovers can be viewed as an example of shareholders collectively exercising the 'exit' option.[129] The rationale for a takeover offer is that the bidder believes that a company is being run inefficiently and that benefits can be gained through a change of control. In order to gain control, it is likely that a bidder will have to pay a premium over the prevailing market price. The premium reflects the special circumstances in which the 'exit' option is being exercised and the value attached to control of a company. While the sale of a shareholding normally does not carry with it any real control over a company, a takeover offer is designed to transfer control and therefore a bidder will attach a higher value to shares that deliver control of a company. In an unregulated environment it is likely that the premium would increase in line with the size of the shareholding of the bidder, as the marginal benefits of each acquisition would increase as the shareholding grew. In principle, the size of the premium that a bidder should be prepared to pay to gain control should be less than the benefits that result from the change in control. If it were otherwise, the bidder would be over-paying for the target and while the target

---

[128] See J Franks and C Mayer, 'Hostile Takeover and the Correction of Managerial Failure' (1996) 40 *Journal of Financial Economics* 163–81 and M Maher and T Anderson, 'Corporate Governance: Effects on Firm Performance and Economic Growth' in L Renneboog *et al* (eds) *Convergence and Diversity of Corporate Governance Regimes and Capital Markets* (Oxford, OUP, 2000) pp 29–32.

[129] See 8.4 (above) for a discussion of the 'voice' and 'exit' options.

shareholders would benefit, shareholders of the bidder would suffer loss as a result of the transaction.[130]

Several conditions must be met for takeovers to operate as an effective disciplining mechanism. First, there must be a liquid capital market. If there is not, it is unlikely that a bidder will be able to acquire sufficient shares in the target company to gain control. For this reason, takeovers are relatively rare in countries with 'bank-centred' systems of corporate governance, in which share ownership is often heavily concentrated. They are more commonly associated with countries such as the UK and USA, in which share-ownership is relatively dispersed and there are large and liquid capital markets. Second, there must be rules in place that ensure fair and equal treatment of the shareholders in target companies. If there are not, it is likely that arbitrary treatment of different shareholders will lead to widespread resistance to takeovers on the part of shareholders who do not fall within the favoured group. Third, there must be adequate disclosure to the shareholders of the target company to enable them to make a decision on the offer. This is particularly the case when the offer is a 'share-for-share'[131] offer under which the shareholders in the target company are being offered shares in the bidder. Unless the target shareholders have adequate information they will be unable to judge whether the benefits claimed by the bidder as a result of the takeover can realistically be achieved.

The second and third conditions mentioned above are the main concern of the Takeover Code, which is discussed below.

8.8.2 The Takeover Panel and Code

The Takeover Panel and Code were established on a self-regulatory basis to regulate the conduct of takeovers and mergers.[132] They have survived in that form to the present day notwithstanding the demise of the principle of self-regulation in most other areas of financial market regulation.[133] The objective of the Takeover Code is to deal with the conduct of takeovers and in particular their effect on shareholders in the respective companies. Other aspects of takeovers, such as their impact on competition, are dealt with through a separate legal framework in which the Competition Commission and the European Commission play the leading roles.[134]

---

[130] For the relevance of this issue to the social costs of takeovers and regulation based on competition considerations, see C Bradley, 'Corporate Control: Markets and Rules' in S Wheeler (ed) *A Reader on the Law of the Business Enterprise* (Oxford, OUP, 1994).

[131] See Ch 7.7 for an explanation of this term.

[132] See Ch 7.7 as to the meaning of these terms and generally *Boyle & Birds' Company Law* (above n 48) ch 18.

[133] See Ch 2 regarding the history of self-regulation.

[134] The legal framework is that created by the Enterprise Act 2002 and the EC Merger Control Regulation 139/2004 OJ L24/1, replacing the previous EC Merger Regulation (4064/89, [1990] OJ L257/14).

Although the Panel is not a statutory body and its decisions do not have legal force, its decisions remain fully effective unless and until they are set aside by a court of competent jurisdiction. It is acknowledged by government and other regulatory bodies that those who seek to take advantage of the facilities of the securities market in the United Kingdom should conduct themselves in matters relating to takeovers in accordance with the best business standards and so according to the Code. Therefore, for those who do not do so, by way of sanction, the facilities of those markets may be withheld. The Financial Services and Markets Act 2000 gives effect to this principle by permitting the FSA to 'endorse' the Takeover Code and the Substantial Acquisition Rules (SARs). The FSA has done so[135] and the result is that breaches of the Code or SARs can lead to enforcement action being taken by the FSA, such as the imposition of fines or the withdrawal of authorisation to engage in regulated activity.

The provisions of the Code fall into two distinct categories. First, there are the General Principles, of which there are ten. These are intended to be 'general principles of conduct to be observed in takeover and merger transactions'. They are a 'codification of good standards of commercial behaviour and should have an obvious and universal application'. A major concern is that shareholders should be treated equally and fairly during a takeover, and that changes of control should not come about through limited offers made to favoured groups of shareholders. The second and larger part of the Code consists of Rules (of which there are now thirty-eight).[136] Some of these

> are no more than examples of the application of the general principles whilst others are rules of procedure designed to govern specific forms of takeover and merger transactions practised in the United Kingdom.

The Code emphasises that a legalistic and literal interpretation should not be given to any part of the Code. It is framed

> in non-technical language and is, as a measure of self-discipline, administered and enforced by the Panel, a body representative of those using the securities markets and concerned with the observance of good business standards and not the enforcement of the law.

Following 14 years of negotiations, an EC directive on takeovers was recently approved.[137] Contrary to fears that were expressed in respect of

---

[135] See FSA Handbook MAR 4.2.1R. Endorsement applies equally to altered provisions of the Code: see FSMA 2000 s 143(6), in respect of which the FSA has issued the relevant notification (see FSA Handbook MAR 4.2.2G).

[136] There are also notes to the rules which are intended to furnish a more detailed guidance as to how the Rules are to operate.

[137] Dir 2004/25/EC [2004] OJ L142/12. For the history of the proposal see *Gore-Browne on Companies,* 44th edn (Jordans, loose-leaf) at 40.5–40.16.

earlier drafts,[138] the Directive is unlikely to have a major impact on the role of the Takeover Panel and the operation of the Takeover Code in the UK. Political disagreements over the role and regulation of takeovers within the EU resulted in the Directive being framed more at the level of broad principle than detail, thus giving considerable freedom to Member States as regards implementation. For example, although the Directive follows the approach of the Takeover Code in adopting a mandatory bid rule,[139] definition of the control threshold that triggers a mandatory bid is left to Member States.

The Directive is a minimum standards directive and does not attempt to introduce extensive harmonisation of takeover rules throughout the EU. In principle, Member States can therefore adopt more stringent national provisions provided they comply with the minimum requirements. Provision is also made for Member States to opt out of/into two of the most significant and controversial provisions of the directive: article 9, which relates to defensive measures taken by the board of an offeree company, and article 11 (the so-called 'breakthrough' provision), which allows restrictions in respect of transfer and voting rights to be disapplied for certain purposes. That provision clearly opens up the possibility of very different systems of takeover regulation being preserved in the different Member States and the objective of establishing a single market in capital and financial services being frustrated.

---

[138] The United Kingdom reacted strongly to early drafts, fearing that the Takeover Panel might have to be established on a statutory footing and thus would lose the benefits of its non-statutory status. In particular, the DTI expressed concern that the proposal would have the result that litigation could be used as a tactic for delaying or preventing takeovers.

[139] Rule 9 of the Takeover Code contains the mandatory bid rule. It is designed to ensure that any 'control' premium paid by a bidder to acquire control of a company (defined as a 30% shareholding) is made available to all shareholders.

Part 4

Markets and Participants

9

Investment Markets

Investment markets have been at the centre of much of the discussion that has already been presented in this book. The purpose of this chapter is to examine in more detail the operation and regulation of such markets. It begins by considering the different types of organisational structure to which the term 'market' is applied and the impact that technological innovation is having on regulatory developments. The meaning and role of transparency in financial markets is then analysed. Attention is then turned to the issue of how the regulatory system promotes 'clean' financial markets, which are now widely regarded as playing a central role in generating investment and economic growth. The role of regulation in clearing and settlement, the 'back office' of the investment business, is then considered. The chapter ends with an outline of the law governing the insolvency of participants in investment markets.

9.1 Investment markets: nature and typology

The main function of investment markets is to provide a forum for the trading of securities.[1] The operation of investment markets is dependent on the transferability of securities and this is reflected in the requirement of the UKLA Listing Rules that shares in public listed companies must be freely transferable.[2] In private and unlisted public companies, the articles of association may and often do restrict transfer. This reflects the absence, in most cases, of an organised market for shares in such companies and the fact that small

---

[1] See R Lee, *What is an Exchange?* (Oxford, OUP, 2000) ch 1. Lee defines a market's structure to include the full set of rules governing data dissemination, order routing and order execution. A broader definition is given by S Valdez at p 156 of *An Introduction to Global Financial Markets*, 4th edn (Basingstoke, Palgrave, 2003):

> It [a stock exchange] provides the regulation of company listings, a price formation mechanism, the supervision of trading, authorisation of members, settlement of transactions and publication of trade data and prices.

[2] See Listing Rules para 3.15 (available at www.fsa.gov.uk (22 Nov 2004)).

companies often operate on a basis similar to a partnership and therefore wish to restrict share-ownership to persons with whom the existing shareholders feel comfortable in running the business.

There is no legal or regulatory requirement for transfer of securities to take place through an organised or regulated market.[3] The attraction of markets, especially regulated markets, is that they provide liquidity and ensure some degree of investor protection. Liquidity refers to the ease with which investors can buy or sell securities.[4] Investors value liquidity because it enables securities to be converted into cash: all things being equal, investors will therefore pay more for a liquid security than an illiquid one. Protection of investors who trade in investment markets is an important issue because it creates confidence in the operation of markets and therefore encourages the process of investment. Investor protection encompasses issues such as transparency and market integrity, which are discussed in greater detail below.

Investment markets also have a role in raising new capital for companies, but in comparison with other sources of corporate finance, that function is quite limited. In other words, there is relatively little 'new' capital raised by companies through the process of 'floating' their shares or through subsequent share issues.[5] The more common pattern is for a 'flotation' to serve as a mechanism through which existing shareholders can sell their shares to the public. In this sense, the market provides liquidity to those shareholders and serves a vital function in encouraging their initial investment in the knowledge that success will bring with it the opportunity to 'float'.

A basic distinction can be drawn between organised and unorganised or 'over-the-counter' (OTC) markets. An organised market operates under a set of standard rules relating to admission to trading, the process of trading and the settlement of transactions. It may have a central location or may simply link the various participants together electronically. 'Over-the-counter' markets operate on an *ad hoc* basis with no regulatory infrastructure. The 'market' is simply a collection of individual transactions relating to similar securities. There may be established market customs and practices but there is no organised market. The Eurobond, derivatives and money markets are the main examples of OTC markets. Their operation is characterised by the use of

---

[3] See Ch 4 for more details on the transfer of shares and debentures.

[4] See generally M O'Hara, *Market Microstructure Theory* (Oxford, Blackwell, 1995).

[5] See the data presented by the International Federation of Stock Exchanges (at www.fibv.com (22 Nov 2004)) under 'Stock Markets' Importance in the National Economy'. This data shows the significance of stock markets as a source of finance for companies by expressing new capital raised on stock markets as a percentage of gross fixed capital formation (on an annual basis). For the UK, the ratio in 2001 was 12.2%, which was high by international standards (the ratio for the US was only 7.0%). Nevertheless, the clear implication is that capital raised on stock markets makes a relatively small contribution to the financing needs of business. See also R La Porta *et al*, 'Legal Determinants of External Financing' (1997) 52 *Journal of Finance* 1131.

standard form documentation[6] and reliance on trade customs which, if sufficiently well established, are considered to be implied contract terms.[7]

Markets can also be distinguished by reference to the securities traded on the market. The market for debt instruments with a maturity of less than a year is referred to as the money market, while the market for debt instruments with more than a year to maturity is referred to as the debt capital market. The market in ordinary shares is referred to as the equity capital market. A distinction is made in the case of both the equity and debt capital markets between the primary market, in which securities are offered to the public for the first time, and the secondary market in which trading of those securities subsequently takes place.

Another distinction is between regulated and unregulated markets. The Investment Services Directive[8] (ISD) uses the term 'regulated market' to mean a market that is regulated by the competent authority in each Member State. In the UK, the equivalent term is a recognised investment exchange (RIE). The essential feature of a regulated market is that it operates subject to rules set by the ISD and the national system of regulation (such as FSMA 2000 in the UK). There is no requirement that an exchange operator secures recognition as a 'regulated market' but there are several incentives that encourage operators towards that outcome. First, 'regulated market' status carries with it the assurance that the exchange operates under a formal system of regulation that is intended to promote fair and efficient markets. This is likely to appeal to companies because they will be keen to attract investors and ensure that there is a liquid market in their securities. Second, there are incentives within the regulatory system that encourage (and sometimes require) investment intermediaries (eg brokers) to use regulated markets.[9] Third, there are tax advantages for intermediaries registered with an RIE in the UK, in the form of exemption from Stamp Duty.[10]

It is possible for markets to operate without being regulated in this manner and when they do so they are generally referred to as alternative investment exchanges or electronic communication networks.[11] Such markets are

---

[6] For example, the forms devised by the International Swaps and Derivatives Association (ISDA, see www.isda.org (22 Nov 2004)) are the standard terms for derivatives transactions.

[7] See generally GH Treitel, *The Law of Contract,* 11th edn (London, Sweet & Maxwell, 2003) pp 201–14.

[8] See Ch 2.5.2 for discussion of the ISD and EC regulatory regime.

[9] For example, capital adequacy requirements are lower for transactions undertaken on regulated markets.

[10] Exemptions from stamp duty on trades in UK equities (at the rate of 0.5% on the value of purchases) are only available to RIE registered intermediaries and only in respect of 'on-exchange' transactions.

[11] An additional category is a 'service company' which is not authorised as a broker/dealer but is subject to a special 'light-touch' regulatory regime, reflecting the limited range of activity in which it is authorised to engage and its lack of direct contact with private investors. Such

unregulated in the sense that they are not regulated as markets but their operators, who are normally broker/dealers, are regulated in respect of the activity of dealing in investments (as a principal) and arranging deals in investments (as an agent). In other words, the essential difference is that alternative markets are regulated in a different way to recognised markets. To date, recognised exchanges have generally been subject to more onerous obligations than alternative markets and hence have incurred higher regulatory costs.[12]

Markets can also be distinguished on the basis of their dealing systems. Order-driven systems are those in which buyers and sellers are directly matched together, usually via a computer system. The precise manner in which matching occurs can vary (eg by reference to price considerations or the time at which an instruction is input) but the essential point is that there is no third party involvement in the pricing process (although third parties such as brokers may be responsible for inputting investors' instructions). Quote-driven systems are based around buy/sell quotes made on a continuous basis by market-makers, who trade as principals and provide liquidity to the market.[13] Historically, the London Stock Exchange has been a quote-drive market, but a substantial volume of trade is now conducted through the order-matching system SETS (Stock Exchange Trading System).[14]

Distinctions can also be drawn by reference to the investors in different markets. The term 'wholesale market' refers to the market in which institutional investors purchase securities while the term 'retail market' refers to the purchase of securities (directly or indirectly through investment funds) by private individuals. Within the wholesale market there exists a market that is termed the 'inter-professionals' market by the FSA Handbook. This is a market in which investment professionals authorised under the FSMA 2000 deal with each other.[15] The retail market is characterised by the presence of 'packaged' products. These are financial products such as investment funds or investment-linked life assurance that offer indirect investment in securities.[16]

---

companies are mainly technology companies who provide order-routing and post-trade processing (settlement) to market participants.

[12] See eg pp 39–44 of FSA Discussion Paper, *The FSA's Approach to Regulation of the Market Infrastructure* (Jan 2000).

[13] See Ch 10.3.2.

[14] See Valdez (above n 1 at p 172–79) for more detail.

[15] See Ch 10 for more detail.

[16] See Ch 4 on investments and Ch 6 on the retail investment market.

9.2 Market regulation: overview

From the economic perspective, a major concern is that markets should operate efficiently. This can be understood in different ways.[17] Allocative efficiency refers to the manner in which the capital market allocates capital to competing uses. It should operate so as to allocate capital to the projects with the highest present value (broadly speaking those that will generate the highest return on capital) and if it does not, it will not be operating efficiently. Informational efficiency refers to the ability of the market to price securities by reference to available information.[18] Operational efficiency refers to the extent to which markets are able to minimise the transaction costs (eg brokerage and administrative costs) associated with dealing in securities.

These underlying economic principles are linked to the historical development of market regulation. Disclosure obligations were first introduced when the Companies Act 1844 required information to be disclosed to the Registrar of Companies prior to incorporation. In the modern context, disclosure (at different levels) is mandated by the Companies Act 1985 for all companies and by the Listing Rules for listed companies.[19] The objective is to promote allocative and informational efficiency by providing the information necessary for investors to choose between competing uses for their capital.[20] They also promote informational efficiency by allowing the market to price securities at the time of an initial listing/offer and on an on-going basis.

Market transparency obligations require the reporting and publication within defined time limits of transactions that take place on a market.[21] They promote informational efficiency in that they allow investors to make pricing decisions by reference to the prices at which other investors are trading. More controversial are prohibitions against insider dealing. While they may be seen to limit informational efficiency, by preventing prices moving to their true level, they can be justified on two grounds.[22] First, they address an

---

[17] See generally K Pilbeam, *Finance and Financial Markets* (Basingstoke, Palgrave, 1998) ch 10.

[18] The efficient market hypothesis (in its strong form) holds that the market is efficient in pricing securities on the basis of all known information. If true, it would render pointless any attempt to discover information (eg through fundamental analysis) that is not already discounted in the price of a security. See generally Pilbeam (above n 17) ch 10.

[19] Disclosure obligations for listed companies are dealt with in more detail in Ch 7.

[20] Allocative efficiency refers to the role of financial markets in allocating capital to competing uses (companies) whereas informational efficiency refers to the role of financial markets in supplying information to participants who trade in the market.

[21] They are discussed in more detail in 9.3 below.

[22] Plus the more general reason that insider dealing is simply not fair because it represents a wealth transfer to insiders. See H McVea, 'What's Wrong with Insider Dealing?' (1995) *Legal Studies* 390. Insider dealing is dealt with in more detail in 9.4 below.

information asymmetry problem (as between 'insiders' and 'outsiders') that has the potential to damage confidence in the operation of capital markets and thereby limit their potential role in the financial system. Second, they reduce the cost of capital for companies because the presence of insider-dealing is likely to raise transaction costs for investors.

9.2.1 Recognised investment exchanges and clearing-houses

Market regulation in the UK is based on the provisions of FSMA 2000 relating to recognised investment exchanges (RIEs) and recognised clearing-houses (RCHs). The relevant provisions largely continue the regime established under FSA 1986 and reflect the longer tradition of self-regulation under which exchanges set and enforced their own trading rules. The starting point is that a RIE is exempt from FSMA 2000. To be recognised, an exchange must comply with the requirements set by the Act and regulations made by the Treasury under the Act.[23]

These regulations require an exchange applying for 'recognised' status to satisfy, inter alia, the following conditions:

1 The exchange must have adequate financial resources.
2 The exchange must be a fit and proper person to perform the functions of a recognised investment exchange.
3 The exchange must ensure that business conducted by means of its facilities is conducted in an orderly manner and so as to afford proper protection to investors.
4 The rules of the exchange must allow the exchange to take effective measures against an issuer who does not comply with disclosure obligations.
5 The exchange must have effective arrangements for monitoring and enforcing compliance with its rules.
6 The exchange must have an effective complaints procedure.
7 The exchange must have default rules which, in the event of a member of the exchange being or appearing to be unable to meet his obligations in respect of one or more market contracts, enable action to be taken in respect of unsettled market contracts to which he is a party.
8 The exchange's rules must make provision for payment to be required (subject to netting) from a defaulter in respect of unsettled market contracts.

Once recognised, an exchange operates without the controls imposed on authorised persons but the FSA can nevertheless veto rule changes and issue directions to an exchange. The description of RIEs as 'exempt' is somewhat misleading in that the recognition process brings them clearly within the scope

---

[23] The FSMA 2000 (Recognition Requirements for Investment Exchanges and Clearing Houses) Regulations 2001, SI 2001/995.

of the FSMA 2000 system of regulation and the FSA's residual powers ensure that ultimately it is the FSA which determines the manner in which they operate. The FSA has power to impose notification requirements[24]; give directions requiring compliance with legal and regulatory obligations[25]; revoke a recognition order[26]; and deal with complaints relating to recognised status[27]. Moreover, for certain purposes (see eg the reduction of financial crime objective in section 6 FSMA 2000) recognised investment exchanges are treated as regulated persons. The scope of their exemption is limited as it relates to activities carried on as part of the business of an exchange or in connection with the provision of clearing services. There is no exempt person status in respect of other activities undertaken by RIEs.[28]

Until recently, there was a link between RIE status and regulatory responsibility for listing and public offers in the sense that the London Stock Exchange (LSE) was designated as the 'competent authority' by the relevant EC directives.[29] However, following the change in status of the LSE when it became a company listed on the exchange, its function as 'competent authority' for listing and public offers was transferred to the FSA. The rationale was that it was not appropriate for regulatory functions to be undertaken by a commercial organisation that ran (on a 'for profit' basis) the market it regulated. The United Kingdom Listing Authority (UKLA, a division of the FSA) now makes and monitors compliance with the listing and public offers rules. RIEs do however retain a role in that they are responsible for 'admission to trading' (which is now a separate regulatory process from admission to the official list) and are also responsible for setting and enforcing trading rules.

The RIE regime does not directly regulate participants who trade on the relevant exchange as its focus is on the exchange itself as a regulated entity. Participants include broker/dealers, banks and institutional investors, who are already regulated by the FSA in respect of their investment activities, as well as private investors. In respect of trading on exchanges by these participants, the FSA Handbook focuses on capital adequacy (solvency), the standards to be observed in trading and the manner in which client assets and money are safeguarded. Three broad categories of market participant can be distinguished for this purpose.[30] The first is professional investors who trade as principals for

---

[24] FSMA 2000 s 293.

[25] FSMA 2000 s 296.

[26] FSMA 2000 s 297.

[27] FSMA 2000 s 299.

[28] Any application for permission in respect of such other activities is treated as an application relating only to that other activity.

[29] See Ch 2.5.2.

[30] This categorisation is adopted to illustrate the broad objectives of FSA regulation of market participants. The more technical regulatory categorisation and the relevant rules applicable to each category are dealt with in Ch 10.

their own account (eg market-makers). The main concern of the regulatory system is that such traders have adequate capital to meet their obligations. The second category is professional investors who deal on behalf of others (eg fund managers or stockbrokers). The main focus of the regulatory system in this area is to safeguard the interests of the clients of the professional investor through rules relating to client assets and conflicts of interest. The third category is private investors and in this area the regulatory system adopts a protective stance in recognition of the limited knowledge and expertise of most private investors.

Nor does the RIE regulatory regime directly control the manner in which dealing in securities is organised, although the system will be scrutinised by the FSA for compliance with recognition requirement (3) (above) prior to the making of a recognition order. In principle therefore, there is no regulatory preference at the recognition stage in favour of order-driven or quote-driven systems. The general movement towards order-driven markets is largely a function of advances in technology, lower costs and the greater scope for anonymity on the part of buyers and sellers offered by such systems.

Recognised investment exchanges enjoy a favoured position in relation to competition law. They are exempt from the prohibitions contained in chapter 1 (anti-competitive agreements) and chapter 2 (abuse of a dominant market position) of the Competition Act 1998.[31] The rationale for the exemption is the separate system of competition scrutiny established by FSMA 2000[32] in respect of recognised bodies. This approach avoids the possibility of routine challenge to the validity of market contracts on the basis that the rules of the exchange under which the contract is made are anti-competitive. The following are exempt from the chapter 1 prohibition:

(a) the constitution of a recognised body;
(b) the constitution of an applicant for recognition;
(c) the regulatory provisions of a recognised body;[33]
(d) a decision of a regulatory body in respect of its regulatory provisions or practices;
(e) the practices of a recognised body;
(f) an agreement the parties to which include an RIE or RCH (recognised clearing-house) or persons subject to its rules to the extent that the agreement is required or encouraged by the recognised body's regulatory provisions or practices.

---

[31] There is no exemption from the equivalent provisions of EC competition law contained in arts 81 and 82 of the EC Treaty.

[32] ss 302–11.

[33] See s 302(1) FSMA 2000 for the meaning of regulatory provisions.

Despite their exemption, RIEs are nevertheless subject to a separate system of competition scrutiny established by FSMA 2000.[34] This involves submission of their rule-book (at the time of recognition) and subsequent rule changes to the Office of Fair Trading and potentially also the Competition Commission. The Treasury is empowered to order an RIE to rectify any anti-competitive conduct or rules.

RIEs (as well as their officers and staff) have immunity from liability in damages. The liability in damages can be based on any cause of action (such as negligence, breach of statutory duty, defamation, breach of confidence). The immunity is in respect of anything done or omitted in the discharge of the recognised body's regulatory functions[35] unless it is shown that the act or omission was in bad faith. There is no immunity in respect of acts or omissions which are unlawful as a result of section 6(1) of the Human Rights Act 1998 (a public authority acting in contravention of a Convention right). There was no comparable immunity provided to RIEs under the FSA 1986. The formulation of the immunity in this section is similar, but not identical, to that provided to the FSA.[36] The section leaves open the possibility of judicial review and court orders other than damages being sought against an RIE.

The FSMA 2000 makes provision for clearing-houses to become recognised and 'exempt' in the same manner as investment exchanges. The recognition requirements are very similar to those applicable to investment exchanges.[37] The central requirement is that a RCH should ensure 'the timely discharge . . . of the rights and liabilities of the parties to the transactions in respect of which it provides such services'.[38] The main clearing-house operating in the UK is the London Clearing House, which offers clearing in exchange-traded futures and options, cash equity business undertaken on the LSE's SETS platform, European government bonds and interest-rate swaps.[39]

9.2.2 Alternative trading systems

While regulated markets and OTC markets have co-existed in one form or another since securities were first traded, alternative trading systems (ATS) are

[34] See M Blair (edn) *Butterworths Annotated Guide to FSMA 2000* (London, Butterworths, 2002) pp 523–41. The rationale is presumably to avoid routine challenge of market transactions on the basis that they are anti-competitive and hence potentially void under the Competition Act 1998.

[35] Regulatory functions, as defined in s 3 FSMA 2000, cover obligations arising from recognition requirements made by the Treasury under s 286 FSMA 2000.

[36] By s 1 and sch 1 (para 19) FSMA 2000.

[37] See the FSMA 2000 (Recognition Requirements for Investment Exchanges and Clearing Houses) Regulations 2001, SI 2001/995, Schedule Part III.

[38] Schedule to the Recognition Requirements Regulations para 19(2)(b).

[39] The mode of operation of a clearing-house and the related regulatory requirements are considered in more detail in 9.6 below.

a relatively new development.[40] They have emerged mainly over the past 15 years as a result of new technology, which has encouraged securities firms to compete with regulated markets by cutting transaction costs for investors.[41] An ATS has been defined by the Committee of European Securities Regulators (CESR) as follows:

> a multilateral system, operated by an entity, which without being operated as a regulated market, brings together multiple third party buying and selling interests in financial instruments—in the system and according to non-discretionary rules set by the system's operator—in a way that results in a contract.

This definition focuses regulatory attention on those systems that replicate the 'functionality' of regulated markets by creating facilities for trading between buyers and sellers.

ATS raise a number of regulatory issues.[42] First, as they operate without the full rigour of the recognition or transparency requirements applicable to regulated markets, there is a 'level playing-field' issue in respect of the regulation of organisations that perform similar functions. As ATS derive at least some of their competitive advantage from a lower burden of regulation, the regulated exchanges have some grounds for arguing that they face unfair competition. Moreover, although ATS have in the main aimed to attract professional investors (who are assumed to be well informed as to market practices), there remains scope for confusion over the terms on which they transact business, particularly if the ATS is within a securities firm operating as a broker/dealer. In these circumstances there may be confusion regarding when the firm is acting as principal or agent for a customer when a transaction is being executed through an 'in-house' ATS. There may also be confusion over regulatory obligations such as 'best execution'.[43]

Second, there has been concern over the impact which ATS have on transparency and liquidity.[44] In a securities market in which virtually all securities transactions take place in a single regulated market (the model which applied in most of Europe in the 1980s) transparency is ensured through transaction reporting and publication rules such as those contained in the Investment Services Directive. In such a market, the absence of alternative dealing venues

---

[40] See generally S Prigge, 'Recent Developments in the Market for Markets for Financial Instruments' at http://ssrn.com/abstract=258593 (22 Nov 2004).

[41] See S Claessens, T Glaessner and D Klingebiel, 'Electronic Finance: Reshaping Financial Landscapes around the World' Financial sector Discussion Paper no 4, World Bank, September 2000 (see www.worldbank.org (22 Nov 2004)).

[42] See generally FSA Discussion paper at n 12 above.

[43] See Ch 6.2.

[44] See FSA Consultation Paper 153, *Alternative Trading Systems* (Oct 2002) and H Allen, J Hawkins and S Sato, 'Electronic Trading and its Implications for Financial Systems' Bank for International Settlement Papers no 7, available at www.bis.org (22 Nov 2004).

for investors ensures that liquidity in the regulated market will be maximised as all dealing is centralised in that market. The position changes when, as occurred in the late 1990s, the market structure changes to one in which regulated markets are competing with alternative systems. Transparency for the market as a whole will decline if ATS are not subject to transparency obligations as there will be a part of the market in which transactions are not visible. Liquidity may also decline if the market for particular securities fragments into segments traded on regulated markets and others on ATS. It is thus possible to envisage a scenario in which ATS deliver benefits in the form of lower transaction costs for investors but exert a negative influence on the securities market as a whole by lowering its transparency and reducing liquidity.

The response of regulators has been to bring ATS within the scope of the regulatory system without subjecting them to the full rigour of the regulation applicable to regulated markets. The Committee of European Securities Regulators (CESR) has adopted seven standards applicable to ATS that are intended to give effect to this principle. They cover the following areas:

1 Investment firms are required to register an ATS with their home country regulator.
2 Investment firms should be required to establish trading arrangements that result in fair and orderly trading on an ATS (as required for RIEs under the recognition requirements).
3 Investment firms must make ATS trading information available for publication on a reasonable commercial basis.
4 Investment firms must monitor user compliance with the (contractual) rules of the system.
5 Investment firms must, if required, submit to monitoring by the home country regulatory authority.
6 Investment firms must ensure that an ATS has the capability to deliver the proposed service.
7 Investment firms operating qualifying systems should ensure that there is clarity of obligations and responsibilities for the clearing (where applicable) and settlement of transactions.[45]

These principles have been given effect in the UK through changes to the FSA rule-book.[46]

---

[45] Clearing and settlement are discussed in more detail at 9.6 (below).
[46] See FSA Consultation Paper 153 *Alternative Trading Systems* and the FSA Alternative Trading Systems Instrument 2003 (FSA 2003/45).

9.3 Market regulation: transparency

Transparency refers to the extent to which investors are able to observe activity in markets. It is an important regulatory issue because transparency influences the efficiency of markets. Economic theory holds that for markets to operate efficiently, investors must be fully informed when making investment decisions.[47] Disclosure obligations imposed on listed companies[48] attempt to ensure that this is the case with regard to information concerning the business of an issuer but the activity of other investors is also relevant in rendering investors fully informed. This can arise in two ways. First, information regarding the price and size of transactions informs investors about the likely terms on which they will be able to trade. Transparency in this sense has two dimensions: pre-trade information on order sizes and quotes[49] and post-trade information on prices and quantities of executed trades. Second, information regarding the identity of substantial holders of a particular security provides information to investors regarding potential changes of control. Each aspect is dealt with by a different part of the regulatory system.

The Investment Services Directive[50] imposes transaction-reporting obligations on investment firms operating in regulated markets within the EC. These obligations are framed at a high level of generality, leaving considerable discretion to Member States in their implementation. As a 'minimum standards' directive, the ISD also allows Member States to impose stricter obligations. The ISD is implemented in the UK by the FSA Handbook,[51] which sets reporting requirements by reference to the nature and scale of a firm's business. The ISD also requires the regulator to ensure that this information is published to the market within certain time limits.[52] In the UK, this is given effect through the recognition requirement for RIEs that:

> appropriate arrangements are made for relevant information to be made available (whether by the exchange, or where appropriate, by issuers of the investments) to persons engaged in dealing in investments on the exchange.[53]

---

[47] See PD Spencer, *The Structure and Regulation of Financial Markets* (Oxford, OUP, 2000) pp 1–3 or Pilbeam (above n 17) ch 10 for a discussion of the conditions under which financial markets can be expected to operate efficiently.

[48] See generally Ch 7.4.

[49] The reference to quotes is relevant for quote-driven markets. In order-driven markets, pre-trade transparency refers to the price (and possibly other) conditions attached to orders that are directly entered into the execution mechanism through which dealing instructions are matched.

[50] Art 20.

[51] See FSA Handbook SUP 17; see Ch 3.6 regarding the FSA Handbook of Rules and Guidance.

[52] See art 21 of the ISD.

[53] Para 4(1) Pt 1 of the Schedule to the FSMA 2000 (Recognition Requirements for Investment Exchanges and Clearing Houses) Regulations 2001, SI 2001/995.

The FSA Handbook makes clear that this is taken to mean that RIEs must ensure that there is adequate pre-trade and post-trade transparency.[54]

Disclosure relating to the identity of substantial shareholders is mandated by both company law (in respect of all public companies) and the Listing Rules (in respect of listed companies only). The company law provisions[55] are based on the principle that investors in all public companies (not just listed companies) are entitled to know the identity of substantial shareholders as they are in a position to exercise influence over the company's affairs.[56] The relevant provisions require that an interest of 3 per cent or more in the 'relevant share capital' of a company must be disclosed to the company.[57] Subsequent changes from that level must also be disclosed. It is also possible for a company to discover the true identity of the holder of shares which are held by nominees or in trust.[58] Shareholdings held on behalf of investors by various types of investment manager and custodian are excluded from the disclosure obligation.[59] If they were included in the disclosure requirement, it would lead to disclosure of substantial shareholdings which comprise multiple small holdings held for different purposes and with different arrangements regarding voting.

While information relating to 3 per cent shareholders is in principle public information as it is held in the company's register of interests, company law imposes no obligation on the company to disseminate the information to the market. The Listing Rules[60] do impose such an obligation, with the result that information disclosed to the company is quickly transmitted to the market. It may also be the case when a substantial acquisition of shares is made that the rules administered by the Takeover Code relating to substantial acquisitions will take effect.[61]

Finally, there are disclosure requirements relating to directors' shareholdings. A director is required to notify the company of interests in shares held by him (or members of his family) and the company is obliged to keep a register

---

[54] FSA Handbook 'Recognised Investment Exchanges and Clearing Houses' (REC) 2.6.6G.

[55] Contained in Pt VI of the Companies Act 1985 (as amended to comply with the EC Directive on Major Shareholdings, 88/627 [1988] OJ L348/62).

[56] The government has recently consulted on extending the regime for mandatory disclosure of substantial shareholdings in public companies to private companies on the basis that concealment of beneficial ('true') ownership of companies provides a mechanism for money laundering and terrorist funding: see Joint DTI/ HM Treasury Consultation Document, 'Beneficial Ownership of Unlisted Companies' (2002) available at www.hm-treasury.gov.uk (22 Nov 2004). No action has yet been taken.

[57] Companies Act 1985 s 198.

[58] Companies Act 1985 s 212. A notice can be issued under this section by a company to any person who the company knows or has reasonable cause to believe has been interested in the shares of the company in the preceding three years.

[59] See s 199(2A) Companies Act 1985. The category includes operators of authorised unit trusts and open-ended investment companies.

[60] See FSA Listing Rules Ch 9 paras 9.11–9.15.

[61] See Ch 8.8.2.

of such information.[62] A listed company is obliged to pass that information on to a recognised exchange on which its shares are traded.[63] The rationale for such a disclosure requirement is twofold. First, it reinforces the prohibitions on insider dealing by recording changes in directors' interests in the share capital of the company. Second, directors' dealing provides an important signal to investors as regards the directors' evaluation of the company's prospects.

9.4 Market regulation: insider dealing and market manipulation

Insider dealing did not attract formal regulatory attention in the UK until legislation was introduced in 1980.[64] By that time, there was already a long history of regulating insider dealing in the United States. Statutory regulation was introduced in the United States by the Securities Exchange Act 1934, and even before then the common law in some states had already begun to control insider dealing. Why should there have been such a difference in approach in two countries which shared a common legal heritage and led the world in the development of financial (and particularly equity) markets in the nineteenth and twentieth centuries? Two explanations can be offered. First, the tendency in the UK to permit self-regulation in financial markets meant that insider dealing was regarded as a matter of internal market discipline rather than a matter of public interest. Hence, insider dealing was not viewed as being in the same category as other forms of 'white collar' crime. A second explanation, linked to some extent with the first, is that the state courts in the US adopted an interventionist stance in respect of insider dealing. This was achieved by extending fiduciary duties to dealings between company directors and share-holders so that directors with inside information were required either to disclose the relevant information or refrain from dealing.[65] The emphasis in company law in the UK on directors' duties being owed to the company alone largely ruled out the possibility of the common law regulating insider dealing in this way.[66]

---

[62] Companies Act 1985 ss 324–29.

[63] Companies Act 1985 s 329.

[64] The relevant provisions were contained in the Companies Act 1980.

[65] See generally S Bainbridge, 'The Law and Economics of Insider Trading: A Comprehensive Primer' at hhttp://papers.ssrn.com/abstract=261277 (22 Nov 2004).

[66] See *Percival v Wright* [1902] 2 Ch 421, a case in which directors of a company bought shares from shareholders without disclosing that the company was in takeover negotiations. It was held that as the directors did not owe a fiduciary duty to the shareholders disclosure was not required. Company law in the UK does not rule out the possibility of directors owing fiduciary duties to

There are three different grounds on which prohibitions against insider dealing have been based. In the EC, the rationale for the prohibition has been that insider dealing has a negative effect on market integrity, resulting in a loss of confidence in the market and a therefore an unwillingness to use the market to transform savings into investments.[67] The negative effect on market integrity results from the information asymmetry caused by the presence of 'insiders' in a market. The result of 'insiders' being routinely present in a market is that 'outsiders' are likely to adjust their price expectations to reflect the likelihood of dealing with better-informed buyers or sellers. The aggregate effect of this across the market as a whole is likely to be that transaction costs will increase (eg market-makers will widen spreads) and therefore the cost of capital for companies will rise.[68] This will be the case even if investors are confident that full information is provided when a company first makes a public offer as trading in the secondary market will reflect the presence of 'insiders' and new share issues will have to be priced consistently with valuations in the secondary market. Another consideration is that large controlling shareholders might be tempted to make profits from insider dealing (as they are likely to have access to inside information) rather than engage in monitoring, which would benefit all shareholders equally. There may also be a depressing effect on valuations as investors lose confidence in the likelihood of being treated fairly in a market in which insiders are routinely trading.

In the United States, two different grounds for a prohibition have been identified. The first is that investors should have equality of access to information, a principle which lay behind the 'disclose or abstain' rule which has formed an important thread in the development of insider dealing case-law.[69] An alternative basis developed in the US courts has been the concept of 'misappropriation', which holds that insider dealing is objectionable because it is a wrong (breach of fiduciary duty) done to the person from whom the information is taken.[70] These grounds reflect the private law (derived from fiduciary duty) origins of the regulation of insider dealing in the United States, on which the statutory regulation introduced by the Securities Exchange Act 1934 was superimposed.

shareholders in specific circumstances, but there is no instance of this principle being applied to insider dealing in the way that occurred in the US.

[67] This is evident in the preambles to both the 1989 Directive on insider dealing (89/592, [1989] OJ L334/30) and the 2003 Market Abuse Directive (2003/6, [2003] OJ L96/16). The 1989 Directive was implemented in the UK by Pt V of the Criminal Justice Act 1993. It is superseded by the 2003 Directive as from October 2004.

[68] See U Battychara and H Daouk, 'The World Price of Insider Trading' (2002) 57 *Journal of Finance* 75–108. On one measure, the authors conclude that enforcement of insider dealing laws reduces the cost of equity by around 6% per year.

[69] See, for example, the cases of *Cady Roberts*, *Texas Gulf Sulphur* and *Chiarella*, discussed in Bainbridge (above n 65).

[70] See the *O'Hagan* case discussed in Bainbridge (above n 65).

In the United Kingdom, the criminal law prohibition of insider dealing is contained in Part V of the Criminal Justice Act 1993 (CJA 1993).[71] It establishes three separate offences:[72]

- dealing;
- encouraging another person to deal; and
- disclosing information.

In each instance the person must have information as an insider. This will be the case only if the information is inside information and the person has it and knows he has it from an inside source. Inside information is defined as information which:[73]

(a) relates to particular securities or to a particular issuer of securities or to particular issuers of securities and not to securities generally or to issuers of securities generally;
(b) is specific or precise;
(c) has not been made public; and
(d) if it were made public would be likely to have a significant effect on the price of any securities.

A person has information as an insider if and only if:[74]

(a) it is, and he knows that it is, inside information; and
(b) he has it, and he knows that he has it, from an inside source.

A person has information from an inside source if and only if:

(a) he has it through—
    i. being a director, employee or shareholder of an issuer of securities; or
    ii. having access to the information by virtue of his employment, office or profession; or
(b) the direct or indirect source of his information is a person within paragraph (a).

For any of the offences to be established, the relevant securities must be price-affected securities, meaning that publication of the relevant inside information would be likely to have a significant effect on the price of the securities.[75] This is not to say that the inside information must relate to the

---

[71] These provisions implement the 1989 EC directive on insider dealing. See P Davies, *Gower and Davies' Principles of Modern Company Law*, 7th edn (London, Sweet & Maxwell, 2003) ch 29 for a more detailed discussion.

[72] s 52.

[73] s 56.

[74] s 57.

[75] Information falling within this category is subject to the obligation imposed by the Listing Rules to publicise the information to the market. See Ch 7.4.2.

securities relevant to the offence. It is possible for the offence to be committed by dealing in other securities if they are price-affected (eg dealing in the shares of a competitor whose shares are likely to fall when the inside information becomes public).

It is also necessary to establish that the dealing occurred on a regulated market or that the person dealing relies on a professional intermediary[76] or is himself acting as a professional intermediary. The Act contains a number of defences, some of which are general in their scope, others which apply to specific situations (eg the exemption given to market-makers allowing them to continue trading even when in possession of inside information).

Prosecutions for insider dealing are undertaken by the FSA in England[77] and the Lord Advocate in Scotland. Few prosecutions have been pursued. The main problem is that the prosecutor is required to produce evidence that shows beyond reasonable doubt that the offence has been committed. The presence of any reasonable doubt will result in acquittal of the accused. There are problems in collecting the necessary evidence to sustain a prosecution as in many cases 'insiders' will go to considerable trouble to cover their tracks (eg dealing through nominees and offshore companies). Even when evidence can be collected, it may be difficult to corroborate it.[78]

Market manipulation is, in certain circumstances, a criminal offence under FSMA 2000.[79] Manipulation is not defined in the Act[80] but is generally understood to refer to devices such as transactions in which there is no change of ownership (giving a false impression of liquidity in the relevant security) or price positioning (such as heavy buying of a security to influence the level of an index at a particular time).

9.5 Market regulation: market abuse

The perceived failure of the criminal law to deal with cases of insider dealing and market manipulation led to calls for powers to be given to the FSA to impose sanctions for such behaviour. The FSA (and the regulatory bodies

---

[76] eg when a deal involves either a broker (acting as agent for the accused) or a dealer (trading on her own account) operating outside the regulated markets.

[77] FSMA 2000 s 402. The FSA must comply with any conditions or restrictions imposed by the Treasury. See FSA Handbook ENF 15 for FSA policy on prosecuting offences (especially ENF 15.5.1G).

[78] See eg *Mackie v HMA* 1994 SCCR 277.

[79] See s 397(3) for a definition of the offence and sub-sections 4 and 5 for defences.

[80] s 397 does not refer explicitly to 'market manipulation' but to 'any course of conduct which creates a false or misleading impression as to the market in or the price or value of any relevant investments'.

which preceded it) already had such powers under the FSA 1986 regulatory framework in that such behaviour was prohibited either by Core Rule 28 or by the Statements of Principle made under the Financial Services Act 1986.[81] It was therefore possible for regulators to take disciplinary action under those provisions.[82]

However, there were three main problems associated with this system of regulatory sanctions. First, action against insider dealing based on Core Rule 28 was limited to behaviour falling within the definition of insider dealing in the CJA 1993. This was seen as unduly restrictive by comparison with the type of behaviour that could be regarded broadly as 'market abuse'. Second, disciplinary action was limited to authorised firms and their employees as the relevant rules (above) did not apply to the public at large (they applied only to authorised firms and their employees). Third, reliance on the high-level principles as a basis for disciplinary action against behaviour considered to be 'market abuse' would, even if it were legally possible,[83] leave the FSA open to the criticism that is was failing to specify in sufficient detail conduct which it regarded as contrary to high-level principles.

The market abuse regime was introduced to resolve these problems.[84] It applies to qualifying investments traded on specified markets. All investments traded on Recognised Investment Exchanges in the UK have been specified for this purpose.[85] For behaviour to constitute market abuse it must occur in the UK or in relation to qualifying investments traded on a specified market which is situated in the UK or which is accessible electronically in the UK.[86]

The main innovation of the market abuse regime lies in the introduction of a 'regular user' test for determining if behaviour constitutes market abuse. The definition of the relevant behaviour, while different from that which forms the basis of the criminal offences of insider dealing and market manipulation, is analogous to them. There are three types of behaviour that are covered by the market abuse regime:

---

[81] See I MacNeil and K Wotherspoon, *Business Investigations* (Bristol, Jordans, 1998) paras 4.4 and 4.58.

[82] See for example *R v SFA ex p Fleurose* [2001] EWHC Admin 1085, a case in which the SFA (the Securities and Futures Association, a self-regulatory organisation under FSA 1986 and the FSA's predecessor as regulator of broker/dealers) took disciplinary action against a trader on the basis of FSA Statements of Principle 1 and 3.

[83] *R v SFA ex p Fleurose* (above n 82) lent support to the view that it was possible.

[84] It is contained in Pt VIII of the FSMA 2000, *Penalties for Market Abuse*.

[85] SI 2001/996 and SI 2001/3681.

[86] This would cover, subject to the other tests below, behaviour comprising the use of 'inside information' to purchase, outside the UK, qualifying securities issued by UK listed companies or derivatives in respect of which those securities represent the underlying instruments.

(a) behaviour based on information which is not generally available to those using the market but which, if available to a regular user of the market, would or would be likely to be regarded by him as relevant when deciding the terms on which transactions in investments of the kind in question should be effected ('misuse of information');

(b) behaviour likely to give a regular user of the market a false or misleading impression as to the supply of, or demand for, or as to the price or value of, investments of the kind in question ('misleading impression');

(c) behaviour likely to distort the market in investments of the kind in question ('market distortion').

In each case the relevant behaviour must be likely to be regarded by a regular user of that market who is aware of the behaviour as a failure on the part of the person or persons concerned to observe the standard of behaviour reasonably expected of a person in his or their position in relation to the market. The FSA has stressed that the regular user is a hypothetical person (not the FSA itself).

As required by the Act, the FSA has produced a Code of Market Conduct.[87] The purpose of the Code is to define more clearly the types of behaviour that will and will not be considered to be market abuse. Behaviour that will not be considered to be market abuse falls into two categories:

• Conclusive descriptions of behaviour, made under section 119(2) FSMA.
• Behaviour conforming with other rules, specified under section 118(8) FSMA.

Taken together, these two types of provision represent all the 'safe harbours' contained in the Code.[88] They are conclusive in the sense that a person can be sure that behaviour falling within the rule does not constitute market abuse.

The definition of behaviour representing market abuse is more open-ended. This is because it comprises provisions which do not have the conclusive character of the 'safe harbour' provisions above. Those provisions are evidential provisions and guidance. Evidential provisions are in effect presumptions that can be rebutted.[89] It follows that while such provisions may point to the likelihood of certain behaviour being considered market abuse, it is in principle possible to convince the FSA that the behaviour is not in fact market abuse. Guidance consists of information and advice given by the FSA with respect to the Act and rules made under it.[90] There is no obligation to follow guidance

---

[87] See generally M Blair (ed) (above n 34) pp 182–87.

[88] They are designated 'C' in the Code. See eg MAR 1.7.7C and MAR 1.7.8C for 'safe harbours' in respect of behaviour conforming with the City Code on Takeovers and Mergers.

[89] See s 149 FSMA for a definition of evidential provisions. They are designated 'E' in the Code.

[90] It is indicated by the letter 'G' in the Code.

and failure to follow it does not automatically mean that a person has engaged in market abuse.

The FSA can take enforcement action when a person has engaged in market abuse or required or encouraged another person to engage in such behaviour. The normal warning and decision notice procedure associated with FSA disciplinary action must be followed in these circumstances.[91] Where the response to a warning notice indicates that the relevant person believed on reasonable grounds that his behaviour was not market abuse (or requiring or encouraging market abuse) or that he took all reasonable precautions and exercised all due diligence to avoid such behaviour, the FSA may not impose a penalty.[92] This comes close to but does not expressly create a requirement for intent in respect of behaviour constituting market abuse.

Disciplinary proceedings for market abuse are civil in character.[93] While this was the intention of the government at the time of the introduction of FSMA 2000, doubts were expressed at the Committee stage of the FSMA Bill as to whether the market abuse regime was sufficiently different from the criminal law of insider dealing to be considered civil in character for the purposes of the European Convention on Human Rights (ECHR).[94] The significance of the categorisation of the market abuse regime as civil or criminal lies in the safeguards which are available to the defence in criminal cases. While the ECHR requires a fair hearing in all cases before courts and tribunals, there are specific safeguards which apply to criminal cases. Moreover, the determination of whether an 'offence' is criminal or civil is ultimately determined under the ECHR and not under national law. In recognition of the potential for legal challenges to the market abuse regime based on its criminal character, the FSMA provides two important protections to the 'defence'. First, legal assistance is available to a person who appeals an FSA decision on market abuse to the Financial Services and Markets Tribunal.[95] Second, compelled evidence is not admissible in market abuse cases.[96] Such evidence arises when there is an obligation on a person to answer questions posed by an FSA investigator.[97] The availability of these two safeguards does raise some doubt as to whether the market abuse regime can properly be considered civil in character. It also reduces the likelihood that the issue will be tested as it has considerably narrowed the grounds on which it could be argued that the safeguards associated with a criminal trial have not been provided.

[91] See s 126 FSMA 2000.

[92] FSMA 2000 s 123(2).

[93] *R v SFA ex p Fleurose* (above n 82).

[94] See Annex C to the First Report of the Joint Parliamentary Committee on the Financial Services and Markets Bill (HC 328–I).

[95] FSMA 2000 s 134 provides for the creation of such a scheme.

[96] s 174(2).

[97] ss 171 and 172 require persons under investigation to answer questions.

In principle the FSA has discretion as to the penalties it imposes for market abuse.[98] It is, however, required to issue a statement of policy with respect to the imposition of penalties and the amount of penalties. The policy must take account of:[99]

(a) whether the relevant behaviour had an adverse effect on the market in question and, if so, how serious that effect was;
(b) the extent to which that behaviour was deliberate or reckless;
(c) whether the person on whom the penalty is to be imposed is an individual.

The FSA's policy statement on penalties in market abuse cases is published at ENF 14 in the FSA Handbook.

Implementation in the UK of the EU market abuse directive[100] will require some changes to be made to the Market Conduct sourcebook of the FSA, the UK Listing Rules and the FSA's Conduct of Business Rules.[101] Many of the provisions of the directive are already part of the UK regulatory system but there are differences as regards the scope of each regime and in respect of some of the detailed provisions. The directive is a 'minimum standards' directive, meaning that it requires Member States to adopt its provisions but leaves them free to set additional requirements. The government has proposed that the additional requirements that are in place in the UK as a result of the scope of the UK regime being broader than that of the EU directive will be maintained following implementation of the directive.[102]

9.6 Clearing and settlement

The term 'clearing' is used in different senses in relation to banking and investment exchanges. In banking, clearing is used in a narrow sense to refer to the calculation of payment obligations:

---

[98] s 123. A recent example is the penalty of £17m imposed on Shell Transport and Trading Company plc—see www.fsa.gov.uk/pubs/press/2004/074.html (22 Nov 2004).

[99] s 124(2).

[100] Dir 2003/6EC, [2003] OJ L96/16. The directive was the first to be agreed under the so-called 'Lamfalussy process', according to which new EU legislation is to be created within a four-tier approach: framework principles, implementing measures, regulatory co-operation and enforcement. The market abuse directive is the framework and the implementing measures are: Commission Dir 2003/124/EC [2003] OJ L339 70 on the Definition and Disclosure of Inside Information; Commission Directive 2003/125/EC [2003] OJ L339 73 on the Fair Presentation of Investment Recommendations; and Commission Regulation 2273/2003 on Exemptions for Buy-back Programmes and Stabilisation of Financial Instruments. The implementing measures were adopted following advice from the Committee of European Securities Regulators.

[101] See HM Treasury/FSA Consultation Paper *UK Implementation of the EU Market Abuse Directive* (June 2004).

[102] *Ibid* ch 3.

> In its narrow sense, 'clearing system' is a mechanism for the calcuation of mutual positions within a group of participants ('counterparties') with a view to facilitate the settlement of their mutual obligations on a net basis.[103]

In this context the main function of clearing is to reduce (through netting) the number of payments that have to be made by participants to each other. Without netting, each payment would be treated separately (gross payments) resulting in many individual payments between banks. Netting can operate on either a bilateral or multilateral basis. In the former case, netting operates separately between each pair of counterparties in the system. In the latter case, netting operates so as to result in each participant having to make only one payment into the system in respect of all transactions for which payment is due at a particular point in time.[104]

'Clearing' in the context of investment exchanges encompasses the narrow banking definition above but also refers to the process by which a clearing-house becomes a counterparty to transactions undertaken on the exchange and thereby guarantees performance of the contract.[105] This function of clearing-houses evolved first in commodities markets in the nineteenth century, was later adopted in relation to transactions on exchanges trading futures and options and has now been extended to some forms of trading on standard investment exchanges and also some OTC transactions.[106] The rationale for clearing-houses assuming the role of counterparty (in return for a fee) is that it avoids the credit risk associated with the default of a counterparty. This has been a particular concern in derivatives markets where the prices of the relevant contracts are subject to greater volatility than is the case in the securities market generally. Clearing-houses undertake their counterparty function only in relation to members, who are required to meet on-going financial requirements, which serve the function of limiting the exposure of the clearing-house to potential defaults.[107]

---

[103] B Geva, 'The Clearing House Arrangement' (1991) 19 *Canadian Business Law Review* 138, 138, quoted in R Cranston, *Principles of Banking Law,* 2nd edn (Oxford, OUP, 2002) p 279.

[104] See Cranston *ibid* p 287 for more detail. He observes that bilateral netting reduces payments in a system with n participants to $n(n - 1)/2$ while multilateral netting reduces payments to n.

[105] For a description of the manner in which this occurs see London Clearing House Publication, *Market Protection* under 'Legal and Contractual Obligations'. The process involves trades made by non-clearing members being registered in the name of a clearing member and trades undertaken for clients being 'mirrored' by a separate contract between member and client (replicating the exchange contract for which the clearing-house acts effectively as guarantor).

[106] See R Kroszner, 'Can the Financial Markets Privately Regulate Risk? The Development of Derivatives Clearing Houses and Recent Over-the-Counter Innovations' at http://ssrn.com/abstract=170350 (22 Nov 2004).

[107] See the London Clearing House Publication, *Market Protection* (at www.lchclearnet.com (22 Nov 2004)).

Another important development has been the creation of a central counter-party system for trading on SETS, the London Stock Exchange's electronic order book. LCH acts as counterparty to such transactions, thereby allowing anonymous trading on SETS without any risk being posed to participants resulting from the fact that they do not know the identity of the other side to the transaction. In this sense a central counterparty is a guarantor who has been described as the seller's buyer and the buyer's seller.[108] Virtually all order-driven markets operate some form of central-counterparty system as it is vital to provide some security to transactions in which buy/sell instructions are matched electronically without revealing the identity of the parties. The oper-ation of this central counterparty system at relatively low cost is made possible by limiting its availability to clearing members of LCH and integrating it into the CREST settlement system.

The term 'settlement' is also used differently in banking and investment contexts. In banking, settlement is the transfer of value to discharge a payment obligation.[109] In the investment context, settlement can also bear this meaning (eg in respect of exchange-traded derivatives which are settled by a monetary transfer) but it also refers to the performance of the mutual obligations of buyer and seller under a contract for the transfer of legal title to securities. The buyer's obligation is to pay the price and the seller's is to deliver a valid legal title to the buyer (irrespective of the form in which legal title is recorded).

The timing of settlement in securities markets is determined by the design of the system, which can take two forms.[110] Rolling settlement involves settle-ment on a given number of days after trade date $(t + x)$. In 1989 the G30[111] rec-ommended that final settlement of cash transactions[112] should occur on $t + 3$, that is three days after settlement date. This is the system currently in use on the London Stock Exchange (LSE). Account settlement involves all transac-tions within a set period being settled on a fixed day after the end of the period. Such a system was operated in the past by the LSE, with all transactions

---

[108] Although analogous to a guarantee, the legal mechanism under which the CCP operates is novation (see Ch 1.2.5). A trade between buyer and seller is subject to novation at the point of execution, being replaced by two new contracts, between buyer and LCH as seller and seller and LCH as buyer respectively. These transactions are then passed on to CREST for settlement.

[109] Cranston (above n 103), p 278.

[110] See generally IOSCO Consultative Report (2001), *Recommendations for Securities Settlement Systems* (at www.iosco.org (22 Nov 2004)). The report notes that the longer the period from trade execution to settlement, the greater is the risk that (a) one of the parties may become insolvent or default on the trade and (b) prices of securities will depart from contract prices, cre-ating the potential for non-defaulting parties to incur a loss in replicating the unsettled contract.

[111] The Group of Thirty is an international non-profit body that researches and advises on choices available to market practitioners and policymakers: see www.group30.org (22 Nov 2004).

[112] If settlement occurs immediately or shortly after a trade (eg 3 days as occurs in the UK equity market) a market is described as a cash market: if it is in the future it is a forward or futures market.

during a two-week period being settled on the following Monday. In principle, it is also possible to operate 'real time' settlement, in which transfer of legal title and payment occur simultaneously with the making of a contract, but that poses technical and logistical problems which are difficult to resolve, at least in the context of the equity market.

Settlement plays a key role in the operation of investment markets. Routine failures in the settlement system pose a number of risks. First, they create credit and liquidity risk for the party whose counterparty defaults on a transaction (eg A does not pay B the agreed price for securities on the agreed date and B is therefore forced to borrow to meet other commitments). Second, settlement defaults on a sufficiently large scale have the potential to create systemic risk across the whole financial system. Third, settlement problems may result in investors withdrawing from particular types of investment or particular countries in which settlement problems cause a significant rise in transaction costs.

These issues have been addressed in several different ways by both regulators and market participants. The International Organisation of Securities Commissioners (IOSCO) has stressed the importance of the principle of 'delivery versus payment' (DvP) as a method of minimising the risks associated with settlement. The essence of the principle of DvP is that if delivery of legal title to securities occurs simultaneously with payment, the credit and liquidity risks associated with settlement are minimised.[113] The CREST/Clearstream settlement system, which settles most transactions in the UK, operates a form of DvP.

The capital adequacy rules derived from the Capital Adequacy Directive[114] also promote the honouring of settlement obligations by requiring securities firms to allocate capital against transactions that have not settled by the due date. This is achieved by requiring firms to include in their calculation of financial resources[115] an allowance ('counterparty risk requirement') for transactions on which a counterparty has defaulted by not settling on the due date.[116] In effect this results in a financial penalty being applied in respect of unsettled transactions in the sense that the allocation of capital (financial resources) to cover settlement risk means that it cannot be used to support the firm's business (eg by using that capital to trade in securities). Moreover, as the 'counterparty risk requirement' increases the longer a trade remains unsettled

---

[113] See *Delivery versus Payment in Securities Settlement Systems* (Basle: Bank for International Settlements, 1992 available at www.bis.org (22 Nov 2004)).

[114] Directive 93/6/EC, [1993] OJ L141/1 implemented in the UK by the FSA Handbook. See A Winkler (ed) *A Practitioner's Guide to the FSA Handbook* (Old Woking, City & Financial Publishing, 2001) pp 139–54.

[115] Firms are required to calculate their financial resources (capital supporting their business) on a daily basis for the purposes of regulatory reporting and on an intra-day basis to verify their capability to enter into transactions.

[116] See FSA Handbook IPRU(INV) 10-170.

(i.e. as the period of default increases) there is a strong incentive for firms to ensure that settlement occurs as quickly as possible.

In the UK, as elsewhere, settlement nowadays typically takes place in dematerialised form.[117] Secondary legislation introduced in 1995 resulted in the establishment of the CREST transfer system and the replacement of most share certificates by electronic records. CREST is owned by its users, which include stockbrokers, banks, investment institutions and registrars. It offers settlement facilities in securities traded on the London and Irish Stock Exchanges, the Eurotop 3000, NASDAQ 5000 and S&P 500 indices as well as unit trusts and OEICs.[118]

Securities are transferred within CREST by the operation of an account system that parallels the register maintained by the issuer. CREST maintains such accounts for members showing the same information as the issuer's register. A transfer is made by debiting the CREST account of the seller and crediting the account of the buyer. At this stage the buyer's account will show the relevant shares as being held in trust by the seller for the buyer.[119] This means that in English law the buyer already has a property right in the respect of the relevant securities and not just a contractual right. While the buyer is not yet at this stage the legal owner, she becomes so relatively quickly as CREST simultaneously instructs the registrar of the relevant issuer to amend its register to give effect to the transaction. At this point the buyer becomes the legal owner of the security and the equitable interest is merged with the legal interest.[120]

It should be noted, however, that this system does not involve immobilisation of securities and that CREST does not act as a depositary.[121] The records maintained by CREST for each member[122] are mirror-images of the registers of companies, which themselves form the basis for determining membership of the company and legal title to securities.[123] It is therefore CREST members rather than CREST itself that hold legal title to securities.[124] Nor does CREST hold cash for members to settle transactions. It records payment entitlements

---

[117] See Ch 4 re transfers of securities in certificated and dematerialised form.

[118] Settlement of foreign securities is achieved through links with foreign settlement systems. Foreign securities cannot be admitted to CREST as the Uncertificated Securities Regulations (see Ch 4.4.3) are effective only in the UK.

[119] Art 25 of the Uncertificated Securities Regulations.

[120] This comment relates to English law, which will normally govern transactions on a recognised investment exchange in the UK.

[121] See Ch 10.3.3 and 10.3.4.

[122] Re CREST membership see J Benjamin, *Interests in Securities* (Oxford, OUP, 2000) para 9.61.

[123] See Ch 4.4.2.

[124] See Ch 10 for an analysis of the position of the 'ultimate investor' (ie the person who has acquired the security but whose legal rights are derived from a chain of ownership rights) in this scenario.

and obligations in members' cash memorandum accounts but payments are effected through settlement banks.

9.7 Insolvency

The insolvency of a market participant who trades on an investment exchange gives rise, in principle, to two main problems. The first is that the relevant person is likely to default on settlement obligations. RIEs and RCHs are required to have rules to deal with this contingency. In the case of the London Stock Exchange, the rules provide for a member firm to be declared a defaulter if it is unable to fulfil its obligations in respect of one or more market contracts or appears to be or is likely to become so unable.[125] The significance of that process is that responsibility for the calculation of amounts due to and from the defaulter is transferred to the exchange.[126]

The second problem is whether, and if so how, the general principles of insolvency law should be applied to such contracts.[127] A particular concern is that if market participants are exposed to the risk that a payment due to them from a counterparty may become the subject of competition among the general creditors of that counterparty following insolvency, the credit risk associated with market transactions will be increased and the market will operate less efficiently than if they are protected from that risk.[128] This concern is reflected in the legal provisions governing 'market contracts'.

Part VII of the Companies Act 1989 established a special regime modifying the general law of insolvency for 'market contracts'.[129] That regime is based on several principles.

1 The procedures of a recognised exchange or clearing house take precedence over insolvency proceedings. To this end, it is made clear that none of the following shall be regarded as to any extent invalid at law on the grounds of inconsistency with insolvency law:

---

[125] See the Rules of the London Stock Exchange, default procedures, section D020, available at www.thelondonstockechange.com.

[126] The exchange is entitled to fix 'hammer' prices in respect of unsettled contracts with a defaulter, which may deviate from the contract price. The practice has given rise to the description of a defaulter as having been 'hammered'.

[127] On the general principles of insolvency law see R Goode, *Corporate Insolvency Law*, 2nd edn (London, Sweet & Maxwell, 1997).

[128] This will be so as the market is likely to the reflect credit risk of market participants in setting prices as well as the underlying fundamentals of a security.

[129] Market contracts are defined by s 155 of the Companies Act 1989. The definition requires the contract to be between a member of the recognised exchange and a third party and to be subject to the rules of the exchange. The definition does not apply to contracts made on an ATS (as it is not a recognised exchange).

(a) a market contract;
(b) the default rules of an RIE or RCH;
(c) the rules of an RIE or RCH as to the settlement of market contracts not dealt with under its default rules.[130]

2 A person with control over the assets or documents of a defaulter is required to give an RIE or RCH such assistance as it may reasonably require for its default proceedings. This applies notwithstanding any duty of that person under the enactments relating to insolvency.[131]

3 On completion of default proceedings an RIE or RCH is required to report to the FSA on its proceedings stating in respect of each creditor or debtor the sum certified by them to be payable to or from the defaulter or, as the case may be, the fact that no sum is payable.[132]

4 The sum so certified can be claimed on the bankruptcy/insolvency of the defaulter.[133]

5 The law relating to transactions at an undervalue, unfair preferences and transactions defrauding creditors is disapplied in respect of market contracts entered into by an RIE or RCH under its default rules and a disposition of property in pursuance of such a market contract.[134] This allows an RIE or RCH to act under its default rules free from the threat that transactions made under those rules may be challenged by a defaulter's general creditors.

The general approach established by the Companies Act 1989 is developed further by the EC Directive on Settlement Finality in Payment and Securities Settlement Systems.[135] The purpose of the directive is to reduce the risks associated with participation in payment and securities settlement systems by minimising the disruption caused by insolvency proceedings brought against a participant in such a system. It pursues this objective by requiring that the rules of a designated settlement system will prevail over the provisions of national insolvency laws. The scope of the Directive is defined by reference to participants in designated[136] payment and settlement systems. This differs from the provisions of Part VII of the Companies Act 1989, whose provisions apply to 'market contracts' (see above). There is, however, substantial overlap

---

[130] Companies Act 1989 s 159.
[131] Companies Act 1989 s 160.
[132] Companies Act 1989 s 162.
[133] Companies Act 1989 s 159.
[134] Companies Act 1989 s 162. See Goode (above n 127) re transactions at an undervalue, unfair preferences and transactions defrauding creditors.
[135] Directive 98/26/EC [1998] OJ L166/45, implemented in the UK by the Financial Markets and Insolvency (Settlement Finality) Regulations 1999 (SI 1999/2979). See generally L Sealy, 'The Settlement Finality Directive—Points in Issue' [2000] *Company Financial and Insolvency Law Review* 221.
[136] Designation in the UK is by the FSA or Bank of England.

between these two sets of legal rules as the insolvency of a participant in a designated settlement system will normally have implications for 'market contracts' entered into by that participant.[137]

The effect of the Directive is to protect practices such as netting[138] of payments and the giving of collateral, which are common in settlement systems, from challenge under national insolvency law. In particular it is provided that none of the following shall be regarded as invalid on the grounds of inconsistency with the rules of insolvency law:

- a transfer order relating to money or securities;
- a designated system's default arrangements;
- a designated system's rules as to the settlement of transfer orders;
- a contract for the purpose of realising security.[139]

The special regime applicable to financial collateral arrangements is also relevant in the context of insolvency of market participants.[140] The regime applies to arrangements under which cash or financial instruments are transferred outright or by way of a security interest as collateral in a capital market transaction. The purpose of such arrangements is to provide an additional right to a counterparty in the event of default. The special regime facilitates the creation of such arrangements by dispensing with some of the formalities normally associated with the creation of such arrangements.[141] It also facilitates their enforcement by disapplying the operation of various provisions of insolvency law that would otherwise limit or prevent the enforcement of financial collateral arrangements.[142]

---

[137] Art 13 of the Settlement Finality Regulations expressly state that the Regulations do not disapply Pt VII of the Companies Act 1985.

[138] As to the meaning of this term see n 104 above and accompanying text.

[139] Art 14(1) of the Settlement Finality Regulations.

[140] The regime is derived from the EC Directive on Financial Collateral Arrangements, 2002/47, [2002] OJ L168/43, implemented in the UK by the Financial Collateral Arrangements (no 2) Regulations 2003, SI 2003/3226.

[141] See eg arts 4 and 5, dispensing with the requirement for charges (security interests) granted by a company to be registered with the Registrar of Companies.

[142] See art 10.

10

Market Participants

The term 'market participants' is used here to refer to persons who are involved in a professional capacity in the transaction of investment business. It excludes investors on the basis that their primary concern is with the ownership of investments. The term 'market participant' therefore applies to persons or organisations with a professional involvement in the process of investment. It covers stockbrokers, market-makers, custodians[1], central securities depositaries, merchant banks, investment banks, commercial banks and credit-rating agencies. Persons involved in the transaction of investment business primarily in the 'retail market' (such as independent financial advisers and appointed representatives) are dealt with in Chapter 6.

Market participants differ from 'investors' in that, although they do sometimes act as investors in their own right,[2] they act more frequently in the role of agents for investors (eg a stockbroker) or as parties to a contract with investors (eg a market-maker). The nature of their business and the incentives under which they operate therefore differ from those of investors. Market participants are generally more concerned with valuation and trading of securities and transaction costs than with exercising ownership rights. This is because their role is primarily to facilitate the acquisition and transfer of ownership of investments by investors.

In section 10.1 of this chapter, the general principles adopted by the FSMA 2000 system of regulation in respect of market participants is examined. This part should be read in conjunction with Chapter 3, which sets out the overall framework of regulation under FSMA 2000, including the sanctions that are available to the FSA in the event of breaches of the Act or rules made under it. There follows a discussion in 10.2 of the main types of common-law claims that are likely to be made against market participants by their customers. In

---

[1] Custodians are categorised for this purpose as market participants rather than investors because, although they are often the registered owners of shares (and therefore the legal owners), they are not the beneficial owners of shares.

[2] Market-makers and other proprietary traders become owners of the securities they trade on their own account, but they generally hold these securities for very short periods. The purpose of their ownership is to provide liquidity to the market (and by doing so make trading profits) rather than to exercise ownership rights.

10.3, the role of different market participants is discussed and specific regulatory rules and forms of common-law liability relevant to each are considered.

10.1 Regulatory structure and principles

10.1.1 Customer classification

A distinction between investors and market participants is relevant for the regulatory system because the traditional role of the regulatory system has been to provide investor protection. This has meant, among other things, protecting investors from the information asymmetry problems that they face in entering into investment transactions with market participants. There are, however, also many transactions in financial markets between professionals, in respect of which the information asymmetry rationale for regulation does not apply. The main problem for the regulatory system is to distinguish the two types of transaction, so as to supply investor protection when it is required and to allow parties to contract freely when it is not.

The FSMA system of regulation undertakes this task by using client classification to allocate regulatory rules to transactions according to the parties to the transaction and the context within which it occurs. This means that, in respect of different transactions, clients of market participants can be considered to fall within different classifications.[3]

It is the responsibility of an authorised firm to categorise its clients.[4] The possibilities are as follows.

Market counterparty

This category is not considered a 'customer' for the purposes of the FSA Handbook. It is intended to cover clients who are able to look after their own interests and who do not, in the main, require protection through regulatory rules. It comprises mainly authorised firms who are market participants (as defined above) and includes governments, central banks and supranational bodies.[5] It does not include collective investment schemes.

---

[3] In most cases, authorised firms will be categorised as market counterparties but there are circumstances in which this need not be the case: eg see FSA Handbook COB 4.1.7R. See Ch 3.6 regarding the structure of the FSA Handbook of Rules and Guidance.

[4] See FSA Handbook COB 4.1.4R.

[5] See the definition of 'market counterparty' in the Glossary to the FSA Handbook.

Intermediate customer

This category covers customers who are not market counterparties and who fall within other conditions.[6] It includes local authorities, listed companies, large (unlisted) companies and partnerships, trustees of large trusts or large occupational pension schemes and unregulated collective investment schemes. It does not include regulated collective investment schemes.[7] This category comprises mainly institutional investors.

Private customer

This category covers clients who are not market counterparties or intermediate investors.[8] It includes individuals who are not authorised under FSMA 2000, regulated collective investment schemes and companies and partnerships who are not considered 'large' for the purposes of the 'intermediate customer' definition.

The regulatory rules applicable to different types of client are grafted on to the existing common law framework, which is considered in section 10.2. In some cases, the regulatory rules have absorbed much of the common law but this is not always clear, not least because of the relatively undeveloped nature of the common law in this field and the fundamental changes in the structure and regulation of the financial markets that have occurred in the last twenty years. The result is that the legal position of market participants has to be considered from the perspective of both the regulatory rules and the common law.

10.1.2. The Inter-Professionals Code

The purpose of the Inter-Professionals Code (IPC) is to create a 'light touch' regulatory regime for dealings between market professionals.[9] The rationale is that the parties to such transactions are well-informed and able to assess risk for themselves, with the result that they do not require the protection provided by Conduct of Business Rules (COBs). In this respect it continues the approach that had previously been adopted in the 'Grey Paper' regime adopted by the Bank of England for listed money market institutions operating under

---

[6] See the definition of 'intermediate customer' in the Glossary to the FSA Handbook.

[7] But note that Split Capital Closed End Funds (SCCEFs, see Ch 4) are likely to be considered 'intermediate' customers. See FSA Discussion Paper 10—*SCCEFs*.

[8] See the definition of 'private customer' in the Glossary to the FSA Handbook.

[9] It forms part of the Market Conduct Sourcebook (MAR) in the FSA Handbook of Rules and Guidance. See generally T Little, 'The Inter-Professional Conduct', ch 6 in A Winkler and Ernst & Young LLP, *A Practitioner's Guide to the FSA Handbook* (London, City & Financial Publishing, 2001) and FSA Consultation Paper 47, *The Inter-Professionals Code*.

the provisions of section 43 of the Financial Services Act 1986.[10] The IPC is, however, much broader in scope than the old 'Grey Paper' regime.

The IPC comprises mainly guidance on the FSA's interpretation of the Principles for Business and contains only two substantive rules. They relate to non-market price transactions (NMPTs) undertaken off-exchange and payments made to wholesale market brokers who act as arrangers.[11] The FSA does not endorse individual codes of practice applying to inter-professional business but will take into account the differing standards and practices operating in markets when interpreting the Principles as they apply to inter-professional business.

There is a three-fold test for determining whether the IPC applies:

- *The nature of the parties.* The IPC only applies to business between an authorised firm[12] and a market counterparty.
- *The type of business activity.* The IPC applies only to dealing in investments as principal or agent, acting as an arranger[13] or giving transaction-specific advice. The IPC does not apply to the approval of financial promotions, in-house business of collective investment schemes, corporate finance business or safeguarding and administering investments or agreeing to carry out that activity.
- *The type of instrument.* All financial instruments that are 'investments' for the purposes of FSMA 2000 are included within the IPC, irrespective of where they are traded (on or off a regulated market). Instruments that are not investments for the purposes of FSMA 2000 (eg wholesale deposits) are dealt with in the FSA's Non-Investment Product Code. The code applies to wholesale market dealings in sterling wholesale deposits, foreign currency wholesale deposits, gold and silver bullion deposits, spot and forward foreign exchange and spot and forward gold and silver bullion. Although the code has no statutory basis (having been drawn up by participants in the wholesale markets) the FSA participates in its development and non-compliance may raise issues (such as the integrity or competence of the firm) that are relevant to the FSA's authorisation requirements.

The IPC guidance clarifies the application of the FSA's Principles for Business to inter-professional business. It makes clear that the Principles do

---

[10] The 'Grey Paper' was the (1995) Bank of England publication 'The Regulation of the Wholesale Cash and OTC Derivatives Markets'. It operated in association with the *London Code of Conduct for Principals and Firms in the Wholesale Markets* (Bank of England, 1995). See FSA Consultation Paper 68, *Section 43 Firms—Prudential Regime.*

[11] See FSA Handbook MAR 3.5.4R and MAR 3.7.5R.

[12] Subject to the exclusion of the following from the IPC regime: service companies; non-directive friendly societies; non-directive insurers; a UCITS qualifier. See the Glossary to the FSA Handbook (at www.fsa.gov.uk) for the meaning of these terms.

[13] This includes investment managers who instruct brokers to act on their behalf.

not require a firm to assess the suitability of a particular transaction for its client once it has established that it is dealing with a market counterparty.[14] Similarly, a firm is not obliged to give advice to a market counterparty. If a firm volunteers information to a market counterparty, but no formal advisory arrangement is agreed, the firm need not advise a market counterparty about the reliability, relevance or importance of that information. The guiding principle of the IPC is therefore very much *caveat emptor* ('buyer beware'), but contractual or fiduciary duties may arise in particular circumstances. For example, a firm acting as an agent for a market counterparty owes a fiduciary duty to the market counterparty and a firm that has agreed to advise a market counterparty is bound by the terms of its contract.

10.1.3 Generally applicable regulatory rules

Only a relatively small part of the FSA Handbook is generally applicable to business falling within the scope of any particular regulated activity. For example, many of the FSA's Conduct of Business Rules apply only when firms are conducting business with private customers. This reflects a combination of a number of statutory provisions:

(a) that regulation should be proportionate to the benefits it provides[15];
(b) that the FSA should take into account the differing degrees of experience and expertise of investors[16];
(c) that the FSA may make rules that make different provision for different cases and may, in particular, make different provision in respect of different descriptions of authorised person, activity or investment.[17]

The following are generally applicable rules:

The Principles for Businesses (PRIN)[18]

The Principles (PRIN) are a general statement of the fundamental obligations of firms under the FSMA 2000 regulatory system. They derive their authority from the FSA's general rule-making powers as set out in the Act and reflect the regulatory objectives.[19] Breach of the Principles may lead to enforcement

---

[14] See in this regard *Bankers Trust International plc v PT Dharmala Sakti Sejahtera* [1996] CLC 481.
[15] FSMA 2000 s 2(3)(c).
[16] FSMA 2000 s 5(2)(b).
[17] FSMA 2000 s 156.
[18] See the FSA Handbook at www.fsa.gov.uk (22 Nov 2004).
[19] See Ch 2 for a discussion of the FSA's rule-making powers and the regulatory objectives.

action by the FSA but does not affect the validity of a transaction or give rise to a claim in damages under section 150 FSMA 2000.[20]

Statements of Principle and Code of Practice for Approved Persons (APER)

Section 64 FSMA 2000 empowers the Authority to issue statements of principle with respect to the conduct expected from approved persons. If it does so, it is also required to issue a code of practice for the purpose of helping to determine whether or not a person's conduct complies with the statement of principle. Principles or codes made under this section may make different provision in relation to persons, cases, or circumstances of different descriptions. The Authority has used this power to issue (7) principles and a code of practice.[21] The statements of principle are mainly concerned with an approved person's performance of a controlled function.[22] The code comprises mainly evidential provisions but also includes some guidance. The code, in its entirety, may be relied on so far as it tends to establish whether or not conduct complies with a statement of principle. The code is not, however, a 'safe harbour' (a definitive statement of compliant conduct). Failure to comply with a statement of principle does not of itself give rise to any right of action by persons affected or affect the validity of any transaction.

The Code of Market Conduct[23]

The statutory provisions relating to market abuse and the Code of Market Conduct apply to all persons trading relevant securities on markets in the UK. They are discussed in Chapter 9.

COB 4 Accepting customers

This section of the FSA Handbook requires a firm to classify persons for whom it intends to carry on designated investment business[24] as a private customer, intermediate customer or market counterparty.[25] It also requires a firm to

---

[20] See PRIN 3.4.4R.

[21] See FSA Handbook APER 2.1.2P for the principles and APER 3 and 4 for the Code of Practice.

[22] See s 59 FSMA 2000 regarding controlled functions. FSA Handbook AUTH 6.1.2G and SUP 10.4.5R list controlled functions.

[23] The Code is part of the Market Conduct (MAR) section of the FSA Handbook, which is itself part of the Business Standards block.

[24] 'Designated investment business' (see the glossary to the FSA Handbook) is business relating to a sub-set of 'specified activities' (see Ch 3). The definition serves the purpose of distinguishing 'mainstream' investment business from the other activities (such as banking) that are included within the scope of regulation of FSMA 2000. It corresponds to what was termed 'investment business' under the FSA 1986 (see FSA Consultation Paper 45a *The Conduct of Business Sourcebook*, Feb 2000).

[25] See 10.1 above.

provide a customer with its terms of business, setting out the basis on which designated investment business is to be conducted with or for the customer.

COB 9 *Client assets and client money*

Several types of market participant, principally stockbrokers, fund managers and banks, assume responsibility for the safekeeping of investments under various types of contractual arrangement. Some arrangements involve the firm itself undertaking the safekeeping, others provide for this task to be delegated to a professional custodian. The purpose of the rules in this section of the FSA Handbook (Client Assets, abbreviated to CASS) is to restrict the co-mingling of client and firm assets and minimise the risk of the client's assets being used by the firm without the client's agreement or contrary to the client's wishes, or being treated as firm assets in the event of insolvency.

There are special rules applicable to the holding of client money.[26] The effect of the statutory provision and relevant rules is that a statutory trust is created in respect of clients' money, which has the effect of 'ring-fencing' the money in the event of the firm's insolvency.[27] In the event of a deficiency in client funds, a 'pooling' system operates so that the deficiency is shared among clients, with payments being made *pro rata* according to entitlement.[28] Provision is made for market counterparties and intermediate customers to opt out of the client money rules.[29]

10.1.4 Regulatory rules applicable to business conducted with 'customers'

The following regulatory rules are applicable to designated investment business[30] conducted with all 'customers' (intermediate customers and private customers). Rules applicable only to private customers are dealt with in Chapter 6.

---

[26] These rules are made under s 139 FSMA 2000 and are contained in CASS 4. As was the case with the relevant provision of FSA 1986 (s 55(5)), FSMA 2000 s 139(3) states that, as regards Scotland, the reference to money being held on trust is to be read as a reference to its being held as agent for the person on whose behalf it is held. In the past, this served the purpose of avoiding the complications, real or imagined, associated with the Blank Bonds and Trusts Act 1696. Following the repeal of that Act by the Requirements of Writing (Sc) Act 1995, it is not clear why it is necessary to for s 139 to apply in a different way to Scotland.

[27] See FSA Consultation Paper 38 *Protecting Client Money on the Failure of an Authorised Firm* (Jan 2000) Annex B for more detail and the history of client money rules.

[28] The creation of a pooling system expressly disapplies the rule in *Clayton's Case* (*Devaynes v Noble* (1816) 1 Mer 572, 35 ER 767), which adopts a 'first-in-first-out' approach to credit and debit transactions in a (banking) current account. See R Cranston, *Principles of Banking Law*, 2nd edn (Oxford, OUP, 2002) pp 160–63 for more detail.

[29] See COB 9.3.9R.

[30] See n 24 above for the meaning of this term.

COB 2 Clear fair and not misleading communication

The purpose of these rules is to expand the part of Principle 7 (Communications with clients) that relates to communication of information. They do not apply to most forms of financial promotion[31] (within the meaning of section 21 of FSMA 2000) as there are special rules (in COB 3) dealing with this. The types of communication covered by COB 2 are client agreements, periodic statements, financial reports and telephone calls that are not financial promotions.

COB 2.2 Inducements and soft commissions

This part of the FSA's Conduct of Business Rules deals with the conflict of interest that can arise if an authorised firm accepts an inducement or enters into other arrangements that may interfere with any duty that it may owe to its customers. The Myners Report[32] identified the potential for two practices to give rise to such conflicts and to distort the market for dealing services and investment research. They are 'bundled brokerage' and 'soft commission'. The former is an arrangement in which a broker provides a client (eg a fund manager) with a combination of trade execution services and other services, such as investment research, paid for through the commission payable to brokers for executing orders on behalf of clients. The components of the bundle are not usually offered or priced as separate services. There is an expectation, but no obligation, that the fund manager will deal through the broker. Under a 'soft commission' arrangement, the fund manager receives goods and services (usually from third parties) which are paid for by the broker. There is an explicit prior agreement that links the value of the 'softed' goods and services to a specified volume of commission from dealing orders.

Following the Myners Report, the FSA reviewed the manner in which the regulatory regime dealt with these issues. Its report[33] identified a number of regulatory concerns:

(a) The contractual basis under which UK fund managers typically operate permits dealing costs to be incurred (at the discretion of the manager) over and above the fee agreed for investment management. The resulting costs are often opaque and accountability to customers (typically pension funds and collective investment funds) is poor.

---

[31] See Ch 3.5 for an explanation of 'financial promotion'.

[32] *Institutional Investment in the United Kingdom: A Review*, prepared for the Treasury by Paul Myners (March 2001, see www.hm-treasury.gov.uk (8 Nov 2004)).

[33] See FSA Consultation Paper 176, *Bundled Brokerage and Soft Commission Arrangements* (April 2003).

(b) Bundled brokerage and soft-commission arrangements distort fund managers' decisions on the routing of business because additional services provided by brokers may be a more significant factor than execution quality.

(c) Competition between fund managers focuses on the management fee and not on dealing costs. Moreover, there is only very limited disclosure of the effect of transaction costs on fund performance (the main criterion against which fund managers are judged).

The FSA proposed two regulatory measures to resolve these problems. The first was that the nature of goods and services that can be bought from a broker with commission payments should be limited to trade execution (dealing) and investment research.[34] The rationale was that the fund manager should be incurring these costs directly rather than including them in transaction costs to be paid by the customer. The second proposal was that where a fund manager buys any services additional to trade execution with his customer's commission, he should determine the cost of those services and rebate an equivalent amount to his customers' funds. This was envisaged as providing fund managers with an additional incentive to control the purchase of additional services.

However, in its more recent policy statement,[35] the FSA decided to pursue only the first option. The abandonment of the second option reflected a number of considerations including:

(a) The concern expressed by fund managers regarding the practical aspects of calculating rebates across a varied customer base.

(b) A desire not to stifle market developments in view of changing attitudes among industry participants to their traditional business models.

(c) Industry-led developments that are likely to result in greater disclosure by fund managers to customers as to how costs incurred by the manager are broken down. This is being led by the Investment Management Association (IMA), which has put forward a comparative disclosure proposal to provide information to trustees, on a fund-by-fund basis, on the proportions of commission spent on execution and research.

---

[34] This would exclude services such as market information provided by third parties (eg the Reuters news agency), custody services, computer hardware, telephone lines and payment of fees for seminars and publications.

[35] FSA Policy Statement 04/13, *Bundled Brokerage and Soft Commission Arrangements* (May 2004).

COB 2.3 Reliance on others

This part of the Conduct of Business Rules deals with the extent to which an authorised firm can meet the requirement of Principle 2[36] by relying on others. If it is reasonable[37] to rely on information provided by another person, a firm will be taken to be in compliance with any requirement under the Conduct of Business Rules that the firm obtain information.

COB 2.4.4 Chinese walls

A 'Chinese wall' is a an arrangement that requires information held by a person in the course of carrying on one part of its business to be withheld from, or not to be used for, persons with or for whom it acts in the course of carrying on another part of its business.[38] The need for regulatory rules relating to Chinese walls arises from a combination of the law relating to the attribution of information to companies and the establishment of financial conglomerates, which became possible after the 'Big Bang' in 1986. Chinese walls are, in the main, applicable to financial conglomerates (aka investment banks) and are discussed in more detail in section 10.3.5 later in this chapter.

COB 3 Financial promotion

As discussed earlier,[39] the Financial Promotion Regime established by FSMA 2000 is intended to restrict the promotion (advertising etc) of certain financial instruments by unauthorised persons. However, this restriction does not apply if an authorised person approves the content of a communication. The purpose of COB 3 is largely to establish rules applicable to the approval process.

COB 4 Accepting customers

COB 4 is mainly concerned with customer classification, which was discussed earlier.[40] It requires a firm to provide a customer with its terms of business, setting out the basis on which designated investment business is to be conducted with or for the customer. The time at which this must be done and the form

---

[36] Principle 2 of the FSA's Principles for Business requires a firm to conduct its business with due skill, care and diligence.

[37] Steps must be taken to ensure that the provider of information is not connected with the firm and is competent to provide the information.

[38] This is the definition contained in the Glossary to the FSA Handbook.

[39] See Ch 3.5.

[40] See 10.1.1 above.

that the terms of business must take vary as between different types of customer.[41]

COB 7 Dealing and managing

The rules in this section apply when a firm is conducting designated investment business with or for a customer. Taken together, they are intended to protect customers from a range of possible abuses that can occur when authorised firms manage funds or deal on behalf of their customers.

(i) Conflict of interest and material interest
The rules require that, when a firm has a material interest in or a conflict of interest in respect of a transaction, the firm must not knowingly advise or deal in the exercise of discretion in relation to that transaction unless it takes reasonable steps to ensure fair treatment for the customer. A firm may manage a conflict of interest by taking one or more of the following steps:

- disclosure of an interest to a customer;
- relying on a policy of independence;
- establishing internal arrangements (Chinese walls);
- declining to act for a customer.

Examples of conflicts of interest that should be disclosed include a recommendation to buy or sell a designated investment in which the firm has respectively a long or short position.[42]

(ii) Churning and switching
The purpose of these rules is to ensure that transactions are in the best interests of a customer. In particular, the rules attempt to ensure that firms do not deal for a customer with unnecessary frequency having regard to the customer's agreed investment strategy.

(iii) Dealing ahead
This section applies to a firm when it intends to communicate a written recommendation or a piece of research or analysis to customers that relates to a designated investment. The purpose of the rules is to ensure that customers have the opportunity to act on the recommendation before the firm deals for its own account. The firm is prohibited from 'front-running' the customer in this situation.[43]

---

[41] See Ch 6 for more detail on private customers and terms of business.
[42] See further 10.3 below (investment banks).
[43] The exceptions to this rule include a market-maker undertaking the transaction in good faith in the normal course of market-making: see COB 7.3.4(2)R. The FSA has recently amended this rule so as to remove other exemptions.

(iv) Customer order priority

This section requires a firm to execute customer orders and own account orders in designated investments fairly and in due turn and to manage any conflict of interest accordingly. Order priority may affect the interests of customers as own account orders (or other customer orders) may move the price of a security against a customer.

(v) Best execution

As stated by the FSA:

> In most major jurisdictions in the world, regulation of best execution is acknowledged as having two main purposes: providing consumer protection and contributing to market efficiency.[44]

Except in some limited circumstances, a firm must provide best execution when it executes a customer order[45] in a designated investment.[46] To provide best execution a firm must take care, inter alia, to ascertain the price[47] which is the best available for the customer order in the relevant market at the time and, unless there are special circumstances, deal at that price. A firm need not have access to all competing exchanges and trading platforms but, if it does, they are encompassed by the best-execution principle. The firm is required to pass on to the customer the price at which it deals for the customer. It is possible for a firm to 'internalise' an order, meaning that the firm is both the execution venue for the transaction and the contractual counterparty to the customer. This occurs in broker/dealer firms that offer both execution (broking) and market-making (dealing) services. When this occurs, the requirement for 'best execution' remains relevant and the firm must carry out the transaction by reference to the outcome (price and other considerations) available through execution on alternative venues.

The FSA has, however, stressed that the obligation of best execution is more than the achievement of best price.[48] It requires attention to the overall costs of trading, both implicit and explicit, which are ultimately borne by the cus-

---

[44] FSA Consultation Paper 154, *Best Execution* p 7.

[45] Best execution applies irrespective of whether a firm acts as a principal or agent on behalf of a customer. The former situation can occur in those cases where a firm acts for a customer by buying (or selling) securities from the customer (as principal) and then selling on (or buying) in the market.

[46] See n 24 above. Best execution does not, however, apply to purchases of life policies and purchases and sales of units in regulated collective investment schemes from or to the operator of the scheme. Specific regulatory rules apply to these transactions.

[47] For securities traded on SETS (eg the entire FTSE 100 constituents), execution through SETS—or elsewhere at the equivalent of the SETS price—will be sufficient to meet the firm's obligations, unless it is able to execute the trade through another execution venue at a better price (see COB 7.5.6(3) and (4)).

[48] See FSA Consultation Paper 154, *Best Execution* (Oct 2002).

tomer. A decision on how to execute an order will therefore require a firm to consider the order type, size, settlement arrangements and timing along with any other conditions set by the customer.

It is likely that the FSA will in the near future adopt regulatory measures that implement the requirements of the EU Markets in Financial Instruments Directive[49] relating to best execution.[50] Much of the substance of those requirements has already been foreshadowed by the extensive consultation undertaken by the FSA in the past few years on this issue.

(vi) Timely execution

This section requires that once a firm has agreed or decided in its discretion to execute a current customer order in a designated investment, it must do so as soon as is reasonably practicable.

(vii) Aggregation and allocation

This section applies when a firm aggregates a customer order with an own account order or with an order from a market counterparty or another customer order while conducting designated investment business. In this situation, the allocation of the investment to the individual accounts must be in accordance with a written policy on allocation that is consistently applied and fulfils the requirements of this section. The intention is to ensure that the benefits of aggregation (typically better prices for larger transactions) are allocated equitably between a firm and its customers.

(viii) Customer order and execution records

This section requires a firm to ensure by the establishment and maintenance of appropriate procedures that it promptly records adequate information in relation to customer orders and own account transactions.

(ix) Personal account dealing

This section reflects the requirements of the Investment Services Directive (see above Ch 2.5.2) and requires a firm to take reasonable care to organise and control its affairs responsibly and effectively with a view to ensuring that the firm's customers are not disadvantaged by the personal dealings of the firm's employees.

(x) Programme trading

The purpose of this section is to ensure that a customer is informed when a firm intends to deal with it, whether as principal or agent, by executing a programme trade. The term is used here to describe a single transaction or series

---

[49] Dir 2004/39/EC, [2004] OJ L145/1. See Ch 2.5.2 for a discussion of the directive.
[50] See art 21 of the directive.

of transactions executed for the purpose of acquiring or disposing, for a customer, of all or part of a portfolio or basket of securities.

(xi) Non-market-price transactions

A firm should not enter into non-market-price transactions unless it has taken reasonable steps to ensure that the transaction is not illegal or otherwise for an improper purpose.

(xii) Investment research

This rule applies where a firm publishes or distributes investment research that it holds out as being an impartial assessment of the value or prospects of its subject matter. In these circumstances, a firm must establish and implement a policy for managing the conflicts of interest that might affect the impartiality of its investment research.

10.1.5 Financial resources

Principle 4 of the FSA's Principles for Business requires firms to maintain adequate financial resources. The purpose of this requirement is to minimise the risks to investors arising from the failure of a firm.[51] The basic principle is that financial resources should be sufficient to absorb losses suffered by a firm, with the result that investors' assets or money are not threatened.

The FSA rules[52] that give effect to this principle are to a substantial extent derived from the Capital Adequacy Directive[53], which establishes common financial resources (also referred to as capital adequacy) rules for investment firms operating in the EC. The definition of investment firms for this purpose includes stockbrokers (both when acting as agents in dealing on behalf of clients and when acting as investment manager for clients), market-makers and banks who engage in 'core investment services'.[54]

The rules require investment firms to satisfy three tests of capital adequacy. The first relates to the level of initial capital when a firm is first authorised. The level of initial capital required reflects the nature and scope of a firm's business: in particular, firms that are not authorised to hold clients' money or securities

---

[51] Potential causes of failure include: a general decline in the firm's markets affecting income levels; adverse movements in positions in securities held by the firm; default by a customer or counterparty; adverse currency or interest rate movements.

[52] Contained in the Business Standards Sourcebook, section IPRU(INV) for investment firms other than banks and IPRU(BANK) for banks.

[53] Dir 93/6/EC [1993] OJ L141/1.

[54] These services are defined in the Annex (Section A) to the Investment Services Directive (93/22/EC, [1993] OJ L141/27. They include reception and transmission on behalf of investors of orders in securities, execution of such orders, dealing for own account, managing investments on a client-by-client basis and underwriting issues of securities.

have a lower initial capital requirement, reflecting the lower risk that failure of such a firm poses to investors. The second test requires that at all times a firm's own funds[55] must exceed the initial capital requirement. The third test requires that at all times a firm's financial resources[56] must exceed the financial resources requirement. The implication of requiring the latter two tests to be met at all times is that the capacity of investment firms to enter into transactions must always be verified by reference to the financial resources available to the firm.

Calculation of the financial resources requirement is quite complex.[57] It incorporates requirements relating to position risk, counterparty risk and foreign exchange risk. The purpose of these requirements is to increase the financial resources that are available to a firm as each of these categories of risk increases. Position risk is the risk arising from the net position of an investment firm across the securities in which it trades on its own account. Calculation of the position risk requirement involves separate calculation of the specific and general risk associated with each type of financial instrument.[58] Moreover, the position risk requirement reflects the inherent risk associated with different types of instrument (eg government bonds carry a much lower specific risk requirement than do equities). Counterparty risk reflects the risks posed to a firm by the scale of the obligations it has undertaken and that are owed to it. It acts as a proxy for the scale of the business being conducted by a firm and requires financial resources to be adjusted accordingly. Moreover, it penalises firms by requiring additional financial resources to be available when a firm has unsettled transactions. Foreign exchange risk is the risk that arises when a firm's trading book or more generally its balance sheet, income and expenses are denominated other than in the currency of its books of account. In these circumstances, adverse exchange rate movements pose a potential risk and therefore financial resources are required to cover this risk.

10.2 Common-law liability

Market participants potentially face a wide range of common-law claims from their customers. They can be split into four categories.[59] The first are those that

[55] Own funds comprise principally share and loan capital.

[56] Financial resources includes share capital and loans plus the profit or loss arising on the firm's 'trading book' (ie trading on its own account).

[57] See FSA Handbook IPRU(INV) rule 10.70.

[58] See Ch 1.1 for an explanation of general and specific risk.

[59] This treatment adopts the three categories identified by A Hudson, *The Law on Financial Derivatives*, 3rd edn (London, Sweet & Maxwell, 2002) with the addition of breach of contract, which, it is submitted, cannot be subsumed within any of the other three categories.

arise from the failure of a contract to represent the intentions of the parties (vitiated consent). The second are those arising from a breach of contract. The third are claims in damages arising from wrongful acts[60] of a market participant. The fourth are claims for the recovery of property wrongfully taken from a customer (restitution or unjustified enrichment). Each will now be considered.

10.2.1 Vitiated consent

Contracts are based on the consent of each party, freely given. When consent is not freely given, the law responds by providing, in effect, that the innocent party is released from the obligations contained in the contract. There are three circumstances in which this can occur.

The first is where one party breaches a condition precedent to the contract.[61] The essence of such a condition is that it has to be satisfied before a contract comes into existence.[62] For example, it might be made a condition precedent to a contract that a borrower or an issuer of shares has no outstanding litigation being pursued against it. If the condition is not satisfied, there can be no contract because the consent of each party is predicated on the satisfaction of the condition. Breach of a condition precedent therefore results in there being no contract and no obligations on either side.

The second is where a seller of a financial product makes a misrepresentation that induces a customer to enter into a contract. A distinction is drawn between misrepresentations that are made fraudulently (intentionally), negligently and innocently. In each case, the innocent party is entitled to rescind the contract.[63] Rescission involves the innocent party giving notice to the other party that he regards the contract as terminated. The legal effect of rescission is that the contract is voidable, meaning that it remains valid until set aside by the process of rescission. For this to occur, each party must be able to restore to the other benefits that have been obtained under the contract (*restitutio in integrum*). For example, in the case of a sale of shares induced by misrepresentation the buyer would be required to transfer the shares to the seller in return for repayment of the purchase price.

A misrepresentation has no effect unless it is material, meaning that it would affect the judgment of a reasonable person in deciding whether to enter into

---

[60] Torts in England, delicts in Scotland.

[61] In Scots law, this is referred to as a contract subject to a suspensive condition. See W McBryde, *Contract*, 2nd edn (Edinburgh, W Green, 2001) para 5–35.

[62] See *Bettini v Gye* (1876) 1 QB 183 and *Murdoch & Co Ltd v Greig* (1889) 16 R 396 for analysis of the law in England and Scotland respectively.

[63] See, as regards English Law GH Treitel, *The Law of Contract*, 11th edn (London, Sweet & Maxwell, 2003) pp 371–77 and as regards Scots Law McBryde (above n 61) paras 15–69 to 15–76.

the contract. This issue was considered in *Bankers Trust International plc vs PT Dharmala Sakti Sejahtera,*[64] a case involving an interest rate swap. The court concluded, on the basis of the facts, that a case for rescission had not been established. In explaining the circumstances in which a misrepresentation might be made, Mance J said:

> A description or commendation which may obviously be irrelevant or may even serve as a warning to one recipient, because of its generality, superficiality or laudatory nature, or because of the recipient's own knowledge and experience, may constitute a material representation if made to another less informed or sophisticated receiver.[65]

The relevance of the recipient's actual and apparent expertise in the assessment of whether a misrepresentation was made was explained as follows:

> Whether there was any and if so what particular representation must thus depend on an objective assessment of the likely effect of the proposal or presentation on the recipient. In making such an assessment, it is necessary to consider the recipient's characteristics and knowledge as they appeared, or ought to have appeared, to the maker of the proposal or presentation. A recipient holding himself out as able to understand and evaluate complicated proposals would be expected to be able to do so, whatever his actual abilities.[66]

This case suggests that the courts are likely to take a more robust view of transactions between commercial organisations dealing with each other as principals than they would do if one party were a private investor. A similar approach is evident in respect of the issue of whether a duty of care is owed by one party to the other in the context of principal-to-principal transactions between commercial organisations.[67]

10.2.2 Breach of contract

Claims arising from beach of contract relate to the failure of one of the parties to perform their obligations under a contract. In respect of financial market transactions this could take the form of a buyer failing to pay the agreed price or a seller failing to deliver a good title to the investment that is the subject of the transaction. The risks posed to market participants from such a breach of contract have always been a concern in the markets and have led to the development of market practices and procedures that minimise such risks.

---

[64] [1996] CLC 518. See, for discussion of this case, T Little, 'Suitability the Courts and the Code' (1996) *European Financial Services Law Review* 119 and S Greene, 'Suitability and the Emperor's New Clothes' (1996) *European Financial Services Law Review* 53.
[65] At p 530.
[66] *Ibid.*
[67] See 10.2.3 (tort/delict) below.

Examples are the operation of the principle of 'delivery versus payment' in settlement systems, which attempts to ensure simultaneous performance of obligations by buyer and seller, the taking of security interests as collateral in OTC derivative transactions and the payment of margin in exchange-traded derivatives transactions.[68]

10.2.3 Claims in tort/delict[69]

Claims arising in tort in respect of financial transactions are most likely to be for damages in respect of misrepresentation. It is possible, when the innocent party has suffered loss, for damages to be recovered in respect of fraudulent and negligent misrepresentations. Such a claim can be pursued either as an alternative or in addition to a claim for rescission of a contract as a result of misrepresentation.[70] In the case of an innocent misrepresentation, no damages are available in Scotland,[71] but in England damages may be awarded in lieu of rescission.[72]

The general conditions applicable to a claim in damages for negligent misrepresentation were established in the case of *Hedley Byrne & Co Ltd v Heller*.[73] The plaintiff in that case suffered a loss as a result of extending credit to a firm in reliance on a banker's reference given by the defendant. While the decision in the case was that the defendant bank was not liable as the reference was given 'without responsibility', the House of Lords made clear the circumstances in which liability would arise. The central issue was the definition of circumstances in which a duty of care can arise as between two parties. The House of Lords made clear that a duty of care arises when there is a 'special relationship' between two parties. It has been said in a number of cases that three conditions must be met for this to occur. First, it must be reasonably foreseeable by the representor that the representee will rely on the relevant statement. Second, there must be a sufficiently close relationship between the parties ('proximity'). Third, it must be reasonable in all the circumstances for the law to impose such a duty. Moreover, even if a duty of care is shown to exist, the plaintiff must show a causal link between breach of the duty and the loss which he has suffered.

---

[68] See Ch 4 for a discussion of these issues.

[69] The Scots law counterpart of liability in tort is liability in delict.

[70] *Newbigging v Adam* (1886) 34 Ch 582, 592, *Archer v Brown* [1985] QB 401, 415. See also Companies Act 1985 s 111A, which reverses the common law rule (established in *Houldsworth v City of Glasgow Bank* (1880) 5 App Cas 317) that a person induced by fraud to subscribe for a company's shares could not claim damages unless he rescinded (and thereby ceased to be a shareholder).

[71] *Manners v Whitehead* (1898) 1 Fraser (Court of Session Reports) 171.

[72] Misrepresentation Act 1967 s 2(2).

[73] [1964] AC 465.

Several cases have applied these principles in the context of dealings in the financial markets. The most far reaching in terms of its analysis of the existence and scope of a duty of care as between a market participant and its customers is *Bankers Trust International plc vs PT Dharmala Sakti Sejahtera*.[74] This case arose from the sale by Bankers Trust International (BTI) of several, ultimately loss-making, interest-rate swaps to the defendant (DSS). Among the defences put forward by DSS to BTI's claim for payment were that (a) misrepresentations made by BTI during the sale of the derivatives gave DSS the option of rescission and (b) BTI was in breach of a duty of care owed to DSS to ensure that the derivatives were suitable and safe products for DSS. The circumstances of the case were that both BTI, a leading player in the derivatives market, and DSS, a substantial commercial organisation with general financial expertise but no special expertise in derivatives, were acting as principals in the transactions, which were exempt from the FSA 1986 but subject to the London Code of Conduct.[75]

As regards DSS's second claim (that BTI owed a duty of care to ensure that derivatives were suitable and safe), the court found in respect of the first transaction that DSS did not ask and were not entitled to expect BTI to act as their advisers generally. In respect of the second transaction, the issue of causality came to the fore in that it was accepted that BTI owed a duty of care not to make inaccurate statements and to make a balanced presentation of the risks arsing from the transaction. However, DSS failed to show that a full and fair presentation would have led to a different result (such as withdrawal from the transaction or negotiation of different terms). There was therefore a failure to show a causal link between BTI's representations and the loss suffered by DSS. It was, moreover, stated that courts should not be too ready to read duties of an advisory nature into the type of (informed principal-to-principal) relationship that existed between BTI and DSS.

In *Possfund Custodian Trustee Ltd vs Diamond and Others*,[76] the court was required to consider whether a common-law duty of care was owed by persons responsible for a prospectus offering shares that were to be quoted and traded on the Unlisted Securities Market (USM). The legal background to the case was that section 150 of the FSA 1986 gave a remedy to anyone who bought securities in reliance on a prospectus (whether in a public offer or in the secondary market), whereas (in the opinion of the judge in this case) the relevant provision of FSA 1986 applicable to unlisted securities[77] did not provide a

---

[74] [1996] CLC 518.

[75] See above n 10.

[76] [1996] 2 All ER 774. The case was for the striking out of the plaintiff's claim on the basis that it disclosed no cause of action. Consideration of the merits was therefore confined to whether there was a cause of action.

[77] FSA 1986 s 166.

remedy to investors who bought in the secondary market. The court reached the view that it was not possible to conclude that there was no common law duty owed by persons responsible for an unlisted prospectus to investors who bought in the secondary market. This followed consideration of the purpose of a prospectus in its modern context as being a document on which investors in the secondary market intend to rely, rather than the narrow view established in the nineteenth century cases, which viewed a prospectus as being limited to providing information in respect of a particular allotment of shares.[78]

While the willingness of the court in the *Possfund* case to consider extension of the traditional common law duty of care associated with a prospectus fits in with the approach taken in *Gorham v British Telecommunications plc*[79], a more cautious approach to extending the common law is apparent in *Bankers Trust v Dharmala*. Given that one of the major concerns of the regulatory system is the delimitation of suitability obligations,[80] this seems an appropriate response. Otherwise, there is a risk of confusion if differing standards of care and suitability are prescribed by the common law and regulatory rules.

10.2.4 Claims in restitution/unjustified enrichment

Claims in restitution (unjustified enrichment in Scotland) arise when property or benefits are transferred other than under a contract and the person holding the property has no legal basis for doing so. There are two main circumstances in which market participants are likely to face claims for restitution of property. The first is where property has been transferred under a contract that is void because of a lack of contractual capacity of one of the parties. This formed the basis of one of the claims arising in the local authority swaps cases. In *Westdeutsche Landesbank Girozentrale v Islington LBC*[81] a derivatives contract was held to be void as a result of the lack of contractual capacity (for the particular contract) of the local authority. The House of Lords held that the local authority could recover money paid under the contract.

The second is where there is a breach of fiduciary duty. Fiduciary duty arises independently of contract as a result of a relationship of trust between two parties.[82] A fiduciary relationship does not arise automatically as between market

---

[78] See *Peek v Gurney* (1873) LR 6 HL 377.

[79] [2000] 1 WLR 2129. See Ch 6.3.2. for a discussion of this case.

[80] See Cranston (above n 28) pp 198–200 and L Lowenfels and A Bromberg, 'Suitability in Securities Transactions' (1999) 54 *Business Law* 1557.

[81] [1996] AC 669.

[82] It may be that there is a contract between them but even if there is, the contract is unlikely to spell out in detail the conduct expected from the fiduciary. A contract can, however, limit fiduciary duty—see *Kelly v Cooper* [1993] AC 205 and Law Commission Report no 236 *Fiduciary Duties and Regulatory Rules* (1995).

participants and their customers.[83] It does, however, arise in circumstances in which a market participant acts as agent or trustee for a customer or as its partner.[84] As discussed earlier[85], the standard of conduct expected from a fiduciary is high. The law prohibits both the use of information gained in the capacity of fiduciary for personal profit and the structuring of transactions with fiduciaries in such a manner that the fiduciary makes a profit for itself. Profits made by a fiduciary in contravention of fiduciary duty are held on trust for the benefit of the fiduciary and may be the subject of a claim in restitution.[86]

10.3 The role of market participants, regulation and the general law

10.3.1 Stockbrokers

Stockbrokers act as agents for investors in the purchase of securities. Prior to the 'Big Bang' in 1986, the London Stock Exchange was organised on the basis of 'single capacity'. This meant that the function of market-makers (or 'jobbers' as they were then known) was separated from that of broker.[87] Investors were not permitted to transact business directly with market-makers[88] and so had to use a broker. When a 'dual capacity' system was introduced in 1986, permitting the functions of broker and market-maker to be performed by the same organisation (hence the term broker/dealer), institutional investors were able to deal directly (on a principal-to-principal basis) with market-makers.[89]

When transacting business, brokers are subject to conduct of business rules according to the category into which the client falls. As indicated above, inter-professional business is subject to few regulatory rules but dealing with or for a customer is subject to considerable regulation. The existence of regulatory rules does not displace the older common-law rules that govern the

---

[83] For example, banks are not automatically in a fiduciary relationship with their customers. However, they may become fiduciaries in specific circumstances such as: becoming a financial adviser or advising a customer on a particular transaction. See Cranston (above n 28 pp 187–91).

[84] The reference here is to a partner in the law of partnership and not any broader usage of that term.

[85] See Ch 1.3.3.

[86] *Boardmann v Phipps* [1967] 2 AC 67.

[87] Historically, the London Stock Exchange did not always require single capacity. See R Michie, *The London Stock Exchange, A History* (Oxford, OUP, 1999) pp 113–15.

[88] Historically, this prohibition did not prevent market-makers having direct contact with investors in overseas markets, see Michie *ibid.*

[89] See eg Ch 27 of J Littlewood, *The Stockmarket, Fifty Years of Capitalism at Work* (London, Pitman, 1998) for an account of the Big Bang.

conduct of stockbrokers. While much of the common law has been absorbed into the regulatory rules, there remain some areas in which it still has the potential to be an important source of redress. Three areas are particularly important. One is the requirement that a stockbroker, as agent, act within the limits of the authority given by the customer. This applies not just to carrying out the client's instruction but also to ensuring that discretion is exercised in the client's best interests.[90]

A second important area of the common law is negligence. In principle a stockbroker can be liable in negligence, irrespective of whether or not there is a contractual relationship with the person alleging negligence.[91] However, the possibility of brokers being found negligent is limited by the general approach of the courts in the UK, which has been to recognise that brokers operating in financial markets are not obliged to be correct in regard to future market movements. For example, it was said in the case of *Stafford v Conti Commodity Services Ltd* that:

> An error of judgment in giving advice on the part of a broker dealing on an unpredictable market like the commodities market would not necessarily be negligence since, in relation to such a market, the broker could not always give correct advice.[92]

A third area is fiduciary duty. Much of the content of the common-law principle of fiduciary duty has been absorbed into the regulatory rules referred to above. It seems likely that a court considering an issue relating to common-law fiduciary duty would take account of these regulatory rules.[93]

Another significant matter is the modification of the common law of agency by the rules of an exchange on which a broker operates. This occurs in the case of the London Stock Exchange through the requirement that members take responsibility for the settlement of transactions notwithstanding that they act as agent on behalf of a client.[94] The common-law rule that an agent acting on behalf of a principal forms a contract between the principal and the third party, to which the agent is not a party, is thereby disapplied. This imposes an onerous obligation on brokers, who are effectively required to assume the risk of default[95] on the part of clients and gives substance to the old adage of the broking community that 'my word is my bond'.

---

[90] See *Jarvis v Moy, Davies, Smith, Vandervelt & Co* [1936] 1 KB 399. While the factual scenario in this case has become outdated, the principles relating to the exercise of discretion remain relevant.

[91] *Hedley Byrne & Co v Heller and Partners* [1963] 2 All ER 575. Liability could arise in a non-contractual situation as a result of the making of a negligent statement.

[92] [1981] 1 All ER 691, [1981] 1 Lloyd's Rep 466.

[93] See Law Commission Report no 236 (above n 82).

[94] See rule 2100 of the rules of the London Stock Exchange for the precise wording.

[95] The risk can be mitigated by making provision in client agreements for the power to sell a client's holdings following default so as to make funds available to meet settlement obligations.

Stockbrokers also perform the function of acting as sponsor (or corporate stockbroker) for listed companies. The Listing Rules require that each listed company appoint a sponsor whose role is to liaise between the UKLA and listed companies and to advise the companies on compliance.[96]

10.3.2 Market-makers

Market-makers trade as principals in securities on exchanges where they are members. They are required to register with the relevant exchange the securities in which they trade and then become subject to an obligation to make a continuous two-way (buy/sell) market in those securities.[97] It is this requirement that provides liquidity to the market. The quote must be made in the minimum number of shares applicable to that security (normal market size). The 'spread' between the bid and offer prices is the profit made by the market-maker and is determined by competition in the market. The best bid/offer spread available in the market from all the market-makers in a particular security is referred to as the 'touch price'.

As members of an exchange, market-makers are subject to the rules of the exchange and may also be subject to regulatory rules made under FSMA 2000, depending on the type of person they deal with. Many deals between market-makers and other market participants will fall within the IPC, but there are circumstances where this will not be the case.[98] Institutional investors dealing on a principal-to-principal basis with market-makers will typically be classified as intermediate customers. An important exception, however, is regulated collective investment schemes, which are always categorised as private customers.

10.3.3 Custodians

Custodians safeguard and administer assets on behalf of others. A substantial proportion of securities are now held through custodians, the main attractions being:

---

[96] See Ch 2 of the UKLA Listing Rules para 2.6.

[97] See rule 5100 and rules 5210–14 respectively of the London Stock Exchange, which apply to the operation of the quote-driven trading service provided by SEAQ (Stock Exchange Automated Quotation System) and SEAQ International.

[98] The definition of market counterparty excludes business with or for a firm or institution classified as an intermediate customer under COB 4.1.7R. This might occur for example when a firm (F) which would otherwise be classified as a market counterparty decides that it (F) needs to be classified as an intermediate customer to protect its (F's) underlying customer (C). This could occur for example when F relies on another person to provide best execution in respect of a transaction for C.

(a) security of paper documents of title from loss or theft;
(b) specialist services such as record-keeping, valuation and performance measurement;
(c) savings in transaction costs resulting from the custodian's investment in specialist systems and the possibility of some transfers of securities being effected simply by changes in the records of the custodian;
(d) the simplification of legal and regulatory issues by holding securities through a custodian established in the country of the issuer.

A distinction can be drawn between intermediary and non-intermediary custody.[99] The former refers to the deposit with a custodian of a share certificate or certificate of negotiable securities indorsed to the investor. In this situation, there remains a direct link between the issuer of the security and the investor because the investor remains the legal owner of the security.[100] Non-intermediary custody refers to a situation in which a custodian becomes the legal owner of the relevant securities (eg the registered owner of company shares). In this situation, the direct ownership link between the issuer and the ultimate investor is broken.

This is not to say that the investor in non-intermediary custody becomes irrelevant. Three mechanisms ensure that the investor continues to have a significant link with the investment. First, the custody contract between investor and custodian will often specify the manner in which the custodian is to hold the investment on behalf of the investor. Such rights are, however, personal in their nature and do not give the investor an ownership link with the investment.[101] Second, it will often be clear from the circumstances in which custody is created that a custodian holds investments on trust for the investor, with the result that the investor has a beneficial interest in the rights held by the custodian.[102] This will be the case even if it is not possible for the existence of the beneficial interest of the investor to be formally recorded.[103] Third, the relevant conduct of business rules (below) protect the investor by creating a number of safeguards in the creation and performance of custody.

Non-intermediary custody can be either single- or multi-tier. The former, as the name suggests, involves a single custodian holding legal title to investments

---

[99] See generally, AO Austen-Peters, *Custody of Invetsments, Law and Practice* (Oxford, OUP, 2000) and SL Schwarcz, 'Intermediary Risk in a Global Economy' (2001) 50 *Duke Law Journal* 1541.

[100] This form of custody was traditionally termed 'bailment'.

[101] See N Papasyrou, 'Immobilisation of Securities—Part Two: Personal Rights of Indirect Holders' (1996) 11 *JIBL* 459.

[102] See Austen-Peters (above n 99) ch 3.

[103] s 360 of the Companies Act 1985 prevents any beneficial interest from being recorded in the shareholders' register of a company registered in England.

in which the investor has a beneficial interest. Multi-tier custody (or 'sub-custody') involves more than one custodian holding investments on behalf of an investor. Such arrangements are common in respect of overseas investments, with local custodians often being used by a global custodian (or 'lead custodian') to simplify investment in a particular country, region or category of security. As immobilisation of securities is often encountered in overseas investment, it will also often be the case that the local custodian holds through a central securities depositary that is the legal owner of the securities.

Two critical issues arise in non-intermediary custody. First, what is the nature of the investor's interest in the investment, and second, what rights does the investor have against the custodian(s)? Many different contractual permutations are possible, but several general points can be made:

(a) The investor will usually have a contractual relationship with only one custodian (the 'lead custodian').

(b) It will often be possible to infer the creation of a trust at each level of custody, with each party's respective interest being passed down to the investor.[104]

(c) Each investor shares common ownership of the pool of a particular security held by the custodian. When an investor deposits securities with the custodian, he has a claim to have returned an equal amount of the same securities, but not the same securities that were deposited. In other words, the pool held by the custodian for investors in a particular security comprises fungibles and the investor has no right to require the return of the deposited securities *in specie*.[105]

(d) Because there are separate trusts at each level, only the lead custodian owes a fiduciary duty to the investor.

(e) It is possible for the fiduciary duty owed by a custodian to be modified by contract.[106]

(f) The existence of a trust in principle precludes the custody assets being claimed by creditors of the custodian should the custodian become insolvent, although problems may arise if the investments are held in a pooled fund that does not have segregated client-specific holdings.

---

[104] See Austen-Peters (above n 99 at para 4.40).

[105] See R Goode, 'The Nature and Transfer of Rights in Dematerialised and Immobilised Securities', ch 7 in Oditah F (ed) *The Future for the Global Securities Market: Legal and Regulatory Aspects* (Oxford, OUP, 1996).

[106] *Kelly v Cooper* [1993] AC 205. Exclusions of liability in standard form documentation are subject to a reasonableness test under s 3 (England) and s 17 (Scotland) of the Unfair Contract Terms Act 1977. J Benjamin, *Interests in Securities* (Oxford, OUP, 2000) p 45 notes that it is customary for custodians to accept liability for ordinary negligence.

While some of these issues remain subject to some doubt in the United Kingdom,[107] other jurisdictions have adopted measures to clarify matters. This is particularly true of the nature of the investor's interest in a pool of securities held by a custodian for investors. In the United States, a revised version of Article 8 of the Uniform Commercial Code[108] makes clear that investors have (real) property rights in securities held on their behalf by custodians, not merely personal claims.[109] Belgium and Luxembourg have adopted similar measures, primarily to support respectively the operations of Euroclear and Cedel Bank, who hold in custody the majority of internationally-traded securities.[110]

Custody is a 'regulated activity' for the purposes of FSMA 2000 if the relevant assets include 'investments' or 'contractually based investments'.[111] Principle 10 (Clients' assets) requires a firm to arrange adequate protection for clients' assets when it is responsible for them. The relevant conduct of business rules are, in the main, applicable to market counterparties as well as 'customers'. Their objectives are:

(a) To protect clients by restricting the commingling of client and firm assets. This is achieved through rules relating to the segregation of firm and client assets, registration and recording of ownership.

(b) To minimise the risk of client assets being used by a firm without the client's agreement or contrary to the client's wishes.[112] This is achieved mainly through a requirement that the terms on which safe custody is provided are notified to the client and a general prohibition against firms using clients' assets for their own account.[113]

(c) To prevent the client's assets being treated as the firm's assets in the event of insolvency. This is mainly achieved through the agreements that must be made between firms and custodians who hold the assets of the firm's clients. Those agreements must detail the manner in which assets are held, following the principle of segregation of firm and client assets.

---

[107] See Financial Markets Law Committee, 'Property Interests in Investment Securities' (at www.fmlc.org (22 Nov 2004)) for background and proposals to clarify the legal regime in the UK.

[108] The UCC is a uniform law intended for separate enactment by each state of the United States. The revised Article 8 has, according to Schwarcz (above n 99 at fn 49), been enacted in almost all the states of the USA.

[109] As regards the distinction between real and personal rights see Ch 1.2.

[110] See, on the structure and operation of Euroclear and Cedel Bank, F Christie and H Dosanjh, 'The Practical Elements of Settlement and Custody', Ch 8 in Oditah (above n 105).

[111] See art 40 of the Regulated Activities Order (RAO, SI 2001/544).

[112] eg the risk that a firm might use client assets for stocklending.

[113] FSA Handbook, CASS 2.3.2R.

Before a firm provides safe custody services to a client it must notify the client of the terms under which the service is provided.[114] Those terms must cover, inter alia:

- registration of the safe custody investments if they will not be registered in the client's name;
- the extent of the firm's liability in respect of default by a custodian;
- the circumstances in which the firm may realise a safe custody investment held as collateral to meet the client's liabilities.[115]

Some modifications are made to the scope of the conduct of business rules governing custody in particular cases. A trustee firm or depositary acting as custodian for a trust or collective investment scheme is required to comply with only a limited number of the rules, reflecting the extensive regulation of this activity under the relevant regulations[116] as well as common-law duties. A firm that merely arranges safeguarding and administration of assets is subject to a limited set of rules, including a requirement that it undertake a proper risk assessment of the custodian.

10.3.4 Central securities depositories

Central securities depositories (CSDs) are a key component of systems of immobilised securities.[117] They hold legal title to immobilised securities and record transfers between the underlying investors. Such transfers have no effect on the legal ownership of immobilised securities, which remain with the depository, but give the ultimate investor an ownership right in relation to the deposited securities.[118] Depositories differ from custodians as legal title to immobilised securities always remains with the relevant depository, whereas it may be transferred between custodians.

CSDs are found in countries in which issuers of securities in immobilised form are resident. In the US, a large proportion of securities are issued in this form and are held by the Depositary Trust Corporation. In the UK, Euroclear (which has absorbed the CREST settlement system) provides depositary services. Euroclear and Cedel Bank provide depositary services in respect of internationally traded securities such as Eurobonds.

---

[114] FSA Handbook, CASS 2.2.2R.
[115] See also COB7.8 regarding private customers.
[116] See Ch 4.
[117] See Ch 1.2 for an explanation of the principle of immobilisation.
[118] In English law, this takes the form of beneficial ownership. See Goode (above n 105) p 125.

10.3.5 Merchant and investment banks

The terms 'merchant' and 'investment' bank are sometimes used interchangeably nowadays but their derivation reflects different regulatory and corporate finance traditions in the UK and USA. Merchant banks in the UK were historically merchants who diversified into banking principally through the provision of finance.[119] The Accepting Houses Committee developed from this background as a body representing their interests as acceptors[120] of Bills of Exchange, which were commonly used as a means of payment in international trade. The merchant banks were also historically involved in taking deposits and making short-term loans, principally in connection with international trade. Corporate finance became an important part of the business of merchant banks that were members of the Issuing Houses Association.

Investment banks in the USA were so named so as to distinguish them from commercial banks during the period when there was a prohibition on combining banking and securities business. That prohibition was introduced by the Glass–Steagall Act 1934 in the wake of the Wall Street crash of 1929 as a result of concern over the involvement of commercial banks in the speculative stockmarket boom of the late 1920s.

Two developments led to the distinction between merchant and investment banks on the one hand, and commercial banks on the other, becoming blurred. First, the relaxation of ownership restrictions in the London Stock Exchange, combined with the 'Big Bang' in 1986 meant that it was possible for financial conglomerates to be formed in the UK comprising merchant and commercial banking, broker/dealing in securities and fund management. Conglomerates also emerged in the US. While the Glass–Steagall Act of 1934 prohibited the combination of banking and securities business, its effect was mitigated by exceptions and liberal court decisions.[121] The partial repeal[122] of the Act in 1999 further assisted the emergence of conglomerates. Whether one refers to such conglomerates as merchant or investment banks makes little difference in most cases. However, there do remain some banks in the UK who continue the older 'merchant' banking tradition and therefore the distinction does still carry some significance.

The involvement of investment banks in securities markets takes a number of different forms. First, they often act as financial advisers to companies

---

[119] See generally C Clay and B Wheble, *Modern Merchant Banking* (Cambridge, Woodhead-Faulkner, 1976).

[120] See s 54 of the Bills of Exchange Act 1882 for more detail on the position of an acceptor of a bill of exchange.

[121] See Cranston (above n 28) p 99.

[122] As a result of the Gramm–Leach–Bliley Act of 1999 (also referred to as the Financial Services Act of 1999). See generally KA Summe, 'The repeal of Glass–Steagall and the modernisation of the US Financial System' (2000) 21 *Company Lawer* 189.

whose shares are being listed. In this capacity they organise the writing of the prospectus and assume responsibility (and therefore also legal liability) for some of the contents of the prospectus.[123] They often also act as underwriter of the share issue made by such a company at the time of listing. Second, investment banks often acts as stockbrokers and market-makers. They assumed this role when the Stock Exchange relaxed the ownership restrictions for member firms in the early 1980s and many of the previously independent stockbroking and jobbing firms were bought by banks. When they act as stockbrokers or market-makers they are subject to the regulatory regime outlined above. Third, investment banks act as fund managers. In this capacity they are subject to the regulatory regime applicable to that activity.[124]

A major concern resulting from the combination of a number of different functions in a single organisation is the possibility that the interests of different clients may differ and the organisation may find itself unable to serve all those interests simultaneously. The COBs require that when a firm has a material interest or a conflict of interest in respect of a transaction it must not knowingly advise or deal in the exercise of discretion, in relation to that transaction, unless it takes reasonable steps to ensure fair treatment for the customer.[125] Quite apart from this regulatory rule, there will often be common law fiduciary duties arising from a principal/agent relationship between an investment bank and a client. Under the common law, fiduciary duty requires that the agent act at all time in the best interests of the client.

Problems are particularly likely to arise in a conglomerate because, even if there is functional segregation within the firm, knowledge possessed in one part of a single corporate entity or partnership is treated in law as known in all parts of that entity.[126] Even where the conglomerate is not a single entity (eg because it has a group structure) common directorships may result in attribution of knowledge between group companies. This approach to attribution of knowledge can lead to a number of problems. For example, an investment bank dealing as principal for its own account in company A may have been given information by company B relating to A. If B passed the information to the bank in the context of a fiduciary relationship, the bank is prohibited from using the information for its own purposes.[127] A conflict of interest would also exist in this situation when an analyst working for the bank advises a client on company A. While the analyst is obliged, in principle, to use all the information

---

[123] Principally any profit-forecast included in the prospectus. See Ch 7.4 for more details on prospectuses.

[124] See Chs 3 and 6 for more detail.

[125] COB 7.1.3R.

[126] *Harrods Ltd v Lemon* [1931] 2 KB 157.

[127] The basic principle is derived from *Boardmann v Phipps* [1967] 2 AC 46.

that the law attributes to the bank in framing the recommendation, the duty of confidentiality owed to B creates a conflict of interest.

The Conduct of Business Rules identify several possible solutions to the presence of a material interest or a conflict of interest.[128] First, the customer can be informed of the circumstances.[129] Second, a firm can rely on a policy of independence, under which the relevant employee disregards the firm's interest. Third, a firm may establish and maintain Chinese walls, an organisational arrangement for restricting information flows within a firm to prevent information confidential to one department being communicated (deliberately or inadvertently) to another department. The objective is to prevent the attribution of knowledge between departments in a firm on different sides of the wall, so that they can act independently and so avoid real conflicts of interest.[130] In this sense Chinese walls are like information firewalls that separate a conglomerate into different regulatory components. Finally, the firm may decline to act for a customer.

The FSMA enables the FSA to make 'control of information' rules, which are in effect rules recognising Chinese walls.[131] The only rule made by the FSA under this power is a rule providing that where a firm establishes and maintains a Chinese wall it may withhold information or not use the information held and limit the transfer of information between departments.[132] The result of this rule is that:

(a) acting in conformity with this rule provides a defence against a prosecution (under s 397 FSMA) for making misleading statements or practices or engaging in a course of conduct creating a false or misleading impression;
(b) behaviour conforming with this rule does not amount to market abuse;
(c) acting in conformity with this rule is a defence to an action for damages under s 150 FSMA, where that action is based on a breach of a relevant requirement to disclose or use information.

Another rule deals with attribution of knowledge. It provides that when any of the COB rules apply to a firm that acts with knowledge, the firm will not be taken to act with knowledge for the purposes of that rule if none of the relevant individuals involved on behalf of the firm acts with that knowledge as a

---

[128] See FSA Handbook, COB 7 and more generally Law Commission Consultation Paper no 124, *Fiduciary Duties and Regulatory Rules.*

[129] See COB 7.1.6E, which requires the firm only to demonstrate that the customer does not object to the material interest or conflict of interest. As Cranston observes (above n 28 at p 26), this is a lower standard than that required from a beneficiary of a fiduciary duty consenting to a breach of that duty under the common law.

[130] See generally N Poser, 'Chinese Wall or Emperor's New Clothes' (1997): *Company Lawyer,* Part 1 Vol 9(6) 119, Part II vol 9(8) 159, Part III vol 9(10) 203.

[131] FSMA 2000 s 147.

[132] COB 2.4.4(1)R.

result of arrangements established under the above rule.[133] This means that when a Chinese wall is in operation, individuals on the 'other side of the wall' will not be regarded as being in possession of knowledge denied to them as a result of the effective operation of the Chinese wall.

Following the bursting of the 'dotcom' bubble in the year 2000, regulators around the world became particularly concerned over the impartiality of investment research produced and distributed by regulated firms such as investment banks. In the United States the SEC took legal action against ten of the nation's top investment firms and secured a $1.4 billion dollar settlement.[134] In the UK, the FSA began a process of consultation with a view to ensuring that research held out to clients as impartial or objective is produced according to appropriately high standards for conflict management.[135] Following that consultation the FSA has taken the following action:[136]

(i)   It has amended the Conduct of Business Sourcebook to provide guidance on the management of conflicts of interest in particular situations arising in the context of corporate finance business.[137] The most obvious conflict in this area arises when a firm owes duties both to a client for whom it is carrying out a public offer of securities and to investment clients who may be interested in buying those securities.

(ii) It has amended the COB Rules relevant to investment firms dealing ahead of investment research.[138] The dealing ahead rules are aimed at ensuring that a firm does not use knowledge of the content, and timing of publication, of a research report to inform its proprietary dealing and thereby to prefer its own interests above those of its clients. The rules contained a number of exemptions which have now been closed.[139]

---

[133] COB 2.4.6R.

[134] See www.sec.gov/litigation/litreleases/lr18438.htm (22 Nov 2004). In its complaints, the allegations of which the defendants neither admit nor deny, the Securities and Exchange Commission alleged that, from approximately mid-1999 through mid-2001 or later, all of the firms engaged in acts and practices that created or maintained inappropriate influence by investment banking over research analysts, thereby imposing conflicts of interest on research analysts that the firms failed to manage in an adequate or appropriate manner. The complaints also alleged supervisory deficiencies at every firm.

[135] See FSA Discussion Paper 15 *Investment Research—Conflicts and Other Issues* (July 2002), FSA Consultation Paper 171 *Conflicts of Interest: Investment Research and Issues of Securities* (Feb 2003) and FSA Consultation Paper (CP) 205 *Conflicts of Interest: Investment Research and Issues of Securities* (Oct 2003).

[136] For general background see FSA Policy Statement 04/6, *Conflicts of Interest in Investment Research* (March 2004).

[137] See COB 5.10 and the Conflicts of Interest (Corporate Finance and Investment Analysts) Instrument 2003 (attached to CP 205, above n 135).

[138] See COB 7.3.

[139] See the Conflicts of Interest (Corporate Finance and Investment Analysts) Instrument 2003 (FSA 2003/70, attached to CP 205, above n 135) for a comparison of the old and new text of COB 7.3.

(iii) It has amended the COB Sourcebook so as to require investment firms to establish and implement a policy, appropriate to the firm, for managing effectively the conflicts of interest that might affect the impartiality of investment research that is held out as being impartial.[140]

Further action on the part of the FSA is likely, as the UK will be required to implement the relevant provisions of the market abuse[141] and MiFID[142] directives. The former requires investment research to be fairly presented and relevant conflicts to be disclosed. The latter requires that firms introduce organisational and administrative arrangements such that conflicts of interest that may arise in the provision of investment services are identified, managed and/or disclosed.

10.3.6 Commercial banks

Commercial banks are those whose business is primarily lending money raised from deposits or from other banks.[143] Commercial banking business is regulated mainly through the system of prudential supervision, which focuses on the solvency of financial institutions. Historically, the Bank of England was responsible for the authorisation and supervision of banking business, but this role was transferred to the FSA in 1998. In contrast to investment business, conduct of business rules are of little relevance to mainstream commercial banking business.

Increasingly, however, commercial banks also have an involvement in the investment markets, through stockbroking, fund management or life assurance and pensions subsidiaries. When they carry on such business, they are subject to the relevant regulatory regime in addition to the system of prudential supervision that applies to banking. The regulatory provisions relating to material interests and conflicts of interest (see above) are applicable when the bank acts in different capacities for different clients or acts as a principal in a transaction with a client. A common pattern in recent years has been for banks to act as a sales outlet for a life assurance and pensions company with which

---

[140] See COB 7.16 and the Conflicts of Interest (Investment Research) Instrument 2004 (FSA 2004/24, attached to FSA Policy Statement 04/06 (n 136 above)).

[141] See article 6(5) of the Market Abuse Directive ('MAD', 2003/6/EC, [2003] OJ L96/16) and Commission Directive 2003/125 implementing article 6(5) of the MAD. The MAD is subject to the 'Lamfalussy' process, under which the commission has responsibility for detailed implementation of directives in consultation with the Committee of European Securities Regulators. The objective is to limit the technical complexity of directives that contain basic principles (termed 'level 1').

[142] The Markets in Financial Instruments Directive, 2004/39/EC, [2004] OJ L145/1, art 18.

[143] Banks lend to each other in the 'inter-bank' money market. Banks that rely primarily on this type of funding for their lending activity are referred to as 'money-centre' banks.

they have an ownership link, an arrangement commonly referred to as 'bancassurance'.[144]

10.3.7 Credit-rating agencies

Credit-rating agencies are private-sector organisations that assess the likelihood of timely payment on debt securities.[145] They have been described as 'the universally feared gatekeepers for the issuance and trading of debt securities'.[146] Investors in domestic and international debt securities markets increasingly rely on the credit rating attached to an issue of such securities. It avoids the need for investors to engage in their own assessment of creditworthiness. While there is generally no form of regulation applicable to credit-rating agencies,[147] they trade on and are subject to the discipline resulting from the capital markets' view of their reputation for integrity and accuracy.

Rating agencies use similar, though not identical, ratings. Standard & Poor's ratings for long-term debt securities can be referred to as an example. Their highest rating is AAA, followed by AA, A, BBB and below. Marginal modifications within these ratings are indicated by the attachment of + and – designations. The higher the rating, the lower the risk of default associated with the particular issue.[148] Ratings below BBB– are deemed 'non-investment grade' (or 'junk bonds'), indicating considerable risk associated with full and timely payment on the securities. This categorisation can have considerable implications for the type of investor who is able to purchase such securities and may increase the interest rate payable by a borrower.[149]

Credit-ratings are generally solicited by and paid for by issuers of debt securities. This undoubtedly creates a potential conflict of interest in that there may be a temptation to overstate the capacity of the issuer to meet its obligations.

---

[144] This business model operates in the retail market subject to the regulatory regime outlined in Ch 6. See also the Sandler Report (*Medium and Long-Term Retail Savings in the UK: A Review*, July 2002, available at www.hm-treasury.gov.uk (22 Nov 2004)) p 80, noting that expectations that 'bancassurance' would eventually dominate the retail investment market have failed to materialise.

[145] The best-known credit-rating agencies are Standard & Poor's, Moody's Investors Service Inc and Fitch Investors Service Inc, all based in the US, but with worldwide operations. See K Pilbeam, *Finance and Financial Markets* (Basingstoke, Palgrave, 1998) pp 104–106 for a more detailed description of the rating systems used by Moody's and Standard & Poor's.

[146] S Schwarcz, 'Private Ordering of Public Markets: The Rating Agency Paradox', (2002) *University of Illinois Law Review* 1, 2.

[147] See Schwarcz (above n 146) as to arguments for and against regulation of credit-rating agencies.

[148] A rating relates to a particular issue of debt securities and not the credit-worthiness of the issuer.

[149] For example, insurance companies and investment funds may be restricted to investment in 'investment-grade' debt securities.

In reality, the concern of the agencies with their reputation has resulted in this potential conflict of interest being subordinated to the need to maintain their reputation in the market.[150] The freedom afforded to rating agencies to issue unsolicited ratings has been challenged as abusive in the US (on the basis that they effectively force unwilling issuers to pay for a rating) but has been upheld on the basis of the US constitutional provisions relating to freedom of speech and the press.[151] The liability of rating agencies for negligence is a matter that appears to be untested in the UK courts. In the US, the courts have held that in order for liability to be attached to a rating agency, it must be shown that they acted recklessly and not simply negligently.[152]

---

[150] See Schwarcz (above n 146 at p 13), citing research on the long-term default rates of debt securities with different credit ratings.

[151] See Schwarcz (above n 146) p 17.

[152] See the cases cited by Schwarcz (above n 146 at fn 78).

INDEX

Index